Barron's Regents Exams and Answers

Global History and Geography

MICHAEL J. ROMANO, Ph.D.
Former District Chairperson, Northport School District, Northport, New York

WILLIAM STREITWIESER, B.A., M.A.
Former Social Studies Teacher, Northport High School, Northport, New York

Glossary by
MARY MARTIN
Social Studies Teacher, Greene Central School, Greene, New York

D1261057

Barron's Educational Series, Inc.

All inquiries should be addressed to:
Barron's Educational Series, Inc.
250 Wireless Boulevard
Hauppauge, New York 11788
www.barronseduc.com

ISBN-13: 978-0-8120-4344-0
ISBN-10: 0-8120-4344-8
ISSN 1069-2932

PRINTED IN CANADA
9 8 7 6 5 4 3 2 1

Contents

Regents Examinations, Answers, and Self-Analysis Charts   91

Introduction

THE TWO-YEAR GLOBAL HISTORY AND GEOGRAPHY COURSE

After the two-year Global History and Geography course in New York State, there is a Regents examination. All 10th-grade students are required to take the Regents examination if they want to receive a Regents diploma. The focus of social studies is to help students understand how history, geography, economics, government, and civics have influenced the past, present, and future. The Global History and Geography courses that are given in the 9th and 10th grades are part of a required K-12 social studies program in New York. On the elementary and middle school level, students learn about their community, state, and nation. Global History is built on the premise that we live in an interdependent world and that no nation can isolate itself from the world. What happenes in other nations impacts our lives and the way we live. Thus, to have a better understanding of our country's history and growth, it is important to understand the events that are occurring in the world today. In September 1998 the Global History and Geography course replaced the Global Studies course. The old Global Studies approach divided the world into eight regions, such as Africa and the Middle East. Students studied the particular areas from ancient times to the present. After seven or eights weeks, students moved on to a different area of the world. *The new Global History approach is chronological and highlights major themes and concepts by studying what is happening in different world regions during the same time period.*

The two-year Global History course is divided as follows:

Unit 1: Ancient World (400 B.C. to 500 A.D.)—A study of the Ancient Civilizations of Asia, Africa, and Europe

Unit 2: Expanding Zones of Exchange and Encounter (500 to 1200)—A study of how different regions of the world encountered and exchanged ideas with each other from the Gupta Empire to the Crusades

Unit 3: Global Interaction (1200 to 1650)—A study of how the interaction of Japanese, Mongol, and African Civilizations and the spirit of the Renaissance led to the exchange of ideas, trade, and changes in society

Unit 4: The First Global Age (1450 to 1750)—A study of how the encounter among the Ming, Ottoman, Spanish, Portuguese, and Mesoamerican empires led to changes in the world

Unit 5: Age of Revolution (1750 to 1914)—A study of how the Scientific Revolution, the Enlightenment, political revolution, nationalism, industrialism, and imperialism influenced the world

Unit 6: A Half Century of Crisis and Achievement—A study of how World War I, the Russian Revolution, rise of dictatorship in Europe, the rise of nationalism in Asia and the Middle East, and World War II affected the world

Unit 7: The 20th Century Since 1845—A study of the political, economic, and social changes that influenced Europe, Asia, Latin America, the United States, and the Middle East

Unit 8: Global Connections and Interactions—A study of how overpopulation, urbanization, globalization, ethnic rivalry, and other economic and political issues are influencing the world

The underlying theme of Global History and Geography is the importance of geography in studying a society as well as the fact that the world has been coming closer together since the 13th century. The Global History and Geography Regents examination is also designed to reflect the five social studies standards that are: U.S. History, World History, Geography, Economics, Civics, Citizenship, and Government.

WHAT IS THE FORMAT OF THE GLOBAL HISTORY AND GEOGRAPHY REGENTS?

The Global History and Geography Regents is a three-hour test that contains questions on topics, concepts, skills and themes from each historical era that is covered in the two-year Global History and Geography course. Be sure to review information from units in Grades 9 and 10.

Each examination will include:

Part I:	Multiple-Choice Questions:	50 items	55% of the test
Part II:	Thematic Essay	1	15% of the test
Part III:	Document-Based Question	1	15% scaffolding
			15% analytical essay
			100% of the test

Unlike the former Global Studies Regents, there will be no choices for the essay question. The Thematic Essay, the Scaffolding question of the Document-Based Question and the Analytical Document-Based Essay will be scored holistically, using a specific standard that is outlined in the scoring rubric. The passing score will be based on the student's average on the entire test.

How to Use This Book to Study

This book contains various features that will enable you to get the most out of your review and help you score well on the Regents. The book is divided into the following sections: **Test-Taking Tips, Glossary of Important Terms, International Organizations and Agreements, and Important People, Previous Regents Examinations and Answers, and Self-Analysis Charts.** Read each of these sections carefully and you will be on the road to success.

TEST-TAKING TIPS

These hints, suggestions, and practice questions will help you become a better test taker and enable you to develop the skills that will lead to success on the Regents. The sample Multiple-Choice Questions, the Thematic Essay, and the Document-Based Question will provide you with specific strategies on how to answer these questions. Review this section after you have taken two or three practice Regents. This step will help you realize how these hints have improved your score.

GLOSSARY

The Glossary contains important terms, people, and international agreements and organizations that are part of the Global History and Geography course of study. The Glossary should be used as a study guide to help you focus on the key turning points, terms, and people in Global History.

PREVIOUS REGENTS EXAMINATIONS AND ANSWERS

This third section contains previous Global Studies and History Regents with an analysis of the right and wrong answers. These Regents are an excellent study guide because they focus on the key content areas of the course. Answer the multiple-choice questions first. This step will provide you with an overview of your strengths and weaknesses. Review the answers because they will provide you with additional information about a particular question.

Carefully read the model answers for the Thematic Essay and the DBQ. This step will help you understand how the scoring rubric is used to determine the essay score on a scale of 1–5.

SELF-ANALYSIS CHART

The self-analysis chart following the Answers Explained for each Regents has been designed to help you note the number of questions and the frequency of the questions in each of the five social studies standards. You should use the chart to analyize your strengths and deficiencies in each of the historical periods.

STEPS FOR SUCCESS

1. Read your notes, review packets, and material on the topics in the course.
2. Read the Test-Taking Tips.
3. Check the Glossary to make sure that you are familiar with the information that it contains.
4. Look over past examinations to become familiar with the format and types of tests.
5. Take the most recent Regents examination and try to complete it within the specified time period.
6. Check all your answers in Part I and carefully read all explanations for the correct and incorrect answers as well as questions you were unable to answer.
7. Complete the Self-Analysis Chart; this will help you focus on the areas in which you need more review.

8. Read your essay answer for each question and compare your response with the one given in the book; check the rubric to determine how you have scored on this part of the examination.
9. Recheck your notes, review Test-Taking Tips, and continue to take more practice regents
10. Always think positive—you will succeed!

Test-Taking Tips

HELPFUL HINTS FOR ALL TESTS

TIP 1
Be prepared and have an optimistic approach.

- Organize/review your notes.
- Don't cram; develop good study habits throughout the year.
- Complete all your written and reading assignments on time.
- Be familiar with the format of the test.
- Review past examinations under test conditions (no headphones, CD players, etc.).
- Visit *www.barronseduc.com* for the latest information on the Regents.
- Come prepared for the test; bring pens and pencils.
- Focus on the test.
- Relax and be positive.

TIP 2
Carefully read the directions and questions.

- Be familiar with the test directions before you take the exam.
- Know how much time is allocated for each part of the exam.
- Become familiar with the grading of the test and which questions are worth more points.
- Circle or highlight important terms or phrases.
- Know how many questions you must answer from each part of the test.
- Ask for assistance from the proctor when the directions are unclear.

TIP 3

Budget your time.

- Make a note of when the test began and when it will end.
- Wear a watch or make sure that the clock in the room is working so that you can keep track of the time.
- Quickly look over the entire examination first before you begin to answer any questions.
- Outline a time frame. It makes sense to spend more time on the parts that are worth more points; a good guide would be to spend one hour on the short answers and two hours on the Thematic and DBQ essays.
- Answer the easy questions first. Don't get stuck on one question. Move on to the next questions; you might find a clue or hint in other sections of the test.
- Don't leave early if you finish before the three-hour limit. Recheck your answers; you may want to add information or you may have omitted something asked for in the question.

TIP 4

Don't give up on your reasoning abilities.

- Don't leave out any questions.
- Restate the question in your own words so that you understand it.
- Try to connect the question with some ideas or topic that you have covered in class or on your test.
- Check the whole test to determine if you can use any information from one part to help you answer a question on another part.
- Make a list of the Global History Connections: cultural diffusion, migration, regional empire, belief systems, trade/conflict. See if any of these topics can help you answer a question.

TIP 5

When in doubt, guess.

- Answer all questions. Remember that an unanswered question receives no credit; there is no penalty for guessing.
- Go with your first choice.
- Eliminate the least obvious choices; try to use a 50–50 lifeline, then make an educated guess.

Let's review the **Helpful Hints** for all tests:

1. Be confident and optimistic.
2. Carefully read the directions and questions.
3. Budget your time.
4. Don't give up on your reasoning abilities.
5. When in doubt—guess.

SPECIFIC HELPFUL HINTS FOR ANSWERING MULTIPLE-CHOICE QUESTIONS

The Global History and Geography Regents has many kinds of multiple-choice questions. They require knowledge of some basic facts and analysis or application of the facts.

TIP 1

Read the questions carefully and underline the key words.

WHY WILL THIS TIP HELP YOU?
- It helps you avoid making careless mistakes.
- It focuses on the key ideas.
- It directs your answer to what is being tested.

WHEN SHOULD YOU UTILIZE THIS TIP?
- When taking any multiple-choice test.

The example below shows the importance of key words. The key words provide the specific meaning of the question and point you to the correct response.

EXAMPLE

The Silk Road was important to China because it provided
1 contact with other cultures through trade
2 a means of administering civil service examinations
3 a military route for the defense of the northern border
4 a means for the country to expand its borders
                          (from Test Sampler Draft Spring 1999)

By underlining *Silk Road* and *China*, you are focusing on the key points of the question. You are being asked to show the connection between the Silk Road and its importance to China. The correct answer is Choice 1. It contains the only statement that has a direct connection with Silk Road and trade route. The other choices deal with topics concerning military or political issues.

PRACTICE

Underline the key words in the following question:

Which term is used to describe the spread of Buddhism from India through Southeast Asia?

1 ethnocentrism
2 isolationism
3 imperialism
4 cultural diffusion

(from June 2000 Regents)

You should have underlined *spread*, *Buddhism*, *India*, and *Southeast Asia* because they are the important terms in the question. The correct choice is 4 because cultural diffusion is a term used to describe the spread of ideas to different societies. The other terms are not related to religion.

TIP 2

Answer the easy questions first and leave the difficult questions for later.

WHY USE THIS TIP?
- It instills confidence.
- It enables you to use your time more efficiently.
- It provides an opportunity to find clues/ideas in other answers that can be useful in answering the ones left blank.

WHEN DO YOU USE THIS TIP?
- This tip is helpful whenever you take a test that contains difficult or unfamiliar questions

Easy questions are those that contain limited vocabulary, short statements, and are readily answered from the given information.

EXAMPLE

Which aspect of a nation's culture is most directly influenced by the physical geography of that nation?
1 form of government
2 religious belief
3 population distribution
4 social class system

(from January 1998 Regents)

Choice 3 is the obvious answer; it is the only choice that is connected to physical geography. The other choices are not related to the main idea of the question and have little to do with a nation's geography.

PRACTICE

> An aspect of society that an economist would study in depth would be the
> 1 development of self-image and causes of mental illness
> 2 problem of scarcity of resources
> 3 origins of religion, legends, and festivals
> 4 migratory patterns of animals
>
> (from Test Sampler Draft Spring 1999)

The correct answer is 2. Economics is the only social science that deals with scarcity and resources. The other choices relate to different types of social sciences.

TIP 3

Read all choices. Look out for decoys.

WHY USE THIS TIP?
- It encourages you to read all possible answers before making a selection.
- It makes you aware that initial choices may seem correct but sometimes are not.

WHEN DO YOU USE THIS TIP?
- When taking a multiple-choice test.

Be a patient test taker. Very often, the decoy precedes the correct choice and the careless student will choose the incorrect answer.

EXAMPLE

Which slogan expressed the ideals of the Bolshevik
Revolution of 1917?
1 Liberty, Equality, and Fraternity
2 Bread, Land, and Peace
3 Land and Liberty
4 Nationalism, Democracy, and the People's Livelihood

(from January 1998 Regents)

The correct choice is 2. It is the only choice that applies specifically
to the Bolshevik Revolution. However, all three choices are historical
slogans and represent other revolutions that occurred in history.

PRACTICE

One reason for both the French Revolution (1789) and the
Cuban Revolution (1959) was that
1 people often rebel when they are governed by a foreign
   power
2 the monarchs did not meet the needs of culturally
   diverse populations
3 the writings of Karl Marx encouraged workers and the
   industrialists to unite
4 existing governments failed to address the major
   economic differences between social classes

(from January 1997 Regents)

Did you select number 3? It is an attractive choice, but the French
Revolution took place *before* Karl Marx wrote, and indicated that the
workers would revolt against the industrialists. However, Choice 4 is
correct because revolutions take place when governments ignore the
needs of the people.

TIP 4

Check for clues found in other questions and among the choices in the actual question.

WHY USE THIS TIP?
- It helps you to make connections and associations among various questions.
- It helps you to utilize the test as an educational tool.
- It enables you to find information that can help in answering other questions in the test.

WHEN DO YOU USE THIS TIP?
- Whenever necessary; all tests should be an assessment of your knowledge as well as an educational tool.

Sometimes you can find clues to the correct answer in other questions on the same test. The two questions below demonstrate how connections and associations can be made between different questions on the same Regents.

EXAMPLE (CLUE IN ANOTHER QUESTION)

In many Latin American nations, the leadership roles assumed by the military and by the Roman Catholic Church evolved from
1 Native American beliefs
2 the development of the triangular trade
3 the effects of matriarchal societies
4 Spanish colonial rule

(from January 1998 Regents)

The correct response is 4. You can get a clue to the right answer from the question below, which appeared on the same exam.

Which statement best illustrates the contradictory actions of the Catholic Church in colonial Latin America?

1 The Jesuits destroyed the temples of the Native Americans, but allowed them to continue their religious rituals.
2 The Church expressed concern over the mistreatment of Native Americans, but supported the encomienda system
3 The Church moved many Native Americans from Spanish territory to Portuguese territory, but encouraged the importation of African slaves.
4 The Pope endorsed the Treaty of Tordesillas, but outlawed further exploration

(from January 1998 Regents)

The correct choice is 2. Most students will remember that the Spanish controlled Latin America and that the Church converted the Native Americans, but also resented their being mistreated by the Spaniards. The role of the Spanish would provide a clear hint to the correct answer for the first question.

Practice (Clue found among choices)

What would most likely be included in a description of an area's physical geography?
1 customs and traditions
2 distribution of goods and services
3 systems of government
4 landforms of continents and currents of oceans

(from Sampler Spring 1999)

The correct choice is number 4. Landforms of continents and currents of oceans are the only terms that deal with physical geography. Choice 1 is cultural, choice 2 is economic, and choice 3 deals with an area's government.

TIP 5

Use the process of elimination.

WHY USE THIS TIP?
- It helps you discard the wrong choices.
- It narrows down the possible correct choices and increases the possibility of getting the right answer.

WHEN DO YOU USE THIS TIP?
- Whenever you face a tough question and are unsure about the correct response.

Always use the process of elimination to arrive at a conclusion when you are uncertain about the answer. Look at the example below and begin using this process.

EXAMPLE

"Archduke Franz Ferdinand Assassinated!"
"Germany declares war on Russia and France!"
"Peace Treaty signed at Versailles!"

Which event is referred to in these headlines?
1 Franco-Prussian War
2 Crimean War
3 World War I
4 Cold War

(from June 2000 Regents)

You may not be familiar with all the headlines, but you can eliminate Choice 4 because Russia and the United States opposed each other in the Cold War. If you know that Archduke Ferdinand was from Austria, you can rule out the Franco-Prussian War. You can eliminate Choice 2 if you remember that England and Russia fought in the Crimean War. Thus, you have arrived at your answer—Choice 3.

PRACTICE

One similarity in the Mesopotamian, Egyptian, Ancient Indian (Harappan), and Ancient Chinese civilizations was that they each developed
1 democratic governments
2 monotheistic religions
3 irrigation systems
4 industrialized economies

(from Test Sampler Draft 1999)

Congratulations if you selected Choice 3! Questions that ask for similarities between groups are good because if you know a fact about one, you know that it is the same for all. You remember that none of the ancient civilizations was democratic or monotheistic (with the exception of the Hebrews) and all developed an agricultural society. Thus, the only similarity is that all of these civilizations developed irrigation systems.

TIP 6

Identify differences among the choices.

WHY USE THIS TIP?
• It helps you decide between general and specific answers.
• It helps you identify decoys.

WHEN DO YOU USE THIS TIP?
• When several choices seem correct.
• When you have reduced the answer to two choices.

How do you answer a question when several choices seem to be correct? Tip 6 provides you with a way to recognize the difference among these choices. Try the following examples.

EXAMPLE

The Native American population of Mexico in 1492 has been estimated at 25 million; the population in 1608 has been estimated at 1.7 million. This decrease in population was mainly a result of
1 crop failures brought on by poor weather conditions
2 emigration of Native Americans to Europe and Africa
3 wars between various native groups
4 diseases introduced by the Spanish

(from January 1997 Regents)

This is a difficult question because it mainly implies that to some extent more than one of these choices are correct. Choice 2 does not fit since there was no emigration of Native Americans to Europe and Africa. Crop failures, Choice 1, and wars between Native Americans,

Choice 3, did result in the death of some Native Americans; however, diseases, such as smallpox and measles, introduced by the Spanish, were the main factor that led to the decimation of the Native American population. Choice 4 is the best answer.

PRACTICE

> The strong showing by the Communist Party in the Russian Presidential election of 1996 suggests that large numbers of Russian people
>
> 1 favored a return to Stalin's policy of imprisoning dissidents
> 2 feared continuing economic instability and high inflation
> 3 wanted the Russian Orthodox Church to play a larger role in government
> 4 supported a return to isolationist policies
>
> (from January 1999 Regents)

This again is a difficult question because two of the wrong choices have elements of truth. While some people did want a return to stability, as stated in Choice 1, they rejected Stalin's strict policies. Choice 3 is a possible option because the Russian people have resumed worshiping in the Russian Orthodox Church; however, there is no evidence to suggest an end to separation of church and state. Choice 4 is incorrect because Russian leaders wanted to reject isolationism and play a greater role in world politics. Therefore, this leaves Choice 2 as the correct answer because many Russian people do indeed fear inflation and instability.

TIP 7

Don't select an answer that is correct in itself but is wrong as it relates to the question.

WHY USE THIS TIP?
- It assists you in relating answer choices to the question.
- It guides you in focusing on the question and its connection to the answer.

WHEN DO YOU USE THIS TIP?
• Whenever answering a multiple-choice question.

Quite often one or more of the options are accurate, but are the wrong answer for that question. Always keep in mind which choices best relate to the specific question. Try the following.

EXAMPLE

Which economic policy of the Soviet Union in the 1980s was the most different from the economic policies of Stalin?
1 government ownership of the means of production
2 the development of heavy industry
3 central planning of basic economic decisions
4 private management

(from June 1991 Regents)

All of the choices describe the Soviet economy in the 1980s; however, Choice 4 is the one that best answers the question. Gorbachev's policy of perestroika was a direct rejection of Stalin's command economy.

PRACTICE

The amount of carbon dioxide in the atmosphere has increased in recent years. Environmentalists suggest this change is a direct result of the

1 improper storage of solid and nuclear wastes
2 overcutting of forests and the increased use of fossil fuels
3 dumping of inorganic material into lakes and rivers
4 use of herbicides and toxic substances such as asbestos and DDT

(from June 1996 Regents)

Choices 1, 3, and 4 are all regarded as environmental hazards that reduce the quality of life and may cause death. However, they do not contribute to the increase in the level of carbon dioxide. Choice 2 is the correct statement for this question because overcutting of forests leads to global warming.

TIP 8

Always pick the broader encompassing option.

WHY USE THIS TIP?
- It is helpful when two choices are accurate but one choice more fully answers the question.

WHEN DO YOU USE THIS TIP?
- When two or more choices are correct but one of the choices includes the other.

This is a valuable tool when answering questions that call for inclusive answers. Below is a sample of this type of question.

EXAMPLE

People in both Japan and India eat very little meat. A study of these cultures would show that

1 although these cultures have similar practices, the reasons for these practices differ
2 the raising of cattle in both nations is very different due to the extreme climate
3 neither culture is concerned with health issues
4 the governments of both nations enforce strict dietary laws

(from January 1993 Regents)

Use the process of elimination in answering the question (Tip 5). You could have eliminated Choice 2 because you know that Indians do not eat meat because of religious reasons. You can cross out Choices 3 and 4 because both of these governments are secular democratic governments. They would not ignore health issues nor impose dietary laws. The most general answer is Choice 1 and is likely to be true of both countries.

PRACTICE

Which factor is the best indicator of the wealth of a nation?
1 Gross National Product (GNP)
2 Prime Interest Rate
3 Number of millionaires
4 Defense spending

(from January 1996 Regents)

Choices 2, 3, and 4 have some validity since they indicate certain characteristics of an economy. However, Choice 1 is a broader statement and a more accurate way to measure the total economic activity during a set time period.

TIP 9

Have an idea about the answer before looking at the answer choices.

WHY USE THIS TIP?
• It helps you to recall an idea or term associated with the question.
• It helps you to stimulate your memory.

WHEN DO YOU USE THIS TIP?
• Whenever you answer a multiple-choice question.
• When interpreting cartoons.

When you read a question you should put it in the context of the time period and associate the important events in that era. Try the following example.

EXAMPLE

As a result of the Glorious Revolution and the English Bill of Rights of 1689, the government in Great Britain gradually became a
1 theocracy
2 limited monarchy
3 direct democracy
4 socialist republic

(from June 1994 Regents)

As you read this question, you should have thought how the Glorious Revolution and the Bill of Rights brought about an end to absolute power and established a limited monarchy. There was little interest in Great Britain in a theocracy or a direct democracy. Therefore, Choice 2 is correct.

Try this tip when you look at a cartoon. Interpret the meaning of the cartoon before looking at the choices.

PRACTICE

Base your answer to this question on the cartoon below and on your knowledge of social studies.

Gorrell, Richmond Times-Dispatch

What is the main idea of this 1994 cartoon?
1 Haiti's lack of industrialization has led to economic stagnation
2 Haiti's limited experience with democracy has made it difficult to establish this form of government
3 The desire for democracy has led Haiti to neglect its development of modern technology
4 The presence of American industry has failed to improve Haiti's economy

(from January 1999 Regents)

The cartoon suggests that Haiti has to put many parts together to develop a democracy. The words "Some assembly required" provides the focus of the cartoon. Focusing on these words will enable you to select Choice 2 as the correct answer.

TIP 10

Make educated guesses.

WHY USE THIS TIP?
- Because there is no penalty for guessing.
- Because any answer is better than no answer.
- Because using the process of elimination helps you to arrive at the right answer.

WHEN DO YOU USE THIS TIP?
- When there is no penalty for guessing.
- When there is nothing to lose; a blank answer is wrong anyway.

Remember, you should use guessing as a last resort! The question below will give you an opportunity to use the technique of intelligent guessing to arrive at the correct answer.

EXAMPLE

The contributions of the Golden Age of Islamic civilization include
1 advances in mathematics
2 irrigation systems
3 polytheistic beliefs
4 gunpowder and guns

(from June 2000 Regents)

Even if you are not certain of the choices, you can make an informed guess that Choice 1 is the correct answer. You probably realize that Arabic numbers are used worldwide and that we borrowed them from the Muslims.

PRACTICE

Which practice was similar under the rule of the Bolsheviks in Russia and of the Nazi Party in Germany?
1 establishing communism in their respective nations
2 permitting a series of multiparty elections
3 increasing the power of the middle class
4 limiting government opposition through intimidation and fear

(from January 1999 Regents)

Choice 4 is the correct answer. It contains the key words—*limiting, intimidation*, and *fear*—all essential features of the two ideologies. Communism and Fascism are opposed to each other and thus Choice 1 is eliminated. A series of multiparty elections would not exist in a dictatorship so you can rule out Choice 3.

CHECKLIST FOR ANSWERING THE MULTIPLE-CHOICE QUESTIONS

1. Read the questions carefully and underline key words.
2. Answer the easy questions first.
3. Read all the choices. Look out for decoys.
4. Check for clues found in other questions and among the choices in the question.
5. Use the process of elimination.
6. Identify differences among the choices.
7. Don't select an answer that is correct in itself but is wrong as it relates to the question.
8. Always pick the broader encompassing option.
9. Have an idea about the answer before looking at the answer choices.
10. Make educated guesses.

STRATEGIES FOR ANSWERING THE THEMATIC ESSAY QUESTION

There will be one Thematic Essay on the Regents. It will count for 15 percent of the examination. The Thematic Essay requires you to **interpret, understand, and explain key concepts that link several events in Global History**.

THEMES	EXAMPLES
Major Belief Systems	Judaism; Confucianism
Turning Points in History	Fall of Rome; French Revolution; Birth of Islam
Forms of Government (Political System)	Monarchy; Democracy
Economic Systems	Communism; Capitalism
Geography and the Environment	Early River Civilization; Global Economy
Justice/Human Rights	Code of Hammurabi; Justinian Code; Violations (i.e., Holocaust, Apartheid)
Science/Technology	Invention of Printing Press; Neolithic Revolution
Movement of People/Goods (Cultural Diffusion)	Crusades; Silk Road
Nationalism	Italian/German Unification; Zionism
Imperialism	British in India; European Partition of Africa
Conflicts	Political (World War I, World War II) Religious (Northern Ireland, Middle East, India)
Culture/Intellectual Life	Roman, Gupta Civilizations; Renaissance

Most Thematic Essays will have the following parts:

THE THEME: Identifies the broad concept that will be the topic of the essay. Usually, there is a general explanation statement that provides more focus to the question.

THE TASK: Provides the instruction for what you will need to write about your topic or concept.

SUGGESTIONS: Provide you with a specific area that you might choose to discuss in your essay. **Note:** These are only suggestions and you are not limited to these examples. **Beware:** Pay attention if the suggestions caution you not to choose the United States as your topic. Students will lose credit if they do not follow the directions.

THEMATIC ESSAY QUESTION—June 2000

Directions: Write a well-organized essay that includes an introduction, several paragraphs addressing the task below, and a conclusion.

Theme: Justice and Human Rights

> Throughout history, the human rights of certain groups of people have been violated. Efforts have been made to address these violations.

Task:

> • Define the term "human rights"
> • Identify *two* examples of human rights violations that have occurred in a specific time and place
> • Describe the causes of these human rights violations
> • For *one* of the violations identified, discuss *one* specific effort that was made or is being made to deal with the violation

You may use any example from your study of global history. Do *not* use the United States in your answer. Some suggestions you might wish to consider include: Christians in the early Roman Empire, native peoples in Spain's American colonies, untouchables in India, blacks in South Africa, Jews in Nazi Germany, Muslims in Bosnia, Kurds in Iraq or Turkey, or Tibetans in China.

You are *not* limited to these suggestions.

STEP 1

Read the entire question first.

This will help you focus on what is expected of you in the essay.

STEP 2

Analyze the task.

Review key phrases and words in the task directions that you must include in your essay. In the sample Thematic Essay of June 2000, you should underline the key words in the directions:

- *Define* human rights.
- *Identify* two examples of violations in different time periods.
- *Describe* the causes of these violations.
- *Discuss* one specific effort to deal with the violations.

By listing these items, you can begin to organize your outline.

STEP 3

Check the suggestions.

This will help you recall the importance of themes in different places and time periods.

STEP 4

Organize the information.

Begin to outline the information you could include in your essay. In the sample Thematic Essay of June 2000, you might include:

- Definition of human rights: rights and liberties guaranteed by birth; freedom of religion; right to vote
- Identify two human rights violations: Apartheid (South Africa); Holocaust (Germany)
- Causes: White minority control; black majority; separation of races; Hitler's extermination of Jews; Nuremberg Laws; Kristallnacht
- Effort to deal with violations: Role of Nelson Mandela and Bishop Tutu; economic boycott in South Africa

STEP 5

Identify the main ideas of the essay.

Use the theme or the task of the Thematic Essay to create your topic or thesis statement. An example of a thesis statement might be as follows:

Throughout history, the human rights of certain groups such as the blacks in South Africa and the Jews in Germany have been violated.

STEP 6
Write the introductory paragraph.

The introductory paragraph should connect the thesis or topic to the main idea of the essay. You might include in your paragraph a definition of human rights and two examples, such as the blacks in South Africa and the Jews in Germany. Below is an example of an introductory paragraph:

Human rights are those rights and liberties that are guaranteed to everyone from birth by virtue of belonging to a civil society. These rights include freedom of religion, the right to vote, and freedom of expression without fear of abuse by government officials. In 1948 the United Nations adopted a Universal Declaration of Human Rights, which set forth those basic liberties and freedoms to which all people are entitled. Throughout history, the human rights of people such as the blacks in South Africa and the Jews in Nazi Germany have been violated. (**Note:** the introductory paragraph concludes with the thesis statement.)

STEP 7
Write the supporting paragraphs.

Each of these paragraphs should deal with one aspect or part of the task. These paragraphs should explain your answer with facts, details, and examples. Check the facts from the outline as you are writing. Remember the following:

1. Develop your essay logically.
2. Do not list facts. Analyze, evaluate, compare, or contrast various aspects.
3. Do not use meaningless facts unrelated to the theme.
4. Use concrete examples to support your ideas.
5. Make sure that you have completed all the assigned tasks listed in the question.

STEP 8

Write the concluding paragraph.

Restate or rewrite the thesis summarizing the essay. Make sure that your essay has both a strong introduction and a strong conclusion. You will not receive full credit if either of these pieces is missing or weak. A good concluding paragraph would be as follows:

> Human rights violations such as those in South Africa and Nazi Germany have existed throughout history. It is is important to be aware of these violations and for society to make an effort to ensure that they never happen again. History has shown that the global community does not benefit when any group of people becomes victims of intolerance or injustice.

STEP 9

Check the essay against the generic scoring rubric.

Depending on time, reread your essay to check for errors of facts, spelling, or grammar. Check to see if the essay is organized, reads clearly, and makes sense. The following scoring rubric will appear after the Thematic Essay Question in your Regents exam booklet. It shows exactly what an essay must contain to receive a particular score. For example, in order to abtain a score of 4, the rubric indicates your essay must contain relevant facts and examples. If, while checking your essay against the rubric, you discover you've neglected to include relevant facts, you can add them at this time.

THEMATIC ESSAY
GENERIC SCORING RUBRIC

Score of 5:
- Shows a thorough understanding of the theme or problem
- Addresses all aspects of the task
- Shows an ability to analyze, evaluate, compare and/or contrast issues and events
- Richly supports the theme or problem with relevant facts, examples, and details
- Is a well-developed essay, consistently demonstrating a logical and clear plan of organization
- Introduces the theme or problem by establishing a framework that is beyond a simple restatement of the task and concludes with a summation of the theme or problem

Score of 4:
- Shows a good understanding of the theme or problem
- Addresses all aspects of the task
- Shows an ability to analyze, evaluate, compare and/or contrast issues and events
- Includes relevant facts, examples, and details, but may not support all aspects of the theme or problem evenly
- Is a well-developed essay, demonstrating a logical and clear plan of organization
- Introduces the theme or problem by establishing a framework that is beyond a simple restatement of the task and concludes with a summation of the theme or problem

Score of 3:
- Shows a satisfactory understanding of the theme or problem
- Addresses most aspects of the task or addresses all aspects in a limited way

- Shows an ability to analyze or evaluate issues and events, but not in any depth
- Includes some facts, examples, and details
- Is a satisfactorily developed essay, demonstrating a general plan of organization
- Introduces the theme or problem by repeating the task and concludes by repeating the theme or problem

Score of 2:
- Shows limited understanding of the theme or problem
- Attempts to address the task
- Develops a faulty analysis or evaluation of issues and events
- Includes few facts, examples, and details, and may include information that contains inaccuracies
- Is a poorly organized essay, lacking focus
- Fails to introduce or summarize the theme or problem

Score of 1:
- Shows very limited understanding of the theme or problem
- Lacks an analysis or evaluation of the issues and events
- Includes little or no accurate or relevant facts, examples, or details
- Attempts to complete the task, but demonstrates a major weakness in organization
- Fails to introduce or summarize the theme or problem

Score of 0: Fails to address the task, is illegible, or is a blank paper

CHECKLIST FOR WRITING THE THEMATIC ESSAY

1. Read the entire question first.
2. Analyze the task.
3. Check the suggestions.
4. Organize the information.
5. Identify the main ideas of the essay.
6. Write the introductory paragraph.
7. Write the supporting paragraphs.
8. Write the concluding paragraph.
9. Check the essay against the generic scoring rubric.

Here is your task: Use these steps to answer the following Thematic Essay question from the Spring 1999 Test Sampler Draft. Use the Thematic Essay Rubric (pages 31–32) to evaluate your answer.

Thematic Essay

Directions: Write a well-organized essay that includes an introduction, several paragrphs explaining your position, and a conclusion.

Theme: Belief Systems

> At various times in global history, members of different religions have acted to bring people together. Members of these same religions have also acted to divide people and have caused conflict.

Task:

> Choose *two* religions from your study of global history and geography.
> For *each* religion:
> • Describe *two* basic beliefs of the religion
> • Explain how members of the religion, at a specific time and place, acted either to unify society or to cause conflict in society

You may use any example from your study of global history and geography. Some suggestions you might wish to consider include: Judaism in the Middle East, Roman Catholicism in Latin America, Hinduism in India, Islam in Iran, Protestant Reformation and the Counter Reformation in Europe, animism in Africa, Shintoism in Japan, and Buddhism in Southeast Asia.

You are *not* limited to these suggestions.

STRATEGIES FOR ANSWERING THE DOCUMENT-BASED ESSAY QUESTION (DBQ)

There will be one Document-Based Essay question on the Regents. It will count for 30 percent of the examination. The Document-Based Essay question requires students to write an essay incorporating information from several documents. The documents may consist of both primary and secondary sources including maps, charts, political cartoons, graphs, or photographs. Remember, the documents may look different but they are all related to a single subject or theme. The DBQ tests a student's ability to **interpret and draw conclusions from historical documents**.

Most DBQ questions will have the following parts:

GENERAL DIRECTIONS: The directions tell you what to do for each part of the question.

HISTORICAL CONTEXT: This is the theme of the question. Read the historical context before you start to answer the question. Each document is related to or takes a position on that theme.

TASK: This statement defines what you must do as you examine the documents. The task is usually in the form of a question.

PART A—SHORT ANSWERS: In this part, you study between six and eight documents. Each document will be followed by one or more possible questions to which you will provide a short response. This portion of the test is worth 15 percent of the exam grade.

PART B—ESSAY: In this part, you will answer an essay question on the same topic as the documents. This portion of the test is worth 15 percent of the exam grade.

STEP 1

Read the question carefully.

Determine what you must do. Read the Historical Context and underline or box the main topic of the question.

Historical Context:

> Economic systems attempt to meet the needs of the people. Capitalism and communism represent two different ways to meet people's economic needs.

(from June 2000 Regents)

The key words to underline would be: *Economic systems; capitalism; communism; different ways; economic needs.*

STEP 2
Read the task.

As you read, circle key words and phrases and try to identify the theme or issue in the question.

Task:

> • Describe how these two economic systems attempt to meet the needs of the people.
> • Evaluate how successful each system has been at meeting the economic needs of the people.

(from June 2000 Regents)

You should have circled the following: *Describe; two economic systems; evaluate; successful.*

Write down any information that you know about the theme, task, or issue.

STEP 3

Read and analyze each document.

Highlight key words and phrases. Take note of the author, date of the document, and the place. When reviewing each document, assess "How is the document related to the theme?" How does Document 1 compare with or contrast to ideas in Document 4?"

Document 1

> Capitalists are rich people who own factories and have lots of money and workers. . . . A factory can belong to one person in Capitalism but in [Communism] it belongs to the government. . . . I am for the idea of [Communism]. It seems to me that you have more of an opportunity to live well. You won't lose your job in [Communism] . . . I've heard about the unemployment problem in America. People can't find any kind of job. . . . That's the way we heard about it—that [in] the West, unemployment, everything there is bad, a real mess.
> —"Katia," a 16-year-old ninth grader from Moscow, 1980s

(June 2000 Regents)

Document 4

> Andrei, his wife, his father, and [his] elder son all have to work on the collective farmlands . . . He is not stupid and sees that almost all the produce ends up in the hands of the Government. The local Communist party boss is always coming back . . . for more and more. Andrei and his family know ahead of time that they are going to get [a] very small return for working on the collectivized fields. Naturally this condition [changes] their attitudes. They are constantly on a sort of slow-down strike . . .
>
> —T. P. Whitney, "The Russian Peasant Wars on the Kremlin," 1954

(June 2000 Regents)

In Document 1, you should have noted that it was written by a 16-year-old ninth grader from Moscow in the 1980s. Compare the statement with Document 4 written in the 1950s. How are they different? What other outside information can be applied to them?

STEP 4
Begin to answer Part A.

Summarize the main viewpoints expressed in each document and answer the question following each document. These short-answer questions are called **Scaffolding** because Scaffolding provides the foundation for answering the essay portion (Part B).

NOTE: Answers to the Scaffolding questions should be *concise* and *straightforward*—one or two sentences are sufficient.

Document 3

> Above all, [the government] . . . will have to take the control of industry and of all branches of production out of the hands of . . . competing individuals, and instead institute a system as a whole, that is for the common account [good], according to a common plan, and with the participation of all members of society. It will . . . abolish [eliminate] competition. . . . Private property must therefore be abolished.
>
> —Friedrich Engels, *Principles of Communism*

(June 2000 Regents)

3a) Who controls the means of production and all property in a Communist system?

You would receive a score of 1 if you stated the following: Government, not the individual, controls the means of production and all property.

3b) What happens to competition in a Communist system?

You would receive a score of 1 if you stated the following: Competition is abolished.

STEP 5

Begin to organize your essay for Part B.

Make an outline or chart of key ideas from each document, separating them to reflect both sides of the task. Below is a summary of the key ideas from the documents in the June 2000 Regents.

Capitalism
   Unemployment—Document 1
   Success to industrious and hard-working—Document 2
   Supply and demand—Document 2

Rewards talent—Document 2
Laissez-faire—Documents 2 and 5
Private ownership—Document 3
Economic class distinction—Document 6
Negative aspects of factory system—Document 6
Free enterprise—Document 7

Communism
Classless society—Documents 1 and 6
Concept of common good—Document 3
Government control of industry—Document 3
Elimination of private property—Document 3
Collectivization—Document 4
Exploitation by leadership—Document 4
Five-year plan—Document 7
Free social and medical services—Document 8
No unemployment—Document 8

STEP 6

Begin to write your essay for Part B

You can approach this part as you would a Thematic Essay, but you should try to incorporate outside information from your Global History and Geography course. Write an introductory paragraph in which you state your position (if necessary) and the varying issues that your essay will discuss. Below is an example of an introductory paragraph that you might use in answering the DBQ on the June 2000 Regents that contains these points:

Capitalism and communism are two types of economic systems that have attempted to meet the needs of the people. Each of these economic systems must address the following three questions: What goods and services should be produced? How should these goods and services be produced? Who should consume these goods and services?

STEP 7

Write the body of your essay.

Refer to the documents to provide the conflicting views and to support your position or thesis. Include specific historical examples and refer to the documents you analyzed in Part A. **Do not merely copy the documents or use long passages from them**. Try to summarize the documents in your own words in one or two sentences.

Document 5

The Wealth of Nations carries the important message of *laissez faire*, which means that the government should intervene as little as possible in economic affairs and leave the market to its own devices. It advocates the liberation of economic production from all limiting regulation in order to benefit the people . . .
—Adam Smith, *The Wealth of Nations*

A good way to summarize this document is to refer to Part A in which your response included the idea that government should leave business alone (laissez-faire).

STEP 8

Evaluate/analyze the different viewpoints expressed in the documents.

Note that the documents contain a variety of ideas on the topic, in this case, capitalism and communism. Some documents are contradictory. This is not done to confuse you but to assess how you will analyze different points of view. In your answer, you should know how the documents support/oppose your thesis or viewpoints.

Remember you must use at least **four** documents to receive full credit.

STEP 9

Write your conclusion.

Restate or rewrite the thesis summarizing the essay. Make sure that you have responded to all parts of the question, check for a strong introduction, and include a judgment in your conclusion if the question warrants it. Below is a conclusion that you might use in answering the June 2000 DBQ.

Capitalism has become the dominant economic system in the world today because it has been successful in providing a stable economic environment that gives society basic needs as well as allowing freedom for each individual. However, there are concerns that capitalism has resulted in widening the gap between the rich and the poor in our industrial society and between the developed and underdeveloped nations of Africa and Latin America. Pope John Paul II has applauded the fall of communism and the freedom associated with capitalism. However, he has also reminded all capitalistic countries that we must insure that capitalism meets the social needs of the people.

STEP 10

Check the essay against the generic scoring rubric.

Proofread the essay to see if it is clear and logical and that the facts are accurate. The following scoring rubric will appear after the Document-Based Essay question in your Regents exam booklet. It will help you decide if your essay has enough detail, relevant outside information, and facts to receive a score with which you will be satisfied. Notice that to receive a score of 4 or 5 you must correctly analyze and interpret at least **four** documents. Comparing your essay to the rubric will make sure you have included four documents in your essay.

DOCUMENT-BASED QUESTION
GENERIC SCORING RUBRIC

Score of 5:
- Thoroughly addresses all aspects of the *Task* by accurately analyzing and interpreting at least **four** documents
- Incorporates information from the documents in the body of the essay
- Incorporates relevant outside information
- Richly supports the theme or problem with relevant facts, examples, and details
- Is a well-developed essay, consistently demonstrating a logical and clear plan of organization
- Introduces the theme or problem by establishing a framework that is beyond a simple restatement of the *Task* or *Historical Context* and concludes with a summation of the theme or problem

Score of 4:
- Addresses all aspects of the *Task* by accurately analyzing and interpreting at least **four** documents
- Incorporates informatioin from the documents in the body of the essay
- Incorporates relevant outside information
- Includes relevant facts, examples, and details, but discussion may be more descriptive than analytical
- Is a well-developed essay, demonstrating a logical and clear plan of organization
- Introduces the theme or problem by establishing a framework that is beyond a simple restatement of the *Task* or *Historical Context* and concludes with a summation of the theme or problem

Score of 3:
- Addresses most aspects of the *Task* or addresses all aspects of the *Task* in a limited way, using some of the documents
- Incorporates some information from the documents in the body of the essay
- Incorporates limited or no relevant outside information
- Includes some facts, examples, and details, but discussion is more descriptive than analytical
- Is a satisfactorily developed essay, demonstrating a general plan of organization

- Introduces the theme or problem by repeating the *Task* or *Historical Context* and concludes by simply repeating the theme or problem

Score of 2:
- Attempts to address some aspects of the *Task*, making limited use of the documents
- Presents no relevant outside information
- Includes few facts, examples, and details; discussion restates contents of the documents
- Is a poorly organized essay, lacking focus
- Fails to introduce or summarize the theme or problem

Score of 1:
- Shows limited understanding of the *Task* with vague, unclear references to the documents
- Presents no relevant outside information
- Includes little or no accurate or relevant facts, details, or examples
- Attempts to complete the *Task*, but demonstrates a major weakness in organization
- Fails to introduce or summarize the theme or problem

Score of 0: Fails to address the *Task*, is illegible, or is a blank paper

CHECKLIST FOR WRITING THE DBQ ESSAY

1. Read the question carefully.
2. Read the task.
3. Read and analyze each document.
4. Begin to answer Part A.
5. Begin to organize your essay for Part B.
6. Begin to write your essay for Part B.
7. Write the body of your essay.
8. Evaluate/analyze the different viewpoints expressed in the documents.
9. Write your conclusion.
10. Check the essay against the generic scoring rubric.

Here is your task. Use these steps to answer the following DBQ Essay question from the Spring 1999 Test Sampler. Use the Document-Based Specific Rubric (pages 53–54) to evaluate your answer.

Document-Based Essay

This task is based on the accompanying documents (1–6). Some of these documents have been edited for the purposes of this task. This task is designed to test your ability to work with historical documents. As you analyze the documents, take into account both the source of each document and the author's point of view.

Directions: Read the documents in Part A and answer the questions after each document. Then read the directions of Part B and write your essay.

Historical Context:

Throughout history, societies have held different viewpoints on governmental decision making and the roles of citizens in this decision-making process. The decision-making process can range from absolute control to democracy.

Task:

Using information from the documents and your knowledge of global history and geography, write an essay in which you
- Compare and contrast the different viewpoints societies have held about the process of governmental decision making and about the role of citizens in the political decision-making process.
- Discuss the advantages and disadvantages of a political system that is under absolute control or is a democracy.

NOTE: The scoring rubric for this essay appears on pages 53–54.

Part A: Short Answer

Directions:
- Analyze the documents and answer the questions that follow each document in the space provided.

Document 1

> The Wise Man's policy, accordingly,
> Will be to empty people's hearts and minds,
> To fill their bellies, weaken their ambition,
> Give them sturdy frames and always so,
> To keep them uninformed, without desire,
> And knowing ones not venturing to act.
>
> Be still while you work
> And keep full control
> Over all.
>
> —Lao Tzu (6th century B.C.)

1. What role does the citizen play in this political system?

_____

_____

Document 2

> "We are a democracy because the power to make the laws is given to the many rather than the few. But while the law gives equal justice to everyone, it has not failed to reward excellence. While every citizen has an equal opportunity to serve the public, we reward our most distinguished [best] citizens by asking them to make our political decisions. Nor do we discriminate against the poor. A man may serve his country no matter how low his position on the social scale.
>
> An Athenian citizen does not put his private affairs before the affairs of the state; even our merchants and businessmen know something about politics. We alone believe that a man who takes no interest in public affairs is more than harmless—he is useless."
>
> —"Pericles' Funeral Oration"
> Athens, 5th century B.C.

2. According to Pericles, what is a responsibility of a citizen in a democracy?

_____

_____

Document 3

"... Whereas ... King James II, ... did attempt to undermine ... the laws and liberties of this kingdom ...

Therefore, the Parliament declares:

1. That the King's supposed power of suspending laws without the consent of Parliament is illegal.

4. That the levying of taxes for the use of the king without the consent of Parliament is illegal.

8. That the king should not interfere with the election of members of Parliament.

13. And that to redress grievances and amend, strengthen, and preserve the laws, Parliament ought to be held [meet] frequently."

—The English Bill of Rights, 1689

3. How did the English Bill of Rights change governmental decision making?

_____

_____

Document 4

"But what happens when the sun sets?"

4. Based on this cartoon, who controlled the government of France from the mid-1600s to the early 1700s?

_____

_____

Document 5

After Socialism, Fascism combats the whole complex system of democratic ideology [theory], and repudiates [denies] it, whether in its theoretical premises [basis] or in its practical application. Fascism denies that the majority, by the simple fact that it is a majority, can direct human society; it denies that numbers alone can govern by means of a periodical consultation [elections], and it affirms the . . . beneficial, and fruitful [useful] inequality of mankind, which can never be permanently leveled through . . . universal suffrage.

—Benito Mussolini, 1932

5. What was the basis of Mussolini's argument against democracy?

_____

_____

Document 6

> "We the Japanese people, acting through our duly elected representatives in the National Diet [legislature], resolve that never again shall we be visited with the horrors of war through the action of government, do proclaim that sovereign power resides with the people and do firmly establish this Constitution. Government is a sacred trust of the people, the authority for which is derived from the people, the powers of which are exercised by the representatives of the people, and the benefits of which are enjoyed by the people. This is a universal principle of mankind upon which this Constitution is founded. We reject and revoke all constitutions, laws, ordinances, and rescripts in conflict herewith."
>
> —The Japanese Constitution of 1947

6. Which universal principle is the basis for the Japanese Constitution?

_____

_____

Part B: Essay

Directions:
- Write a well-organized essay that includes an introduction, several paragraphs, and a conclusion.
- Use evidence from the documents to support your response.
- Do not simply repeat the contents of the documents.
- Include specific related outside information.

Historical Context:

> Throughout history, societies have held different viewpoints on governmental decision making and the role of citizens in this decision-making process. The decision-making process can range from absolute control to democracy.

Task:

> Using information from the documents and your knowledge of global history and geography, write an essay in which you
>
> - Compare and contrast the different viewpoints societies have held about the process of governmental decision making and about the role of citizens in the political decision-making process.
> - Discuss the advantages and disadvantages of a political system that is under the absolute control of a single individual or a few individuals, or a political system that is a democracy.

Be sure to include specific historical details. You must also include additional information from your knowledge of global history and geography.

DOCUMENT-BASED ESSAY
SPECIFIC RUBRIC

5

- Uses at least half of the documents provided
- Places documents in historical context
- Incorporates relevant outside information related to document
- Uses the terms "absolute monarch," "democracy," and "fascism" correctly
- Either compares or contrasts societies' viewpoints on the process of governmental decision making
- Either compares or contrasts the citizen's role in the decision-making process
- Analyzes advantages and disadvantages of each political system
- Weaves documents into body of essay
- Writes a well-developed essay, consistently demonstrating a logical and clear plan of organization
- Includes a strong introduction and conclusion

4

- Uses at least half of the documents provided
- Places documents in historical context
- Incorporates relevant outside information related to documents
- Uses the terms "absolute monarch," "democracy," and "fascism" correctly
- Either compares or contrasts societies' viewpoints on the process of governmental decision making
- Either compares or contrasts the citizen's role in the decision-making process
- Discusses advantages and disadvantages of each political system
- Discussion of documents may be descriptive or analytical
- Writes a well-developed essay, demonstrating a logical and clear plan of organization
- Includes a good introduction and conclusion

3

- Uses at least two of the documents provided
- Use of documents within the historical context may be in error
- Incorporates limited outside information related to documents
- Has limited understanding of political terms

- Understands some aspect of the process of governmental decision making
- Understands some aspect of the citizen's role in the decision-making process
- Has limited understanding of different political systems
- Generally discusses advantages and disadvantages of a political system
- Reiterates information from documents
- Writes a satisfactorily developed essay, demonstrating a general plan of organization
- Restates the theme in the introduction and concludes with a restatement of the task

2

- Attempts to address task with at least one document
- No relevant outside information is apparent
- Knowledge of political terms and systems is vague, general, or incorrect
- Reiterates contents of document
- Does not understand process of governmental decision making or citizen's role
- Writes a poorly organized essay lacking focus
- Has vague or missing introduction or conclusion

1

- Demonstrates a very limited understanding of the task
- Cannot distinguish between aspects of the task
- Fails to use or vaguely refers to documents
- Contains factual errors
- Essay demonstrates a major weakness in organization
- Vague or missing introduction or conclusion

0

- Fails to address the question
- No response
- Blank paper

Glossary

The Glossary that follows contains a list of terms, international organizations, and important people that are an integral part of the Global History and Geography course of study. The Glossary should be used as a device to help you recall some significant terms, people, and concepts in Global History and Geography. It is not all-inclusive but is one study tool to prepare you for the Global History and Geography Regents.

IMPORTANT TERMS

absolute monarchy   system in which a ruler (king or queen) has complete authority over the government without limits on his/her powers.

absolutism   political system in which the monarch has supreme power and control over the lives of the people in the country.

acid rain   toxic pollution that is produced by the burning of fossil fuels. It affects plants, animals, and people who have a respiratory illness.

African National Congress (ANC)   group formed in 1912 to work for blacks' rights in South Africa. This group led the fight against apartheid and continues to encourage independence for the black majority.

Age of Exploration   period from 1400 to 1600 during which European monarchs sent explorers to find new trade routes, resources, and land in Asia, Africa, and the Americas.

agrarian economy   economic system that centers on agriculture as the chief source of wealth.

Agrarian Revolution   change in the farming method in England during the 1600s that dramatically increased farm production.

alliance   agreement between two or more countries that provides for their mutual defense or protection.

animism   traditional African religion; a belief that the spirit dwells in all living and nonliving things.

anthropologist   social scientist who studies the physical characteristics, origins, cultures, and artifacts of human beings.

anti-Semitism   prejudice against the Jewish people.

apartheid (Afrikaans word—apartness)   an official policy of strict segregation of the races; practiced in South Africa from 1945 until it was repealed in 1991.

appeasement   policy of giving in to the demands of the aggressor to avoid war; policy used by England and France to satisfy Hitler's demands for land during the 1930s.

Arabic numerals   numbers first developed by mathematicians in Gupta, India, and adapted by most of the Western world (counting 1, 2, 3, etc.).

archaeologist   social scientist who studies past human life by examining the monuments and relics left by ancient people.

archipelago   chain or group of islands.

aristocracy   government ruled by nobles or the upper class.

armistice   temporary agreement to stop fighting.

astrolabe   instrument that determines latitude by measuring the position of the stars; one of the technological improvements that the Europeans borrowed from the Muslims that contributed to the Age of Exploration.

balance of power   distribution of military and economic powers among rival nations so that one nation does not have more power than its neighbors or other nations.

balance of trade   difference in value between a nation's imports and exports over a period of time.

Black Death   bubonic plague or contagious disease during the 14th century whose death toll is estimated to have exceeded 100 million in Europe, Asia, and Africa.

Bolsheviks   left-wing majority group of the Russian Socialist Democratic Party under the leadership of Nikolai Lenin, which seized control of the government by revolution in November 1917; the group was later called Communists.

bourgeoisie   middle class between aristocrats and workers. This term was used by Marx and Engels in the *Communist Manifesto* to describe the capitalists, or factory owners, who exploit the worker, or the proletariat. In the Middle Ages, the bourgeoisie were members of the merchant class or the townspeople of the city.

Buddhism major religion of eastern and central Asia founded in 6th century B.C. and based on the teaching of Siddhartha Gautama, who believed people must reject the material world and follow a philosophy of self-denial and meditation.

Bushido traditional code of the Japanese warrior class (the samurai) during the feudal period; emphasizes loyalty and honor to the local warlord over allegiance to the Emperor.

Byzantine Empire eastern part of the Roman Empire; existed from 330 A.D. to 1453 A.D.; preserved the rich cultural heritage of the ancient Greeks; saved Roman texts from destruction after the fall of the western part of the Roman Empire in 476 A.D.

caliph title for the successor to Muhammad as the political and religious leader of Islam.

calligraphy elaborate handwriting that Chinese and Arab scholars turned into an art form; characters or symbols represent words or ideas.

capitalism economic system in which the means of production and the distribution of goods and wealth are controlled by individuals and operated for profit. Consumers have freedom of choice to buy or not buy goods.

caste system division of society into four major groups based on occupation or birth; a rigid social system that was characteristic of traditional Hindu Indian society.

Christianity belief system based on the teachings of Jesus Christ that began in the Middle East about 2,000 years ago and was rooted in the monotheistic religion of Judaism.

citizen member of a state or country.

city-state small independent state that consists of a city and the territory surrounding it; associated with Ancient Greece.

civil disobedience nonviolent or passive resistance; refusal to obey unjust laws that are morally wrong.

civilization advanced form of society characterized by a complex social system, some form of writing, and advances in science and technology.

clan extended family unit or groups of families that have a common ancestor or family ties.

Classical Period name for the period in history that pertains to the artistic style of ancient Greece and Rome; their civilization was at its highest and was considered the Golden Age.

class system social division of society based on wealth, birth, education, occupation, or race.

codified law organized and written set of rules or laws.

Cold War period of tension and hostility between the United States and the Soviet Union after 1945 because of their different political and economic systems; worldwide struggle without actual fighting between the two powers; ended in 1991 with the collapse of the Soviet Union.

collectivization system under communism in which many small farms were combined into large farms owned and operated by the government and worked by the peasants; started by Stalin in the late 1920s.

command economy economic system in which the central authority makes all the production decisions on what and how to produce goods.

Commercial Revolution changes in the economies of Europe in the Middle Ages in which there was a growth of towns, banking systems, and trade among nations; the economic changes that opened up Europe to a global economy based on worldwide trade.

communism form of socialism proposed by Karl Marx and Friedrich Engels; characterized by a classless society that supports a common ownership of the means of production and equal distribution of the products of society; no class struggle and the government will wither away.

Confucianism belief system based on the teaching of the Chinese philosopher Confucius, also known as Kung Fu Zi; emphasizes traditional values such as obedience, knowing each person's role in society, and respect for education, elders, and leaders.

conquistadors Spanish explorers who conquered land in the Americas for Spain during the 1500s and 1600s.

Constitutional Monarchy system of government in which the power of the king or queen is limited or defined by the legislature or parliamentary body.

consumer goods tangible economic products used to satisfy the wants and needs of a society.

containment policy of the United States toward the Soviet Union during the Cold War to prevent the spread of communism in the world.

coup d'état (French term) swift overthrow of the government by force or by a small group of people.

Crusades religious wars between Christian Europe and the Muslims for control of the Holy Lands lasting from 1096 A.D. until 1246 A.D.

cultural diffusion spread of ideas, customs, and technology from one group or region to another culture.

Cultural Revolution program organized by Mao-Zedong in China in the 1960s against those who opposed the Communist government. Mao used the Red Guards (Chinese Youths) to purge China of anyone who disagreed with his ideas or policies.

culture people's way of life, which includes language, customs, religion, traditions, and institutions.

cuneiform ancient Sumerian form of writing developed around 3000 B.C. The wedge-shaped characters were formed by pressing a stick into wet clay.

Czar title of the Russian Emperor; also spelled tsar.

decolonization process by which European colonies in Africa and Asia became independent countries after World War II ended.

deforestation destruction of a forest, especially the tropical rain forest, to clear the land to raise food or sell the lumber. The remaining soil is of poor quality because heavy rains wash away the nutrients; the land becomes barren.

democracy system of government in which the people rule.

demographic pattern population distribution.

depression period of drastic economic decline, characterized by a large increase in unemployment, falling prices, and wages.

desalination process of removing salt from sea water in order to make it drinkable.

desertification process by which fertile land becomes a desert due to natural causes or sometimes by man's destructive use of the land.

détente relaxation of tension between the United States and the Soviet Union during the 1970s. The policy was developed by U.S. President Richard Nixon and Soviet leader Leonid Brezhnev.

developed countries highly industrialized nations that have advanced technology.

developing countries countries that are in the process of industrializing, have limited resources, and poor educational and health systems; mainly located in Africa, Asia, and Latin America.

dharma religious duties and rights of each individual of each class within the Hindu belief system.

Diaspora forced scattering of the Jewish people from their homeland in Palestine by the Chaldeans in 586 B.C. and later by the Romans in

70 A.D., resulting in the establishment of Jewish communities throughout Europe and North Africa; scattering of African people because of the slave trade.

dictatorship system of government in which one person or one party rules the government with absolute control.

disarmament reduction or limiting weapons and military forces as outlined in a treaty.

dissident a person who openly disagrees with the policies or methods of a political party or government, such as those who disagree with the policies of the Communist Party in China or Cuba.

divine right belief that the king or queen was God's earthly representative and received all power directly from God.

domestic system system of manufacturing prior to the Industrial Revolution in which weavers and craftsmen produced goods at home.

dynasty series of rulers from the same family or line of descent.

economics study of how people make a living; how goods and services are produced and distributed to satisfy people's needs.

embargo government order restricting the selling of a particular product to or trading with another nation.

empire groups of territories controlled by one ruler or government.

encomienda system established by the Spanish government in the Americas that enabled the colonists to tax or get labor from the Native Americans.

enlightened despot absolute ruler who bases decisions on the Enlightenment ideas; uses absolute power to begin social changes.

Enlightenment period known as the Age of Reason in 18th-century Europe. Enlightenment thinkers believed that one could use reason to understand the universe; they rejected traditional ideas based on authority.

Estates-General legislative assembly of France composed of clergy, nobles, and commoners.

ethics standards or rules that guide human behavior.

ethnic cleansing term used to describe the forcible removal or murder of Muslims from former Yugoslav provinces of Bosnia and Herzegovina by the Serbian Christian majority during the years 1992–1995; similar policy used by Serbs in Kosovo against the Muslims in 1998.

ethnic group group of people sharing a common language, religion, history, and cultural heritage.

ethnocentrism   prejudicial belief that one's culture or standards are superior to those of other societies.

Eurodollar   uniform currency introduced in Europe in 1999.

expansionism   policy of increasing a nation's territory at the expense of another nation.

exploitation   term used to describe how the mother countries took advantage of their colonies to insure that their own economies grew.

extended family   family made up of grandparents, parents, children, aunts, uncles, and cousins whose members may live in the same household or area; this type of family structure exists primarily in a traditional society.

extraterritorality   special right of citizens of a foreign country to be tried for a crime by the laws and courts of their own nation; applied to Westerners in China during the 19th and 20th centuries.

factory system   system that brought workers and machines together to produce goods in large quantities; began in the British textile industry during the Industrial Revolution.

famine   drastic shortage of food that results in severe starvation and hunger.

fascism   political philosophy that glorifies the nation over the individual. A dictator has complete control, suppresses all opposition, promotes a policy of extreme nationalism and racism, and has no regard for democracy.

Fertile Crescent   large arc of land in the Middle Eastern area between the Tigris and Euphrates Rivers; mostly desert or semiarid land; called the Cradle of Civilization.

feudalism   political, economic, and social system developed in Europe and Japan during the 1100s in which land is controlled by the local lord, who owed allegiance to a higher lord or monarch. The lord allowed serfs to work the land in exchange for protection.

Five Pillars of Wisdom   basic beliefs of Islam that include: one God, Allah, praying five times a day, fasting during the month of Ramadan, making a pilgrimage to Mecca, and giving alms to the poor.

Five-Year Plan   series of economic goals set by the government in either a Communist or Socialist system; instituted by Joseph Stalin in Russia in 1927 to build up industry and improve farm production.

fossil fuels   fuel such as oil, coal, wood, and natural gas.

free enterprise   economic system in which individuals and businesses have the freedom to operate for profit with little or no government interference.

free trade   removal of trade restrictions among nations.

genocide   deliberate effort to kill all members of an ethnic or religious group.

geography   one of the social sciences that studies the people, the environment, and the resources of an area.

glasnost   Russian term for "openness"; refers to Mikhail Gorbachev's effort in the 1980s to introduce political reform in the Soviet Union by providing freedom of speech and press.

globalization   integration of capital, technology, and information across national borders, creating a single global market and, to some degree, a global village.

Great Depression   worldwide economic decline that began in 1929 and ended in 1940; businesses and banks failed and there was widespread joblessness.

Great Leap Forward   five-year economic program introduced by Mao Zedong in China in 1958; designed to improve China's agricultural and industrial production.

greenhouse effect   rise in the global temperature due to excessive carbon dioxide and pollutants that create a layer in the atmosphere that traps the heat.

Green Revolution   twentieth-century technological advances in agriculture that have led to increased food production on a limited parcel of land.

gross national product (GNP)   total value of goods and services produced in one year; indicator of a country's standard of living.

heavy industry   industries requiring complex machinery in the production of iron, steel, and coal.

heliocentric theory   belief that the sun is the center of the universe and that earth and the planets revolve around it.

hierarchy   group of people or things arranged or organized by rank or level of importance.

hieroglyphics   ancient Egyptian writing system that uses pictures and symbols to represent sounds, words, or ideas.

Hinduism   major religion of India based on a rigid caste system containing rules for proper behavior. Karma, or a person's behavior, influences his or her reincarnation after death into a higher or lower caste. An endless cycle of rebirth is created for each soul.

Holocaust Nazi genocide against Jews and other minorities during World War II, resulting in the death of millions of people.

Holy Land sacred Israel/Palestine area where Christian, Islamic, and Judaic shrines are located commemorating the birth of their religions.

humanism intellectual and cultural movement of the Renaissance stressing the significance of each individual; focused on the secular world and a return to a study of the classical works of Greece and Rome.

human rights freedom and rights that all people belonging to a society are entitled to, such as freedom of expression, life, religion, right to vote, and equal protection before the law.

ideology system of beliefs and ideas that guide a nation or group of people.

illiteracy inability to read or write; one measure of a country's industrial development and standard of living.

imperialism policy whereby one nation dominates by direct or indirect rule the political, economic, and social life of a foreign country, region, or area.

indemnity payment of damages or losses suffered in war.

Industrial Revolution historical event that began in the textile industry in England in the 18th century resulting in the shift from the manufacturing of goods by hand to the use of machinery, along with social and economic changes accompanying this change.

inflation economic cycle resulting in a general rise in prices and a decline in the purchasing power of money.

interdependence mutual way in which the economies of countries are dependent on the goods, resources, and knowledge from other parts of the world.

Internet global computer connection using telephone lines or modems providing on-line contact with people and information on most subjects.

intifada Palestinian uprising against the territory held by Israel that lasted from 1987 until 1988.

Iron Curtain term coined by Winston Churchill in 1946 to describe an imaginary line dividing Soviet Communist-dominated Eastern Europe and the democracies of Western Europe.

Islam name that means submission to the will of God; major religion of the Middle East founded in the seventh century A.D. by the prophet Muhammad whose teachings include belief in one God—Allah.

Islamic Fundamentalists Muslims who believe that public and private behavior should be guided by the principles and values in the Koran. They are against the materialism of Western society.

isolationism policy of avoiding or limiting involvement in the affairs or conflicts of other nations.

jihad Muslim holy war to spread the Muslim faith.

Judaism monotheistic religion of the Hebrews whose spiritual and ethical principles are rooted in the Old Testament of the Bible and in the Talmud.

junta group of military officers who rule a country after seizing power.

Justinian Code codification of Roman law by the Emperor Justinian in the 6th century that greatly influenced the Western legal system.

kaiser German word for emperor used in the 1870s and early 1900s.

karma belief in Hinduism, that people's lifelong deeds and actions affect their fate in their future life.

kibbutz collective farms established by Jewish settlers in Israel that are based on socialist principles of shared ownership and communal living.

Koran sacred book of Islam containing the revelations made by Allah to Muhammad.

kulak group of wealthy peasants in the Soviet Union who opposed the collectivization of agriculture in the 1920s and 1930s.

laissez-faire economic policy stating that there should be a "hands off" or limited government involvement with private business.

Law of Twelve Tablets basis of Roman law written on twelve tablets around 450 B.C. and displayed in the marketplace for all to see and know.

less-developed countries (LDC) countries with few industries and poor health and educational systems.

liberalism political philosophy supporting social changes, democracy, and personal freedom.

liberation theology movement in the Catholic Church in Latin America in the late 1970s and 1980s urging the clergy to take an active role in changing the social conditions of the poor.

limited monarchy system of government in which the king's powers are not absolute but specifically guided by a constitution or legislative body.

literacy rate   percentage of people in a country with the ability to read and write; method used to measure the standard of living of a country.

mandate of heaven   belief in ancient China that the Emperor received the authority to rule from heaven (God), and in return, the people owed compete obedience to the ruler; divine right theory.

manoralism   economic and social system in Medieval Europe; a self-sufficient community in which the serfs were bound to the land and were required to work on the lord's manor or estate that consisted of farmland, a village, the lord's castle, and surrounding lands administered by the lord.

market economy   economic system in which the laws of supply and demand and the price system influence the decisions of the consumer and the producers of goods.

Marshall Plan   formally known as the European Recovery Act; American economic aid package proposed by Secretary of State George Marshall in 1947 to assist European countries in rebuilding after World War II as a way to strengthen democratic governments against communism. The United States gave $17 billion in aid from 1947 to 1951.

Marxism   political and economic theory developed by Karl Marx and Friedrich Engels in support of an economic interpretation of history that contributed to a class struggle between the haves and have nots; belief that private ownership must be abolished in favor of collective ownership.

matriarchy   system in which ancestry is traced through the mother and her descendants.

medieval   historical period known as the Middle Ages lasting from about 500 A.D. until the beginning of the 1400s.

Meiji Restoration   period lasting from 1868 to 1912 when Japan adopted Western ways in order to become a modern and industrialized nation.

mercantilism   economic theory developed during the 17th and 18th centuries in which the colonies existed for the benefit of the mother country; wealth and power of a country based on exporting more than it imported through strict regulation of colonial trade.

mestizo   people of mixed European and Native American ancestry in the Spanish colonies of Latin America.

militarism   policy glorifying the armed forces; support of aggressive military preparedness.

mixed economy   economic system combining government regulation of industries with private enterprise or capitalistic characteristics.

modernization   change in a nation from a traditional economy or way of life to modern ideas, methods, and technology.

monopoly   complete control by one person or group over a particular product or market resulting in the ability to set or fix market prices.

monotheism   belief in one God.

monsoons   seasonal winds from the Indian Ocean that bring heavy rain. They dominate the climate of South Asia, the Middle East, and East Africa.

Mosque   Muslim house of worship.

multinational corporation   large business enterprises such as Coca-Cola and McDonald's that have branches in many countries.

Muslim   follower of the Islamic religion.

nationalism   feeling of pride in and loyalty to one's nation or group and its traditions; belief that each group is entitled to its own nation or government.

nationalization   government seizure of private businesses or industries.

nation-state   political state that developed in Western Europe at the end of the Middle Ages with the decline of feudalism. At that time, the strong monarchs of England and France united people of a common nationality who began to transfer their loyalty from the local lord to the monarch who molded a unified national state. Today it refers to a country with a strong central government and a common history and culture.

natural laws   rules of human behavior based on reason and an inborn sense of morality. Enlightenment philosophers thought these laws were universal.

Nazism   policies associated with German dictator Adolf Hitler of the National Socialist Party stressing militarism, racism, and extreme nationalism.

Neolithic Revolution   the New Stone Age (8000–300 B.C.) or the Agricultural Revolution; changes brought about when people began to settle in small communities, domesticated animals, and secured food by farming.

neutrality   policy of not supporting any one side in a conflict.

New Economic Policy (NEP)   policy introduced by Lenin in 1921 in the Soviet Union providing for some restoration of private enterprise and capitalism in order to ease the economic crisis created by the civil war in Russia (1918–1921).

nomad   person who has no fixed home and travels from place to place in search of food and other necessities of life.

nonaggression pact   agreement between two nations to not attack each other.

nonalignment   policy that some Third World nations followed during the Cold War of not supporting either the United States or the Soviet Union.

nuclear family   family structure usually found in industrial societies consisting of only parents and their children.

oligarchy   form of government in which a small group or elite has power.

oral tradition   the practice of passing on history and culture of a society through the spoken word.

overpopulation   condition in many developing countries where the population is too large to be supported by the available resources of the region.

Palestine Liberation Organization (PLO)   group formed in 1964 and led by Yasir Arafat whose goal was to establish a Palestinian homeland by the use of terrorist tactics in the lands occupied by Israel. The PLO later renounced terrorism and became the official organization to negotiate with Israel over the creation of a Palestinian state.

Pan-Africanism   nationalist movement that began in the early 1900s encouraging unification and cooperation among all African nations.

Pan-Arabism   mid-twentieth-century movement promoting the unification of all Arab countries based on cultural and political ties.

Pan-Slavism   nationalist movement promoting the cultural and political unification of Slavic people.

parliamentary system   type of government in which representatives to the legislative branch of government (Parliament) are democratically elected by the people and the majority party in Parliament selects a prime minister from their ranks. Parliament has supreme legislative powers.

passive resistance   form of civil disobedience using nonviolent methods; technique used by Indian leader Mohandas Gandhi, included the boycott of British goods and refusal to pay taxes or serve in the army as a way to promote Indian independence. A similar approach was adopted by Dr. Martin Luther King, Jr., in the civil rights movement in the United States during the 1960s.

patriarchy family organization in which the father or eldest son heads the household.

patricians wealthy landowners or nobles of the ancient Roman Empire.

Pax Mongolia brief period of peace and prosperity in Eurasia during the Mongol rule of Kublai Khan.

Pax Romana time of Roman peace and relative prosperity in the Mediterranean world beginning in 27 B.C. and lasting over 200 years during the time of the Roman Empire.

peaceful coexistence Soviet policy adopted by Nikita Khrushchev in the 1950s, believing that communism and democracy could exist with each other peacefully and avoid hostility.

peasants small farmers or laborers who work the land.

peninsular person born in Spain or Portugal who was eligible for the highest position in the Latin American colonies.

per capita income average income per person of all the citizens in a country; one way to measure the standard of living of a country.

perestroika Russian term for reconstructing; Gobachev's economic policy of the 1980s promoting private enterprise and the free market system instead of a strict government-planned economy.

pharaoh title of rulers of ancient Egypt who had absolute power.

planned economy system in which the government determines what, how much, and who is allowed to receive the goods that are produced; used by the Soviet Union starting in 1927 and lasting until the 1980s.

pogroms organized attacks or persecutions against a minority group, particularly the Jews in czarist Russia.

polis independent city-state in ancient Greece.

polytheism worship or belief in many gods.

population distribution average number of people in a particular area or region.

population explosion large increase in the world's population due to the availability of better medical technology contributing to a longer life expectancy for children and adults.

prehistoric referring to a period of time prior to written history, around 3000 B.C.

primary source eyewitness account or firsthand information about people or events such as diaries or legal documents.

privatization returning or selling of government facilities to private individuals or investors.

proletariat term used by Marx and Engels to describe the industrial working class in capitalist countries.

propaganda spreading of ideas, information, and rumors to promote a cause or damage an opposing cause.

protectorate form of imperial control in which the foreign country allows the local ruler to remain in power but controls affairs behind the scenes.

Protestant Reformation period beginning in 1527 in Europe when Martin Luther challenged the authority of the Pope resulting in the formation of new Christian churches that opposed the rules and doctrines of the Roman Catholic Church.

racism prejudice and discrimination based on the premise that one group is superior to another because of race.

reactionary political leader who is opposed to change or wants to restore the old order such as those leaders at the Congress of Vienna in the 1800s.

recession decline in economic activities that lasts for a limited amount of time.

reform to try to make things better by change.

reincarnation Hindu belief that the soul is reborn in different forms that indicate whether a person led a good or bad life.

Renaissance French word meaning rebirth; period of reawakened interest in the classical works of art, literature, and architecture of Greece and Rome that originated in Italy and spread throughout all of Europe from the 1300s until the 1600s; challenged the ideas and structure of the Middle Ages.

reparation payment for war damages.

republic form of government in which the people choose their officials.

revolution sudden and drastic change resulting in the overthrow of the existing government or political system by force, as in the Russian Revolution; changes in cultural systems, as in the Industrial or Computer Revolution.

Russification policy adopted by Russian Tsar Alexander III in 1882. Its purpose was to unite the empire's many provinces. It became an official policy of intolerance and persecution of non-Russian people. Jews were singled out in particular for persecution.

samurai members of the Japanese warrior class during the medieval period.

sanctions penalties or actions imposed on a nation by other countries for breaking international laws in order to end its illegal activity.

satellite countries   countries politically and economically controlled by a nearby country such as the Eastern European countries that were dominated by the Soviet Union after World War II.

savanna   broad grassy plain with few trees in a tropical or subtropical region that has an irregular rain pattern.

scapegoats   people who are made to bear the blame for the actions of others; technique used by the Nazi Party in Germany against the Jews for problems confronting the country in the 1920s and 1930s.

scarcity   fundamental economic problem describing limited resources combined with unlimited wants and needs.

Scientific Revolution   period in science during the 16th and 17th centuries in which scientists challenged traditional authority and used observations and reason to reach conclusions; contributed to advances in medicine and mathematics.

scramble for Africa   time period from 1890 to 1914 when European imperialistic countries divided up the continent for markets and raw materials.

secondary source   information about past historical events based on the knowledge collected from several sources.

secularism   rejection of the importance of religion in favor of worldly matters.

self-determination   right of the people to make their own decisions about their political and economic development.

serf   peasant in feudal times who was legally bound to the land, owned by the lord and subject to the will of the lord.

Shintoism   native Japanese religion stressing the connection between people and the forces of nature. In the 18th century it became the national religion of Japan extolling nationalism, ancestor worship, and divinity of the emperor.

shoguns   military generals who ruled Japan from the 12th century to the 1800s.

Sikhs   people who live primarily in the Punjab area of Northern India; followers of a religion formed in the early 1500s that blends elements of Islam and Hinduism, rejects the caste system, and is monotheistic.

Silk Road   ancient Chinese commercial route that stretched for over 4,000 miles, allowing China to exchange its silk for Middle Eastern and European products.

social contract   political theory of 17th- and 18th-century Europe stating that there is an agreement between the people and the government, with people giving up power to their leader in return for life, liberty, and property; governments that fail to fulfill their agreement can be changed.

socialism   system in which the government owns and operates all the essential means of production, distribution, and exchange of goods; society as a whole, not the individuals, owns all the property.

social mobility   ability to move from one social class to another through education or improvement in income or occupation.

Solidarity   independent trade union movement led by Lech Walesa of Poland contributing to the demise of communism.

Soviet bloc   countries in the Cold War that were allied with or supported the Soviet Union.

sphere of influence   area or region of a country in which a foreign country had exclusive trading privileges such as the right to build railroads and factories; special regions along the coast of China in the 19th century controlled by European imperial countries.

standard of living   measure of how well people are living based upon the availability of resources and wealth.

status quo   describing a state of affairs existing as they are at the present time.

subsistence agriculture   type of farming in which the farmer and his family can barely make a living.

suffrage   the right to vote.

Superpowers   the United States and the Soviet Union, which dominated world politics from the end of World War II until the late 1980s.

supply and demand   economic theory of a market economy that prices reflect the demand for a product and its availability.

tariff   tax on goods coming into the country usually to protect industries from foreign competition.

technology   use of science and inventions to help society achieve its basic needs or improve a way of living.

Ten Commandments   religious and moral laws of Judaism; also adopted by the Christians as part of their moral laws.

terrorism   deliberate use of force or violence by an organized group to achieve its political goals.

theocracy   nation ruled by religious leaders who base their power on the Divine Right.

Third World   term used to describe the developing nations of Africa, Asia, and Latin America.

totalitarianism government in which one person or group controls all aspects of the political, economic, social, religious, educational, and cultural life of the nation with no regard for individual rights.

total war commitment of a nation's entire military and civilian resources to the war effort.

trade deficit excess of imports over exports.

traditional economy economic system that meets the basic needs of its people through fishing, hunting, and gathering; basic economic decisions are made according to customs or habits.

tyrant ruthless and unfair ruler in ancient Greece who gained power by force and established a one-man rule.

untouchable (harijan) name derived from the ideas that others would be made dirty and impure from touching them; social group belonging to the lowest caste in Hinduism who do all the undesirable work; outlawed by the Indian Constitution but still prevalent in some communities.

urbanization development of cities due to the movement of people from rural areas in search of jobs and better opportunities.

utopian 19th-century socialist who believed in the ideal society in which all members of society worked for the common good and shared equally in the economic success of the group.

vassal lord in medieval Europe who received land from a more powerful lord in exchange for loyalty and service.

vernacular language of the people in a country; language used by Renaissance writers to replace Latin, which was the language of the church or scholars.

war crimes atrocities committed by the military or the government against the civilian population during armed conflicts; they include mass murders, genocide, rape, or persecution of religious or racial groups. Since World War II, war crime tribunals such as Nuremburg and The Hague have been set up to deal with these crimes against humanity.

welfare state system under which the government assumes responsibility for the people's social and economic well-being.

Westernization process of adapting Western culture and technology; adapted by Peter the Great of Russia in the 18th century and during the Meiji Restoration of Japan in the 19th century.

zero population growth   situation in which the birth rate of a country equals the death rate.

Zionism   worldwide organized movement to build or gain support for a Jewish homeland in Palestine.

INTERNATIONAL ORGANIZATIONS AND AGREEMENTS

Antarctic Treaty   treaty signed in 1959 by the United States, the Soviet Union, and ten other nations forbidding the building of military bases, testing of nuclear weapons, or disposing of radioactive wastes by these nations in the area near the Antarctic. It was meant to foster cooperation among scientists from all nations who conduct research on the continent; other nations later signed this treaty.

ANZUS Pact   mutual defense agreement among Australia, New Zealand, and the United States, signed in 1951 to contain communism; considered an attack upon one of the others as dangerous to its own safety.

Arab League   organization founded by Arab nationalists in 1945 to promote Arab unity during times of crisis; worked jointly for common economic, political, and social goals; presently, all sixteen nations in the Middle East are members along with four other African nations in which the majority of the population is Arab.

Asia Pacific Economic Cooperation Group (APEC)   group formed by the nations of the Pacific Rim including countries in Southeast Asia, East Asia, and the Americas that border the Pacific Ocean; goal is to promote trade and investment across the Pacific region and the world.

Association of Southeast Asian Nations (ASEAN)   organization consisting of seven members that are archipelago nations in Southeast Asia and nations on the Indochina peninsula; seeks to promote economic and cultural cooperation as well as solve regional disputes.

Camp David Accords   agreement negotiated by President Jimmy Carter between Prime Minister Menachem Begin of Israel and President Anwar Sadat of Egypt; later became the basis of the peace treaty in 1979 calling for diplomatic recognition of Israel by Egypt and normalization of relations, the return of the Sinai Peninsula to Egypt in exchange for the opening of the Suez canal to Israel, and discussion on Palestinian self-rule in the West Bank and the Gaza Strip.

Caribbean Community and Common Market (CARICOM) formed in 1973 to promote cooperation in the areas of economics and foreign policy among the 13 Caribbean countries.

Commonwealth of Independent States (CIS) association created in December 1991 to replace the government when the Soviet Union collapsed; consisted of 12 of the 15 independent republics including Russia, Ukraine, and Belarus, whose city of Minsk became CIS headquarters; designed to promote economy and political cooperation among the former Communist republics.

Commonwealth of Nations (originally known as the British Commonwealth of Nations established by the Statute of Westminster enacted in 1931); voluntary association linking Great Britain and its former colonies on an equal basis; 47 members try to coordinate economic, political, social, and military matters.

Council of Europe old European organization established by the Treaty of London; an international organization in Strasbourg comprised of 41 democratic countries of Europe. Its purpose is to promote democratic stability and economic and social progress for Europe; composed of a committee of ministers, a secretariat, selected for five years, and an assembly of delegates; council advises on social, political, and economic matters but has no power of enforcement. It is an influential organization because all European nations are members and participate in activities.

Dayton Accord agreement negotiated to end the conflict in Bosnia-Herzegovina in November 1995 at Dayton, Ohio by three presidents: Slobodan Milosevic of Serbia, Aliza Izetbegovic of Bosnia-Herzegovina, and Franjo Tudjman of Croatia, with strong diplomatic assistance from U.S. President Bill Clinton; signed in December; provided for the partition of Bosnia and Herzegovina into two distinct areas—a Serb republic and a Muslim Croat federation; 60,000 multinational forces were provided to safeguard the peace.

European Economic Community (EEC) organization established in 1958 by Belgium, Luxembourg, France, Italy, the Netherlands, and West Germany, which agreed to form a Common Market to expand free trade by eliminating internal tariff barriers and allowing labor and capital to move freely among member nations. Now called the European Union, it includes Great Britain, Ireland, Spain, Portugal, Greece, and Denmark; by the 1990s, membership increased to 15 countries with the addition of Finland, Sweden, and Austria.

European Parliament   legislative branch of the European Union found-ed in 1958; composed of 518 representatives elected by the votes of member nations for five years; powers are advisory with all final deci-sions requiring approval of the ministers of the Council of Europe.

European Union   group that includes the countries that were members of the European Coal and Steel Community, European Atomic Energy Commission, and the European Economic Community (Common Market); official name since 1967 after the merger of these three organizations into one governing unit.

General Agreement on Tariffs and Trade (GATT)   agreement signed in 1947 to provide for free trade among member nations and to settle trading disputes; consists of 110 members; Group of Seven (G7) rep-resenting the seven most productive economies—Britain, Canada, France, Germany, Italy, Japan, and the United States—meet annually to discuss common economic problems. In 1995, the World Trade Organization (WTO) was formed as the successor to GATT.

Helsinki Accords   major diplomatic nonbinding agreement signed on August 1, 1975, at Helsinki, Finland, among the United States, Canada, the Soviet Union, and 32 European nations except Albania; agreed to legitimize the USSR's World War II territorial gains (status quo in Europe), agreed to respect human rights, and to promote scientific and cultural exchanges with each other.

International Court of Justice   agency of the United Nations consisting of 15 judges; power to settle disputes among nations by majority vote; nations that submit disputes must agree in advance to accept all decisions.

International Monetary Fund (IMF)   financial agency of the United Nations established after World War II to promote international trade, help developing nations with troubled economies, and provide balance for currencies of member nations.

Israeli-PLO Accord (The Oslo Accord)   agreement negotiated by Israeli Prime Minister Yitzhak Rabin and Palestinian Yasir Arafat in Sept-ember 1993; provided for Israel and PLO recognition of each other, eventual Palestinian self-government in the West Bank and Gaza Strip, and the gradual withdrawal of Israeli troops from these areas; implemented in May 1994 in the West Bank city of Jericho and the Gaza Strip. In 1995, following difficult negotiations with the PLO, Israel agreed to the removal of forces from other Palestinian areas and the establishment of a Palestinian police force to govern these regions.

League of Nations world peace organization with headquarters in Geneva, Switzerland, created by the Versailles Treaty at the end of World War I. Failure of the United States to join and the lack of power to enforce decisions contributed to its demise as a peacekeeping organization; precursor of the UN, which replaced the League at the end of World War II.

Montreal Protocol agreement signed in 1987 at Montreal, Canada, by 46 nations; urged that the world's nations reduce the use of chemicals that were damaging the earth's ozone layers.

North Atlantic Treaty Organization (NATO) defensive alliance formed in 1949 as a way to contain communism in Europe; members Britain, France, Belgium, the Netherlands, Luxembourg, Denmark, Iceland, Italy, Norway, Portugal, Canada, and the United States agreed that an attack on one was an attack on all and they would assist each other; Greece, Turkey, West Germany, and Spain later became members; extended membership to Poland, Hungary, and Czech Republic in 1997.

North American Free Trade Agreement (NAFTA) agreement signed by the United States, Canada, and Mexico in 1991 and implemented in 1993; designed to remove all tariffs, quotas, and trade barriers among the three nations over a 15-year period.

Northern Ireland Peace Accord agreement reached on April 10, 1998 (Good Friday) to bring peace to Northern Ireland; representatives of United Kingdom, Republic of Ireland, and leaders of Protestants and Catholics of Northern Ireland participated in the negotiations; agreed to a 108-member Northern Ireland Assembly in which Protestants and Catholics would share power, ending 26 years of direct rule from London; encouraged cooperation between Northern Ireland and the Republic of Ireland on issues of agriculture and tourism; renunciation of the Irish Republic to territorial claims in Northern Ireland; accord approved in May in a referendum by 71 percent of voters in Northern Ireland and 94 percent of voters in the Republic of Ireland.

Nuclear Test Ban Treaty signed in 1963 by Great Britain, the Soviet Union, and the United States prohibiting the testing of nuclear weapons in the atmosphere; underground testing was still permitted; nations could withdraw from the treaty if the test ban jeopardized national interest; the United Nations voted in 1996 to prohibit all future nuclear testing; only Pakistan and India failed to agree to it.

Organization of African Unity founded in 1963 by Kwame Nkrumah of Ghana to promote African unity, end colonialism, and foster cooperative approaches in foreign policies, economics, education, and defense; by 1994, with the end of white dominance in South Africa, there were 53 members with the admission of South Africa into the group.

Organization of American States (OAS) regional organization set up in 1948 to promote common defense of Western Hemisphere, democracy, economic cooperation, and human rights; headquarters in Washington, D.C.; members include the United States and 31 South American, Central American, and Caribbean countries; pressure by the United States led to the expulsion of Cuba, an original member, in 1962.

Organization of Petroleum Exporting Countries (OPEC) organization founded in 1960 by Iran, Iraq, Kuwait, Saudi Arabia, and Venezuela to control production and price of oil; membership expanded to include Algeria, Ecuador, Gabon, Indonesia, Iraq, Libya, Nigeria, Qatar, and United Arab Emirates.

SALT I and SALT II (Strategic Arms Limitations) agreements signed in 1972 and 1979; designed to limit the spread of nuclear weapons and reduction of specific types of new missile systems such as ICBM and SLBM; limits set on the number of heavy bombers carrying nuclear weapons and air-to-surface ballistic missiles with ranges of more than 375 miles.

START I (Strategic Arms Reduction Treaty) treaty signed by President George Bush and Soviet leader Mikhail Gorbachev on July 31, 1991, to reduce their strategic nuclear forces over a seven-year period by 25 to 35 percent; agreed to destroy their nuclear arsenals; ratified by the United States and Russia in 1992. Later, the former Republics of the Soviet Union Belarus, Kazakhstan, and Ukraine agreed to transfer their nuclear forces to Russia.

START II treaty signed by Presidents George Bush and Boris Yeltsin in January 1993; called for reduction of Russian nuclear warheads to 3,000 and those of the United States to 3,500 by the year 2003 or by the end of 2000, if the United States agreed to finance the dismantling of weapons in Russia; ratified by the United States in 1996; rejected by the Russian Parliament in 1997.

United Nations (UN) world peace organization established in 1945 with 185 members; included six major components: General Assembly, Secretariat, Economic and Social Council, International Court of Justice, Trusteeship Council (largely inactive with the end of colonialism), and Security Council. The Security Council keeps world peace and has five permanent members: China, France, former USSR, United Kingdom, and the United States, with ten rotating members. It has many specialized and autonomous agencies such as the World Bank, World Health Organization, and World Trade Organization.

Universal Declaration of Human Rights adopted by the United Nations General Assembly on December 10, 1948; outlined the basic rights of all individuals without regard to race, color, sex, or nationality.

Warsaw Pact mutual defense alliance formed in 1955 by Russia and its satellite nations of Eastern Europe; agreed to assist each other if attacked by Western powers; Cold War answer to NATO. The treaty is no longer operational since the collapse of communism in 1991.

World Bank specialized agency of the UN (International Bank for Reconstruction and Development) established in 1944; created to provide economic and technical help for developing nations to improve their condition; single most lending agency in international development.

World Health Organization (WHO) UN agency whose main activities include setting of international health standards. It provides information on fighting infectious diseases such as AIDS.

World Court (International Court of Justice) court consisting of 15 judges who meet in The Hague, Netherlands, and decide cases by majority votes; judges settle disputes between nations according to the principles of international law; nations submitting disputes to the court agree in advance to accept its decisions.

World Trade Organization (WTO) successor to GATT; organization with a membership of 117 countries; purpose is to make global trade free for all. The agency monitors trade agreements so that a trade benefit granted to one member must be extended to all other members; tries to settle disputes and foster the development of prospering economies by keeping tariffs low and promoting fair competition.

IMPORTANT PEOPLE

Akbar the Great (1542–1605)   greatest Mogul Emperor of India; Muslim leader who promoted religious toleration with the Hindu majority; married a Hindu princess; established a strongly centralized rule and competent civil service.

Alexander the Great (356–323 B.C.)   became king of Macedonia in 336 upon assassination of his father Philip; proceeded to control Greece and conquered the entire Persian Empire (Egypt, Asia Minor, the Fertile Crescent, and India); laid the foundation for the fusion of Greek and Middle Eastern cultures during the Hellenistic period; maintained peace and unity in the Middle East, which later influenced the Romans.

Annan, Kofi (1938–   )   elected UN secretary-general in 1997 for a five-year term of office; first secretary-general to rise through the ranks of the organization; first black African from sub-Saharan area (Ghana) to serve as head of the United Nations; educated in the United States; proposed UN reform such as consolidation of offices and revision of the UN charter to improve efficiency.

Arafat, Yasir (1929–2004)   chief spokesman and leader of the Palestine Liberation Organization (PLO) since 1969; chief goal—destruction of the state of Israel. In 1974 he was the first representative of a nongovernmental agency to address the UN General Assembly; in 1988 he renounced terrorism; supported UN-sponsored resolution for a peaceful resolution of the Arab-Israeli crisis; formally recognized Israel's right to exist in 1993 and negotiated an accord with Israeli Prime Minister Rabin, providing for gradual implementation of Palestinian self-rule in the West Bank and Gaza Strip (over the next five years). In 1996 he was elected president of Palestinian-controlled areas of Gaza and the West Bank. The peace process has stalled over the issue of control of Jerusalem. Arafat promised to proclaim a Palestinian State in the West Bank by September 2000.

Aristotle (384–322 B.C.)   Greek philosopher who wrote works on philosophy, science, government, and literature; served as personal tutor to Alexander the Great; his works influenced European thinking for over 200 years.

Assad, Hafez-al (1928–2000)   president of Syria from 1971 to 2000; defense minister and leader of nationalist Ba'ath Party who led a successful coup after Syria's loss of the Golan Heights to Israel in the 1967 Six-Day War; domestic popularity rose after the 1973 Arab-

Israeli war in which Syria failed to gain the Golan Heights but the
army performed creditably; authoritarian ruler who faced opposition
at home from Muslim fundamentalists; supported the United States
in the Gulf War of 1990; prior to his death expressed a willingness to
negotiate with Israel over the Golan Heights.

Ataturk, Kemal (1881–1938)   means Father of Turks; military officer
who led the revolution in 1923 to overthrow the sultan; first president
of Turkey from 1923 to 1938; introduced reform to create a secular
state based on Western customs; Islamic law and Arabic script
replaced by Western laws and alphabet; women were given the right
to vote; separation of church/public schools; encouraged Western
dress.

Augustus (63 B.C.–14 A.D.)   first emperor of Rome; attained sole power
after defeat of Mark Antony; Pax Romana, administrative reform that
laid the foundation for growth of the Empire that lasted for
centuries.

Begin, Menachem (1913–1992)   Israeli prime minister from 1977 to
1983; signed Camp David Accords with Egypt calling for recognition
of Israel, discussion of self-rule for Palestine, and withdrawal of
Israeli troops from Sinai Peninsula; shared the Nobel Peace Prize in
1978 with Egyptian President Anwar Sadat.

Bismarck, Otto von (1815–1898)   Prussian-born landowner known
as the Iron Chancellor; responsible for unifying the German state
into the German Empire in 1871 by a policy of Blood and Iron;
unified Germany; dominated central Europe; upset the balance
of power leading to an alliance between England and France in
1904.

Bolívar, Simón (1783–1830)   Creole leader of the South American
independence movement against Spanish rule; liberator of South
America; led a series of campaigns resulting in independence for
Venezuela, Colombia, Ecuador, Peru, and Bolivia.

Bonaparte, Napoleon (1769–1821)   general and emperor of France;
called "Son of Revolution"; gained control of France by a coup d'état
in 1799; crowned emperor in 1801; very popular due to his reform of
the French legal system (Napoleonic Code) and educational system
(state-controlled education); improved finance system; conquered and
dominated most of Europe except England; defeated by Allied Forces
of Prussia, Russia, and England; exiled to Elba; returned and defeated
at Waterloo; exiled to Saint Helena. He influenced the growth of
nationalism in Europe.

Boutros Boutros-Ghali (1922–   )   first African and Arab to serve as secretary-general of United Nations; served from 1992 to 1997; member of Egyptian delegation that helped to negotiate Camp David Accords in 1978.

Brezhnev, Leonid (1906–1982)   Soviet leader from 1964 to 1982 who succeeded Nikita Khrushchev; longest-ruling Communist leader after Stalin; followed the policy of détente; signed SALT, Helsinki Accords; harsh policy toward dissidents; invaded Czechoslovakia (1968) and Afghanistan (1980) to protect Soviet interests.

Castro, Fidel (1927–   )   Cuban revolutionary leader; premier since 1959 when he overthrew the Fulgencio Batista dictatorship; established Communist state; one of the last Communist leaders in the world; aided Communist movements in Africa and Latin America.

Catherine the Great (1729–1796)   German-born empress of Russia who ruled from 1792 to 1796; extended Russia's border to the south against Ottoman Turks by securing a warm water port on Black Sea; in the West took part in the partition of Poland; efficient ruler who codified laws; began state-sponsored education for boys and girls; ruthless toward serfs; last of the great absolute monarchs of the 1700s.

Cavour, Camillo di (1810–1861)   Italian political leader of Piedmont Sardinia from 1852 to 1859 and 1860 to 1861; considered the "Brains of Italian unification."

Charlemagne (742–814)   king of the Franks; emperor of Holy Roman Empire from 800 to 814; founder of the first empire in the West after the fall of Rome; oversaw a cultural revival of arts and learning.

Chiang Kai-shek (1888–1975)   also known as Jiang Jieshi; military leader of Chinese Nationalist Party (Kuomintang) after the death of Sun Yat-sen in 1925; involved in a civil war with Communist forces of Mao Zedong from 1927 to 1949; exiled to Taiwan after being defeated by Communists in 1949; strongly supported by the United States during his presidency of the Nationalist government of Taiwan from 1950 to 1975.

Churchill, Winston (1874–1965)   prime minister of England during World War II; strongly condemned England's policy of appeasement toward Germany prior to World War II; coined the term "Iron Curtain" describing Eastern European countries under communism after 1945.

Columbus, Christopher (1451–1506)   Italian explorer in the service of Spain who in 1492 attempted to reach Asia by sailing west and found the Western Hemisphere, thereby opening up continents to European exploration.

Confucius (551–479 B.C.)   Chinese philosopher, teacher, and political advisor; founded Confucianism, a system of ethical conduct stressing the importance of tradition, respect for learning, obedience, reverence to family, and golden rule. His teaching's dominated China for over 2,000 years.

Copernicus, Nicolaus (1473–1543)   Polish astronomer who advanced the heliocentric theory that earth and the other planets revolve around the sun; rejection of traditional view of earth as the center of the universe.

Darwin, Charles (1809–1882)   British naturalist; wrote *The Origin of the Species*, stating the theory of evolution that human beings are evolved by natural selection or survival of the fittest; theory used by Europeans to justify Imperialism, "White Man's Burden," in the scramble for Africa.

Da Vinci, Leonardo (1452–1519)   central figure of Italian Renaissance; artist, painter, engineer, scientist; most famous paintings are *Mona Lisa* and *The Last Supper*.

Deng Xiaoping (1904–1997)   Chinese Communist political leader from 1976 to 1997; implemented economic reforms modernizing industry and allowing some privatizing of agriculture and consumer industries; allowed increased contact with the West; harsh treatment for the protest movement for political freedom at Tiananmen Square.

Descartes, René (1596–1650)   French scientist, mathematician, and philosopher; considered the Father of Analytic Geometry; stressed power of reason: "I think, therefore I am."

Diaz, Porfirio (1830–1915)   Mexican dictator, or *caudillo*, from 1876 to 1880 and from 1884 to 1911; brought foreign investments and economic stability to Mexico; prosperity for the rich and poverty for the lower classes.

Elizabeth I (1533–1603)   absolute monarch of England from 1588 to 1603; restored the power of the Anglican Church; defeated the Spanish Armada in 1588; established England as a power in Europe; began colonization of the New World; brought peace and prosperity to the country.

Engels, Friedrich (1820–1895)   German philosopher, socialist, and associate of Karl Marx; wrote the *Communist Manifesto*.

Frederick the Great (1712–1786)   king of Prussia; ruled from 1740 to 1786; doubled the size of his kingdom through foreign wars and converted the country into an important European power; enlightened despot who supported educational and legal reforms and religious freedom.

Gama, Vasco da (1469–1524) Portuguese explorer who in 1498 sailed around southern Africa to India; first successful water journey from Europe to Asia; established Portuguese monopoly of Indian trade replacing Arab domination of the trade route.

Galilei, Galileo (1564–1642) Italian physicist and astronomer; discovered the law of falling bodies; used a telescope to confirm Copernicus' theory; Catholic Church condemned him as a heretic and forced him to recant.

Gandhi, Mohandas (1869–1948) Hindu nationalist leader of India's independence movement from Great Britain; revered as a prophet; called *Mahatma* (saintly one); advocated civil disobedience and passive resistance to achieve his goals; against mistreatment of women and Untouchables; assassinated in 1948 by a Hindu extremist.

Garibaldi, Giuseppe (1807–1882) Italian general and nationalist who led his volunteers (Red Shirts) in the capture of Naples and Sicily; the conquest led to the formation of a united Italy; known as "Sword of Italian Unification."

Genghis Khan (ca. 1167–1227) name means Universal Ruler; Mongol warrior; founded the largest land empire by unifying the Mongols; empire extended to Korea, Northern China, Central Asia, Middle East, and parts of European Russia; it had disintegrated by the late thirteenth century.

Gorbachev, Mikhail (1931–) Soviet leader of Communist Party who ruled from 1986 to 1991; introduced liberal policies of *glasnost*, or openness, for more democracy, and *perestroika*, economic reforms encouraging more free-market activities; was awarded Nobel Peace Prize in 1990 for permitting self-rule in Eastern Europe; resigned when Soviet Union collapsed in 1991.

Hammurabi (ca. 1792–1750 B.C.) king of Babylon who conquered city-states in the Tigris-Euphrates Valley forming the Babylonian Empire; responsible for the Code of Hammurabi, the oldest legal written code of laws that established rules for property, trade, slavery, and fair treatment of women.

Hitler, Adolf (1889–1945) German chancellor from 1933 to 1945; leader of the Nazi Party; brutal dictator whose policies led to the murder and persecution of Jews, and other minorities and dissidents; promoted extreme nationalism contributing to World War II; conquered Europe except for England; defeated by allied forces of United States, England, France, and Russia in 1945.

Ho Chi Minh (1890–1969) president of North Vietnam; founded Vietnamese Communist Party; Nationalist leader against French and United States in the Vietnam War.

Hussein, ibn Tala (King Hussein) (1935–1999) called Father of Modern Jordan, he ruled from 1955–1999; instrumental in drafting UN Resolution 242 in 1967 calling for Israel to withdraw from all occupied lands; resolution served as a benchmark for future negotiations; a shrewd political leader who survived the demands of Arab neighbors, Israel and Palestinian refugees, who are a majority in his country; in 1994 signed a peace treaty with Israel becoming the second Arab leader to end a state of war with Israel which had technically existed since 1945.

Hussein, Saddam (1937–) president and dictator of Iraq from 1979–2003; expansion policies led to war against Iran and the United States (Persian Gulf War 1990); despite disastrous defeat in both wars, maintained power by destroying all opposition, especially Kurd minority; development of chemical weapons led to problems with the United Nations and war with the United States starting in 2003.

Ivan IV (1533–1584) grandson of Ivan the Great; called Ivan the Terrible; created secret police to subdue *boyars* (aristocracy); extended Russian territories; attained absolute power and first to be crowned as tsar; ruled from 1547–1584; his death led to a civil war and foreign invasion of Russia.

Ivan the Great (1440–1505) ruled Russia from 1462–1505; ended Mongolian domination of his Moscow kingdom; first to assume title of tsar as a mandate from God.

Jefferson, Thomas (1743–1826) American statesman; third president of the United States (1801–1809); drafted Declaration of Independence borrowing from John Locke's idea of natural rights and the social contract; a child of the Enlightenment.

Jiang Zemin (1926–) Communist leader of China since 1997; introduced economic reforms to increase private ownership; little toleration for political dissenters.

Khomeini, Ayatollah (1900–1989) Islamic Fundamentalist who returned from exile in 1978 to lead a revolution resulting in the overthrow of the Shah of Iran; established an Islamic republic based on ideas contained in the Koran; rejected Westernization, particularly the United States, which he called "The Great Satan"; supported militants who held 52 American hostages for 444 days.

Khrushchev, Nikita (1894–1971) Stalin's successor, who became the first secretary of the Communist Party after Stalin's death in 1953; eliminated all opposition in a power struggle to become preeminent leader of the country; began the process of de-Stalinization in 1956; tried to increase agricultural production; supported peaceful coexistence but suppressed the Hungarian Revolution and constructed the Berlin Wall.

Klerk, Frederick Willem de (1936–) president of South Africa; released Nelson Mandela from prison in 1990; repealed the apartheid law; negotiated a plan to end white minority rule; shared the Nobel Peace Prize with Mandela in 1993; became a member of Mandela's government in 1994.

Lenin, Vladimir Ilyich (1870–1924) also known as Nikolai; founder of Bolshevik Party in Russia; set up Communist government in 1917; created Union of Soviet Socialist Republics in 1922 after defeating anticommunist forces of the Tsar and foreign nations; his death in 1924 led to a power struggle between Stalin and Trotsky.

Locke, John (1632–1704) seventeenth-century English philosopher; wrote *Two Treatises of Government* to justify the Glorious Revolution; asserted that people possessed the natural right to life, liberty, and property, that people enter a social contract with a government to achieve these goals, and if a government does not live up to these purposes, the people have the right to revolt. His ideas influenced Jefferson's Declaration of Independence and Rousseau's book, *Social Contract*.

Louis XIV (1638–1715) ruler of France known as "The Sun King"; reigned from 1643 to 1715; divine right ruler who exercised unlimited powers, put down nobles' revolts, established loyal middle-class civil servants, built an extravagant palace at Versailles, and developed commerce and industry. His lavish court and endless foreign wars left France almost bankrupt.

L'Ouverture, François (1743–1803) revolutionary leader of Haiti; led struggle for independence from Napoleon; ruled from 1798 to 1802; his success ended Napoleon's dream of an empire in the Americas.

Luther, Martin (1483–1546) German priest and leader of the Protestant

Reformation against the Catholic Church; challenged papal authority and questioned the selling of indulgences in 95 *Theses* in 1517.

Machiavelli, Niccolò (1469–1527)   Italian who served the Florentine Republic as secretary and diplomat; author of *The Prince*, which describes how rulers maintain and hold power: the ruler can ignore right or wrong and accept the idea that "the end justifies the means"; the successful ruler must be lion and fox (powerful and cunning).

Magellan, Ferdinand (ca. 1480–1521)   Portuguese sea captain who led a Spanish-backed expedition sailing west around the southern tip of South America, crossed the Pacific, and was killed in the Philippines; his ship sailed around Africa and returned to Spain in 1522. He proved the world is round by being the first to circumnavigate the globe.

Mandela, Nelson (1918–)   South African statesman; leader of the African National Congress; arrested in 1962 for his opposition to apartheid; spent 27 years in jail; became the international symbol for freedom against white minority rule in South Africa; released in 1990 and negotiated a plan with the white government to turn South Africa into a multiracial democracy; shared the Nobel Peace Prize with Frederick de Klerk in 1993; elected first black president in a free election in 1994; served from 1995 to 1999.

Mao Zedong (also known as Mao Tse-tung) (1893–1976)   Chinese Communist leader who led the struggle against Nationalists from 1927 to 1949; established his regime in 1948 and ruled the People's Republic of China from 1949 to 1976; introduced Great Leap Forward to industrialize China and compelling people to join communes; initiated the Cultural Revolution to diminish all opposition and strengthen his power; his book *Quotations of Chairman Mao* promoted terrorist tactics; became a cult symbol (Maoism).

Marx, Karl (1818–1883)   German philosopher and founder of modern socialism; wrote the *Communist Manifesto* with Friedrich Engels (1820–1895), proposing an economic interpretation of history; wrote *Das Kapital*, an analysis of economic and political aspects of capitalism.

Mazzini, Giuseppe (1805–1871)   Italian patriot and founder of Young Italy, a secret society to promote Italian unity; headed short-lived Republic of Rome in 1849; continued his efforts for independence from Austria from abroad; "Soul of Italian Unification."

Muhammad (570–632)   Arabian prophet; proclaimed himself messenger of Allah; founded Islam, the Muslim religion.

Mussolini, Benito (1883–1945)   Fascist dictator of Italy (1924–1945); called *Il Duce* (leader); ally of Germany (Rome-Berlin Axis) in World War II; shot by Italian partisans in 1945.

Nassar, Gamal Abdel (1918–1970)   president of Egypt from 1956 to 1970; seized power with other military officers by overthrowing King Farouk in 1953; nationalized the Suez Canal, resulting in war with Britain, France, and Israel; promoted economic businesses and irrigation projects such as the Aswan High Dam; supported Pan-Arabism to encourage unity in Arab world.

Nehru, Jawarhalal (also known as Pandit Nehru) (1889–1964)   first prime minister of independent India in 1947, serving until his death in 1964; supported Gandhi's policy of civil disobedience; imprisoned during the 1930s for his activities; rejected Gandhi's proposal for hand production; urged industrialization; set up mixed economy; leader of nonaligned nations in the Cold War; father of Indira Gandhi, India's Prime Minister from 1966 to 1977.

Netanyahu, Benjamin (1949–   )   conservative prime minister of Israel from 1996 to 1999; his party opposed additional concessions to the Palestinians on the issue of the West Bank and Gaza Strip; replaced as prime minister in 1999 by moderate leader Ehud Barak.

Nkrumah, Kwame (1909–1972)   African leader who became the first prime minister of Ghana; American-educated; promoted Pan-Africanism encouraging cooperation among African states; deposed in 1966 due to resentment created by his dictatorial policies.

Nicholas II (1868–1918)   last Romanov Tsar of Russia; ruled from 1894 to 1917; abdicated in the Russian Revolution of March 1917; killed with his entire family by Bolsheviks (Communists) in 1918.

O'Higgins, Bernardo (1778–1842)   Chilean general who led a revolt against Spain in 1816; ruled Chile from 1817 to 1823.

Owens, Robert (1771–1858)   English industrialist and socialist; established utopian communities in New Lanark, Scotland, and New Harmony, Indiana, both of which failed.

Pahlevi, Shah Muhammed Reza (1919–1980)   last shah of Iran who ruled from 1941 to 1978; autocratic ruler; employed secret police (Savak) and permitted no political opposition; encouraged economic and social modernization, including land reforms, literacy, and women's rights; pro-Western foreign policy; special relationship with the United States; overthrown by Ayatollah Ruhollah Khomeini in

1978; workers protested the poor economic conditions; religious leaders opposed his modernization policies.

Perón, Juan (1895–1974)   elected president of Argentina in 1946 with the support of the military; established a dictatorial government; widely popular due to his wife, Eva; instituted economic nationalization of many industries (public works program) and political and social reforms; opposed by the Catholic Church; the poor economic conditions led to his exile to Spain in 1955; returned in 1973 and was reelected President; died in 1974.

Perry, Matthew (1794–1858)   U.S. Navy Commodore; led the fleet that sailed into Tokyo harbor in 1854 and negotiated the reopening of Japan to American trade, which led to the resignation of the Shogun and modernization (Westernization) of Japan.

Peter the Great (1672–1725)   Russian tsar from 1682 to 1725; wanted to model Russia after European culture instead of Byzantine or Asian culture; introduced Western ideas of science, education, and the military to make Russia strong; the need for windows (seaports) in the West led to war against Sweden, resulting in a port on the Baltic Sea; built St. Petersburg; absolute ruler who controlled the Nobles and the Russian Orthodox Church; his Westernization efforts had little impact on Russian masses.

Plato (427–347 B.C.)   Greek philosopher; student of Socrates and teacher of Aristotle; wrote *The Republic* in which he rejected democracy for the ideal state ruled by philosophers.

Polo, Marco (1254–1324)   Venetian merchant who visited China in 1275; lived at the court of the Mongol ruler Kublai Kahn until 1292; his book describing his visit to China aroused European interest in China's riches and led to European overseas exploration.

Rabin, Yitzhak (1922–1995)   Israel's prime minister from 1974 to 1977 and 1992 to 1995; first prime minister to meet with Palestinian leader Yasir Arafat; agreed to set up Palestinian self-rule in the Gaza Strip, the city of Jericho, and the West Bank; negotiated a peace treaty with King Hussein of Jordan; awarded the Nobel Peace Prize in 1994; assassinated in 1995.

Rousseau, Jean-Jacques (1712–1778)   French philosopher of the Enlightenment; wrote the *Social Contract*, claiming that "Man is born free and everywhere he is in chains," and that the people give power to the government (General Will) to act for the good of the people and also have the right to overthrow the government if it fails the people; his ideas were used to support democracy and justify dictatorship under the General Will.

Sadat, Anwar (1918–1981) Egyptian president from 1970 to 1981; directed nation's policy away from dependence on Soviet Union; promoted foreign investments, some privatization of businesses; first Arab leader to visit Israel; signed Camp David Accords with Israeli Prime Minister Menachem Begin in 1978; shared the Nobel Peace Prize with Begin; assassinated in 1981.

Siddhartha Gautama (566–486 B.C.) founder of Buddhism; Indian nobleman who left his comfortable life for one of self-denial and meditation; rejected Hindu caste system; as Buddha, the Enlightened One, he taught Four Noble Truths to achieve Nirvana.

Smith, Adam (1723–1790) social philosopher and economist; founder of modern economics; authored *The Wealth of Nations*; believed in the doctrine of laissez-faire—government should keep a "hands-off" approach to business.

Socrates (469–399 B.C.) Greek philosopher of ancient Athens; advocated the maxim, "Know thyself"; left no written works; refused to renounce his principles even in the face of death when accused of treason for corrupting the minds of youth.

Stalin, Joseph (Josef Dzhugashvili) (1879–1953) dictator of the Soviet Union from 1925 to 1953; used his position as general secretary of the Communist Party to gain absolute power; established a totalitarian state; crushed all opposition by terror and mass executions; introduced a five-year plan to transform Russia into an industrial giant; allied with the West during World War II.

Suleiman the Magnificent (1494–1566) Ottoman sultan who ruled from 1520 to 1566; strong military leader; extended Ottoman control in the Balkans as far as Vienna; conquered North Africa and Mesopotamia; introduced a fair system of justice and strict control of finances; supporter of the arts; made Istanbul into a city of imposing architecture.

Sun Yat-sen (also known as Sun Yixian) (1866–1925) leader of the Chinese revolt against the Manchu Dynasty in 1911; founded the Chinese Republic; briefly served as president; believed in three principles of democracy, nationalism, and people's livelihood to make China strong.

Teresa, Mother (1910–1997) Roman Catholic nun who founded a missionary order to provide food, shelter, and medical help for underprivileged people of India; won the Nobel Peace Prize in 1979 for her humanitarian efforts.

Trotsky, Leon (Lev Bronstein) (1879–1940) Russian revolutionary who worked with Lenin to overthrow the Tsar in November 1917; directed the Red Army in the civil war from 1917 to 1922; lost the power struggle with Stalin after Lenin's death; exiled and assassinated in Mexico by Stalin's order in 1940.

Tutu, Desmond (1931–) Anglican Archbishop in South Africa who won the Nobel Peace Prize in 1984 for his opposition to apartheid; his leadership created worldwide pressure on South Africa to end its repressive policies; appointed head of Truth and Reconciliation by Nelson Mandela to investigate the injustices of apartheid.

Voltaire (François Marie Arouet) (1694–1778) French philosopher; major figure of the Enlightenment; supported control by enlightened absolute rulers and despots; his satirical works mocked the Church and royal authority; exiled to England for three years; praised Britain's limited monarchy; credited with the statement, "I disapprove of what you say, but I will defend to the death your right to say it."

Walesa, Lech (1943–) first democratically elected president of Poland, from 1990 to 1995, in the post-Soviet era; electrician in a Gdansk shipyard who led a strike for better wages and living conditions against the Communist government; formed Solidarity, an independent labor union; arrested for his activities and released; became an international hero; awarded the Nobel Peace Prize in 1983. In 1989 he helped to make Solidarity a legal political party and end Communist rule in Poland.

Yelstin, Boris (1931–) rival of Gorbachev who opposed the slow pace of political and economic reform of the 1980s; elected president of the Russian Republic in 1991; led the resistance to the conservative coup to oust Gorbachev; resigned from the Communist Party and became the first popularly elected president of Russia with the end of communism in 1991; elected in 1996 to a five-year term as president of the Russian federation. Unable to solve Russia's economic problems and ethnic tensions, his poor personal health caused him to resign the presidency in 1999 in favor of Valdimir Putin, his protegé.

Zapata, Emiliano (1879 [?]–1919) Mexican revolutionary and Native Indian leader who helped overthrow the dictator Porfirio Diaz; supported by peasants whose battle cry was "Land and liberty!"; assassinated in 1919.

Regents Examinations, Answers, Self-Analysis Charts, and Regents Specification Grids

Examination
August 2003
Global History and Geography

PART I: MULTIPLE CHOICE

Directions (1–50): For each statement or question, write in the space provided, the *number* of the word or expression that, of those given, best completes the statement or answers the question.

1 In which field of study do people learn about the development of early human beings?

1 economics	3 political science
2 cartography	4 anthropology

1 _____

2 Which document is an example of a primary source?

1 a novel on the Age of Discovery
2 a diary of a Holocaust survivor
3 a textbook on Latin American history
4 an encyclopedia article on Songhai culture

2 _____

3 Hunting and gathering, subsistence agriculture, and the barter system are characteristics of a

1 market economy
2 command economy
3 traditional economy
4 mixed economy

3 _____

4 Hammurabi's code of laws and Qin dynasty legalism are similar in that both promoted the idea that

   1 worship of leaders will maintain the power of an empire

   2 an informed citizenry will help maintain peace and prosperity

   3 equality of the people is the most important goal of government

   4 harsh punishments for crimes will lead to a more orderly society   4_____

5 An important factor that prevented the ancient Greek city-states from uniting to form a single nation was the

   1 lack of a common language

   2 size of the desert regions

   3 mountainous topography of the region

   4 cold, hostile climate   5_____

6 China under the Han dynasty and the Roman Empire were similar in that both grew wealthy because they

   1 developed extensive trade networks

   2 created classless societies

   3 encouraged democratic ideals

   4 established free-market economies   6_____

7 Judaism, Islam, and Christianity share a belief in

   1 papal supremacy

   2 teachings of the Koran (Quran)

   3 reincarnation and the Four Noble Truths

   4 an ethical code of conduct and monotheism   7_____

8 Feudalism influenced Europe and Japan by

1 providing social stability
2 fostering the growth of religion
3 eliminating warfare
4 encouraging formal education   8 _____

9 "... Christian warriors, He who gave His life for you, today demands yours in return. These are combats worthy of you, combats in which it is glorious to conquer and advantageous to die. Illustrious knights, generous defenders of the Cross, remember the examples of your fathers who conquered Jerusalem, and whose names are inscribed in Heaven; abandon then the things that perish, to gather unfading palms, and conquer a Kingdom which has no end."

— St. Bernard of Clairvaux

This statement was most likely used to encourage people to

1 repel a Viking invasion
2 stop advancement of the Huns in Europe
3 join the Crusades
4 force Russians to convert to Catholicism   9 _____

10 One similarity between the Mongols of Central Asia and the Incas of South America was that both societies

1 developed cash-crop farming
2 based their wealth on the slave trade
3 adapted to difficult physical environments
4 practiced monotheistic religions   10 _____

Base your answers to questions 11 and 12 on the map below and on your knowledge of social studies.

Trade Routes (13th—15th centuries)

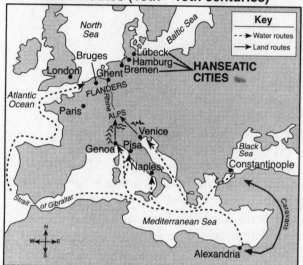

Source: Steven Goldberg and Judith Clark DuPré,
Brief Review in Global History and Geography,
Prentice Hall (adapted)

11 One reason for the success of the cities in the Hanseatic League and the Italian city-states was that both were

  1 protected by mountains
  2 isolated from the rest of Europe
  3 accessible by water
  4 close to a network of navigable rivers

11 _____

12 Which economic practice developed as a result of the growth of the trade routes shown on the map?

  1 capitalism
  2 hunting and gathering
  3 subsistence farming
  4 manorialism

12 _____

13 The Renaissance in western Europe is best described as a period marked by

1 unquestioned reliance on the teachings of Aristotle
2 an advance of Muslim culture
3 Christian unity throughout the region
4 great intellectual and artistic creativity

13 _____

14 ". . . The King is a declared enemy of the Jews. He will not allow any to live in the city. If he hears it said that a Berber merchant frequents them or does business with them, he confiscates his goods. There are in Timbuktu numerous judges, teachers, and priests, all properly appointed by the king. He greatly honors learning. Many handwritten books imported from Barbary are also sold. There is more profit made from this commerce than from all other merchandise. . . ."

— Leo Africanus, *The Description of Africa*, 1526

This passage suggests Timbuktu was a city that

1 participated frequently in war
2 emphasized literacy and trade
3 protected the human rights of all citizens
4 selected political leaders through democratic elections

14 _____

15 After contact with Europeans in the 1500s, millions of native peoples in the Americas died as a result of

  1 new foods, which the native peoples could not digest

  2 religious persecution resulting from the Spanish Inquisition

  3 new diseases to which the native peoples had no natural immunity

  4 slavery and the terrible conditions on their sea journey to Europe   15____

16 During the Age of Absolutism (1600s and 1700s), European monarchs tried to

  1 increase individual rights for their citizens

  2 develop stronger relations with Islamic rulers

  3 encourage the growth of collective farms

  4 centralize political power within their nations   16____

Base your answer to question 17 on the map below and on your knowledge of social studies.

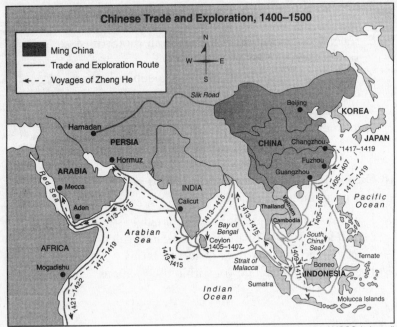

Source: Henry Brun et al., *Reviewing Global History and Geography*, AMSCO (adapted)

17 Based on this map, which statement is accurate concerning China between 1400 and 1500?

1 Most of China's commerce was conducted on overland trade routes.
2 China remained isolated from outside contacts.
3 The Ming dynasty traded more with Persia than with any other culture.
4 China interacted and traded with many diverse cultures.

17 _____

18 The writings of the 18th-century French philosophers Diderot, Rousseau, and Voltaire influenced the

1 policies of the enlightened despots
2 start of the Neolithic Revolution
3 success of the German unification movement
4 spread of imperialism to Africa and Asia   18____

19 A long-term result of the Industrial Revolution in Europe was

1 an increase in the number of small farms
2 a decline in international trade
3 a general rise in the standard of living
4 a strengthening of the economic power of the nobility   19____

Base your answers to questions 20 and 21 on the map below and on your knowledge of social studies.

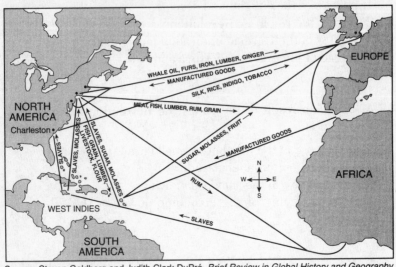

Source: Steven Goldberg and Judith Clark DuPré, *Brief Review in Global History and Geography*, Prentice Hall (adapted)

20 What is the most appropriate title for the map?

   1 The Industrial Revolution
   2 Imperialism in Africa
   3 The Age of Discovery
   4 Atlantic Trade Routes   20 _____

21 Which economic system was responsible for the creation of the situation shown on the map?

   1 feudal system   3 socialism
   2 mercantilism   4 barter system   21 _____

22 ". . . Give Venezuela such an executive power in the person of a president chosen by the people or their representatives, and you will have taken a great step toward national happiness. No matter what citizen occupies this office, he will be aided by the Constitution, and therein being authorized to do good, he can do no harm, because his ministers will cooperate with him only insofar as he abides by the law. If he attempts to infringe upon the law, his own ministers will desert him, thereby isolating him from the Republic, and they will even bring charges against him in the Senate. The ministers, being responsible for any transgressions committed, will actually govern, since they must account for their actions. . . ."

— Simón Bolívar, 1819

In this passage, which type of government is Simón Bolívar proposing for Venezuela?

1 theocracy   3 democracy
2 monarchy   4 dictatorship   22 ____

23 Lenin's promise of "Peace, Land, Bread" during the Bolshevik Revolution of 1917 was made in an effort to

1 end France's occupation of Russia
2 gain popular support to overthrow the government
3 restore Czar Nicholas II to power
4 resolve conflicts between farmers of diverse ethnic backgrounds   23 ____

24 Under Joseph Stalin, peasants in the Soviet Union were forced to

  1 become members of the ruling party
  2 support the Russian Orthodox Church
  3 join collective farms
  4 move to large cities   24 _____

25 Since the late 1940s, Northern Ireland, India, and Israel have all faced which common problem?

  1 the need to adjust to a post-communist political system
  2 continued violent confrontations between different religious groups
  3 economic depression that resulted from rapid industrialization
  4 overpopulation of urban centers   25 _____

26 One reason that Britain and France agreed to appease Hitler at the Munich Conference was to

  1 prevent the start of another world war
  2 stop the Nazis from invading the Soviet Union
  3 obey an order from the League of Nations
  4 obtain advanced German military weapons in exchange   26 _____

27 Nazi Germany, Fascist Italy, and Communist Russia were similar in that each

  1 protected individual rights
  2 elected their leaders through popular vote
  3 supported market-based economies
  4 established totalitarian governments   27 _____

28 A. **Atomic bombs dropped on Hiroshima and Nagasaki.**
B. **Allies invade Europe on D-Day.**
C. **Germany invades Poland.**
D. **Japanese attack Pearl Harbor.**

Which sequence shows the correct chronological order of these World War II events, from earliest to latest?

1 $A \rightarrow B \rightarrow C \rightarrow D$ 3 $C \rightarrow D \rightarrow B \rightarrow A$

2 $B \rightarrow A \rightarrow D \rightarrow C$ 4 $D \rightarrow C \rightarrow A \rightarrow B$ 28 _____

29 The United Nations was created primarily to

1 prosecute persons accused of war crimes
2 contain the spread of communism
3 channel relief aid to war-torn nations
4 provide a means of solving international problems   29 _____

30 During most of the Cold War period, which two nations were divided into communist and noncommunist parts?

1 China and Mongolia
2 Vietnam and Korea
3 Pakistan and Ireland
4 Poland and Cuba   30 _____

31 Pol Pot, Joseph Stalin, and Slobodan Milosevic were similar in that each leader supported actions that

1 modernized their economies
2 introduced democratic ideas
3 supported minority rights
4 violated human rights   31 _____

32 A major goal of the Organization of Petroleum Exporting Countries (OPEC) in world affairs is to

1 encourage development of alternative energy sources
2 promote international free trade
3 provide funds for the World Bank
4 regulate oil policies   32 _____

33 Which concept led to the formation of the North American Free Trade Agreement (NAFTA) and the European Union (EU)?

1 nationalism   3 interdependence
2 imperialism   4 socialism   33 _____

34 In the Soviet Union under Mikhail Gorbachev, the trend toward private ownership of businesses represented a move away from

1 a traditional economy
2 a command economy
3 a free-market economy
4 laissez-faire economics   34 _____

Base your answer to question 35 on the cartoon below and on your knowledge of social studies.

ANOTHER WALL

Source: Dennis Renault, *The Sacramento Bee* (adapted)

35 The main idea of the cartoon was that in South Africa

1 the fall of apartheid ended racial tensions
2 Nelson Mandela was unable to bring about political reform
3 another communist government lost power
4 a significant step was taken toward racial equality   35 ____

36 **"Women of Kuwait Demand the Right to Vote"**
   "Property Inheritance Still Limited for Women of
      Nepal"
   "Women in Jordan Form Alliance to Increase
      Political Representation"

Which conclusion is supported by these headlines?

1 Equal rights for women continues to be a global
   concern.
2 Women are not active in political issues.
3 Women have achieved equality in the area of
   education.
4 Communist governments have insured equal
   rights for women.   36 _____

Base your answers to questions 37 and 38 on the
graph below and on your knowledge of social studies.

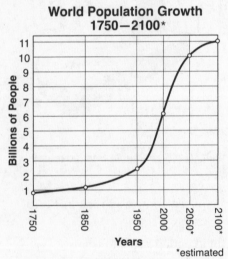

**World Population Growth
1750—2100***

Billions of People

Years

*estimated

Source: United Nations (adapted)

37 The graph shows that between 1950 and 2000 the
world's population increased by approximately

1 1 billion   3 6 billion
2 4 billion   4 8 billion   37 _____

38 What is one explanation for the great change in the world population between 1950 and 2000?

   1 Family planning was successful.
   2 There was an absence of war and conflict.
   3 New medicines and technology were discovered and applied.
   4 Famine and other natural disasters increased.   38 _____

39 What is the primary reason that increasing numbers of Latin American citizens have immigrated to the United States over the last three decades?

   1 escape from the threat of communism
   2 desire for religious freedom
   3 fear of natural disasters
   4 hope for economic opportunities   39 _____

Base your answer to question 40 on the chart below and on your knowledge of social studies.

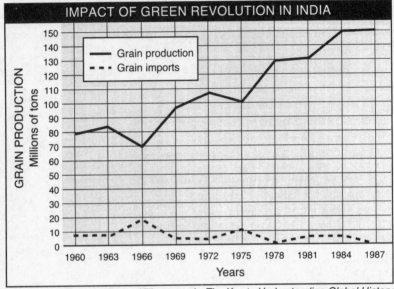

IMPACT OF GREEN REVOLUTION IN INDIA

— Grain production
- - - Grain imports

GRAIN PRODUCTION
Millions of tons

Years

Source: James Killoran et al., *The Key to Understanding Global History*, Jarrett Publishing Co. (adapted)

40 Between 1960 and 1987, a major effect of the Green Revolution on India was

1 a decrease in the production of grain after 1975
2 an increase in grain imports after 1984
3 an overall increase in the production of grain since 1966
4 a steady decrease in grain imports from 1960 to 1966

40 _____

41 Which heading best completes the partial outline below?

> I. _____
>
>   A. Established a direct but limited democracy
>   B. Stressed the importance of the individual
>   C. Considered the political ideas of Socrates, Plato, and Aristotle
>   D. Encouraged all citizens to participate in government

  1 Political Developments of the City-State of Athens
  2 Effects of the Roman Empire on Economic Development
  3 Influence of Belief Systems on Byzantine Society
  4 Achievements of the Age of Enlightenment   41____

42 The spread of Buddhist ideas and customs to China and Southeast Asia was the result of

  1 the Mandate of Heaven
  2 economic dependence
  3 cultural diffusion
  4 the civil service system   42____

43 Meiji reformers of Japan and Peter the Great of Russia were similar in that both emphasized

  1 socialism   3 westernization
  2 isolationism   4 democratization   43____

44 The Sepoy Mutiny in India and the Boxer Rebellion in China were responses to

1 Mongol invasions
2 European imperialism
3 Japanese aggression
4 African slave trading   44 _____

Base your answer to question 45 on the map below and on your knowledge of social studies.

China—Land Use

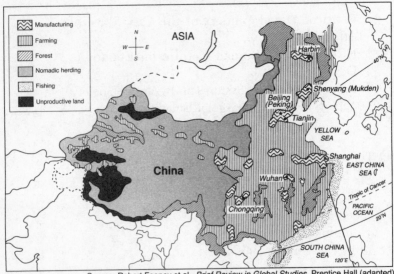

Source: Robert Feeney et al., *Brief Review in Global Studies*, Prentice Hall (adapted)

45 Which inference is best supported with information provided on the map?

1 Most of China's people live in the eastern part of the country.
2 Much of China has a climate that is too hot to allow farming.
3 China has more people than its land can support.
4 Most Chinese people make a living working in factories.   45 _____

46 During the 19th century, industrialization in Great Britain differed from industrialization in Japan mainly because Great Britain

1 had greater deposits of natural resources
2 encountered government resistance to economic growth
3 used isolationism to increase its economic power
4 duplicated the factory systems used in China

46 _____

47 Which statement is accurate about the Hungarian Revolution in 1956 and the Tiananmen Square demonstrations in 1989?

1 These events led to democratic reforms.
2 Repressive action was taken to end both protests.
3 Strong action was taken by the United Nations.
4 Both events brought communist governments to power.

47 _____

Base your answers to questions 48 and 49 on the map below and on your knowledge of social studies.

World Levels of Per Capita Income

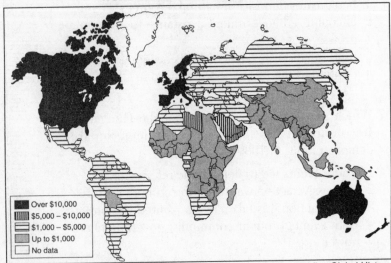

Legend:
- Over $10,000
- $5,000 – $10,000
- $1,000 – $5,000
- Up to $1,000
- No data

Source: James Killoran et al., *The Key to Understanding Global History,* Jarrett Publishing Co., 1998 (adapted)

48 Based on this late 20th-century map, which conclusion is accurate?

1 The worldwide distribution of wealth is unequal.
2 Social mobility between social classes is increasing.
3 The communist movement is growing.
4 Economic self-sufficiency in less developed countries is increasing.

48 _____

49 During the 1800s, which description would have applied to most of those areas shown on the map with a per capita income of up to $1,000?

1 leading industrial powers
2 colonies of western European powers
3 countries of eastern Europe
4 countries with democratic governments

49 _____

Base your answer to question 50 on the map below and on your knowledge of social studies.

Postwar Europe

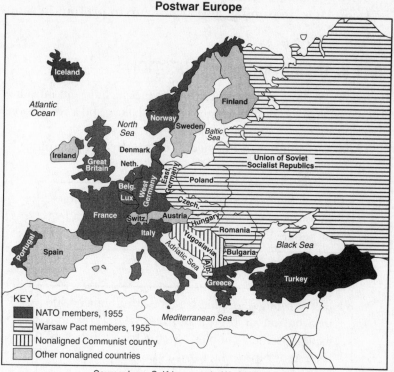

Source: Larry S. Krieger et al., *World History: Perspectives on the Past*,
D.C. Heath and Co. (adapted)

50 Which speech described the political alignment shown on the map?

  1 Pericles' "Funeral Oration"
  2 Bismarck's "Blood and Iron"
  3 Hirohito's "Surrender"
  4 Churchill's "Iron Curtain"

                                             50____

In developing your answer to Part II, be sure to keep these general definitions in mind:

> <u>discuss</u> means "to make observations about something using facts, reasoning, and argument; to present in some detail"

PART II: THEMATIC ESSAY QUESTION

Directions: Write a well-organized essay that includes an introduction, several paragraphs addressing the task below, and a conclusion.

Theme: Human and Physical Geography (Geographic Impact on Societies)

> Geographic factors such as land features, resources, location, and climate of nations and regions affect how people live.

Task:

> - Select *one* geographic factor that influenced life in a nation or region *before* A.D. 1500, and using specific examples. discuss the influence of that geographic factor on the people of that nation or region
> - Select a *different* geographic factor that influenced life in a nation or region *after* A.D. 1500, and using specific examples, discuss the influence of that geographic factor on the people of that nation or region

You may use any examples from your study of global history and geography. You must select a *different* geographic factor for each time period discussed. For example, you may not write about two rivers in different parts of the world. **Do *not* use geographic factors from the United States in your answer.** Some suggestions you might wish to consider include the Nile River in Egypt, the mineral wealth of Africa, the monsoons in South Asia, oil in the Middle East, Japan's location near China, the plains of Northern Europe, rain forests in Latin America, and mountains in eastern Europe.

You are *not* limited to these suggestions.

Guidelines:

In your essay, be sure to:

- Address all aspects of the *Task*
- Support the theme with relevant facts, examples, and details
- Use a logical and clear plan of organization
- Introduce the theme by establishing a framework that is beyond a simple restatement of the *Task* and conclude with a summation of the theme

In developing your answer to Part III, be sure to keep these general definitions in mind:

  (a) <u>discuss</u> means "to make observations about something using facts, reasoning, and argument; to present in some detail"

  (b) <u>evaluate</u> means "to examine and judge the significance, worth, or condition of; to determine the value of"

PART III: DOCUMENT-BASED QUESTION

This question is based on the accompanying documents (1–7). The question is designed to test your ability to work with historical documents. Some of these documents have been edited for the purposes of this question. As you analyze the documents, take into account the source of each document and any point of view that may be presented in the document.

Historical Context:
　　Nationalism is a powerful force that can have positive and negative effects on nations and regions.

Task:
　　Using information from the documents and your knowledge of global history, answer the questions that follow each document in Part A. Your answers to the questions will help you write the Part B essay in which you will be asked to:

> • Define the term *nationalism*
> • Discuss how nationalism has had positive ***and/or*** negative effects on specific nations ***and/or*** regions
> • Evaluate whether nationalism in general has had a more positive *or* a more negative impact on the people of the world

Part A: Short-Answer Questions

Directions: Analyze the documents and answer the short-answer questions that follow each document in the space provided.

Document 1

> . . . Therefore, if we so ardently desire the emancipation [unification] of Italy — if we declare that in the face of this great question all the petty questions that divide us must be silenced — it is not only that we may see our country glorious and powerful but that above all we may elevate her in intelligence and moral development up to the plane of the most civilized nations. . . .

— Camillo di Cavour, 1846

1 According to Camillo di Cavour, what would be *one* positive result of Italian unification? [1]

_____

_____

Document 2

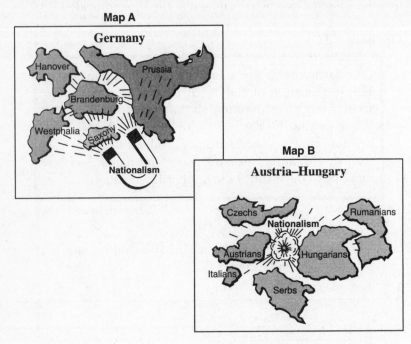

Source: Sol Holt and John R. O'Connor,
Exploring World History, Globe Book Co. (adapted)

2a According to Map **A**, how did nationalism affect the German states? [1]

_____

_____

b According to Map **B**, how did nationalism affect the Austro–Hungarian Empire? [1]

_____

_____

Document 3

A

> As long as the Jewish spirit is yearning deep in the heart,
> With eyes turned toward the East, looking toward Zion,
> Then our hope — the two thousand year old hope —
> will not be lost:
> To be a free people in our land,
> The land of Zion and Jerusalem.

— *Hatikvah* (The Hope), Israel's national anthem

B

> . . . O those who pass between fleeting words
> It is time for you to be gone
> Live wherever you like, but do not live among us
> It is time for you to be gone
> Die wherever you like, but do not die among us
> For we have work to do in our land
> We have the past here
> We have the first cry of life
> We have the present, the present and the future
> We have this world here, and the hereafter
> So leave our country
> Our land, our sea
> Our wheat, our salt, our wounds
> Everything, and leave
> The memories of memory
> O those who pass between fleeting words!

— Mahmoud Darwish, *Those Who Pass Between
Fleeting Words*, Palestinian poet laureate

3*a* How does passage **A** express Israeli nationalism? [1]

_____

_____

b How does passage **B** express Palestinian nationalism? [1]

_____

_____

Document 4

. . . Attention: all people in markets and villages of all provinces in China — now, owing to the fact that Catholics and Protestants have vilified [made damaging statements about] our gods and sages, have deceived our emperors and ministers above, and oppressed the Chinese people below, both our gods and our people are angry at them, yet we have to keep silent. This forces us to practice the I-ho magic boxing so as to protect our country, expel the foreign bandits and kill Christian converts, in order to save our people from miserable suffering. After this notice is issued to instruct you villagers, no matter which village you are living in, if there are Christian converts, you ought to get rid of them quickly. The churches which belong to them should be unreservedly burned down. Everyone who intends to spare someone, or to disobey our order by concealing Christian converts, will be punished according to the regulation when we come to his place, and he will be burned to death to prevent his impeding [interference with] our program. We especially do not want to punish anyone by death without warning him first. We cannot bear to see you suffer innocently. Don't disobey this special notice.

Source: Ssu-Yü, Teng and Fairbank, John K., *China's Response to the West: A Documentary Survey, 1839–1923*, Harvard University Press

4 Identify *one* expression of Chinese nationalism in this passage.
[1]

_____

_____

_____

Document 5

> . . . Why do you want to drive away the English?
>
> . . . Because India has become impoverished by their Government. They take away our money from year to year. The most important posts are reserved for themselves. We are kept in a state of slavery. They behave insolently [disrespectfully] towards us and disregard our feelings. . . .

Source: M. K. Gandhi, *Indian Home Rule*, Navajivan Publishing House

5 Based on the document, identify *one* criticism Gandhi expressed about British rule. [1]

_____

_____

Document 6

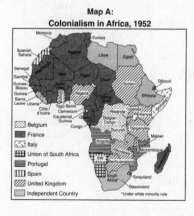

Map A:
Colonialism in Africa, 1952

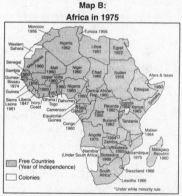

Map B:
Africa in 1975

Source: Sidney Schwartz and John R. O'Connor,
Imperialism and the Emerging Nations,
Globe Book Company, Inc. (adapted)

6 According to these maps, how did nationalism affect the continent of Africa between 1952 and 1975? [1]

_____

_____

Document 7

. . . From Iraq to the former Soviet empire to the Balkans, the authoritarian state exists as a piece of machinery, man-made, breakable, the borders etched by diplomats ignorant of or indifferent to ancient claims and tribal hate. Kurds fight for their freedom from Iraq and Turkey; Tamils battle Sinhalese in Sri Lanka; Armenians fight Azerbaijanis in Nagorno-Karabakh; Albanian Muslims and Serbs circle each other in Kosovo. Last week Yemen was the latest country to break apart, as those in the south accused the northerners of attempting to further impoverish [weaken] them. The struggles can be ancient and visceral [deep], religious and racial, the oppressed against the oppressors. Where the valves of democracy allow for ethnic pressures to escape, differences are settled by discussion; in the embattled outposts of the new world order, it is the tribes that rule, and the nature of war and peace in the next century may be largely determined by their ambitions. . . .

— *Time*, May 16, 1994

7*a* Based on this document, identify *two* examples of nationalistic conflict. [2]

(1) _____

(2) _____

b Based on this document, identify *one* cause of these nationalistic conflicts. [1]

_____

_____

Part B: Essay

Directions: Write a well-organized essay that includes an introduction, several paragraphs, and a conclusion. Use evidence from at least *four* documents in the body of the essay. Support your response with relevant facts, examples, and details. Include additional outside information.

Historical Context:

Nationalism is a powerful force that can have positive and negative effects on nations and regions.

Task:

Using information from the documents and your knowledge of global history, write an essay in which you:

- Define the term *nationalism*
- Discuss how nationalism has had positive *and/or* negative effects on specific nations *and/or* regions
- Evaluate whether nationalism in general has had a more positive *or* a more negative impact on the people of the world

---

Guidelines:

In your essay, be sure to:

- Address all aspects of the *Task* by accurately analyzing and interpreting at least *four* documents
- Incorporate information from the documents in the body of the essay
- Incorporate relevant outside information
- Support the theme with relevant facts, examples, and details
- Use a logical and clear plan of organization
- Introduce the theme by establishing a framework that is beyond a simple restatement of the *Task* or *Historical Context* and conclude with a summation of the theme

Answers
August 2003
Global History and Geography

Answer Key

PART I (1–50)

1. 4	14. 2	27. 4	40. 3
2. 2	15. 3	28. 3	41. 1
3. 3	16. 4	29. 4	42. 3
4. 4	17. 4	30. 2	43. 3
5. 3	18. 1	31. 4	44. 2
6. 1	19. 3	32. 4	45. 1
7. 4	20. 4	33. 3	46. 1
8. 1	21. 2	34. 2	47. 2
9. 3	22. 3	35. 4	48. 1
10. 3	23. 2	36. 1	49. 2
11. 3	24. 3	37. 2	50. 4
12. 1	25. 2	38. 3	
13. 4	26. 1	39. 4	

PART II: Thematic Essay   See answers explained section.

PART III: Document-Based Essay   See answers explained section.

Answers Explained

PART I

1. **4** People learn about the development of early human beings in the field of anthropology. Anthropology is the study of the customs, beliefs, and folkways of different societies and ethnic groups, especially on a comparative basis. An anthropologist is a social scientist who examines the origins and development of man and society. An anthropologist will study how the lives of the Neolithic farmers differed from those of Paleolithic hunters and gatherers or how social and economic differences began to develop in settled farm communities.

WRONG CHOICES EXPLAINED:
(1) Economics is the study of how people make a living. An economist also studies how goods and services are produced and distributed to satisfy people's needs.
(2) Cartography is the art of drawing or compiling maps or charts.
(3) Political science is one of the social sciences that examines the purpose of government and how power, law, and authority are distributed within a political society.

2. **2** A diary of a Holocaust survivor is an example of a primary source. Primary sources are original records of an event. Primary sources include official documents and firsthand accounts of events by people who witnessed, participated in, or observed these developments. Primary sources also include letters, speeches, reports, and photographs by people involved in the events.

WRONG CHOICES EXPLAINED:
(1), (3), and (4) A novel on the Age of Discovery, a textbook on Latin American history, and an encyclopedia article on Songhai culture are examples of secondary sources. Secondary sources are written after the events have occurred by people who did not witness or participate in them. A novel, textbook, and encyclopedia article are secondary sources that obtain their information from primary sources. Secondary sources provide convenient summaries of events found in primary sources.

3. **3** Hunting and gathering, subsistence agriculture, and the barter system are characteristics of a traditional economy. Hunting and gathering, farming, and herding cattle are also the basis of a traditional economy in which economic needs are met and economic decisions are made according to customs and habits. The role of each individual and economic activity within the society is determined by ritual and custom. In many countries,

parents taught their children how to hunt, fish, and farm, and in turn, their children taught their skills to the next generation. In a traditional economy, people produce just enough food to meet the needs of their immediate family. This is known as subsistence agriculture, which in most cases is based on ritual and custom and leads to the barter system. The barter system is an exchange of one set of goods and services for another. The advantage of a traditional economy is that everyone has a role and it tends to produce stability. However, the main disadvantage of a traditional economy is that it fails to meet the needs of changing economic times and fails to promote new ideas by discouraging change.

WRONG CHOICES EXPLAINED:

(1) A market economy is a system in which economic decisions are influenced by supply and demand and not by customs or rituals.

(2) A command economy is an economic system in which the national government controls all the means of production and makes all the economic decisions.

(4) A mixed economy is an economic system that combines government regulation of industries with private enterprise or capitalistic characteristics.

4. **4** Hammurabi's code of laws and Qin dynasty legalism are similar in that both promoted the idea that harsh punishments for crimes will lead to a more orderly society. Hammurabi, ruler of the Babylonians, developed the first written law codes around 1705 B.C. Hammurabi's Code consists of 282 sections dealing with most aspects of daily life. It lists criminal laws dealing with murder, as well as theft, and civil laws dealing with private rights and matters such as marriages, divorces, and property. The code provides a specific punishment for each violation. Hammurabi's Code was designed to insure order and strengthen the government, protect the weak, and establish the legal rights of citizens. Instead of fining the violators, the code enacted harsh punishments for crimes. If a house collapsed because of poor construction and someone was killed, the builder of the house could be put to death.

By 221 B.C. a leader of the Qin dynasty united all of the warring factions into China's first centralized empire. The Qin king adapted the title of Shi Huangdi (first emperor). He believed in legalistic principles. Some of the main ideas of legalism were that a highly efficient government was the key to social order, and harsh punishments were necessary to ensure social order. Shi believed that people were not necessarily good and needed a strong government to punish those who committed bad acts. For example, anyone caught outside his own village without a travel permit would have his ears or nose chopped off. To silence criticism of his government, Shi murdered hundreds of Confucian scholars and ordered that so-called useless books be burned. These books were the works of Confucian thinkers and poets who disagreed with legalists. Only books on medicine, agriculture, and technology were spared. Through such harsh measures, Shi Huangdi established a government with unlimited power and used it in an arbitrary manner. The government created a uniform system of writing and weights and measurements through-out the empire. Shi Huangdi's sweeping program of centralization, which included the building of a highway network of more than 4,000 miles, result-ed in peasants working on the roads against their will. Shi Huangdi unified China and brought order but at the expense of human freedom. Following his death, the people rebelled against his harsh rule.

WRONG CHOICES EXPLAINED:

(1) Neither Hammurabi's Code nor the legalism of the Qin dynasty was designed to promote the idea that the worship of leaders would maintain the power of the empire. Hammurabi and the Qin emperor had absolute power and wanted to establish a system to maintain order in their empire.

(2) Hammurabi's Code and the legalism of the Qin dynasty were directed to keep the people under direct control and promote social order. Hammurabi's Code provided a standard of justice and the Qin dynasty used legalism as a way to end civil disorder by establishing an efficient absolute government. The belief of an informed citizenry was never considered as a way to maintain peace and prosperity.

(3) Hammurabi's Code and the legalism of the Qin dynasty did not pro-mote the idea that equality of the people was the most important goal of gov-ernment. Hammurabi's Code favored the higher class over the lower ones and the legalists taught that a ruler should provide rich rewards for people who successfully carried out their duties.

5. **3** An important factor that prevented the ancient Greek city-states from uniting to form a single nation was the mountainous topography of the region. About three-fourths of Greece is covered with mountains, the highest of which is Mount Olympus. These mountains divide Greece into a number of different regions and the rugged terrain made transportation difficult. For example, the city-state of Sparta was only 60 miles from Olympia, the site of the Olympic Games; yet it took Spartans nearly a week to travel that distance. The mountains influenced Greek political life. The Greeks never created a large empire like the Egyptians or Mesopotamians. The mountainous geo-graphic barrier led Greeks to organize many independent communities that in time grew into city-states. Each prized its own freedom and resisted out-side interference. The mountainous regions created political disunity because the first loyalty of the people was not to Greece as a nation but to their own city-states.

WRONG CHOICES EXPLAINED:

(1) The Greeks did have a common language but that was not enough to overcome the isolation created by the rugged mountain terrain.

(2) Greece does not have a desert region. Greece is part of the Balkan Peninsula and extends southward into the eastern Mediterranean.

(4) It was the mountainous terrain and not the climate that isolated the Greeks. Greece does not have a cold, hostile climate; Greece has a Mediterranean

climate: temperatures are moderate and rains fall only in winter. This climate promoted an outdoor life, which in many city-states led the Greeks to participate in civic life.

6. **1** China under the Han dynasty and the Roman Empire were similar in that both grew wealthy because they developed extensive trade networks. Under the Han dynasty, which ruled China from 202 B.C. to 220 A.D., China expanded across Asia. Powerful emperors such as Wudi, who ruled from 141 B.C. to 87 B.C., used their armies to keep peace and protect trade. Wudi and other emperors developed the Silk Road that carried Chinese jade, bronzes, and silk westward in exchange for the goods of India and the Mediterranean world. Chinese travelers returned home with new seeds such as grapes and alfalfa. New foods, such as oranges, pears, and peaches, also flowed to China. The Silk Road, which eventually stretched for 4,000 miles, helped to make the Han dynasty the Golden Age for China. Trade within China expanded and tea growing spread from the south to other parts of China. Travelers and merchants also introduced new ideas, such as Buddhism, into China.

The Roman Empire, like the Han dynasty, also grew wealthy because of its extensive trade routes. During this 200-year period known as the Pax Romana, which occurred at the same time that Han rulers were uniting China, Emperor Augustus brought peace and prosperity to the empire. Under Augustus, who ruled from 31 B.C. to 14 A.D., Rome established an efficient system of roads that enabled it to expand its trade and to establish order. Roman expansion allowed the empire to take over prosperous trade routes throughout the Mediterranean. Trade flowed freely from distant parts and brought wealth to the empire. Grain from the Nile Valley, ivory and gold from Africa, gems from India, and silk from China via the Silk Road were shipped into the empire. Rome and China shared goods through the Silk Road but they never made formal contact. However, their control of the extensive trade routes enabled their empires to prosper.

WRONG CHOICES EXPLAINED:

(2) Classless societies did not exist under the Han dynasty and the Roman Empire. The emperor was chosen because he was born into the ruling class. During the Han dynasty and the Roman Empire, there was a civil service system, through which officials gained jobs by merit, not by birth or wealth. However, none of these government officials could ever become rulers.

(3) Neither the Han dynasty nor the Roman Empire encouraged democratic ideals. The emperors had absolute power and ruled with an iron fist.

(4) The Han dynasty and the Roman Empire did not establish free market economies. The extensive trade routes depended upon the protection by these two countries and not upon the control of the economies of these areas.

7. **4** Judaism, Islam, and Christianity share a belief in an ethical code of conduct and monotheism. Judaism is monotheistic, teaching a belief in one God. At the heart of Judaism are the Ten Commandments, laws that the Jews

believe God gave them through Moses. These laws set out the religious duties toward God and rules for moral conduct toward other people, such as "Thou shall not kill; Thou shall not steal." Christianity was founded by Jesus and is deeply rooted in Jewish tradition. Like Judaism, Christianity fosters the belief in one God as the father of all humanity. Jesus emphasized religious morality and ethics. He accepted the Ten Commandments that God had given to Moses. He taught mercy and sympathy for the poor and preached brotherhood and equality of the people before God. Jesus' disciples believed that he was the son of God sent as the Savior that the Jews were expecting. His teachings presented in the New Testament became the basis of the new religion—Christianity. Islam was a new religion founded in 622 in Arabia by Mohammed. Like Jews and Christians, the people who follow Islam believe in one God. Islam embodies the idea that there is no God but Allah and that Mohammed is the Great Prophet. Muslims, the term used to describe those who follow Islam, are required to follow a code of moral behavior that includes giving alms to the poor, respecting parents, and shunning gambling and alcoholic beverages.

WRONG CHOICES EXPLAINED:

(1) Judaism and Islam do not share a belief in papal supremacy. Neither of these religions have a Pope who sets out the guidelines for their religion. Roman Catholics are the only group of Christians who accept papal supremacy. Other denominations within Christianity do not accept the Pope as the final authority of religions.

(2) The teachings of the Koran (Quran) is the Bible of Islam. The Bible of Judaism is the Old Testament. The New Testament provides the basis for Christianity.

(3) The belief in reincarnation and the Four Noble Truths contain the basic ideas of Buddhism.

8. **1** Feudalism influenced Europe and Japan by providing social stability. During the early Middle Ages in Europe, the central government could not protect its subjects from local warfare or foreign invasion. Thus, small farmers surrendered their lands to powerful local nobles in exchange for their promise of protection. This system became known as feudalism. Feudalism helped people survive the breakdown of central government and order. Feudalism was characterized by key social, economic, and political relationships. A major social feature of feudal society was the development of a strict class structure based on the control of land and military power. There was a rigid class distinction in which the king was at the top and the peasant or serf was at the bottom. Everyone had a well-defined position in medieval European society. Feudal society was sharply divided into the land-holding nobles, the upper class, and the great mass of peasants or serfs. People were born as serfs, knights, or lords and could not change their social position. Local nobles or lords were given lands by their rulers or kings in exchange for military service. These lords had small armies of their own made up of

knights, armed warriors on horseback. During the Middle Ages, most people lived on the manor, which was the noble's estate, and the serfs gave their lords part of the harvest in return for the use of the land. In return, the lords protected the serfs from outside attackers.

During the 1100s in Japan the central authority of the king was weakened and local warlords fought one another. A system of feudalism similar to that in Europe soon arose. All members of society had a defined place. The major feature of Japanese feudalism was the control of the government by noble landlords known as *daimyos*, who owed their loyalty to the *shogun*. The shogun was at the top of the feudal system. To provide military protection for their lands, noble landowners recruited *samurai* warriors. As with European feudalism, the shogun distributed land to the vassal lords, the daimyos, who received land in exchange for a promise to support the shoguns with their armies when needed. In turn, the daimyos granted land to the lesser warriors, called samurais, whose name means "those who serve." The samurais were knights on horseback who lived by a strict code of conduct known as *bushido*, the way of the warrior. The samurais promised loyalty and support to their lords during times of peace and war. If a warrior brought dishonor to his lord or family, he was expected to take his own life. In return for this loyalty the daimyo provided the samurai with social status and economic support. The peasant in Japan, as in Europe, worked the land and served the landowners in exchange for protection. Feudalism in Europe and Japan provided a way for the ruling class to preserve law and order.

WRONG CHOICES EXPLAINED:

(2) Feudalism did not foster the growth of religion in either Europe or Japan. During the Middle Ages in Europe, the Catholic Church had established itself as the dominant institution and provided the main stabilizing force in western Europe. In many cases, the Church exercised control over secular leaders. In Japan, the emperor's role was primarily religious and ceremonial and feudalism was designed to promote social order and not religious growth.

(3) Feudalism did not eliminate warfare in either Europe or Japan. In Europe during the 11th century, the Catholic Church sought to curb the daily violence of feudal warfare by declaring certain days and seasons off-limits for battles. In Japan, as in Europe, local feudal lords fought one another for control of more land or property in their area.

(4) Feudalism did not encourage formal education. Feudalism was designed to provide protection for society and was not concerned about formal education. Under feudalism, formal education was restricted to the upper class.

9. **3** This statement was most likely used to encourage people to join the Crusades. The goal of the Crusaders (1096–1291) was to capture the Holy Land from Islamic rulers. In 1095, the Byzantine Emperor appealed to Pope Urban II for help against the Muslim Turks. The pope agreed to help

because the Muslims had taken control of the Holy Land, and reports of persecution against Christians in the Holy Land also promoted the need for action. In 1096, Pope Urban II called for a Crusade, or Holy War, against the Muslims. Their goal was to capture Palestine, or the Holy Land, as the Christians called it because Jesus had lived and died there. The pope's plan created enthusiasm among religious persons who thought they were doing God's will. If they were killed, they would be sure of salvation. Others were attracted by the prospect of conquest and adventure, and the serfs saw the Crusades as a way to escape feudal oppression. The Crusades lasted more than 200 years and only the first Crusade came close to achieving its goals.

WRONG CHOICES EXPLAINED:

(1) The Viking invasion occurred between 800 and 1000 A.D. and assaults were launched along the western coast of Europe and not the Holy Land (Jerusalem).

(2) The advancement of the Huns in Western Europe took place during the 5th century A.D., nearly 700 years before the Crusades of the 11th century. The Huns were invaders from central Asia who terrorized the Roman Empire until they were defeated in 451.

(4) The Russians were never forced to convert to Catholicism. The Byzantine Empire introduced the Eastern Orthodox Church to Russia in the middle of the 9th century.

10. **3** One similarity between the Mongols of Central Asia and the Incas of South America was that both societies adapted to difficult physical environments. During the late 1100s, the Mongols became the dominant group in Central Asia. Their homeland was Mongolia, a region of forests and steppes northwest of China. In this wild and isolated area, they wandered from pasture to pasture with their herds of sheep and horses. In a few fertile areas, Mongol farmers established small communities. Like most nomads, the Mongols were at first divided into clans and roamed the eastern steppes in loosely organized clans. Each group had its own leader, known as a Khan. Around 1200, they united under the leadership of Genghis Khan, who organized the Mongol armies into disciplined cavalry units. The Mongols were skilled horsemen and fighters and under Khan's leadership they conquered most of Asia from Korea in the east to the Caspian Sea in the west. The Mongol Empire created the largest land empire in history. Their territories extended from China to the frontiers of Western Europe.

In South America, the Incas in Peru adapted terrace farming to adjust to their physical environment. Terrace farming is a method of growing crops on the side of hills or mountains by planting on graduated terraces built into slopes. The mountain ranges of the Andes Mountains in Peru limited the amount of arable lands for farming to the coastal plains and river valleys. Peru's coastal valleys are almost rainless, but where enough water came down their rivers, the Inca farmers used every inch of available land for cultivation, including the river delta near the sea and the narrow plains leading to the

Andes Mountains. Villages were built where they would not intrude on the cropland. Farmers usually raised two crops a year. This degree of production was possible due to the network of irrigation canals that the Incas had developed more than 2,000 years ago.

WRONG CHOICES EXPLAINED:

(1) Neither the Mongols nor the Incas developed cash-crop farming. Cash-crop farming refers to products, such as cotton, rice, coffee, and sugar, which can be sold on a world market. Imperialistic countries encouraged people in Africa and Asia to grow these crops.

(2) The Mongol and Inca empires depended on the strength of their armies. Many West African kingdoms depended on the slave trade, as well as the European countries in the 1500s, which needed slaves for the labor in large plantations in the Americas.

(4) The Mongols and the Incas did not practice a monotheistic religion, or the belief in one God. The Mongols and the Incas followed a polytheistic religion, or the belief in many different gods.

11. **3** One reason for the success of the cities in the Hanseatic League and the Italian city-states was that both were accessible by water. In the late 1200s, a group of towns—Bremen, Hamburg, Lübeck, and other northern German cities—controlled trade in the Baltic and North seas. Because the central government was weak, these states banded together to protect their interests. This group became known as the Hanseatic League. From the 1200s to the 1400s, the league controlled most of the trade among Europe, the Baltic states, and Russia. To promote the commercial interests of its members, the league drove out pirates from the northern cities, maintained regulations for fair trade, and banned non-league cities from trading in the area. The Hanseatic cities dealt chiefly in timber, grain, iron, leather, and salted fish.

The Italian city-states of Venice, Genoa, Pisa, and Naples on the Italian seacoast dominated trade between Europe and the eastern Mediterranean. These cities had the advantages of the Mediterranean location and a commercial tradition dating back to the Roman Empire. Italian ships carried European wheat, wine, lumber, and wool to eastern Mediterranean cities, such as Alexandria and Constantinople. They returned with valuable eastern products. Eventually, Venice, in partnership with Egypt, came to dominate trade with the East. After goods arrived in Venice, traders took them over the Alps and up the Rhine River to Flanders. From there, other traders took the goods throughout Europe as far as the areas along the Baltic Sea.

WRONG CHOICES EXPLAINED:

(1) Neither of these regions was protected by mountain ranges. Traders crossed the mountains, such as the Alps, to ship to other parts of Europe.

(2) These areas became important trading routes because they were not isolated from the rest of Europe. The trading routes near the North Sea and

the Italian city-states contributed to their rise as important economic centers.

(4) The cities in the Hanseatic League and the Italian city-states were not close to a network of navigable rivers. Their success was due to their location surrounded by large bodies of water that enabled them to trade with other parts of the world.

12. **1** Capitalism was the economic practice that developed as a result of the growth of the trade routes shown on the map from the 13th to the 15th centuries. Capitalism is an economic system characterized by the investment of money in business ventures with the goal of making a profit. These economic developments created by the increase in trade led to improvements in business practices that sparked what became known as the Commercial Revolution. The development of new businesses, the increase in the number of trading expeditions, and the ability to raise large sums of money created the need for different types of economic investments such as joint stock companies. These ventures laid the foundation for the economic system known as capitalism.

WRONG CHOICES EXPLAINED:

(2) Hunting and gathering is associated with traditional economy. A traditional economy is an economic system that meets the basic needs of the people through fishing and hunting.

(3) Subsistence farming is one system in which farmers and their families grow just enough food to survive.

(4) Manorialism was an economic system in medieval Europe. The manor was a self-sufficient community in which the serf was required to work for the lord of the manor in return for protection.

13. **4** The Renaissance in western Europe is best described as a period marked by great intellectual and artistic creativity. The Renaissance, which in French means "rebirth," was a period of artistic and cultural achievement in Europe from the 14th to the 16th centuries. The Renaissance began with a reemphasis on the Greco-Roman culture that had been neglected during the Middle Ages. Renaissance writers focused on reason, a questioning attitude, experimentation, and free inquiry, in contrast to the medieval approach that emphasized faith, authority, and tradition. Dante's *Divine Comedy* and Boccaccio's *The Decameron*, written during the Renaissance, are considered literary masterpieces. Renaissance artists rejected the medieval form of art and initiated the classical works of Greece and Rome. Their art was very realistic; the artists studied the human anatomy in detail and worked from live models. They also studied the technique of three-dimensional perspective. The artistic achievements of da Vinci's *Last Supper* and *Mona Lisa* and Michelangelo's *Pietà* and *David* are considered masterpieces of western art.

WRONG CHOICES EXPLAINED:

(1) During the Renaissance, people began to question the teachings of Aristotle. Renaissance writers looked to the teachings of Plato and Socrates as

their guide and rejected many of Aristotle's scientific assumptions that the physical world had to fit into the teachings of the church, such as the belief that the earth was the center of the universe.

(2) The Renaissance focused on the advances of Greco-Roman civilization and not Muslim culture. Western Europe would gain knowledge of Muslim culture through the Byzantine Empire.

(3) During the Renaissance, Christian unity was destroyed throughout the region. The Protestant Reformation, which began in the 1500s, led to a series of religious wars ending the religious unity of Europe. Northern Europe became primarily Protestant and southern Europe became Catholic.

14. **2** This passage suggests that Timbuktu was a city that emphasized literacy and trade. Timbuktu was a flourishing trade city on the Niger River which became a center of learning under the rule of Mansa Musa. Mansa Musa was Mali's greatest ruler who reigned from 1312 to 1337 A.D. He built mosques and other fine buildings in the capital of Timbuktu, which became the center of Muslim culture. At the height of its power, the city had three universities and 50,000 students from Europe, Asia, and Africa. Timbuktu was also an important commercial center. European goods were in great demand as were goods from as far away as India and China. There were a growing number of merchants from many different countries.

WRONG CHOICES EXPLAINED:

(1) The passage does not make any reference to wars that were taking place in Timbuktu. The passage focuses on life in the city revolving around trade and education.

(3) The passage indicates that the human rights of Jews were not protected. The king did not allow them to live in the city.

(4) Political leaders were not selected by democratic elections but were appointed by the king.

15. **3** After contact with Europeans in the 1500s, millions of native peoples in the Americas died as a result of new diseases to which they had no natural immunity. Diseases brought by the Europeans weakened the Aztecs and the Incas. In 1519, when Hernán Cortés landed in Mexico, the native population of Central Mexico was 25.3 million, and by 1523 it was 16.8 million. It continued to decline to 8 million by 1540 and to a low of 1.5 million by the early 1600s. Native Americans had never been exposed to measles, mumps, smallpox, and typhus, and had not developed a natural immunity to these diseases. Like the Spanish in Central and South America, the Europeans who settled North America brought with them several diseases that devastated the native population of North America. One tribe in Massachusetts dropped in population from 24,000 to 750 by 1631.

WRONG CHOICES EXPLAINED:

(1) The new foods introduced by the Europeans in the Americas did not result in the death of millions of Native Americans. The Europeans introduced

new products such as onions, peaches, and coffee beans, which became part of the Native American food supply.

(2) The Native Americans were not part of the Spanish Inquisition. The Spanish Inquisition was a tribunal used to suppress heresy in Spain against those who disagreed with the teachings of the Church. In the Americas, Spanish missionaries, such as Bartolome de las Casas, worked to pass laws forbidding the enslavement of Native Americans. These laws were designed to end abuse against Native Americans.

(4) Native Americans did not die in the millions because of slavery and the terrible conditions on their sea journey to Europe. African slaves, who were used to replace Native American workers on the plantations, suffered this fate on their passage to the Americas.

16. **4** During the Age of Absolutism (1600s and 1700s), European monarchs tried to centralize political power within their nations. Absolutism refers to a political system in which the monarch (king or queen) has supreme power and control without limits over the lives of the people in their country. In England, France, Spain, and Russia, the kings expanded power at the expense of nobles. In England, the Tudor Dynasty, which ruled from 1500 to 1603, strengthened the power of the monarchy. Although Parliament held sessions, it was effectively dominated by the Tudors. Under the leadership of Henry VII, Henry VIII, and Elizabeth I, there was expanded governmental authority over the nation. Henry VIII increased his power by replacing the Catholic Church with the Anglican Church, which was controlled by the king. In France, the Bourbon family, who ruled for more than 200 years, established the foundation of absolutism. Louis XIV of France represented the height of absolutism. He ruled France from 1643 to 1715 and claimed to rule by the Divine Right of Kings. To illustrate this attitude, it is claimed that he said "L'etat, c'est moi," which means, "I am the State." Louis XIV is often referred to as the Sun King. The Hapsburg monarchs of Austria and Spain also established absolute rule in their countries. In Spain, the king increased power by destroying the power of the nobles and enacted laws without the Cortes, the Spanish legislature. In Russia, the Romanov family established control in 1613 and ruled for more than 300 years. Peter the Great, who ruled from 1682 to 1715, established absolute control by creating a strong army loyal to him, extending control over the Russian Orthodox Church and ruthlessly crushing all opposition.

WRONG CHOICES EXPLAINED:

(1) Absolute monarchs did not try to increase individual rights for their citizens. They denied any political freedom for individuals and resisted efforts to provide any sort of rights for their citizens. Louis XIV revoked the Edict of Nantes in 1685, which provided religious freedom for French Protestants.

(2) Absolute monarchs did not develop strong relations with Islamic rulers. During the Age of Absolutism, European countries, such as England

and France, sought to gain control of trading routes that were dominated by the Muslims. For example, in 1571, the Spanish crushed the Ottoman Turks at the Battle of Lepanto.

(3) None of the absolute monarchs tried to encourage the growth of collective farms. Absolute monarchs sought to control the economy through the policy of mercantilism, not by the collectivization of the farms. Totalitarian governments in Russia and China would use collective farms during the 20th century to gain greater control of the economy.

17. **4** Based on this map, the statement that is accurate concerning China between 1400 and 1500 is that China interacted and traded with many diverse cultures. The Ming dynasty experienced a high level of economic prosperity. During the first century of the Ming dynasty, from about 1350 to 1450, China was the greatest naval power in the world and the map shows that it established contact with the people of Southeast Asia, India, and Africa. Between 1405 and 1433, Chinese Admiral Zheng He set out with fleets of ships. His goal was to establish trade with distant commerce centers. On his first three voyages, he visited Southeast Asia and India. On the fourth visit, he went as far as Hormuz, and on the last three the fleets sailed along the East African coast (Mogadishu). These were diplomatic and trade missions. He returned home with new and unfamiliar exotic animals, such as giraffes, for the imperial zoo. He died in Calicut in 1453 during his seventh voyage. After Zheng He's death, the Ming emperor banned the building of large oceangoing ships and halted the voyages of exploration. The Ming emperors believed that the voyages had not brought profit to the empire and that the fleets were too costly to maintain. Ming rulers also believed that limiting contact with foreign influence would best preserve the ancient traditions of China.

WRONG CHOICES EXPLAINED:
(1), (2), and (3) None of these statements can be supported by the map. Most of China's commerce was not conducted by overland trade routes. The map also does not show that the Ming dynasty traded more with Persia than any other culture. The map indicates that China was not isolated from outside contacts because it traded with countries along the Indian and Pacific oceans as well as the Arabian Sea.

18. **1** The writings of the 18th-century French philosophers Diderot, Rousseau, and Voltaire influenced the policies of the enlightened despots. Enlightened despots were rulers who tried to justify their absolute rule by claiming to rule in the people's interest by making good laws, promoting human happiness, and improving society. Enlightened despots were absolute rulers who based their decisions on enlightenment ideas. Enlightenment thinkers believed that just as one could use reason to explain why things happen in the physical universe, there must be natural laws to govern society. French philosophers such as Diderot, Rousseau, and Voltaire sought to use

reason to improve government and society. They criticized the abuses of government and proposed ways to correct it. Diderot published his writings in the *Encyclopedia*, a 25-volume collection of political and social critiques of French society. Voltaire, in his book *Candide*, wrote against the evils of organized religions, while Rousseau, in his book *The Social Contract*, attacked the evils of society that corrupted man. Frederick the Great, who ruled Prussia from 1740 to 1786, invited Voltaire to his court and sought his advice on how to be an enlightened ruler. Frederick the Great did away with the torture of accused criminals, improved the educational system, and allowed his subjects to believe as they wished regarding religion. Maria Theresa, who ruled Austria from 1740 to 1780, tried to implement enlightenment ideas by improving the educational system and limiting the power of the Church and revising the tax system. These enlightened despots did not believe in democracy, but sought to establish a government that was more effective.

WRONG CHOICES EXPLAINED:

(2) The 18th-century French philosophers did not influence the Neolithic Revolution. The Neolithic Revolution occurred between 8000 and 300 B.C. and refers to the changes brought about when people began to domesticate animals and settle in small communities.

(3) The German unification movement was influenced by the ideas of Otto von Bismarck, not by the writings of the French philosophers Diderot, Rousseau, and Voltaire.

(4) The French philosophers of the 18th century did not influence the spread of imperialism to Africa and Asia. The spread of imperialism to Africa and Asia in the late 19th century was influenced by the economic demands of the Industrial Revolution.

19. **3** A long-term result of the Industrial Revolution in Europe was a general rise in the standard of living. The Industrial Revolution greatly increased the production of goods, which raised the standard of living by providing people with cheaper mass-produced goods. Technological advancements provided the hope of improving peoples' lives. Over time conditions in cities improved with better housing, and healthier diets. Due to advances in medicine, there was an increase in the life expectancy of people. Finally, educational opportunities also expanded with the increased demand for professional and clerical workers. The middle and upper classes prospered immediately after the Industrial Revolution. For the workers it took longer but their lives gradually improved during the 1800s. New factories opened, creating new jobs. The workers eventually won higher wages, shorter working hours, and better working conditions. Wages rose so that workers had enough money left over after paying rent and buying food to buy a newspaper or visit a music hall.

WRONG CHOICES EXPLAINED:

(1) The Industrial Revolution led to the decline, not the increase, in the number of small farms. The use of labor-saving machines improved agricultural

production but led to the decline in the number of people involved in agriculture since few people were needed to harvest the land. By 1850, more British workers were employed in factories than on farms.

(2) The Industrial Revolution led to an increase, not a decline, in international trade. Industrial countries, such as Great Britain, France, and the United States, depended on foreign trade to sell their surplus products.

(4) The Industrial Revolution did not strengthen the economic power of the nobility. It led to the rise of a new class structure consisting of the very rich industrial and business families as well as a growing middle class of businesspeople (merchants, factory owners) and professionals, such as lawyers and doctors.

20. **4** The most appropriate title for the map is the Atlantic Trade Routes. The Atlantic Trade began in the 1500s because of the need for labor in the Americas. Africans transported to the Americas were part of a transatlantic network known as the Triangular Trade. Over one trade route, Europeans transported manufactured goods to the west coast of Africa. There traders exchanged these goods for enslaved Africans who were brought to the Americas. Merchants then bought sugar, coffee, and tobacco in the West Indies and sailed back to Europe to sell these products. On another triangular route, merchants carried rum and other goods from the New England colonies to Africa. There, traders exchanged their merchandise for African slaves. The traders than transported the African slaves to the West Indies and sold them for sugar and molasses. They then sold these goods to rum producers in New England. Various other transatlantic routes existed. The Triangular Trade consisted of a network of trade routes crisscrossing the northern and southern colonies, the West Indies, England, Europe, and Africa. A variety of goods were traded including furs, fruit, tar, and tobacco, as well as African slaves.

WRONG CHOICES EXPLAINED:

(1), (2), and (3) None of these historical developments is represented by this map. This map does not provide any information about the Industrial Revolution, Imperialism in Africa, or the Age of Discovery.

21. **2** Mercantilism is the economic system that was responsible for the creation of the situation shown on the map. During the 16th to 18th centuries, European monarchs supported mercantilism as a way of strengthening their national economies in the quest for trade and empires. Mercantilists believed that the wealth of a nation was measured by the supply of gold and silver and the nations had to maintain a favorable balance of trade by exporting more goods than they imported. Colonies existed for the benefit of the mother country. They provided the raw materials not available in Europe and enriched the mother country by serving as markets for manufactured goods. European nations passed strict navigation laws to insure that colonies traded only with the mother country.

WRONG CHOICES EXPLAINED:

(1) The feudal system was a political, economic, and social system that developed in Europe and Japan during the 1100s. In the feudal system land was the source of power.

(3) Socialism is an economic system in which the government controls the production and distribution of goods and wealth in a country.

(4) The barter system is an economic system in which one set of goods or services is exchanged for another.

22. **3** In this passage, democracy is the type of government that Simón Bolívar is proposing for Venezuela. Democracy is a form of government that is controlled by its citizens either directly or through representatives. Simón Bolívar was a Latin American revolutionary leader who earned the title "Liberator" for his role in the struggle for independence from Spanish domination. By 1824, he had liberated his native Venezuela, as well as Colombia, Peru, Ecuador, and Bolivia, from Spanish rule. Bolivar tried to combine Enlightenment political ideas of the French Revolution, ideas from Greece and Rome, and his own original thinking. The result was a system of democratic ideas that influenced revolutions in Latin America. Simón Bolívar sought to incorporate these democratic ideals into the government of Venezuela. Influenced also by the British form of government, he supported a system that provided for an executive chosen by the people who would be accountable to the people.

WRONG CHOICES EXPLAINED:

(1) Theocracy is a government that is controlled by religious leaders.

(2) Monarchy is a system of government in which the power is in the hands of a single ruler (king or queen). This ruler has complete authority over the government.

(4) Dictatorship is a system of government in which one person or one party rules with absolute control.

23. **2** Lenin's promise of "Peace, Land, Bread" during the Bolshevik Revolution of 1917 was made in an effort to gain popular support to overthrow the government. When World War I broke out, the Russian army was unprepared and suffered many military defeats at the hands of Germany. The loss of millions of men at the battlefront combined with food shortages made the Russian people desperate. Nicholas II, the Czar of Russia, ignored demands to withdraw from the war and did nothing about the poverty and starvation caused by war. In March 1917, the Russian Revolution began. Food riots broke out in St. Petersburg, and when the czar's troops refused to fire on the crowd, Nicholas II was forced to abdicate. The new leaders set up a republic and promised constitutional reforms but failed to take Russia out of the war. The hunger and misery continued. The government lost support among the people, especially among the newly organized Soviets, or councils of workers and soldiers. The Bolshevik Revolutionary Party was active in

organizing the Soviets, and under the leadership of Vladimir Lenin, who returned from exile, took control of them. Lenin, who is considered the Father of Russian Communism, was a dynamic speaker who appealed to the hungry, war-weary people. Lenin's slogan of "Peace, Land, Bread" attracted the support of the people. The Bolsheviks promised land reforms and an end to food shortages. On November 7, 1917, Lenin and the Bolshevik Party seized power. Lenin quickly ended the war with Germany by signing the Treaty of Brest-Litovsk. Upon seizing power, the Bolsheviks, now known as the Communists, sought to transform Russia's economic system. Lenin ended private ownership of land and distributed land to the peasants. Workers were given control of the factories and mines.

WRONG CHOICES EXPLAINED:

(1) The French never occupied Russia. After the Russian Revolution, the Allies (England, France, and the United States) sent troops to help the Whites who wanted to continue the war against Germany, but this effort failed.

(3) Lenin did not restore Czar Nicholas II to power. The Communists executed the czar and his family.

(4) Lenin did not make any efforts to resolve conflicts between farmers of diverse ethnic backgrounds. From 1918 to 1922, the Communists, under Lenin's leadership, were involved in a bitter civil war with groups who were still loyal to the czar.

24. **3** Under Joseph Stalin, peasants in the Soviet Union were forced to join collective farms. In 1928, there were more than 25 million small farms in Russia. In that year, Stalin announced that these privately owned farms would be abolished and would be replaced by collective farms. Collectives were large farms owned and operated by peasants as a group. Peasants would be allowed to keep their houses and personal belongings but all farm animals and tools were to be turned over to the collectives. The state set all prices and controlled access to farm supplies. The government planned to provide all the necessary equipment (tractors and fertilizers) and teach farmers modern methods in order to increase the output of grain. Surplus grain would be sold abroad to earn money to invest in industrial growth. The peasants resisted Stalin's policy of collectivization. Many peasants destroyed their crops and livestock in protest. Stalin showed no mercy and ordered the peasants to be shot on sight. Between 5 to10 million peasants died. By 1935, 95 percent of Russian farms had become collectives.

WRONG CHOICES EXPLAINED:

(1) Stalin never made peasants members of the ruling party. Only a small fraction of Soviet citizens were members of the ruling or Communist Party. This elite group included industrial managers, scientists, and military leaders.

(2) Stalin never supported the Russian Orthodox Church. In 1929, Stalin closed churches, synagogues, and mosques.

(4) Soviet peasants were not shipped to large cities but were sent to Siberia if they refused to join collective farms. Peasants were expected to work on collective farms to feed workers in the cities.

25. **2** Since the late 1940s, Northern Ireland, India, and Israel have all faced the common problem of continued violent confrontations between different religious groups. In Northern Ireland, the religious confrontation is between Protestants and Catholics. Although England conquered Ireland during the Middle Ages, Ireland remained Catholic when England became Protestant during the Reformation. In the 1600s, the English sent settlers to Ireland to maintain control. Most of them settled in the north, in Ulster. In 1922, most of Ireland was granted its independence from Great Britain. However, Great Britain retained control of the largely Protestant counties in the north. Northern Ireland contains six of the nine counties that are known as Ulster. Some Catholics objected to the division of Ireland and formed the IRA (Irish Republican Army). Northern Irish Protestants opposed to unification formed their paramilitary groups. During the 1960s, which was known as the "Time of Troubles," rioting erupted in Northern Ireland between Protestants and Catholics. Since that time, violence and terrorism have often occurred in Northern Ireland. Since 1993, efforts have been made by British and Irish leaders and the members of the IRA to reach a compromise. The Good Friday Accord signed in 1998 has provided a framework for Protestants to share political power with the minority Catholics in Northern Ireland. However, the inability of Sinn Fein, the political wing of the IRA, and the Ulster Protestants to resolve differences has hindered the process. Continued violence between Catholics and Protestants has also made the peace process difficult.

A sense of national unity has also been difficult to maintain in India because of the desire of religious groups for greater autonomy. In northeast India, the Naga people claimed the right to a separate state. They formed a small army and waged bloody battles with government forces. In 1960, the government decided that Nagaland should become a separate state of India. The Sikhs are a religious group that began blending elements of Islam and Hinduism in the early 1500s. They make up 2 percent of the population and believe that the government does not provide them with enough aid and resources. Sikh separatists want to break away and form a separate country. In the state of Punjab, where the Sikhs form a majority, they have led many protests. In 1984, they occupied the Golden Temple in Amristar and the government was forced to use violence to remove them. Thousands of Sikhs were killed. The conflict between Muslims and Hindus also continues to exist. Although many Muslims fled to Pakistan, about 100 million still live in India. In 1992, Hindu fundamentalists called for the destruction of a mosque in Ayodhya. This conflict touched off rioting and the mosque was destroyed. Recently, the report of Indian archeologists that they found evidence of a temple under the ruins of a 16th-century mosque has added to the tension between Hindus and minority Muslims. Some believe the two bombings in

Bombay in August 2003 were due to militant Islamic groups who are critical of these findings. At least 45 people were killed in these blasts.

The historic claim of the Israelis and Arabs to the same land has been a key issue in the continuing dispute between the two sides. Israel, once called Palestine, was the home of the Jews until Rome destroyed the country in 70 A.D. Lacking a homeland, most of the Jews in Palestine scattered throughout the world. After the expansion of Islam in the 7th century, the area of Palestine fell under the control of the Arabs, and later the Ottoman Turks. In 1917, the British promised the Jews a homeland in Palestine, but not at the expense of the Arabs who were still living in the area. In 1947, the United Nations drew up a plan to divide Palestine, which was under British rule, into an Arab and Jewish state. In 1948, Israel proclaimed its independence, but the Arabs refused to recognize the partition and invaded Israel. Israel won the war. More than half a million Arabs became refugees. These Arabs still want an Arab Palestinian state. Arab nations went to war with Israel in 1956, 1967, and 1973. The Camp David Accord in 1978 and the Oslo Peace Accord in 1993 have tried to create a framework for Palestinian self-rule but these efforts have failed. In 1987, violent clashes, known as the Intifada, broke out between Israeli police and young Palestinians who had grown up under Israeli control in the West Bank and Gaza Strip. Israel imposed harsh measures to stop the protests but without success. Efforts to implement the Oslo Accord failed as extremists on both sides resorted to violence. Militant Islamist groups, such as the Hamas, staged a campaign of suicide bombings and claimed that it would continue the war against Israel with the goal of creating a fully independent Palestinian state. The Israeli government and the Palestinian Liberation Organization (PLO) authorities have tried to keep the peace process on track. President George W. Bush has met with Israeli and Palestinian leaders to create a road map for peace, but this plan has been shaken by the recent outbreak of suicide bombings in Israel.

WRONG CHOICES EXPLAINED:

(1) These conflicts are religious confrontations and are not related to any adjustments to a post-communist political system.

(3) Northern Ireland, India, and Israel have not suffered economic depression from rapid industrialization. While the Israeli economy has recently declined, India and Northern Ireland have experienced economic growth.

(4) Neither Northern Ireland nor Israel has a problem with the overpopulation of urban centers. Some of India's cities, such as New Delhi and Bombay, are growing rapidly; however, this has not hindered India's economic growth.

26. **1** One reason that Britain and France agreed to appease Hitler at the Munich Conference was to prevent the start of another world war. Under the policy of appeasement, western nations such as Britain and France gave into aggressive demands to maintain peace. The western democracies

responded weakly to German aggression. In 1938, Hitler demanded the Sudetenland, a region in Czechoslovakia inhabited by about three million German-speaking people. Although the Sudeten people were not oppressed, the Nazis circulated stories of Czech cruelties and Hitler promised help. The Czech government, a democracy under President Edvard Benes, refused to yield. He counted on its alliance with France and Russia and expected British support. The Munich Conference, held on September 29, 1938, tried to resolve the problem. Germany, France, Great Britain, and Italy attended but the Czechs were not invited. The British prime minister, Neville Chamberlain, and French premier, Edouard Daladier, agreed to let Hitler seize the Sudetenland in exchange for his respecting Czechoslovakia's new boundaries. The British and French decided not to risk war but to appease Hitler. Six months later, Hitler seized the rest of Czechoslovakia. On September 1, 1939, Hitler invaded Poland, convinced that neither England nor France would risk war. On September 3, 1939, Britain and France honored their guarantee to Poland and declared war on Germany. World War II had started. Appeasement had failed to keep peace.

WRONG CHOICES EXPLAINED:

(2) Germany and the Soviet Union signed a Non-Aggression Act in 1939 in which the two countries agreed not to fight each other. In June 1941, Hitler violated this agreement and invaded Russia.

(3) The League of Nations was not involved with the Munich Conference. Its failure to stop Japanese aggression in Asia, the Italian invasion of Ethiopia, and Germany's violation of the Versailles Treaty had made the organization ineffective.

(4) The Munich Conference did not deal with the exchange of advanced German military weapons. Germany had already rearmed in 1935 in violation of the Versailles Treaty. The Munich Conference addressed the issue of Hitler's demand for the Sudetenland.

27. **4** Nazi Germany, Fascist Italy, and Communist Russia were similar in that each established totalitarian governments. A totalitarian state is one in which the government controls every aspect of a citizen's life through a one-party dictatorship. Adolph Hitler, the leader of the Nationalist Socialist Party, or Nazis, who controlled Germany from 1933 to 1945, built a one-party government that became known as the Third Reich. He had unlimited power. He used his secret police, the Gestapo, to suppress all opposition and had little regard for the civil rights of the people. Schoolchildren were taught Nazi ideas and had to join Hitler's Youth Organization to learn to be good Nazis. Newspapers, radio, and films praised the virtues of Nazism. The Third Reich became one of the most brutal dictatorships in the world.

Benito Mussolini was the leader of the Fascist Party that ruled Italy from 1922 to 1943. As head of the Fascist state, Mussolini (Il Duce) made Italy into a dictatorship. Mussolini allowed the existence of one political party, the Fascist Party, and limited legislative elections to yes/no votes on a single list of Fascist-chosen candidates. The Black Shirts (Mussolini's secret police) crushed all opposition. Unions were abolished, strikes were outlawed, and the press was censored. Mussolini exhorted the people to "believe, fight, and obey."

When Lenin seized power in Russia in 1917, the Communist Party became the only legal party. Lenin's government had a constitution and an elected legislature, but real power was held by the Communist Party. Only members of the Communist Party could run for office. Newspapers were censored. The secret police, the Cheka, ruthlessly killed all enemies of the state. At the time of his death in 1924, Lenin had established the Communists as the one dominant party in Russia.

WRONG CHOICES EXPLAINED:

(1) Individual rights were not protected in Nazi Germany, Fascist Italy, and Communist Russia. Civil rights were denied to individuals who existed for the benefit of the state.

(2) In Nazi Germany, Fascist Italy, and Communist Russia, leaders were not elected through popular vote. There was only one political party in these countries. Hitler in Germany, Mussolini in Italy, and Communist leaders in Russia gained power through repressive measures.

(3) None of these countries supported market-based economies. These countries denied private ownership and the government strictly controlled the economy.

28. **3** The correct chronological order of these World War II events is Germany invades Poland (September 1, 1939); the Japanese attack Pearl Harbor (December 7, 1941); the Allies invade Europe on D-Day (June 6, 1944); atomic bombs dropped on Hiroshima (August 6, 1945) and Nagasaki (August 9, 1945).

WRONG CHOICES EXPLAINED:

(1), (2), and (4) Germany invades Poland must be first in any correct chronological sequence of events.

29. **4** The United Nations (U.N.) was created primarily to provide a means of solving international problems. When the United States, Russia, and Great Britain met at Yalta in February, 1945, the goal was to win Russian support for a worldwide peacekeeping organization. Between April and June, 1945, an international conference in San Francisco drew up a charter for the United States. Five nations signed this charter pledging to work together to protect the members against aggression. The United Nations was to be based in New York and the members also pledged to save succeeding generations from the effects of war. The main purpose of the United Nations is to provide a forum to discuss world problems and to develop solutions. The two main bodies of the United Nations are the General Assembly and the Security Council. The General Assembly is like an international town meeting. Every member nation casts a vote in the General Assembly, which approves new

members, discusses a broad range of issues, and makes recommendations and agreements. The Security Council consists of five permanent members (Britain, China, France, the United States, and Russia) and ten other non-permanent members. Each of the five permanent members can veto any Security Council action. The Security Council can take no action unless all permanent members agree. The role of the Security Council is to authorize economic and military actions in settling international disputes. United Nations peacekeeping forces were used to monitor the first Arab-Israeli war. U.N. troops were used in Korea and have been helpful as peacekeeping forces in the Congo, Cyprus, Angola, the former Yugoslavia, Somalia, and Rwanda. However, the U.N. has had difficulty securing the necessary troops and funding to supply peacekeepers to all the global trouble spots.

WRONG CHOICES EXPLAINED:

(1) The United Nations was not created primarily to prosecute persons accused of war crimes. In 1945, the Nuremberg Trials were set up by Allied leaders to punish 22 surviving Nazi leaders. In 1996, attempts by the United Nations International War Crimes Tribunals to bring those accused of committing atrocities in Bosnia met with limited success.

(2) The United Nations was not designed to contain the spread of communism. In 1947, the United States adopted the policy of containment which was designed to block the growth of Russia's influence and prevent the expansion of communism. Containment policies include creating alliances and helping weak countries resist Soviet advances.

(3) The United Nations was not primarily formed to provide relief aid to war-torn nations. Although U.N. members have made donations to nations in Africa and Europe destroyed by ethnic conflicts, their main function is to resolve these disputes, not to provide relief aid.

30. **2** During most of the Cold War period, Vietnam and Korea were divided into communist and noncommunist parts. The Cold War period lasted from 1945 to 1989. At the end of World War II, Vietnamese forces under Ho Chi Minh occupied parts of North Vietnam. Ho Chi Minh, which means "He Who Enlightens," was the Vietnamese leader who was determined to build a communist movement and win independence. When the French refused to recognize his new nation, he began a war to regain control. After eight years of a bitter struggle, the French were defeated at Dienbienphu in 1954 and were forced to withdraw. The Geneva Agreement in 1954 divided Vietnam at the 17th parallel with elections to be held within two years to unite the country. Ho Chi Minh and his communist followers established a government in the North. South Vietnam came under the control of the noncommunist government led by Ngo Dinh Diem. The Diem Regime rejected plans for an all-Vietnamese election because he feared losing to the Communists. Diem claimed that honest elections were impossible in the North. The United Sates, fearful of a communist takeover in South Vietnam, continued the struggle and provided military support to help South Vietnam.

Although Minh died in 1969, the Vietnamese War continued. In 1975, communist forces captured Saigon, the capital of South Vietnam, and Vietnam became a united country in 1975.

At the end of World War II, North Korea was occupied by Russian troops and South Korea by American troops. Russia and the United States failed to agree regarding Korean unification and Russia resisted the United Nation's attempts to unify the country by free elections. In North Korea, Russia established a communist government and South Korea established an independent anticommunist government. In June, 1950, North Korea invaded South Korea seeking to unify the country by force. Led by General Douglas MacArthur, United Nations forces prevented a northern takeover of South Korea. An armistice was signed in 1953 that ended the war. However, Korea was still divided at the 38th parallel between North and South. Although the Cold War ended in 1989, Korea is still divided.

WRONG CHOICES EXPLAINED:
(1), (3), and (4) None of these nations was ever divided into communist and non-communist parts.

31. **4** Pol Pot, Joseph Stalin, and Slobodan Milosevic were similar in that each leader supported actions that violated human rights. Human rights, such as freedom of expression, life, and liberty, are those freedoms that all people are entitled to as members of society. In 1975, the Khmer Rouge led by Pol Pot took control of Cambodia. He instituted a reign of terror and tried to drive out all Western influence. From 1975 to 1979, he tried to establish a purely agrarian society. Pol Pot forced people out of the cities and resettled them in the country. It is estimated that 1.5 to 1.7 million Cambodians, or nearly one-third of the population, died from forced labor, starvation, or execution in the killing fields.

Joseph Stalin was the Soviet dictator who ruled Russia from 1924 to 1953. His secret police arrested and executed millions of suspected traitors. When wealthy landowners opposed his policy of collectivization, he eliminated them as a class. Many were shot or deported to forced labor camps. Close to 15 million peasants were forced into collective state farms. During the Great Purge of the 1930s, Stalin removed people who threatened his power. It has been estimated that the total number of Russians who died during his dictatorship range between 20 and 30 million.

The breaking up of Yugoslavia in 1991 and 1992 sparked ethnic violence in Bosnia among Serbs, Croatians, and Muslims. Slobodan Milosevic, the Yugoslav president, who was Serbian, began a policy of ethnic cleansing to destroy all non-Serbs. The Serbs dominated Yugoslavia. Milosevic forcibly removed other ethnic groups from the areas that Serbia controlled. Hundreds of thousands of Bosnians became refugees living on food sent by the United Nations and charities. Others were brutalized or killed. Milosevic also waged a brutal campaign of ethnic cleansing against Muslim Kosovans. In November, 1999, NATO forces started a military campaign against

Yugoslavia. Milosevic was forced to retreat and was ousted from power. The International Court at The Hague is trying Milosevic for crimes against humanity.

WRONG CHOICES EXPLAINED:

(1) Joseph Stalin's Five Year-Plan sought to modernize the economy. However, Pol Pot wanted to return to an agrarian society and he rejected Western influence. Slobodan Milosevic did not focus on modernizing the economy. His goal was to expand Serbian control in the former Yugoslavia.

(2) All of these men were dictators and they did not introduce democratic ideas.

(3) These leaders did not support minority rights. Their governments violated the basic civil rights of individuals in society.

32. **4** A major goal of the Organization of Petroleum Exporting Countries (OPEC) in world affairs is to regulate oil policies. In 1960, Iran, Iraq, Kuwait, Saudi Arabia, and Venezuela formed OPEC. It was later expanded to include 13 more nations form Africa, Latin America, and the Middle East. The members of OPEC meet regularly to decide how much oil to produce and at what prices to sell. Their main goal is to increase their profits by regulating the price of oil. The price of oil soared from less than $2 per barrel in the 1960s to more than $30 per barrel in the 1970s. These price increases sent shock waves around the world and triggered high inflation and unemployment throughout the western industrial nations and nonproducing countries. In the 1980s, the surplus of oil allowed prices to fall. In the late 1990s, OPEC again began to limit the production of oil, resulting in an upsurge in oil prices around the world.

WRONG CHOICES EXPLAINED:

(1) The goal of OPEC is to provide countries with a supply of oil at good market prices. The development of alternative energy sources would hurt the economic interests of the OPEC nations.

(2) OPEC is a cartel, which is a formal organization to coordinate price and production. OPEC is not designed to promote international free trade.

(3) OPEC does not provide funds for the World Bank. OPEC's goal is to establish uniformity in the production and price of oil.

33. **3** The concept that led to the formation of the North American Free Trade Agreement (NAFTA) and the European Union (EU) is interdependence. Interdependence is the mutual way in which the economies of countries are dependent on resources and goods from other parts of the world. The principal aim of the North American Free Trade Agreement and the European Union is to increase economic cooperation among member nations. In 1993, Mexico, the United States, and Canada signed NAFTA, the agreement designed to eliminate tariffs and other trade barriers among the member nations within 15 years. The treaty created one huge regional market

of more than 380 billion people. The Common Market, now known as the European Union, was created in 1957 by France, West Germany, Belgium, Italy, the Netherlands, and Luxembourg to expand free trade. By 1993, there were 15 member nations of the European Union and they agreed to eliminate all tariff barriers and to ensure the free movement of manufactured goods, farm products, and people among the member nations. The European Union also introduced a new European currency, the Euro, which so far 11 EU member states have agreed to adopt.

WRONG CHOICES EXPLAINED:

(1) Nationalism is defined as a feeling of pride or loyalty to one's nation or group. Nationalism is also a belief that each group is entitled to its own nation or country.

(2) Imperialism is a policy whereby one nation dominates the political, economic, and cultural life of another country or region.

(4) Socialism is a system under which the government owns and operates the major businesses and controls other parts of the economy.

34. **2** In the Soviet Union under Mikhail Gorbachev the trend toward private ownership of business represented a move away from a command economy. A command economy is an economy in which the government makes all the production decisions on what and how to produce goods. In 1928, Joseph Stalin began a series of Five-Year Plans that brought all economic activities under government control. The purpose of these Five-Year Plans was to build up the heavy industries (steel and iron), improve transportation, and increase farm output. Under Stalin and his successors, the officials of the Soviet Union made all the basic economic decisions. In 1985, Mikhail Gorbachev introduced the idea of *perestroika*. Gorbachev wanted to restructure the failing state-run command economy. In 1986, he made changes to revive the Soviet economy. His goal was to stimulate growth and make the economic system more efficient. Local managers gained greater authority over their farms and factories and people were allowed to open small private businesses. Gorbachev backed free-market reforms. Perestroika had some negative effects. Inflation increased and there were shortages of food and medicine.

WRONG CHOICES EXPLAINED:

(1) A traditional economy is a system in which economic decisions are made according to customs or habits.

(3) A free-market economy is a system in which privately owned businesses decide what to produce and sell, as well as determine the cost of their products.

(4) Laissez-faire economics is a belief that the best policy for the government should be to not interfere in businesses or to limit their involvement in the economy. The government should have a "hands-off policy" toward businesses.

35. **4** The main idea of the cartoon was that in South Africa a significant step was taken toward racial equality. The cartoon indicates that Nelson Mandela was a powerful force in bringing about the end of apartheid. Apartheid is a policy of total separation of the races in South Africa. This policy was practiced in South Africa from 1945 until it was repealed in 1991. In 1990, Nelson Mandela, the leader of the African National Congress who had been imprisoned for 27 years for his antiapartheid actions, was released from prison. Over the next 18 months, the South African Parliament repealed apartheid, which had segregated public facilities and restricted ownership of lands by blacks. The end of apartheid was the first step toward the creation of a new constitution that would grant political equality for all. In 1994, multi-cultural elections were held and the people chose Nelson Mandela as the first South African black president.

WRONG CHOICES EXPLAINED:
(1), (2), and (3) None of these statements are represented in the cartoon.

36. **1** These headlines support the conclusion that equal rights for women continues to be a global concern. In many developing countries, the position of women is less than equal. In 1975, the U.N. announced the Decade of Women to turn attention toward women's issues and their rights. World conferences dealing with international women's issues are held periodically under United Nations sponsorship. In 1995, women from 185 countries met in Beijing for the Fourth World Conference on Women. The conference aimed at empowering women around the world by ensuring that they enjoyed all human rights and fundamental freedoms. In January, 2003, the Fifth World Conference was held in Rome. The conference again called for the international community to focus on developing real social and political equality for women. The struggle is ongoing in many countries. In Kuwait, women have been proposing equal rights since 1971, but it was never approved. Although women in Kuwait are considered the most liberated in the Persian Gulf region and make up 30 percent of the work force, they were denied to right to vote. Finally, in 2003, Kuwaiti women won the right to vote.

Women in Nepal face not only social and cultural bias but are also discriminated against by law in the matter of inheritance rights. According to an existing law from 1963, a daughter is entitled to inherit parental property if she is unmarried and is 35 years of age. Once she gets married, she has to return the property to the family, less the marriage expenses. In March, 2002, after an eight-year struggle, the Nepal Lower House voted in favor of a bill that guaranteed women the right to parental property from the day they were born. However, women activists are still unhappy that this new law has not wiped out the provision that women must return their inheritance to their parents once they marry.

In Jordan, where women constitute more than half the population and have had the right to vote since 1974, only two women have been elected to Parliament. It is alleged that in Jordan women vote according to the instructions of their husbands. Women in Jordan are joining together to ensure that they increase their representation in Parliament. Their hope is to gain six seats in Parliament in the next election.

WRONG CHOICES EXPLAINED:
(2) These headlines indicate that women in Kuwait, Nepal, and Jordan are politically active in trying to obtain equal rights.
(3) None of these headlines addresses the issue of education.
(4) None of these countries had communist governments.

37. **2** The graph shows that between 1950 and 2000 the world's population increased by approximately 4 billion. The world's population in 1950 was approximately 2.5 billion and the world population in 2000 was slightly over 6 billion; this is an increase of approximately 4 billion people from 1950 to 2000.

WRONG CHOICES EXPLAINED:
(1), (3), and (4) The graph does not illustrate that the world's population increased by 1 billion, 6 billion, or 8 billion people between 1950 and 2000.

38. **3** One explanation for the great change in the world population between 1950 and 2000 is that new medicines and technology were discovered and applied. The discovery of penicillin and the subsequent development of antibiotics during World War II brought about major progress in the treatment of diseases such as pneumonia and tuberculosis. Vaccination programs conducted by governments or the World Health Organization made considerable progress in eliminating diseases such as polio and measles. Medical care has led to increased life expectancy in most countries. In Haiti, the life expectancy by the late 1990s was 57 compared to 48 years of age in 1977. In developed countries, organ transplants and laser surgery have lengthened life expectancies. In the United States, life expectancy in 2000 was 78 compared to 71 in 1977. Technological improvements such as the Green Revolution have brought new high-yield crops and better fertilizers. Environmentally safe insecticides are being perfected. However, continued population growth is increasing faster than food production, which is threatening an adequate supply of food for people in developing countries.

WRONG CHOICES EXPLAINED:
(1) Family planning that teaches birth control and limiting the number of children has not been successful. Few countries, other than China, which has a one-child policy, have been able to limit the size of the family. In industrial nations, the population has declined, but in the developing regions of Asia, Africa, Latin America, and the Middle East, children are needed to earn money and assist parents in their old age.
(2) The growth in the world population has not been influenced by an absence of war and conflict. Since 1950, there have been many ethnic conflicts

in Europe, Asia, Latin America, and the Middle East that have contributed to the loss of many lives.

(4) The increase in famine and other natural disasters would have contributed to a decline, not an increase, in the world population.

39. **4** The primary reason that increasing numbers of Latin American citizens have immigrated to the United States over the last three decades is because of their hope for economic opportunities. According to the census of 2000, 51 percent of immigrants in the United States were born in Latin America. This migration is fueled by the hope of jobs, better education for their children, and a higher standard of living. In a recent study conducted by the World Bank, economists found that the per capita income of Mexican workers is about one-half of that of American workers. Throughout Latin and Central American areas, the per capita income in terms of purchasing power is extremely low. In El Salvador, the average per capita income is $4,600; in Ecuador $3,000; in Cuba $2,300; and in Bolivia $2,600. In the United States many of these immigrants will earn much more per hour than they could in their own lands. Furthermore, the opportunities for many unskilled and semiskilled workers are greater in the United States than in their own countries.

WRONG CHOICES EXPLAINED:

(1) Although citizens from El Salvador, Nicaragua, and Cuba migrated to escape the threat of communism, poor conditions in these countries, as well as in Mexico, Bolivia, and Ecuador, have contributed to immigration. Mexicans, who comprise the largest amount of Latin Americans who migrated to the United States, live in a democratic country that has many economic problems.

(2) The desire for religious freedom has not contributed to Latin American immigration. Latin America is a predominantly Catholic region but there is religious toleration for different religious groups.

(3) There have been natural disasters in countries such as Nicaragua, but this has not contributed to immigration to the United States.

40. **3** Between 1966 and 1987, a major effect of the Green Revolution on India was an overall increase in the production of grain. In 1966, India produced 70 million tons of grain. By 1987, India was producing 150 million tons of grain per year—a dramatic increase from the 1966 total.

WRONG CHOICES EXPLAINED:

(1) The chart does not show a decrease in grain production after 1975. In fact, grain production increased after 1975.

(2) After 1984, grain imports in India decreased. In 1984, India imported approximately 5 million tons of grain. By 1987, India did not import significant amounts of grain.

(4) From 1960 to 1966, India's grain importation increased. While India steadily imported approximately 8 million tons of grain from 1960 to 1963,

from 1963 to 1966, India's grain importation increased to its peak of just under 20 million tons of grain.

41. **1** The heading that best completes the partial outline is "Political Developments of the City-State of Athens." Athens, in eastcentral Greece, was the leading Greek city-state. Like other city-states, Athens went through a power struggle between the rich and the poor. Athenians avoided civil war by creating a democracy in which all citizens took part. By 507 B.C., the Athenian constitution stated that all free men were citizens, regardless of what class they belonged to, and that they could participate in the Assembly even if they did not own land. Athens had a direct democracy in which large numbers of male citizens actually took part in the day-to-day running of the government. The Athenians favored a lottery system over the ballot, believing that except for running a military campaign, all citizens were competent to hold public offices. However, it is important to remember that only about one-fifth of the people in Athens were citizens. The rest were slaves, foreigners, and women. Women had no part in the government and had very little intellectual life. Greek philosophers such as Socrates (469–399 B.C.) and Plato (427–347 B.C.), who participated in the cultural life of Athens, stressed the importance of reason and the role of the individual in society. Socrates left no written works but advocated the maxim "Know thyself." He sought truth through persistent questioning—an approach called the Socratic Method. He was tried and convicted for corrupting the minds of youth. He was put to death by poison for his beliefs. Socrates' philosophy is contained in the writings of his student, Plato. In *The Republic*, Plato described the ideal government as an aristocracy of the intelligent who were trained to rule. Plato distrusted democracy and wanted an orderly society run by philosopher-kings. His famous pupil was Aristotle. Aristotle (384–322 B.C.) wrote treatises on philosophy, science, and government, served as a personal tutor to the young Alexander the Great, and stimulated the future leader's interest in Greek culture. The city-state of Athens was the center of political activity during the 5th century B.C. in ancient Greece.

WRONG CHOICES EXPLAINED:
(2), (3), and (4) None of these headings describes events that took place during the periods of the Roman Empire, the Byzantine Empire, or the Age of Enlightenment. These events occurred during the 5th century B.C., which was before the growth of the Roman Empire in the 1st century A.D., the Byzantine Empire which began in the 3rd century A.D., and the Age of Enlightenment in the 18th century.

42. **3** The spread of Buddhist ideas and customs to China and Southeast Asia was the result of cultural diffusion. Cultural diffusion is the spread of ideas and customs from one people to another. The religion of Buddhism began in India around 600 B.C. Prince Siddharta Gautama (563–487 B.C.) lived his youth in comfort and luxury. Upset by the human suffering that he

saw beyond the palace walls, he left his wealth and family and set out in search of the truth. After wandering for six years, he suddenly realized that all suffering was caused by human desires. People must understand that the only way to overcome suffering is to overcome desire. Gautama became known as "The Enlightened One." Buddhist monks moved to China in the 1st century A.D., and later, missionaries carried Buddhism to Vietnam, Korea, and Japan. Although Buddhist principles were absorbed by Hinduism in India, Buddhism still survives in many nations of Southeast Asia, as well as China and Japan.

WRONG CHOICES EXPLAINED:

(1) The Mandate of Heaven is the belief in ancient China that the emperor received power to rule from Heaven (God).

(2) Economic dependence refers to the need that a country has for a particular product or item that might be essential for that country's economy.

(4) A civil service system provides government jobs for candidates based upon a test or standardized procedures.

43. **3** Meiji reformers of Japan and Peter the Great of Russia were similar in that both emphasized westernization. Westernization is the process of adapting Western culture and technology to improve a country. During the Meiji period, the Japanese adapted Western models of industrialization. In the Meiji period from 1862 to 1912, Japan ended feudalism and began to modernize by selectively borrowing from the West. Meiji means enlightened ruler. These reformers rallied around the emperor and unseated the shoguns, who they claimed had weakened the power of Japan. The goal of the Meiji leader, or enlightened ruler, was "a rich country, a strong military." The new leaders sent Japanese students abroad to learn Western government, economies, technology, and customs. In 1889, Japan adapted a written constitution implementing a parliamentary government with the emperor as its head. The Meiji government set up a banking system, improved ports, and organized a telegraph and postal system. The leaders also built a modern army based on a draft and constructed a fleet of steam-powered iron ships. A broad-based program of public education was instituted.

Peter the Great ruled Russia from 1682 to 1725. He wanted to make Russia more powerful by introducing new ideas and technology from Western Europe. After traveling to the West, he brought back many technical experts, teachers, soldiers, and nobles to help him reshape Russia. He introduced new economic policies such as mercantilism, which was popular in Europe during this time. He also supported social changes. He insisted that nobles cut off their beards and replace old-fashioned robes with western style clothing. He ended the practice of women secluding themselves at home and veiling their faces in public. He built up the army modeled on the European organization. The building of St. Petersburg, his new capital city, was the greatest symbol of Peter's policy of westernization. He invited Italian architects and artisans to design his great palaces in Western style.

WRONG CHOICES EXPLAINED:

(1) Neither the Meiji reforms nor Peter the Great supported socialism. Socialism is the economic policy in which the government owns all the means of production. Peter the Great adapted a policy of mercantilism and the Meiji reformers allowed for private ownership of property with the government organizing the banking and other essential systems.

(2) The Meiji reformers and Peter the Great rejected isolationism. These leaders wanted their countries to become more, not less, involved in foreign affairs.

(4) The Meiji reformers and Peter the Great did not support democracy. Peter the Great was an absolute ruler and the Meiji leaders set up a parliamentary government with the emperor as the head.

44. **2** The Sepoy Mutiny in India and the Boxer Rebellion in China were responses to European imperialism. The Sepoys were Indian soldiers serving under British command. These soldiers were protesting the policies of the British East India Company. The British cartridges used by the Sepoys had to be bitten to remove the seal before inserting them into their guns. The coverings were said to be greased with pork and beef fat. In 1857, the Sepoy soldiers refused to accept these cartridges. Both Hindus, who considered the cow sacred, and Muslims, who did not eat pork, were angry. The Sepoy Mutiny (Rebellion) lasted more than a year. The British government sent troops to help the British East India Company. This was a turning point in Indian history. After 1858, the British government took direct control of India. Eventually, the British began educating and training Indians for a role in their own Indian government.

The Boxers were a secret society formed in 1899. Their goal was to drive out the foreigners who were destroying China with their Western technology. In 1900, the Boxers attacked foreign communities in China as well as foreign embassies in Beijing. In response, Western owners and Japan formed a multinational force of 25,000 troops. They crushed the Boxers and rescued the foreigners besieged in Beijing. Both of these rebellions were attacks against Western imperialism.

WRONG CHOICES EXPLAINED:

(1) Mongol invasions were invasions by nomadic herders from Central Asia that began around 1200. Mongol fighters built the largest land empire in the world.

(3) Japanese aggression describes efforts by the Japanese to expand their political and economic influence in Asia by military means. This policy began in the late 19th century and ended with their defeat in World War II.

(4) African slave trading was part of the commerce system of many West African and Eastern African city-states. These kingdoms were influential in global economy between the 9th and 16th centuries. In the 16th century, the Atlantic Slave Trade began when European nations began to forcibly transport large numbers of Africans to satisfy the labor shortage in the Americas.

45. **1** The inference best supported with information provided on the map is that most of China's people live in the eastern part of the country. The eastern part of China contains land that is more useful for farming. In addition, the eastern part of China contains forests as well as the country's centers of manufacturing.

WRONG CHOICES EXPLAINED:

(2) China's climate is not too hot to allow farming. The map clearly indicates that most of eastern China is suitable farming land.

(3) The map does not infer that China's land cannot support its people. There are small patches of unproductive land, but in general, most of China's land is suitable to support its people.

(4) The map shows only scattered patches of manufacturing, which does not support the inference that most Chinese people make a living working in factories.

46. **1** During the 19th century, industrialization in Great Britain differed from industrialization in Japan mainly because Great Britain had greater deposits of natural resources. Japan lacks many mineral resources for industry. The island deposits of copper and coal were not enough to meet Japan's industrial needs. Thus, the scarcity of natural resources led Japan to become an importer of raw material as well as an imperial power in the late 1800s in order to obtain these needed natural resources. Great Britain was a country rich in natural resources, including water power and coal to fuel steam power, and iron ore to make machines, tools, and buildings. Great Britain was also blessed with an abundance of rivers for inland transportation for domestic trade and good harbors for trade with the rest of the continents and the world. All of these factors made the industrial development of Great Britain different from that of Japan.

WRONG CHOICES EXPLAINED:

(2) The English government encouraged economic growth and investment. The government supported the Royal Society of London, which spurred scientific research that could be applied to industry.

(3) Great Britain did not depend upon isolationism to increase its economic power. Great Britain depended upon trade with other countries as well as its colonies to help support its industrial growth. As an island, England was cut off from continental Europe. The country was able to develop its own industries but it needed to trade with other countries.

(4) The factory system began in Great Britain in the late 18th century, not in China. During the 19th century, China rejected industrialization.

47. **2** The statement that is accurate about the Hungarian Revolution in 1956 and the Tiananmen Square demonstrations in 1989 is that repressive action was taken to end both protests. Joseph Stalin, the dictator of the Soviet Union, maintained a tight control over the Eastern European satellite coun-

tries such as Poland and Hungary. After Joseph Stalin's death in 1953, communist leaders in Hungary eased control for two years and reimposed it when Hungary did not achieve their economic goals. Bitter opposition turned into a full revolt. In 1956, Imre Nagy, the new Hungarian communist prime minister, ended one-party rule, got rid of Soviet troops, and withdrew Hungary from the Warsaw Pact, which was a military alliance with Russia. This raised the fear that the Soviet Union was losing control of its satellite countries in Eastern Europe. In response, the Soviet Union poured in troops and tanks. The Western countries did nothing. Thousands of Hungarians died and more than 200,000 Hungarian refugees fled to the United States.

After the death of Mao Zedong in 1976, Xiaoping introduced reforms to modernize the economy. The government was willing to grant economic reform, but not political one. In April, 1989, 100,000 students gathered in Tiananmen Square to protest against official corruption and demand more civil liberties and better conditions at Chinese universities. In the following weeks, factory workers joined the students and demonstrations spread to other cities. Some Communist officials expressed support for the students. After six tense weeks, Xiaoping sent out tanks and troops to crush the demonstrations in Tiananmen Square. Many students were killed or wounded. The government hunted down all dissidents and stifled all political dissent.

WRONG CHOICES EXPLAINED:

(1) These events led to repression, not democratic reforms. In Russia and China, the government severely punished anyone who was involved in these demonstrations.

(3) The United Nations did not take any action. Russia, which sits on the Security Council, would not approve any U.N. intervention that addressed these protests.

(4) Hungary and China were communist countries. These demonstrations were protests against the rule of the Communist party.

48. **1** Based on this late 20th-century map, an accurate conclusion is that the worldwide distribution of wealth is unequal. Following the map's key, the United States, Western Europe, and Australia have per capita incomes of more than $10,000. The rest of the world's per capita income ranges from $1,000 to $10,000.

WRONG CHOICES EXPLAINED:

(2), (3), and (4) None of this information can be supported by the data from this map. The map does not support the conclusions that social mobility between social classes is increasing, the communist movement is growing, or that economic self-sufficiency in less-developed countries is decreasing. The map demonstrates only world levels of per capita income and no other inferences are possible given the data provided.

49. **2** During the 1800s, the colonies of Western European powers would have applied to most of those areas shown on the map with a per capita income of up to $1,000. During the 1800s, European powers exploited the areas in Africa and Asia for their natural resources and as a market for their surplus industrial goods. The European nations set up colonies in Africa and Asia. Great Britain controlled the largest number of colonies including India, South Africa, and parts of the East Indies. Germany, Italy, and France also participated in this scramble for colonies. The people of Asia and Africa provided the natural resources and cheap labor, which enabled their industrial economy to expand and spurred the growth of European industries and financial markets. However, the people in these colonies were treated as inferior and forced to work long hours for little or no pay. These conditions explained why these areas have such low per capita income while the industrial areas in North America and Great Britain have per capita incomes of more than $10,000. The imperial nations stripped these countries of their resources and when the colonies gained their independence, their economy was not developed. Their reliance on a single crop economy, which had been encouraged by the European powers during the 1800s, has continued to affect the economic growth of these countries until the present.

WRONG CHOICES EXPLAINED:
(1) and (4) There is no information on the map to support these statements. This map is about per capita income and does not contain data about industrial powers or democratic governments.

(3) The countries of Eastern Europe have a per capita income from $1,000 to $5,000.

50. **4** Churchill's "Iron Curtain" speech described the political alignment shown on the map. At the end of World War II, the Cold War developed between the United States and Russia. These two countries became rivals as Russia tried to expand its influence in Europe and the United States tried to contain Russia. Winston Churchill, the British prime minister, supported the United States. Churchill coined the phrase "Iron Curtain" in a speech that he gave in Fulton, Missouri, in March, 1946. Churchill proclaimed that an Iron Curtain had descended over Eastern Europe and that Europe was divided between those countries controlled by the Soviet Union and those who followed the West. The Iron Curtain referred to the Soviet-made barrier that split Europe into communist and noncommunist countries. The noncommunist countries, such as France, Italy, West Germany, and Great Britain, became members of NATO, which was established in 1949 to stop the spread of communism. In Eastern Europe, the communist satellites, such as Hungary and Poland, became members of the Warsaw Pact, which was formed as a reaction to NATO. Yugoslavia was the only non-aligned communist country that did not fall under the Iron Curtain. The symbolic Iron Curtain divided Europe for 43 years until communism collapsed in 1989.

WRONG CHOICES EXPLAINED:

(1) Pericles' Oration was given in Athens at the funeral of an Athenian slain in battle.

(2) Bismarck's "Blood and Iron" speech is associated with the unification of Germany.

(3) Hirohito's "Surrender" was drawn up to signify the end of Japanese participation in World War II.

THEMATIC ESSAY: GENERIC SCORING RUBRIC

Score of 5:
- Shows a thorough understanding of the theme or problem
- Addresses all aspects of the task
- Shows an ability to analyze, evaluate, compare and/or contrast issues and events
- Richly supports the theme or problem with relevant facts, examples, and details
- Is a well-developed essay, consistently demonstrating a logical and clear plan of organization
- Introduces the theme or problem by establishing a framework that is beyond a simple restatement of the task and concludes with a summation of the theme or problem

Score of 4:
- Shows a good understanding of the theme or problem
- Addresses all aspects of the task
- Shows an ability to analyze, evaluate, compare and/or contrast issues and events
- Includes relevant facts, examples, and details, but may not support all aspects of the theme or problem evenly
- Is a well-developed essay, demonstrating a logical and clear plan of organization
- Introduces the theme or problem by establishing a framework that is beyond a simple restatement of the task and concludes with a summation of the theme or problem

Score of 3:
- Shows a satisfactory understanding of the theme or problem
- Addresses most aspects of the task or addresses all aspects in a limited way
- Shows an ability to analyze or evaluate issues and events, but not in any depth
- Includes some facts, examples, and details
- Is a satisfactorily developed essay, demonstrating a general plan of organization
- Introduces the theme or problem by repeating the task and concludes by repeating the theme or problem

Score of 2:
- Shows limited understanding of the theme or problem
- Attempts to address the task
- Develops a faulty analysis or evaluation of issues and events
- Includes few facts, examples, and details, and may include information that contains inaccuracies

- Is a poorly organized essay, lacking focus
- Fails to introduce or summarize the theme or problem

Score of 1:
- Shows very limited understanding of the theme or problem
- Lacks an analysis of evaluation of the issues and events
- Includes little or no accurate or relevant facts, examples, or details
- Attempts to complete the task, but demonstrates a major weakness in organization
- Fails to introduce or summarize the theme or problem

Score of 0:
- Fails to address the task, is illegible, or is a blank paper

PART II: THEMATIC ESSAY QUESTION

Throughout history, geographic factors such as land features, location, resources, and climate have affected the area or region in which people live. In ancient times, the Nile River contributed to the development of Egyptian civilization. In the 18th and 19th centuries, the natural and human resources of Great Britain enabled that region to become the first nation to undergo the Industrial Revolution in Europe.

Ancient Egypt, located in northeast Africa, was a narrow strip of land about 550 miles long. It extends 15 miles on each side of the Nile River. From the highlands of Africa to the Mediterranean Sea, the Nile River flows over 4,100 miles, making it the longest river in the world. Every year in June, the Nile floods along its banks. When the river recedes in October, it leaves behind a wet deposit of fertile soil.

Before the scorching sun dried out the soil, the peasants hitched their cattle to the plows and prepared their fields for planting. All summer and fall, they tended the wheat and barley plants. Their crops were watered from an intricate network of irrigation ditches. The welcomed harvest finally arrived. This cycle repeated itself year after year. Since the land would have been a desert without the Nile water, in the 5th century B.C., the ancient Greek historian Herodotus called Egypt "the gift of the Nile." With this rich soil and ample fresh water, Egyptian farmers were able to build settlements along the Nile that were able to support a large number of craftsmen, warriors, and priests. Thus, villages and cities were built along the Nile on a narrow strip of land because it was made fertile by the river.

The river also influenced cultural aspects of Egyptian life. Along the Nile River, Egyptian architects and engineers built magnificent palaces, temples, and statues of stone. The Nile River was so important that the Egyptians worshipped it as a god who was the source of life for the people and seldom turned against them. Governments evolved in ancient Egypt in an effort to control the Nile. The people needed dikes and reservoirs to restrain the annual flooding of the Nile and canals to irrigate the dry lands. These major projects, which were too large for individuals, required a group effort. This led to the development of local governments, usually chiefdoms.

The Nile River was also a major highway providing a reliable system of transportation between Upper and Lower Egypt and helped to unite these regions. The ease of contact made possible by this water highway helped to unify Egypt's villages to promote trade. Egyptian merchants traveled up and down the Nile River on barges, exchanging the products of Africa, the Middle East, and the Mediterranean. The Egyptians traded with people like the Phoenicians and the Greeks. This interaction led to cultural diffusion as different ideas and customs were spread along these trade routes.

The vast and forbidding desert on either side of the Nile acted as a natural barrier between Egypt and other lands. While the Egyptians were forced to stay close to their water lifeline, the desert also shut out invaders. For much of its early history, Egypt was spared the constant warfare of the Fertile Crescent and was able to grow and prosper as a civilization.

In the 1700s, Great Britain was neither the largest nor the smallest country in Europe. However, the Industrial Revolution would begin in Great Britain because of its abundant natural resources. Britain had a large supply of coal and iron ore that became the principal raw materials of the Industrial Revolution.

Coal supplied the energy for the machines developed during the Industrial Revolution. It provided the power necessary for the steam engine, invented by James Watt in 1769, which was adapted for the textile factories that became the foundation of the Industrial Revolution. The steam engine was later adapted for other factories and for transportation. By 1800, almost 500 steam engines were huffing and puffing in various British factories. For the first time, coal allowed people to have a source of power that could be used anywhere and anytime.

Great Britain's supply of iron ore was used to construct machines, tools, and buildings. At first, iron was used because steel, although stronger and less brittle, was costly to produce. In 1856, the English inventor Henry Bessemer devised the inexpensive Bessemer process of refining iron into steel. Steel became the basic metal of our industrial society in the construction of railroads and ships. The British used steel to build up a large fleet of merchant ships that sailed to almost every part of the world. This overseas trade also gave Britain access to raw materials and markets. Both were essential to industrial growth. The need for markets and raw materials also led to the rise of imperialism and the colonization of Africa and Asia.

Great Britain's greatest natural resource was its growing population of workers. Improvements in farming led to an increased availability of food. More nutritious foods allowed people to enjoy longer, healthier lives. In just one century, England's population nearly doubled from about 5 million in 1700 to about 9 million in 1800. The population boom swelled the available work force. Thus, by the middle of the 18th century, Great Britain was ripe for industrial development.

The geographic features of a region directly affect its development. In ancient Egypt, the Nile River helped to determine the economic, political, and cultural life of the region. In Great Britain, its natural and human resources helped make it the birthplace of the Industrial Revolution. Geographic factors in history have always been powerful forces that have had a major influence on how a region, people, or nation develops.

PART III: DOCUMENT-BASED QUESTION

Part A: Short Answers

Document 1

According to Camillo di Cavour, one positive result of Italian unification was to make Italy glorious and powerful.

Note: This response receives full credit because it cites a reason in the document why unification would be good for Italy.

Document 2

2a Map **A** shows that nationalism affected the German states by unifying Germany.

Note: This response receives full credit because it identifies how nationalism pulled Germany together.

2b Map **B** shows that nationalism affected the Austro-Hungarian Empire by leading to the breaking up of the empire and the creation of new nations such as Austria, Hungary, and Romania.

Note: This response receives full credit because it states specifically how the Austro-Hungarian Empire was broken up and the new nations that were created.

Document 3

3a Passage **A** expresses Israeli nationalism by referring to the hope of the Jews to be free in their land and to return to the land of Zion and Jerusalem. The passage is also the Israeli national anthem.

Note: This response receives full credit because it cites specific passages of hope and freedom from the Israeli national anthem as an example of nationalism.

3b. Passage **B** expresses Palestinian nationalism by asking others to leave their land and live wherever they like but not among them.

Note: This response receives full credit because it refers to specific passages that express Palestinian nationalism.

Document 4

One expression of Chinese nationalism in this passage was the demand to expel all foreigners and to practice I-ho magic boxing to protect the country from miserable suffering.

Note: This response receives full credit because it shows examples of how Chinese nationalism would be used to protect the country from foreign influence.

Document 5

One criticism that Gandhi expressed about British rule in India was that it had impoverished the country by taking away their money.

Note: This response receives full credit because it gives a specific criticism from the document, which Gandhi expressed about British rule in India.

Document 6

These maps show that between 1952 and 1975, nationalism affected the continent of Africa by ending colonialism and making almost all of Africa independent and free from foreign rule.

Note: This response receives full credit because it identifies how nationalism made Africa free from colonial or foreign control.

Document 7

7a. Two examples of nationalistic conflict are
  (1) The Kurds fight for their freedom from Iraq and Turkey.
  (2) The Albanian Muslims and Serbs struggle against each other in
      Kosovo.

Note: This response receives full credit because it cites examples of ethnic conflicts in Iraq, Turkey, and Kosovo.

7b. One cause of these nationalistic conflicts is religious differences.

Note: This response receives full credit because it cites one of the examples in the document for the cause of these nationalistic conflicts.

DOCUMENT-BASED QUESTION: GENERIC SCORING RUBRIC

Score of 5:
- Thoroughly addresses all aspects of the *Task* by accurately analyzing and interpreting at least **four** documents
- Incorporates information from the documents in the body of the essay
- Incorporates relevant outside information
- Richly supports the theme or problem with relevant facts, examples, and details
- Is a well-developed essay, consistently demonstrating a logical and clear plan of organization
- Introduces the theme or problem by establishing a framework that is beyond a simple restatement of the *Task* or *Historical Context* and concludes with a summation of the theme or problem

Score of 4:
- Addresses all aspects of the *Task* by accurately analyzing and interpreting at least **four** documents
- Incorporates information from the documents in the body of the essay
- Incorporates relevant outside information
- Includes relevant facts, examples, and details, but discussion may be more descriptive than analytical
- Is a well-developed essay, demonstrating a logical and clear plan of organization
- Introduces the theme or problem by establishing a framework that is beyond a simple restatement of the *Task* or *Historical Context* and concludes with a summation of the theme or problem

Score of 3:
- Addresses most aspects of the *Task* or addresses all aspects of the *Task* in a limited way, using some of the documents
- Incorporates some information from the documents in the body of the essay
- Incorporates limited or no relevant outside information
- Includes some facts, examples, and details, but discussion is more descriptive than analytical
- Is a satisfactorily developed essay, demonstrating a general plan of organization
- Introduces the theme or problem by repeating the *Task* or *Historical Context* and concludes by simply repeating the theme or problem

Score of 2:
- Attempts to address some aspects of the *Task*, making limited use of the documents
- Presents no relevant outside information
- Includes few facts, examples, and details; discussion restates contents of the documents
- Is a poorly organized essay, lacking focus
- Fails to introduce or summarize the theme or problem

Score of 1:
- Shows limited understanding of the *Task* with vague, unclear references to the documents
- Presents no relevant outside information
- Includes little or no accurate or relevant facts, details, or examples
- Attempts to complete the *Task*, but demonstrates a major weakness in organization
- Fails to introduce or summarize the theme or problem

Score of 0:
- Fails to address the *Task*, is illegible, or is a blank paper

Part B: Essay

Nationalism, the feeling of patriotism and pride in one's country, has been a powerful force in the world since the French Revolution of 1789. The intense nationalistic slogan of "Liberty, Equality, and Fraternity" led to the overthrow of the French monarchy. People transferred their loyalty from a king and placed national interests for the country above all other considerations. Nationalism greatly influences the actions of people. The power and force created by nationalism has had a positive effect throughout Europe and on nations and people throughout the world.

In the 19th century, nationalism was a driving force that united both Italy and Germany. Until the 1860s, Italy was divided into a number of small states and was considered a geographic area rather than a united country. Parts of Italy were under the control of Austria. In 1852, Count Camillo di Cavour, the Prime Minister of Piedmont Sardinia, was the driving force in freeing Italy from Austrian control. Cavour is often referred to as "The Brains of Italian Unification." Cavour believed that the unification of Italy would not only elevate Italy's intellectual and moral development but would also make Italy a great nation (Doc. 1). The unification of Italy in 1860 led to the creation of a parliamentary democracy and the decline of papal power in Italy. Later, this spirit of nationalism and unity would be an important force in weakening the control of Benito Mussolini's Fascist dictatorship during the 1920s and 1930s.

Nationalism also led to the unification of Germany in the 19th century. In 1815, there were 38 different independent states, but by 1871, German nationalists, led by Bismarck, unified the country (Doc. 2a). A united Germany would become a powerful political and economic force in the first half of the 20th century.

The spirit of nationalism would also affect the Austrian Empire, which was composed of many subject nationalities. To support their hold over the Empire, Austrians granted equal partnership to the Hungarians. This transformed the Austrian Empire into the Dual Monarchy in 1877. However, the Slavic people (Serbs and Czechs) and the Rumanians remained restless and strived for their own country. These nationalistic feelings eventually led them to win their independence. (Doc. 2b).

Nationalistic movements have affected many different areas of the world. In 1900, the Boxer Rebellion in China called for the Chinese to expel the foreigners because they were destroying their way of life (Doc. 4). The Boxers were a nationalistic group who believed that they could improve the lives of the people by rejecting Western technology and religion (Doc. 4). Later in the century, nationalism would be a rallying force for Dr. Sun Yat Sen (Sun Yixian) who became the leader of the Kuomintag Party. Dr. Sun believed that nationalism was the key to overthrowing the Manchu dynasty and enabled China to survive on its own. In 1911, Dr. Sun succeeded in ending the Manchu dynasty and he became the president of the new Republic of China. A new government was advocated based on the three principles of the people. The main principle was nationalism. It was designed to end foreign control. Nationalism would also be the basis of the Chinese communist demands for the return of the island of Taiwan beginning in the 1950s.

In India, Mohandas Gandhi was a man who resented British colonial rule (Doc. 5). During the 1920s and 1930s, he became leader of the Indian National Congress and led a nonviolent movement or passive resistance for self-government. He claimed that the British policies had impoverished India. He criticized the British for their brute force, their disrespect of Indian culture, and their destruction of the spirit of the Indian people (Doc. 5). Gandhi urged that the people of India return to their native traditions, which would spur economic development and restore national pride. Gandhi urged Indians to boycott British goods and promoted nonviolent demonstrations to end economic exploitation by the British. In 1947, the British finally granted India independence.

Nationalism also contributed to the decline of colonialism in Africa. From 1870 to 1914, European nations (England, France, Italy, Belgium, Spain, and Portugal) seized territory in Africa (Doc. 6). Europeans wanted these colonies because the Industrial Revolution had created the need for raw materials and markets for excess goods (Doc. 6). After World War II, many of these African nations struggled to end foreign domination. Between 1952 and 1975, over 30 nations in Africa declared their independence from their former colonial rulers (Doc. 6). The spirit of Pan-Africanism began to emphasize the unity of the African people and the spirit of freedom. African leaders such as Kwame Nkrumah of Ghana and Jomo Kenyatta of Kenya harnessed this national spirit to gain independence for their countries. This spirit is still a driving force that helps to unite Africa today. Nationalism enabled Nelson Mandela to gain power in South Africa after the Europeans had ruled the country for more than 350 years. Mandela, who was the leader of the African National Congress, had been jailed for moe than 27 years for his activities against the government. During his time in jail, Mandela became a symbol of South Africa's struggle for freedom. After his release from prison in 1991, he became the unifying force to help end the government's policy of racial discrimination. In 1994, Mandela was elected the first president of a free South Africa in an election in which all races could vote.

Current conflicts also stem from centuries-old nationalistic disagreements. In the Middle East, the Jews and Palestinians have been unable to reach an agreement for years. Nationalism contributed to the birth of Zionism, which was founded in the 1890s to promote the establishment of a Jewish homeland in Palestine. The Jews regard Palestine as their Biblical homeland and this belief of returning to their ancient homeland is expressed in their national anthem (Doc. 3a). However, Palestine Arabs resent the efforts to create this new homeland and claim the territory as their land (Doc. 3b). Efforts to negotiate this conflict have been unsuccessful. Militant groups such as the Hamas have exploited nationalism to justify violence, which in turn has led to retaliation by the Israeli government.

Nationalism has also been a powerful force in transforming the former Soviet Empire into independent states (Doc. 7). In the 1980s, Lech Walesa from Poland and other leaders organized an independent trade union named Solidarity. With millions of members, Solidarity called for political change. It demanded that all unions be free of communist control. At first, Solidarity was banned and Walesa was arrested. However, when Mikhail Gorbachev, the leader of the Soviet Union, lifted the ban in 1989, Poland held its first free elections in 50 years. Solidarity won and formed the first noncommunist government in Eastern Europe since World War II. Between 1989 and 1991, Hungary, Czechoslovakia, and Bulgaria held peaceful free elections and the communist governments fell. In 1989, within days, more than two million East Germans poured into West Germany. The crowds were so huge that the government bulldozed new openings in the Berlin Wall, the greatest symbol of the Cold War. The Wall was knocked down by joyous Germans and free elections in 1990 led to the fall of the Communist Party and the reunification of East and West Germany.

The fall of communism led to the breakup of Yugoslavia in 1991 and 1992 (Doc. 7). Yugoslavia was a multinational state created after World War I. It was inhabited by Serbs who were Orthodox Christians, Croats who were Roman Catholics, and Albanians, many of whom were Muslims. In Bosnia, fighting erupted between Serbs and Muslims. Serbs began a campaign of ethnic cleansing, which was designed to drive Muslims out of the part of Bosnia that Serbia claimed. Many Bosnians became refugees and were either brutalized or killed. In 1995, representatives from all warring sides met in the United States and agreed to a peace settlement. NATO troops were sent into Bosnia to enforce the peace.

There have undoubtedly been negative effects to nationalism—the extreme nationalism used to justify the dictatorships of Benito Mussolini in Italy and Adolph Hitler in Germany, tribal conflicts in Africa between Hutus and Tutsis, and the violence in Chechnya and the former Yugoslavia, as well as the continued fighting in the Middle East.

However, the benefits of nationalism have exceeded the negative aspects. A parliamentary democracy established in Italy outlasted the evils of fascism and survived the threat of communism after World War II. The spirit of nationalism also led to the reunification of Germany in 1990 and freedom and independence for many ethnic groups within the former Yugoslavia. A free and independent India has developed into the world's largest democracy and has been able to govern a diverse nation. Economically, India is considered to be a nation that will eventually exert a dominant influence in the 21st century as the center of the technological revolution. The collapse of the Soviet Union has also led to the independence of many of its former satellite states, such as Poland and Hungary. These countries have strengthened their national identities and economies. They are also managing to become part of the European Union and NATO. These steps help insure that the former Soviet satellites are truly integrated into the European economic and political systems. Nationalism is beneficial to a nation or region because it allows people to establish their own identity and control their own destiny and economy.

Topic	Question Numbers	Total Number of Questions	Number Wrong	°Reason for Wrong Answer
U.S. AND N.Y. HISTORY				
WORLD HISTORY	1, 2, 6, 7, 9, 13, 14, 15, 18, 23, 25, 26, 28, 29, 31, 35, 39, 42, 43, 44, 47	21		
GEOGRAPHY	5, 10, 11, 17, 20, 30, 37, 38, 45, 46, 50	11		
ECONOMICS	3, 12, 19, 21, 24, 32, 33, 40, 48, 49	10		
CIVICS, CITIZENSHIP, AND GOVERNMENT	4, 8, 16, 22, 27, 34, 36, 41	8		

°Your reason for answering the question incorrectly might be (a) lack of knowledge, (b) misunderstanding the question, or (c) careless error.

Actual Items by Standard and Unit

	1 U.S. and N.Y. History	2 World History	3 Geography	4 Economics	5 Civics, Citizenship, and Gov't	Number
Methodology of Global History and Geography		1, 2				2
UNIT ONE Ancient World		6, 7, 42	5	3	4, 41	7
UNIT TWO Expanding Zones of Exchange		9				1
UNIT THREE Global Interactions		13, 14, 15	11	12	16	6
UNIT FOUR First Global Age			17	21		2
UNIT FIVE Age of Revolution		18	20, 46	19, 49	22	6
UNIT SIX Crisis and Achievement (1900–1945)		23, 26, 28		24	27	5
UNIT SEVEN 20th Century Since 1945		29, 35, 47	30, 50	32, 33	34	8
UNIT EIGHT Global Connections and Interactions		39	37, 38, 45	40, 48	36	7
Cross topical		25, 31, 43, 44	10		8	6
Total # of Questions		21	11	10	8	50
% of Items by Standard		42%	22%	20%	16%	100%

Examination
June 2004
Global History and Geography

PART I: MULTIPLE CHOICE

Directions (1–50): For each statement or question, write in the space provided, the *number* of the word or expression that, of those given, best completes the statement or answers the question.

1 Which heading best completes the partial outline below?

> I. _____
>
> A. Personal letter
> B. Autobiography
> C. Diary
> D. Driver's license

1 Primary Sources
2 Secondary Sources
3 Official Records
4 Published Records

1 ____

2 A totalitarian society is one in which

   1 the government controls most aspects of life
   2 religious beliefs are supported by the government
   3 the state is considered a servant of the citizens
   4 citizens can publicly criticize the actions of the leaders

2 _____

3 Which geographic factor had the greatest influence on the early history of South Asia and China?

   1 river valleys
   2 island locations
   3 vast coastlines
   4 tropical rain forests

3 _____

4 The Silk Road was important because it allowed for the

   1 exploration of China by the Roman Army
   2 development of agriculture by the nomadic people of Central Asia
   3 movement of Chinese armies through Southeast Asia
   4 exchange of goods between Asia and the Middle East

4 _____

5 Olympic games, the poems of Homer, and Hellenistic culture are associated with which ancient civilization?

   1 Egyptian   3 Roman
   2 Greek   4 Phoenician

5 _____

6 The Code of Hammurabi was a major contribution to the development of civilization because it

   1 treated citizens and slaves equally
   2 ended all physical punishment
   3 recorded existing laws for all to see
   4 rejected the principle of filial piety   6 ____

7 One effect of rugged, mountainous geography on the civilization of ancient Greece was the development of

   1 absolute monarchies
   2 separate, independent city-states
   3 extensive trade with the Persians
   4 belief in one God   7 ____

8 Which heading best completes the partial outline below?

   > I. _____
   >
   >   A. Development of medical encyclopedias
   >   B. Development of algebra and astronomical tables
   >   C. Production of cotton textiles and woolen carpets
   >   D. Production of literature, calligraphy, and geometric art

   1 Achievements of Feudal Societies
   2 Inventions During the Neolithic Revolution
   3 Issues of the Protestant Reformation
   4 Contributions of the Islamic Civilization   8 ____

Base your answer to question 9 on the map below and on your knowledge of social studies.

Movement of People
500 B.C. – A.D. 1500

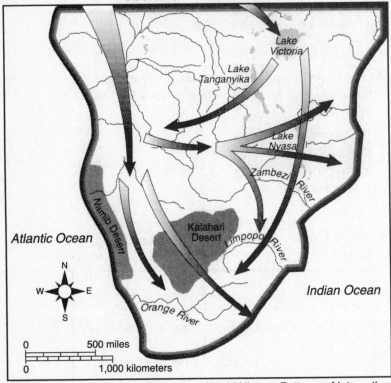

Source: Roger B. Beck et al., *World History: Patterns of Interaction,* McDougal Littell (adapted)

9 The routes shown on the map illustrate the

1 spread of Christianity
2 shift in European population
3 expansion of apartheid
4 pattern of the Bantu migrations

9 ____

10
> • "Most Gracious, Most Merciful;"
> • "Master of the Day of Judgment."
> • "Thee do we worship, And Thine aid we seek."

Source: 'Abdullah Yusuf-Ali, trans.,
The Meaning of the Holy Qur'an,
Amana Publications (excerpted)

This translated quotation from the Qur'an [Koran] refers to

1 Buddha   3 Allah
2 Shiva   4 Muhammad   10 ____

11 Which fact relating to early Japan was a result of the other three?

1 Japan experienced earthquakes and volcanic eruptions.
2 The Japanese developed a nature-based belief called Shinto.
3 Tsunamis and typhoons sometimes destroyed coastal Japanese villages.
4 Mountains are found throughout the islands of Japan.

11 ____

Base your answer to question 12 on the picture below and on your knowledge of social studies.

Source: Q. T. Luong, www.terragalleria.com

12 This statue is most closely associated with which religion?

1 Buddhism   3 Jainism
2 Islam   4 Christianity   12____

13 In his book *The Prince*, Niccolò Machiavelli advises that a wise ruler is one who

1 keeps taxes and food prices low
2 encourages education and the arts
3 allows advisors to speak their minds
4 does what is necessary to stay in power   13____

14 A major reason that the Renaissance began in Italy was that

1 Italian city-states had grown wealthy from trade between Europe and Asia
2 farmers produced great agricultural surpluses on vast plains
3 merchants supported the Green Revolution
4 many European scholars had migrated to this area   14 _____

15 Which action could be considered an effect of the Protestant Reformation?

1 posting of the Ninety-five Theses
2 decline in the power of the Roman Catholic Church
3 sale of indulgences
4 end of religious warfare   15 _____

16 "In 1469, Isabella of Castile married Ferdinand of Aragon. This marriage between the rulers of two powerful kingdoms opened the way for a unified state. Using their combined forces, the two monarchs made a final push against the Muslim stronghold of Granada. In 1492, Granada fell. . . ."

Source: Elisabeth Ellis and Anthony Esler, *World History: Connections to Today*, Prentice Hall

What is being described in this passage?

1 a crusade to the Holy Land
2 the reasons for the voyages of Columbus
3 the Spanish Reconquista
4 the start of the Italian Renaissance   16 _____

17 The archaeological evidence found at the Mesoamerican sites of Tenochtitlan and Machu Picchu
suggests that these societies

   1 consisted of hunters and gatherers
   2 were highly developed and organized cultures
   3 practiced a monotheistic religion
   4 followed a democratic system   17____

18 Which statement describes an impact that the
Columbian Exchange had on the lives of
Europeans?

   1 The transfer of new products and ideas encouraged economic growth.
   2 New diseases were brought to Europe and
resulted in massive deaths caused by a plague.
   3 Native Americans immigrated to Europe and
competed with Europeans for jobs.
   4 Cross-cultural contacts between South America
and Asia declined.   18____

Base your answers to questions 19 and 20 on the map below and on your knowledge of social studies.

Indigenous Civilizations of Africa to 1901

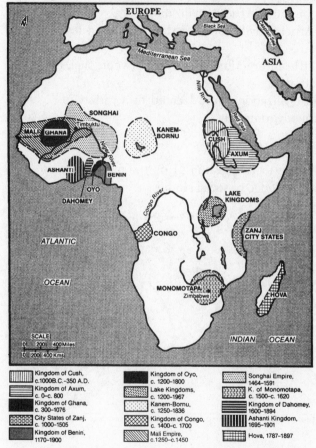

Source: Martin Greenwald Associates, *Historical Maps on File*, Facts on File, Inc. (adapted)

19 Which civilization was located at the mouth of the Niger River?

1 Ghana

2 Congo

3 Benin

4 Ashanti

19 ____

20 Which statement about the civilizations of Africa before 1901 can best be inferred by the information on the map?

1 Christianity and Islam played a minor role in the development of African civilizations.
2 Most African civilizations existed for only a few years.
3 Very little interaction occurred between these civilizations.
4 African civilizations were located in a variety of physical environments.

20 _____

Base your answer to question 21 on the map below and on your knowledge of social studies.

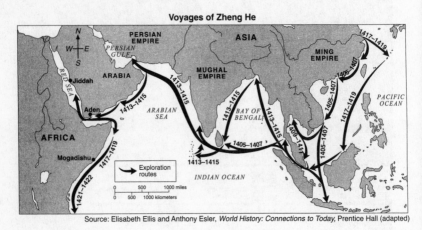

Voyages of Zheng He

Source: Elisabeth Ellis and Anthony Esler, *World History: Connections to Today,* Prentice Hall (adapted)

21 Which conclusion is best supported by the map?

    1 Eastern Chinese cities had extensive contact with the Persian Empire in 1405.

    2 Rivers and mountains prevented the expansion of overland Chinese trade.

    3 The Chinese came into contact with peoples of other cultures between 1405 and 1422.

    4 China was isolated from outside contact under the rulers of the Ming Empire.   21 _____

22 In Europe, joint stock companies, shareholders, entrepreneurs, and the bourgeoisie contributed to the

    1 rise of capitalism

    2 development of feudalism

    3 decline of communism

    4 increase in power of the guilds   22 _____

23 King Louis XIV of France, Peter the Great of Russia, and Suleiman the Magnificent of the Ottoman Empire were all considered absolute rulers because they

    1 broke from the Roman Catholic Church

    2 helped feudal lords build secure castles

    3 instituted programs that provided more power to their parliaments

    4 determined government policies without the consent of their people   23 _____

24 One way in which the Scientific Revolution and the Enlightenment were similar is that they

1 encouraged the spread of new ideas
2 strengthened traditional institutions
3 led to the Protestant Reformation
4 rejected Renaissance individualism

24 _____

25 ". . . Men are born and remain free and equal in rights. Social distinctions may be founded only upon the general good. . . . "

—*Declaration of the Rights of Man and of the Citizen*, 1789

Which principle of the Enlightenment philosophers is expressed in this quotation from the French Revolution?

1 natural law   3 free trade
2 nationalism   4 socialism

25 _____

Base your answer to question 26 on the illustration below and on your knowledge of social studies.

Source: Sue A. Kime et al., *World Studies: Global Issues & Assessments*, N & N Publishing Co. (adapted)

26 All the elements identified in the illustration contributed to German

1 interdependence   3 imperialism
2 unification   4 apathy

26 _____

Base your answer to question 27 on the graph below and on your knowledge of social studies.

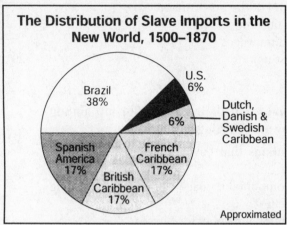

The Distribution of Slave Imports in the New World, 1500–1870

Brazil 38%

U.S. 6%

6%

Dutch, Danish & Swedish Caribbean

Spanish America 17%

French Caribbean 17%

British Caribbean 17%

Approximated

Source: R. W. Fogel and S. L. Engerman, *Time on the Cross: The Economics of American Negro Slavery*, Little, Brown and Company (adapted)

27 Which statement is supported by the graph?

1 Little trade in enslaved Africans took place before the 1500s.
2 Slavery was most widely practiced in Sweden, Denmark, and Holland.
3 Conditions of slavery in Brazil were less harsh than those in the United States.
4 Most enslaved Africans were sent to the Caribbean and Spanish America.   27 _____

28 Which event had the greatest influence on the development of laissez-faire capitalism?

1 fall of the Roman Empire
2 invention of the printing press
3 Industrial Revolution
4 Green Revolution   28 _____

29 In the late 1800s, one response of workers in England
to unsafe working conditions was to

1 take control of the government
2 return to farming
3 set minimum wages
4 form labor unions   29 _____

30 When Koreans call their land "a shrimp among
whales," they are referring to

1 the mountains that cover much of the Korean
peninsula
2 the environmental damage caused by overfishing
in the Pacific
3 their traditional respect for the sea
4 their location between powerful neighbors: Russia,
China, and Japan   30 _____

Base your answers to questions 31 and 32 on the woodblock print below and on your knowledge of social studies.

Ladies with western musical instruments

Source: Published by Ōmori Kakutarō, wood block print (detail), c. 1890, Museum of Fine Arts, Boston

31 This late 19th-century Japanese print illustrates

1 isolationism
2 ethnocentrism

3 cultural diffusion
4 democracy

31 _____

32 During which period of Japanese history was this print most likely created?

1 Tokugawa shogunate
2 Meiji Restoration
3 Russo-Japanese War
4 post–World War II occupation 32 _____

33 During World War I, which group of people were victims of genocide?

1 Arabs in Egypt
2 Palestinians in Syria
3 Algerians in France
4 Armenians in the Ottoman Empire 33 _____

34 The Treaty of Versailles punished Germany for its role in World War I by

1 forcing Germany to accept blame for the war and to pay reparations
2 dividing Germany into four occupied zones
3 supporting economic sanctions by the United Nations
4 taking away German territory in the Balkans and Spain 34 _____

35 The main reason Japan invaded Southeast Asia during World War II was to

1 recruit more men for its army
2 acquire supplies of oil and rubber
3 satisfy the Japanese people's need for spices
4 prevent the United States from entering the war 35 _____

Base your answer to question 36 on the passage below and on your knowledge of social studies.

"It took the Big Four just five hours and twenty-five minutes here in Munich today to dispel the clouds of war and come to an agreement over the partition of Czechoslovakia. There is to be no European war, after all. There is to be peace, and the price of that peace is, roughly, the ceding by Czechoslovakia of the Sudeten territory to Herr Hitler's Germany. The German Führer gets what he wanted, only he has to wait a little longer for it. Not much longer though—only ten days. . . ."

Source: William Shirer, recording of CBS radio report
from Prague, September 29, 1938

36 The policy that France, Britain, and Italy chose to follow at this meeting is known as

1 appeasement   3 liberation
2 self-determination   4 pacification   36 _____

---

37 The political climate of the Cold War caused the world's two superpowers to

1 cooperate in halting the spread of communism
2 colonize Africa and Asia
3 compete economically and militarily
4 protect human rights   37 _____

38 The political ideas of Ho Chi Minh, Fidel Castro, and Pol Pot were strongly influenced by the writings of

1 Confucius   3 Desmond Tutu
2 Mohandas Gandhi   4 Karl Marx   38 _____

39 In India, urbanization affected society by

    1 reinforcing Hindu beliefs
    2 encouraging native arts and crafts
    3 weakening the traditional caste system
    4 increasing the number of farmers   39_____

40 The main purpose of the North American Free Trade Agreement (NAFTA) and the European Union (EU) is to

    1 increase the authority of the United Nations
    2 encourage increased economic development
    3 promote peace between nations
    4 establish and enforce military alliances   40_____

41 • The people of Kashmir demand separation from India.

    • The people of East Timor vote for independence from Indonesia.

    • The Tibetans resent control of their country by China.

    • The Kurds want to establish their own independent state of Kurdistan.

These statements are examples of the efforts of different peoples to achieve

    1 free-market systems
    2 democratic governments
    3 social equality
    4 self-determination   41_____

Base your answer to question 42 on the cartoon below and on your knowledge of social studies.

Source: Dan Wasserman, Tribune Media Services, Inc.

42 The concern expressed in this cartoon is most closely related to the consequences of

1 rapid migration of animals to the Northern Hemisphere
2 further exploration of the Arctic Ocean
3 industrialization and the burning of fossil fuels
4 slow economic growth in developing nations

42 _____

43 The late 20th-century conflicts in Rwanda, Yugoslavia, and India were similar in that each was caused by the

1 deforestation conducted by multinational companies
2 collapse of communism
3 intervention of United Nations peacekeeping forces
4 rivalries between ethnic groups

43 _____

44 The Twelve Tables, Justinian's Code, and the English Bill of Rights are similar in that each addresses the issue of

1 social mobility
2 economic development
3 the individual and the state
4 the importance of religion 44 _____

Base your answer to question 45 on the cartoon below and your knowledge of social studies.

Source: Matt Davies, *Gannett Suburban Newspapers*, United Press Syndicate

45 Which statement best describes the main point of the cartoon?

1 Nuclear proliferation occurs in all societies.
2 Actions of one nation often affect other nations.
3 Nuclear technology should be limited to the global superpowers.
4 Most governments are critical of India's nuclear tests. 45 _____

46 Which heading best completes the partial outline below?

> I. _____
>
>   A. Maurya
>   B. Gupta
>   C. Delhi sultanate

1 Empires of India
2 Latin American Civilizations
3 Empires of the Fertile Crescent
4 Dynasties of China

46 ____

47 Which set of events is in the correct chronological order?

1 Renaissance → Middle Ages → Roman Empire
2 Treaty of Versailles → World War II → Korean War
3 Reformation → Crusades → European exploration of the Americas
4 Bolshevik Revolution → French Revolution → American Revolution

47 ____

Base your answer to question 48 on the cartoon below and on your knowledge of social studies.

The Crime of the Ages—Who Did It?

Source: John McCutcheon, *The Chicago Tribune;* H. H. Windsor, *Cartoons Magazine* (adapted)

48 The cartoon illustrates the tension that led to which war?

1 Franco-Prussian War   3 World War II

2 World War I   4 Cold War   48 _____

49 The Panama Canal and Suez Canal are similar in that both

1 shortened shipping routes between major bodies of water

2 were built by the British to expand their empire

3 replaced the Silk Road as the world's main trade route

4 directly connected the Atlantic and Pacific Oceans   49 _____

50 Which action taken by both Hitler and Napoleon is considered by historians to be a strategic military error?

1 invading Russia with limited supply lines
2 introducing combined ground and naval assaults
3 invading Great Britain by land
4 using conquered peoples as slave laborers   50 _____

In developing your answer to Part II, be sure to keep these general definitions in mind:

(a) <u>describe</u> means "to illustrate something in words or tell about it"

(b) <u>explain</u> means "to make plain or understandable; to give reasons for or causes of; to show the logical development or relationships of"

PART II: THEMATIC ESSAY QUESTION

Directions: Write a well-organized essay that includes an introduction, several paragraphs addressing the task below, and a conclusion.

Theme: Turning Points

> Turning points are major events in history that have led to lasting change.

Task:

> Identify *two* major turning points in global history and for *each*:
> - Describe the historical circumstances surrounding the turning point
> - Explain how *each* turning point changed the course of history

You may use any example from your study of global history. Some suggestions you might wish to consider include the Neolithic Revolution, the Crusades, the Renaissance, the Encounter, the French Revolution, the Russian Revolution of 1917, World War I, creation of the modern state of Israel, Nelson Mandela elected president of South Africa, and the fall of the Berlin Wall.

You are *not* limited to these suggestions.

Do *not* use any turning points in United States history.

Guidelines:

In your essay, be sure to

- Develop all aspects of the task
- Support the theme with relevant facts, examples, and details
- Use a logical and clear plan of organization, including an introduction and a conclusion that are beyond a restatement of the theme

In developing your answer to Part III, be sure to keep this general definition in mind:

> <u>discuss</u> means "to make observations about something using facts, reasoning, and argument; to present in some detail"

PART III: DOCUMENT-BASED QUESTION

This question is based on the accompanying documents (1–8). It is designed to test your ability to work with historical documents. Some of the documents have been edited for the purposes of the question. As you analyze the documents, take into account the source of each document and any point of view that may be presented in the document.

Historical Context:

During the 1800s, Great Britain's empire expanded to include India, other parts of Asia, and parts of Africa. Great Britain's colonial rule had both positive and negative effects on the colonial empire.

Task:

Using information from the documents and your knowledge of global history, answer the questions that follow each document in Part A. Your answers to the questions will help you write the Part B essay in which you will be asked to:

> - Discuss the political, social, **and/or** economic causes of British imperialism
> - Discuss the positive effects **and** the negative effects of British colonial rule

Part A: Short-Answer Questions

Directions: Analyze the documents and answer the short-answer questions that follow each document in the space provided.

Document 1

> . . . The Malay States are not British Territory, and our connection with them is due to the simple fact that 70 years ago [1757] the British Government was invited, pushed, and persuaded into helping the Rulers of certain States to introduce order into their disorderly, penniless, and distracted households [departments of government], by sending trained British Civil Servants to advise the Rulers in the art of administration and to organize a system of government which would secure justice, freedom, safety for all, with the benefits of what is known as Civilization; and, of course, to provide an annual revenue sufficient to meet all the charges of a government which had to introduce railways, roads, hospitals, water supplies, and all the other requirements of modern life. Of nine States south of Siam, four asked for or accepted this help; four others, threatened by Siam, came later under direct British influence; while Johore, nearest neighbour to Singapore had, ever since the occupation of that island by Sir Stamford Raffles in 1819, depended for its development on the wealth and enterprise of Singapore Chinese. . . .

Source: Sir Frank Swettenham, *British Malaya: An Account of the Origin and Progress of British Influence in Malaya*, George Allen and Unwin Ltd., 1906

1 Based on this document, state *two* reasons that help from Britain was needed in the Malay States. [2]

(1) _____

_____

(2) _____

_____

Document 2

> When the missionaries came to Africa they had the Bible and we had the land. They said 'Let us pray'. We closed our eyes. When we opened them, we had the Bible and they had the land.

— Bishop Desmond Tutu, 1984
Source: South Africa Sunday Times, November 26, 2000

2 Based on this document, state *one* effect of British colonial rule on Africa. [1]

_____

_____

Document 3a

> . . . First and foremost among the active imperialist groups come certain business interests. Not the whole so-called "capitalist class," as many an earnest Socialist would have us believe, but only a minority of business interests are directly interested in imperialism. They are easily identified. To begin with, there are the exporters and manufacturers of certain goods used in colonies. The following figures of English exports to India tell the story.
>
> ### English Exports to India (Average 1920–1922)
>
> | | |
> |---|---:|
> | Cotton goods and yarn | £53,577,000 |
> | Iron and steel, tools, machinery, and locomotives | 37,423,000 |
> | Wagons, trucks, and automobiles | 4,274,000 |
> | Paper | 1,858,000 |
> | Brass goods | 1,813,000 |
> | Woolens | 1,600,000 |
> | Tobacco | 1,023,000 |
> | No other item over £1,000,000 . . . . | |

Source: Parker T. Moon, *Imperialism and World Politics*,
Macmillan Co., 1926

Document 3b

> ... Of late years this group of import interests [British merchants] has been enormously strengthened by the demand of giant industries for colonial raw materials—rubber, petroleum, iron and coal, cotton, cocoa. The oil trusts of England and the United States have enlisted the aid of naval and diplomatic officials in their world-wide rivalry. The cotton industry of Germany hoped to obtain from Asiatic Turkey, under German imperialist control, raw cotton for German spindles; the cotton interests of England have been striving for a generation to develop plantations in British colonies; their French and Italian rivals have been hardly less interested in colonial potentialities. The European cotton industry, it may be remarked, as an export business and as an import business, is doubly imperialist. ...

Source: Parker T. Moon, *Imperialism and World Politics*,
Macmillan Co., 1926

3 According to these documents, what were *two* reasons for imperialism? [2]

(1) _____

_____

(2) _____

_____

Document 4a

Source: Andrea and Overfield, *The Human Record*, Houghton Mifflin, 2001

4*a* What does this advertisement show about British interests in Ceylon? [1]

_____

_____

Document 4b

Source: http://www.boondocksnet.com (adapted)

b What does this cartoon show about British interest in Africa? [1]

_____

_____

Document 5

Transforming the Face of India

. . . Failure to answer, nay, refusal to tackle that question has rendered wholly academic the discussion of abandonment. Even were it otherwise we could still look back proudly. British brains, British enterprise, and British capital have, in a material sense, transformed the face of India. Means of communication have been developed: innumerable bridges, over 40,000 miles of railway, 70,000 miles of metalled roads, testify to the skill and industry of British engineers. Irrigation works on a stupendous [huge] scale have brought 30,000,000 acres under cultivation, and thus greatly added to the agricultural wealth of a country which still lives mainly by agriculture. But, on the other hand, the process of industrialization has already begun. The mills of Bombay have become dangerous competitors to Lancashire, and the Indian jute [rope] industry is threatening the prosperity of Dundee. Thanks to improved sanitation (much resented by the more ignorant beneficiaries), to a higher standard of living, to irrigation, to canalization, to the development of transport, and to carefully thought-out schemes for relief work, famines, which by their regular recurrence formerly presented a perennial [continuing] problem to humane administrators, have now virtually disappeared. To have conquered the menace of famine in the face of greater longevity, of diminished death-rate, and the suppression of war, is a remarkable achievement for which India is wholly indebted to British administration. . . .

Source: Sir John A. R. Marriott, *The English in India*,
Oxford University Press, 1932

5 According to this document, what were *two* ways that India changed under British rule? [2]

(1) _____

_____

(2) _____

_____

Document 6

. . . The condition of Africa when Europe entered the continent, which Isaiah so graphically describes as "the land shadowing with wings, which is beyond the rivers of Ethiopia . . . a people scattered and peeled," was deplorable. On the East Coast, Arabs and half-castes were engaged in a lucrative trade in slaves for export to Arabia and to Turkish possessions. In the west, powerful armies of Moslem States depopulated large districts in their raids for slaves. Europe had failed to realise that throughout the length and breadth of Africa inter-tribal war was an ever-present condition of native life, and that extermination and slavery were practised by African tribes upon each other.

It was the task of civilisation to put an end to slavery, to establish Courts of Law, to inculcate in [teach] the natives a sense of individual responsibility, of liberty, and of justice, and to teach their rulers how to apply these principles; above all, to see to it that the system of education should be such as to produce happiness and progress. I am confident that the verdict of history will award high praise to the efforts and achievements of Great Britain in the discharge of these great responsibilities. For, in my belief, under no other rule—be it of his own uncontrolled potentates [rulers] or of aliens [foreigners]—does the African enjoy such a measure of freedom and of impartial justice, or a more sympathetic treatment, and for that reason I am a profound believer in the British Empire and its mission in Africa. . . .

Source: Lord Lugard, *The Dual Mandate in British Tropical Africa*, Archon Books, 1965

6 According to Lord Lugard, what were *two* ways the British helped Africa? [2]

(1) _____

_____

(2) _____

_____

Document 7

In his book *Indian Home Rule*, Gandhi asked the question, **"Why do you want to drive away the English?"**
He replied with the following statement:

> . . . "Because India has become impoverished by their Government. They take away our money from year to year. The most important posts are reserved for themselves. We are kept in a state of slavery. They behave insolently [insultingly] towards us and disregard our feelings. . . ."

Source: Mohandas Gandhi, *Indian Home Rule*, Navajivan Publishing, 1938, reprinted in 1946 (adapted)

7 Based on this document, state *two* reasons Gandhi wanted to drive away the English. [2]

(1) _____

_____

(2) _____

_____

Document 8

> . . . Socially, the ogre [monster] of racial segregation and discrimination makes it extremely difficult for the colonial to develop his personality to the full. Education is obtainable but limited to the privileged. Hospitals are not available to the great number of the people but only to a negligible [small] minority. Public services are lacking in many respects; there are not sufficient water supplies, surfaced roads, postal services and communications systems in most communities of Nigeria. The prisons are medieval, the penal [criminal] code is oppressive, and religious freedom is a pearl of great price. . . .

— Nnamdi Azikiwe, speech on British colonialism in Africa, 1947
Source: *ZIK: A Selection from the Speechs of Nnamdi Azikiwe*,
Cambridge University Press, 1961

8 Based on this document, state *two* ways British colonialism harmed Africa. [2]

(1) _____

_____

(2) _____

_____

Part B: Essay

Directions: Write a well-organized essay that includes an introduction, several paragraphs, and a conclusion. Use evidence from at least *five* documents in your essay. Support your response with relevant facts, examples, and details. Include additional outside information.

Historical Context:

During the 1800s, Great Britain's empire expanded to include India, other parts of Asia, and parts of Africa. Great Britain's colonial rule had both positive and negative effects on the colonial empire.

Task:

Using information from the documents and your knowledge of global history, write an essay in which you

- Discuss the political, social, *and/or* economic causes of British imperialism
- Discuss the positive effects *and* the negative effects of British colonial rule

Guidelines:

In your essay, be sure to

- Develop all aspects of the task
- Incorporate information from at least *five* documents
- Incorporate relevant outside information
- Support the theme with relevant facts, examples, and details
- Use a logical and clear plan of organization, including an introduction and conclusion that are beyond a restatement of the theme

Answers
June 2004
Global History and Geography

Answer Key

PART I (1–50)

1. 1	14. 1	27. 4	40. 2
2. 1	15. 2	28. 3	41. 4
3. 1	16. 3	29. 4	42. 3
4. 4	17. 2	30. 4	43. 4
5. 2	18. 1	31. 3	44. 3
6. 3	19. 3	32. 2	45. 2
7. 2	20. 4	33. 4	46. 1
8. 4	21. 3	34. 1	47. 2
9. 4	22. 1	35. 2	48. 2
10. 3	23. 4	36. 1	49. 1
11. 2	24. 1	37. 3	50. 1
12. 1	25. 1	38. 4	
13. 4	26. 2	39. 3	

PART II: Thematic Essay   See answers explained section.

PART III: Document-Based Essay   See answers explained section.

Answers Explained

PART I

1. **1** Primary Sources is the heading that best completes the partial outline. Primary sources are eyewitness accounts or first-hand information about people or events. They are written or created by people who lived during historical events. A personal letter, an autobiography, and a diary are primary sources because they provide an account by a person who witnessed, participated in, or observed these events. A driver's license is also a primary source because it contains a personal photo of the person who possesses the license.

WRONG CHOICES EXPLAINED:

(2) Secondary Sources are descriptions and interpretations of events or facts written after the events have occurred by people who did not participate in them. Textbooks, almanacs, and encyclopedias are examples of secondary sources.

(3) and (4) Official and Published Records can include primary sources, such as eyewitness accounts or first-person documents. They can also include government investigations or summaries of events that are not written by individuals who actually participated in these events. Published records of the Nuremberg Trials and the recent war crime trials of the Serbian atrocities in Bosnia include published records that are not all primary sources.

2. **1** A totalitarian society is one in which the government controls most aspects of life. In a totalitarian government one person or group dominates the political, economic, social, religious, educational, and cultural life of the nation, such as family life, business, and the arts. Under totalitarianism, individual citizens have no rights. Hitler's Germany, Stalin's Soviet Union, and Mao's China are examples of 20th-century totalitarian states.

WRONG CHOICES EXPLAINED:

(2) A totalitarian government does not support religious beliefs. Freedom of religion is not encouraged because all loyalty is directed to support the aims of the state.

(3) In a totalitarian society, the citizens are considered the servants of the state. The government demands total obedience to authority and personal sacrifices for the state.

(4) In a totalitarian society, citizens cannot publicly criticize the actions of the leaders. Citizens are denied basic liberties and are severely punished for criticizing the government.

3. **1** River valleys had the greatest influence on the early history of South Asia and China. The fertile soils along the river valleys of India's Indus River and China's Huang He (Yellow River) attracted farmers. The overflowing of these rivers deposited rich soils along the banks that enabled farmers to produce surplus food. This surplus food supported growing populations, which contributed to the growth of permanent settlements and fostered the development of civilizations. Food surpluses allowed the people of the Indus Valley to build cities such as Harappa and Mohenzo. Both of these cities had highly advanced drainage systems that were unrivaled until the time of the Roman Empire. Along the Huang He River, under the Sheng Dynasty in 1700 B.C., the Chinese built their first cities, developed the calendar, and constructed an irrigation system.

WRONG CHOICES EXPLAINED:

(2) Island locations had an important geographic influence on the history and development of Japan. Because the islands of Japan are mountainous and difficult to farm, the Japanese learned to use the sea as a source of food.

(3) Vast coastlines influenced the classical civilizations of Greece and Rome. Most Greeks lived along the coast with its excellent harbors, and depended on trade. Through these contacts, the Greeks learned astronomy, mathematics, and building techniques. The location of the Italian peninsula helped the Romans move easily through the land of the Mediterranean and served as a route for Roman trade and expansion.

(4) Tropical rain forests had an influence on the civilizations of Africa and the Americas. Although a large part of Africa is made up of deserts, Africa also has a small belt of rain forests along the Equator that is good for farming. Tropical rain forests influenced the civilizations in the Americas that allowed the people to farm. Three-fourths of Latin America lies in the tropics. They include the Amazon Basin, some Caribbean islands, and parts of Central America.

4. **4** The Silk Road was important because it allowed for the exchange of goods between Asia and the Middle East. The Han Dynasty (206–220 A.D.) in China opened up the Silk Road, which stretched for 4,000 miles and allowed China to exchange goods with different parts of the world. The Silk Road went through central Asia and connected China to the Middle East and Rome. Over these routes, China exported silk, iron, and bronze in exchange for gold, linen cloth, glass, horses, monkeys, and parrots. Contact with India led to the introduction of Buddhism to China, which became popular during the Han Dynasty. The caravan routes in northern Africa and southwestern Asia also led to the spread of new ideas. After the spread of Islam to North Africa and Asia, Muslim merchants built a vast trading network from the 8th to the 14th centuries. Camel caravan routes revolutionized trade across the Sahara Desert. Traders spread both products and technology. Arab merchants introduced mathematical numbers from India to the Western world. Arabs also carried sugar from India and paper-making techniques from China.

WRONG CHOICES EXPLAINED:

(1) The Silk Road was not used by the Roman Army to explore China. China and Rome indirectly shared goods through the Silk Road, but never made formal contact. In 97 A.D. a Han general led an army to the edge of the Caspian Sea, the nearest any Chinese army ever came to Europe.

(2) The nomadic tribes of Central Asia did not develop agriculture along the Silk Road. Nomadic tribes along the Silk Road were used to provide security along the road and were a link for Mediterranean merchants.

(3) The Silk Road was not used for the movement of Chinese armies through Southeast Asia. The Silk Road was a commercial route for Chinese merchants.

5. **2** Olympic Games, the poems of Homer, and Hellenistic culture are associated with ancient Greek civilization. The Olympic Games were part of religious festivals and athletic events in which all Greeks participated every four years. The first Olympic Games were held in 776 B.C. at Olympia. Initially, the only event was the sprint race. Later the discus, the javelin throw, and wrestling were added. These games were so important that even war was stopped at the time they were held. The Olympic Games were held for over 1,000 years in Greece, but were abolished by the Byzantine Emperor Theodosius in 394 A.D. The Olympic Games were revived in Athens, Greece, in 1896 as a symbol of promoting understanding in the world. Homer was a blind Greek poet who provided much of our knowledge of early Greek civilization through his two famous epic poems, *The Iliad* and *The Odyssey*. These poems describe the wars between the Greeks and the Trojans, as well as the wanderings of the Greek hero Odysseus after the Trojan War. These poems are also the sources of many legends that have come down to us, such as Helen of Troy, Achilles, and the Trojan Horse. Hellenistic culture refers to the blending of Greek culture with the cultures of the ancient Middle East. In 334 B.C., Alexander the Great from Macedonia, a mountainous region north of Greece, set out to conquer the world. He conquered Persia, Egypt, and most of the Mediterranean world, and territories as far east as India. Alexander died during his military campaign but his conquest helped pave the way for the spreading of Greek culture throughout the ancient world. The center of Hellenistic culture was Alexandria, Egypt.

WRONG CHOICES EXPLAINED:

(1) Egyptian civilization is associated with the building of pyramids as well as the system of writing known as hieroglyphics.

(3) The Romans are known for their system of laws, aqueducts, and roads.

(4) The Phoenicians are known for the development of the alphabet.

6. **3** The Code of Hammurabi was a major contribution to the development of civilization because it recorded existing laws for all to see. The Code of Hammurabi is the oldest written legal system. Developed by King Hammurabi of Mesopotamia in 1705 B.C., the Code consisted of 282 sections

and set standards of justice. It clearly stated which actions were considered violations and assigned a specific punishment for each. The Hammurabi Code was designed to ensure order, strengthen the government, protect the weak, and establish the legal rights of citizens. All of these factors are important features of a civilization.

WRONG CHOICES EXPLAINED:

(1) Hammurabi's Code did not treat citizens and slaves equally. If a gentleman struck another he was fined. However, if a slave struck a gentleman, his ear was cut off.

(2) Hammurabi's Code did not end all physical punishment. The Code enacted what the Bible later expressed as an "eye for an eye" and a "tooth for a tooth."

(4) Hammurabi's Code was a written legal system that was designed to ensure order and protect the weak. The principle of filial piety refers to the duty and respect that the Chinese philosopher Confucius believes children owe to their parents.

7. **2** One effect of rugged, mountainous geography on the civilization of ancient Greece was the development of separate, independent city-states. Greece is part of the Balkan Peninsula, which extends south into the eastern Mediterranean Sea. It is also a land of high mountains enclosing fertile valleys. These mountains divided the peninsula into isolated valleys since transportation was hazardous and difficult. These geographic barriers led the Greeks to organize many independent city-states, not large empires like the Egyptians or the Mesopotamians. These city-states were cut off from one another by land or water, which led to political disunity. The Greeks felt a stronger loyalty to their tiny city-states rather than to Greece as a nation. In time, endless rivalry between the city-states led to their being conquered by outsiders.

WRONG CHOICES EXPLAINED:

(1) Athens, one of the most important Greek city-states, did not develop an absolute monarchy like the city-state of Sparta. During the Age of Pericles (461–429 B.C.), Athens developed a direct democracy, in which a large number of the male citizens took part in the day-to-day running of the government. Although women were denied the right to vote, slavery was permitted, and citizenship was limited, Athens, more than any other city-state or culture, gave a greater number of people a voice in the government.

(3) Greece was at war with the Persians and did not trade extensively with them. From 500–479 B.C., the Persians fought the Athenians because they had supported the revolt of the Greek colonies against Persian control on the coast of Asia Minor. The Greeks defeated the Persian army at the Battle of Marathon in 490 B.C. and at the Battle of Salamis in 479 B.C. By repelling the Persian forces, the Greeks preserved their freedom.

(4) Ancient Greece did not have a belief in one God. The Greeks shared a polytheistic religion, a belief in many gods. Their deities included Zeus, the chief god, Apollo, the sun god, and Athena, the goddess of wisdom.

8.   **4** Contributions of the Islamic Civilization is the heading that best completes the partial outline. While Western Europe declined during the Middle Ages, the Muslim world developed a flourishing civilization. During the Golden Age of Muslim culture, which lasted from about 750 to 1200 A.D., Baghdad became the center of culture. Muslim medicine became very advanced. The Muslim doctors had to pass difficult tests before they could practice. Physicians used anesthetic drugs to relieve pain and performed difficult surgeries, excelling in eye surgery for the treatment of cataracts. An important physician was Muhammad al-Razi, who was associated with a Baghdad hospital and wrote an encyclopedia called *The Comprehensive Book*, which drew on the knowledge of Greek, Syrian, Arabic, and Indian medicine. He also wrote a book entitled *Treatise on Smallpox and Measles*, which was translated into many different languages. Another outstanding physician was Ibn Sina, known in Europe as Avicenna (980–1037 A.D.). His medical book, *The Canon Medicine*, was a huge encyclopedia from which the Greeks and Arabs learned about the diagnosis and treatment of diseases. In mathematics, Arab scholars borrowed the concept of zero from India and developed the Arabic numbers that were eventually adopted worldwide. Arab mathematicians were pioneers in algebra and created quotations to define curves and lines. Their work in geometry led to the development of trigonometry, which was used in astronomy to calculate the distance to the stars. Muslim observatories charted stars, comets, and planets. Iban al Haytham (Alhazen) developed a set of astronomical tables based on Greek and Indian discoverers. Muslim astronomers observed the earth's rotation and calculated the circumference of the earth within a few thousand feet. The work of these Muslim astronomers helped pave the way for later explorers such as Columbus. Between 750 and 1350 A.D. Arab merchants developed an international trade network that contributed to the production of fine goods. The Muslims produced Cordovan leather, Damascus steel (especially swords), cotton textiles from Egypt, and woolen carpet from Persia, as well as fine glass and tapestries. The Muslims had a high regard for books and maintained extensive libraries. Their famous literary works included *Thousand and One Nights (Arabian Nights)*, which included fables, romances, and humorous anecdotes, and the long poem about the life of the Rubaiyat of Omar Khayyam. Muslim artists were highly skilled in calligraphy or artistic writing. This form of writing was important to the Muslims because it was considered a way to reflect the glory of Allah. Muslim architects were influenced by Byzantine domes and arches. The Muslims designed mosques and palaces typified by rounded domes, elaborate abstract, geometric, and decorative patterns called arabesque. An outstanding example of Muslim architecture is the Alhambra Palace near Granada, Spain.

WRONG CHOICES EXPLAINED:
   (1), (2), and (3) None of these choices can support the outline. During feudal times, Europe was in a state of decline and became acquainted with the Islamic civilization as a result of the Crusades in the 11th century. The

Neolithic Revolution refers to the changes that developed when people began to settle in society. The Protestant Reformation describes the religious and political struggle between Martin Luther and the Roman Catholic Church.

9. **4** The routes shown on the map illustrate the pattern of the Bantu migrations between 500–1500 A.D. The word Bantu means people. These West African people spoke a variety of languages that were derived from a common root language called Bantu. Bantu-speaking people lived south of the Sahara and traveled southward through Africa spreading their language and culture. This migration was one of the greatest in history and populated the southern third of the continent. Bantu-speaking people were groups of people who shared certain characteristics. Scholars have been able to trace their migrations by studying their language patterns. They were farmers and nomadic herders who developed and passed on their farming and ironworking skills. They also adopted their methods to suit their environment as they followed the Congo through the rain forest. They farmed near the riverbanks by the Congo because it was the only area that received enough sunlight to support this activity. Anthropologists believed that as some Bantu farming methods began to exhaust the land, new fertile soil had to be discovered. This constant moving caused the Bantus to displace many groups in Central and Southern Africa. For example, they forced the Khoisans into less desirable areas such as the Zaire rain forest or the Kalahari Desert. Territorial warfare also broke out as the Bantu people spread south into other people's land. However, the Bantu people also exchanged ideas and intermarried with the people they joined. The Bantu migration produced a diversity of cultures in Africa and also left a unifying element on the continent. Due to this migration, more than 60 million people speak one of the hundreds of Bantu languages.

WRONG CHOICES EXPLAINED:
  (1), (2), and (3) None of these statements are supported by the map.

10. **3** This translated quotation from the *Qur'an* (*Koran*) refers to Allah. One of the main principles of Islam is that there is no God but Allah and that Muhammad is the Great Prophet. Muhammad is the founder of Islam and his teaching became the basis of the *Koran*, the Muslim Bible. All persons must submit to and praise and glorify Allah. To a Muslim, Allah is the Almighty creator and sustainer of the universe. Allah is the all-powerful god who will judge all people at the end of the universe. However, in the opening of the *Koran*, Allah is a God who is passionate, compassionate, and all-powerful. The idea of Allah as a monotheistic God who followed a high moral code was drawn from the religions of Judaism and Christianity. The *Koran* was the first book to be written in Arabic since none of the earlier Arabic oral literatures was collected until 600 A.D. Muslims consider every word of the *Koran* to be inspired by God (Allah).

WRONG CHOICES EXPLAINED:

(1) Prince Siddhartha Gautama, who became known as Buddha or the "Enlightened One," was the founder of Buddism, which is a religion based on self-denial and a rejection of the material world. Buddhists do not believe in a single supreme being. Their basic beliefs are found in books called Sutras.

(2) Shiva is a major Indian god associated with Hindus who believed that there are many gods and goddesses. Vishnu is the creator and Shiva is the destroyer. Each of the gods and goddesses is a manifestation of one supreme being.

(4) Muhammad is the founder of Islam and proclaimed himself the messenger of Allah. Muhammad was the last great prophet who wrote down revelations, or his visions. Originally, Muhammad's revelations were written down on leather bits, camel shoulders, and palm leaves and were memorized by his followers. After his death, his followers wrote these revelations in one book, the *Koran*.

11.   **2**   A fact relating to early Japan that was a result of the other three is that the Japanese developed a nature-based belief called Shinto. Shintoism stresses the connection between people and the forces of nature. Shinto has no complex rituals or set of organized beliefs; instead, it is based on a respect for the forces of nature. The early Japanese believed that the spirit or *kami* lived in everything from plants and animals to rocks and mountains. Spirits controlled natural forces such as earthquakes and typhoons. Through prayers and offerings, the Japanese tried to win the favor of the *kami*. The Japanese believed that earthquakes, volcanic eruptions, tsunamis (tidal waves), typhoons, and mountains were part of the spirits that dominated nature. Hundreds of Shinto shrines dedicated to these forces of nature dot the Japanese countryside. It was the Buddhist missionaries who called the local Japanese belief Shinto or "the way of the gods." Later, in the 18th century, Shintoism became the national religion of Japan, extolling nationalism, ancestor worship, and the divinity of the emperor.

WRONG CHOICES EXPLAINED:

(1), (3), and (4)   All of these choices—earthquakes, volcanic eruptions, tsunamis, typhoons, and mountains—contributed to the Japanese belief of Shintoism.

12.   **1**   This statue is most closely associated with the religion of Buddhism. In the 6th century, Siddhartha Gautama, an Indian prince, left his wealth and family and set out in search of the truth. After wandering for six years, Gautama found the answer and became known as Buddha, or the "Enlightened One." As Buddha, he taught that a person's life consisted of suffering caused by desire and that a person can eliminate desire only by following the Eightfold Path of Righteous Living. Buddha describes this Path as renouncing material pleasures, controlling emotions, respecting all living creatures, acquiring knowledge, cultivating goodness, speaking truths, and

acting generously. The Eightfold Path is midway between a life devoted to pleasure and one based on self-denial. Buddhism emphasized moral and ethical rules such as honesty, charity, and kindness to all creatures.

WRONG CHOICES EXPLAINED:

(2) Islam is a major religion of the Middle East that was founded in the 7th century A.D. Islam means submission to the will of God. Muhammad, the prophet, was the founder of Islam, whose teachings include belief in one God, Allah.

(3) Jainism was a religion that grew out of the Hindu tradition. It was founded by Mahavira, who was born in 599 B.C. and died in 579 B.C. Mahavira believed that everything in the universe has a soul and should not be harmed. Jainism emphasized meditation and self-denial. It carries the principles of nonviolence to its logical conclusion. Jainists sweep ants off their paths and wear gauze masks over their mouths to avoid accidentally breathing in an insect.

(4) Christianity is a belief system based on the teachings of Jesus Christ that began in the Middle East about 2000 years ago. Christianity was rooted in the monotheistic religion of Judaism.

13. **4** In his book *The Prince*, Niccolò Machiavelli advises that a wise ruler is one who does what is necessary to stay in power. Machiavelli was an Italian born in Florence in 1469 and lived until 1527. He served the Florentine Republic as secretary and diplomat. In *The Prince,* published in 1513, Machiavelli combined his personal experience of politics with his knowledge of the history of Ancient Rome and offered ways in which a strong ruler might seize and hold power. Citizens were to be given only those rights that the ruler wanted to grant. He advised the rulers to be as powerful as a lion, as cunning as a fox, and kind and generous when necessary. He urged rulers to do whatever was necessary to achieve their goal of power. Machiavelli taught that "the end justifies the means" so long as the ruler gains control. On the issue of honesty in government, he advised that results were more important than the promises. His work continues to spark ethical debates about the nature of government, and the word "Machiavellian" has come to mean "shrewd and cunning."

WRONG CHOICES EXPLAINED:

(1) and (2) Machiavelli believed that a ruler should support low taxes, low food prices, art, and education only if they were for the good of the state. Machiavelli was not concerned about people but how to gain and maintain power.

(3) Machiavelli was not concerned about advisors speaking their minds. The ruler or prince should not worry about what was morally right but what was politically effective. Advisors served at the discretion of the ruler.

14. **1** A major reason that the Renaissance began in Italy was that Italian city-states had grown wealthy from trade between Europe and Asia. The

Renaissance was a period of artistic and cultural achievements in Europe from the 14th to the 16th centuries. The Italian city-states were geographically situated to benefit from the revival of trade that developed as a result of the Crusades. The northern city-states of Florence, Genoa, and Venice acted as middlemen in the lucrative trade with the East. These independent city-states marketed goods such as wool and silk to countries in Europe and Asia. They became prosperous centers of trade, banking, and manufacturing. These city-states also benefited from being able to absorb new ideas received through their trade with the Byzantine and Muslim Empires. By 1350, the city-states of Florence, Venice, and Genoa were urban centers with a population of more than 100,000 people. The conditions were right for these cities to experience a cultural explosion, such as the Renaissance. Furthermore, Italy was the center of ancient Roman history. Architectural remains, statues, and manuscripts excited curiosity about classical civilizations. Merchants in these city-states began to use their wealth to support and promote interest in literature, the arts, and science. The leading Renaissance patrons were the Sforza family in Milan and the Medici family in Florence. Through the efforts of Lorenzo de' Medici, Florence became the cultural center of the Renaissance. By virtue of its artistic leadership and patronage, Florence attracted talented people from other parts of Italy and Europe.

WRONG CHOICES EXPLAINED:

(2) These city-states were centers of trade and were not known for producing great agricultural surpluses.

(3) The Green Revolution refers to technological advances in agriculture in the 20th century that led to increased food production on limited parcels of land.

(4) European scholars migrated to Italy only after it became the center of the Renaissance. Northern scholars traveled to Italy to absorb Italian art and learning and then brought back ideas to their own countries.

15. **2** An effect of the Protestant Reformation was the decline in the power of the Roman Catholic Church. At the beginning of the 1500s, Roman Catholicism was the only Christian religion in Europe. The Protestant Reformation was a religious revolt against the authority and certain doctrines of the Roman Catholic Church. One of the causes of the Protestant Reformation was the selling of indulgences. Indulgences were pardons for sins committed during a person's lifetime. In the Middle Ages, the Church granted indulgences only for good deeds such as going on a Crusade or giving alms to the poor. By the late 1400s, the Church was dispensing indulgences in exchange for monetary gifts. Many Christians protested such practices. In 1517, Martin Luther posted the 95 Theses on the door of the Church at Wittenberg on All Hallow's Eve. This step aroused popular support. Luther condemned the selling of indulgences. He believed that people could gain salvation by faith alone. He also denied Papal supremacy and proclaimed the Bible as the final authority in religious matters. A series of religious wars

broke out between Catholics and the followers of Luther in the 1520s, which led to the peace of Augsburg. This agreement, signed in 1555, allowed the rulers of a country to decide the religion of the people. The religious unity of Europe was ended and the power of the Catholic Church was seriously weakened. Most of northern Europe and northern Germany became Protestant and southern Europe became Catholic. In Protestant countries, monarchs assumed the control of the new Protestant churches and the king seized church property. Even in Catholic countries, monarchs asserted control of the church and weakened papal influence on the appointment of church officials.

WRONG CHOICES EXPLAINED:
(1), (3), and (4) All of these choices—the posting of the Ninety-five Theses, the sale of indulgences, and the end of religious warfare—contributed to the decline in power of the Roman Catholic Church by the middle of the 16th century.

16. **3** The Spanish Reconquista is being described in this passage. Until the 1100s in Spain, Muslims (called Moors) controlled most of the country. The Reconquista was a long effort by the Spanish to drive the Muslims out of Spain. By the late 1400s, the Muslims held only the tiny kingdom of Granada. In 1469, Ferdinand of Aragon married Isabella of Castile, thus uniting the kingdom of Spain. Beginning in 1482, Ferdinand and Isabella set out to reconquer the last Muslim kingdom. After ten years, Granada fell to a Christian army in 1492. In the final battle, Isabella personally led her army and drove the Moors from Europe and Spain. In the same year as the conquest of Granada, Isabella and Ferdinand began a campaign against the 200,000 Spanish Jews who openly practiced their religion. They were forced to become Christians or leave the country. A great majority (about 150,000) chose exile. These steps accomplished the goal of uniting their kingdom under one king and one faith.

WRONG CHOICES EXPLAINED:
(1) The Crusades were a series of religious wars between Christian Europe and the Muslims for control of the Holy Land, lasting from 1096 A.D. to 1246 A.D.

(2) and (4) There are no references to Columbus's voyages nor the start of the Italian Renaissance in this passage

17. **2** The archaeological evidence found at the Mesoamerican sites of Tenochtitlan and Machu Picchu suggests that these societies were highly developed and organized cultures. The Aztecs, who lived in the valley of Mexico, built the capital city of Tenochtitlan in Lake Texcoco in 1325. Aztec engineers connected the city to the mainland by causeways. By 1519, the year the Spanish arrived, the city had a population of more than 150,000 people and covered more than 4.6 square miles, making it one of the largest cities in the world at that time. At the center of the city, people gathered at the Great

Temple, the emperor's palace, the markets, or other public forums. There were also quarters for schools and priests at the Great Temple. Tenochtitlan's busy central market merchants sold goods from all over the empire. The ancient Inca city of Machu Picchu in Peru was built on a mountain top, 8,038 feet above sea level in the Andes. Machu Picchu (which means manly peak) was most likely a religious estate and retreat, which was built between 1460 and 1470 by Pachacuti Inca Yupa, an Inca ruler. The Inca Empire developed along the Andes Mountains and extended from present-day Peru, Ecuador, and Bolivia. The city of Machu Picchu consisted of about 200 buildings. These buildings included private residences, temples, storage structures, and other public buildings. A unique thing about Machu Picchu was the integration of the architecture into the landscape. Existing stone formations were used in the construction of structures, sculptures were carved into the rocks, water flowed through cisterns, and stone channels and temples hung on steep precipices. Most of the blocks in these structures were fitted together perfectly without mortar, although none of the blocks were of the same size. The joints were so tight that even the thinnest knife could not be forced between the stones. The Incas planted crops, such as potatoes and maize. They used advanced terracing and irrigation methods to reduce erosion and to increase the land available for cultivation. Before the Spanish conquistadors arrived in the 1500s, smallpox spread ahead of them. Fifty percent of the population had been killed by the smallpox disease. In 1527, the government began to fail and parts of the empire seceded and civil war erupted. When the Spanish conquered the Incas in 1532, Machu Picchu was never found. In 1911, Hiram Bingham, a professor from Yale, rediscovered Machu Picchu.

WRONG CHOICES EXPLAINED:

(1) The societies of Tenochtitlan and Machu Picchu depended on agriculture and were not hunters and gatherers. Hunters and gatherers existed during the Paleolithic or Old Stone Age. They are nomadic people who moved from place to place in their search for food.

(3) The Aztecs and Incas did not practice monotheism but worshipped many gods. Among the chief Aztec gods was Quetzalcoatl, whom they believed had brought maize to the earth. The Incas worshipped the sun as the most important of the gods.

(4) Neither of these societies followed a democratic system of government. They were ruled by monarchs who had absolute power.

18. **1** The statement that describes an impact that the Columbian Exchange had on the lives of Europeans was that the transfer of new products and ideas encouraged economic growth. Before his death in 1506, Columbus made three voyages to the Caribbean Islands and South America. Columbus's voyages also led to the exchange of items that greatly affected people around the world. The global transfer of foods, plants, and animals during the colonization of the Americas is known as the Columbian Exchange. The Exchange also involved the movement of millions of people.

Settlers came to the Americas from all over Europe, bringing with them their ideas about government, law, and religion. Enslaved Africans also brought their own cultures to the New World. The Spanish introduced many more products from the Americas to the Europeans. These included corn, potatoes, squash, chocolate, peanuts, and tomatoes. From the Americas, Europeans carried sweet potatoes to Africa and pineapples, papayas, and chili peppers to Asia. The new foods enriched the diets of people around the world. The Italians, for example, developed many dishes that included tomatoes, such as pasta. In India, people used chili peppers to spice their curry dishes. Europeans introduced new crops to the Americas, such as wheat, barley, and chick-peas. Columbus brought horses, cows, sheep, chickens, and pigs from Europe. Horses and cattle thrived in Mexico and Argentina. From Asia, Europeans brought rice and bananas to the Americas, while from Africa they carried yams, sugarcane, coffee, and coconuts. Columbus's voyages would open up the way for European colonization, contributing to the economic growth of these nations and enabling them to become powerful countries.

WRONG CHOICES EXPLAINED:
(2) It was the Europeans who carried diseases, such as smallpox, influenza, and measles, into the Americas, which greatly affected the native population.

(3) Native Americans did not migrate to Europe to compete for jobs. Native Americans were used as slave labor in the Spanish colonies. European settlers migrated to the Americas in search of riches and a new life.

(4) The Columbian Exchange led to an increase, not a decline, in cross-cultural contacts as goods were shipped among Asia, Europe, Africa, and the Americas.

19. **3** The Benin civilization was located at the mouth of the Niger River. The mouth of a river is the point where a stream enters into a larger body of water. The Niger River enters the Atlantic Ocean near the Benin civilization. The kingdom of Benin was located to the south and west of Ife, near the delta of the Niger River. The people made their homes in the forest. The forest people carved out farming villages and traded pepper, ivory, and later slaves to their northern neighbors in the savannas. The rulers of Benin organized their kingdom in 1300. By the 1400s, a leader called Ewuare made Benin into a major West African kingdom. He did so by building a powerful army and used it to control an area that extended from the Niger River delta in the east to what is today Lagos, Nigeria. Ewuare also strengthened Benin City by building walls around it. Inside, its broad avenues were dotted by great palaces and tidy houses.

WRONG CHOICES EXPLAINED:
(1), (2), and (4) None of these civilizations was located at the mouth of the Niger River. Ghana and Ashanti civilizations were West African kingdoms that were along the Niger River but not at its mouth. The Congo civilization was more toward the south and near the Congo River.

20. **4** It can be inferred from the map that African civilizations before 1901 were located in a variety of physical environments. This map illustrates the locations of the early African civilizations that flourished before 1901. The physical environment of Africa played a crucial role in their development. The access to rich and fertile lands allowed early African kingdoms to thrive. Africa's vast range of climates provided different environments throughout the country. Rainfall varies to a large degree in Africa. Some areas of Africa experience hot and humid weather with plenty of rainfall, while other areas see very little rainfall. Africa experiences a pattern of alternating wet and dry seasons. Its location near the equator is a major source of the variety. The further a city is from the equator, the shorter the rainy period. This leads to a huge disparity in the physical environment of the country. The Kingdoms of Cush and Axum were forced to deal with the desert areas while the Kingdoms of Oyo and Dahomey could take advantage of the tropical wet climate of Africa. African civilizations that could not rely on the rainfall to help them prosper were forced to rely on other means for survival. Rivers were crucial for their continued existence. Rivers are a source of fish, precious metals and minerals, and water for irrigation, as well as a means of transportation. This map shows that several of the indigenous civilizations, such as the Kingdoms of Cush and Axum, centered on the Nile River, while the Mali Empire flourished near the Niger River.

WRONG CHOICES EXPLAINED:

(1) The map makes no reference to the religions practiced by the indigenous civilizations of Africa before 1901.

(2) The map provides the locations of the early African civilizations as well as the years of existence for such civilizations. Most, if not all, of these kingdoms lasted more than just a few years; for example, the Mali Empire lasted close to 200 years.

(3) No inferences can be made from the map about the type of interaction among the civilizations. Several kingdoms were located very close together and could have had some interaction. However, none of these conclusions can be made solely from this map.

21. **3** This map supports the conclusion that the Chinese came into contact with peoples of other cultures between 1405 and 1422. In the early 14th century, China had cut off trade with other countries. In 1386, the Ming Dynasty assumed power and renewed contact with the outside world. The Emperor thought that China needed to renew trade with the outside world to demonstrate his nation's supremacy over other nations. Between 1405 and 1422, the Ming Emperor sent Admiral Zhen on seven voyages to promote trade. In his voyages, Zhen visited Southeast Asia, India, the Arabian Peninsula, and the eastern cities of Africa. He returned home with new and unfamiliar animals for the imperial court. As a result of these voyages, Chinese merchants established trade links with many distant commercial centers. The reports of his travels provided the Chinese with information and

observations about the countries he had visited. These voyages also provided local rulers with information that confirmed their belief in the superiority of their culture. After Zhen's death in 1453, the Ming Emperor banned ship-building and halted voyages of exploration.

WRONG CHOICES EXPLAINED:

(1) The map shows that the Chinese began to trade with the Persian Empire in 1413, not 1405. Also, the names of Chinese cities are not indicated on the map.

(2) The map provides information about exploration and does not make any reference to overland trade by rivers and mountains.

(4) The map supports the conclusion that China was not isolated but traded with many different parts of the world, such as Africa, India, and Arabia. There is no reference to the rulers of China.

22. **1** In Europe, joint stock companies, shareholders, entrepreneurs, and the bourgeoisie contributed to the rise of capitalism. The expansion of trade and business during the 16th and 17th centuries transformed European economies. The change from a relatively static, localized, and nonprofit economy typical of the Middle Ages led to the beginning of a dynamic worldwide, profit-oriented system called capitalism. Capitalism is an economic system based on private ownership and the investment of wealth for profit. The government was no longer the sole owner of wealth. Entrepreneurs or enterprising merchants engaged in business enterprises, taking risks and facing competition in the hope of making a profit. They hired workers and paid for raw materials, transportation, and production costs. As trade increased, entrepreneurs sought to expand into overseas ventures. Capitalist investors were willing to take risks when the demand and prices were high. Entrepreneurs and capitalists made up the new business class or bourgeoisie that were devoted to the goal of making profits. The joint stock company was a business venture that developed during this period. It allowed people to pool large amounts of capital needed for overseas ventures or colonies. These joint stock companies sold stock to numerous investors (shareholders) who would share in the profits or losses of the business but would leave its management to the top elected officials. Since joint stock companies involved numerous investors, individual investors paid only a fraction of the total colonization costs. If the colony failed, investors lost only their small share, and if the colony prospered the investors shared in the profits. The joint stock company as a form of a business organization was the forerunner of the modern corporation that has become the symbol of capitalism.

WRONG CHOICES EXPLAINED:

(2) Feudalism was a political, economic, and social system that developed in Medieval Europe. Feudalism centered on allegiance to monarchs and lords and is not associated with joint stock companies or shareholders.

(3) Communism is an economic system that is characterized by a classless society and rejects the idea of private enterprise such as joint stock companies. The decline of communism occurred in the late 20th century.

(4) The rise of entrepreneurs and capitalists led to a decrease, not an increase, in the power of the guilds. The guild system limited the production of European textiles that producers needed to meet the demands for goods both in Europe and overseas. Merchant capitalists sent out raw materials to be worked on in the home. This approach enabled the merchants to bypass the guilds, which began to lose their influence in the growing international economy.

23. **4** King Louis XIV of France, Peter the Great of Russia, and Suleiman the Magnificent of the Ottoman Empire were all considered absolute rulers because they determined government policies without the consent of their people. Absolutism is a government in which an individual has total control. Louis XIV, who ruled France from 1643 to 1715, believed in the Divine Right of kings. He said, "I am the state" and took the sun as his symbol of power. He ruled without the Estates General, which is the French Parliament, and crushed all opposition to his government. Peter the Great ruled Russia from 1682 to 1725. Peter's goal was to make Russia more powerful by introducing new techniques and ideas from Western Europe rather than following the Byzantine Asian culture. Although Peter believed Russia needed to change, he knew that many of his people disagreed. To achieve his goals, Peter increased his power as absolute ruler. He strengthened absolutism by creating a strong army loyal to him. He recruited able men from lower-ranking families. He then promoted them to positions of authority and rewarded them with grants of land. Since these men owed everything to Peter, they were loyal to only him. Peter also ruthlessly crushed a revolt of the nobles. Peter appointed royal governors to replace local officials and extended government control over the Russian Orthodox Church. He abolished the office of patriarch, head of the church, and set up a Holy Synod to run the church under his direction. Suleiman the Magnificent was leader of the Ottoman Turks, who ruled from 1520 to 1566. He united all of the Muslim world except for Persia and Afghanistan. Suleiman acted as both the sultan (political ruler) and the caliph (religious leader). He enjoyed absolute power. However, to rule effectively, he needed support from his personal advisers, the bureaucracy, a group of religious advisers known as the Ulema, and a well-trained army. A prime minister headed the bureaucracy that carried out the sultan's decisions throughout the empire. The Ulema ruled on questions of Islamic law. Suleiman maintained an elite corps of soldiers called janissaries who swore complete allegiance to him. Suleiman, also known as "The Lawgiver" for his reforms in organizing Ottoman Law, claimed that he "was the sovereign of sovereigns, the dispenser of crowns to the monarchs on the face of the earth."

WRONG CHOICES EXPLAINED:

(1) None of these leaders broke away from the Roman Catholic Church. Louis XIV supported and controlled the Roman Catholic Church in France. Peter the Great was associated with the Byzantine or Russian Orthodox Church. Suleiman the Magnificent was a Muslim. Neither Peter nor Suleiman had any affiliation with the Western Church.

(2) None of these leaders helped feudal lords build secure castles. Louis XIV destroyed the nobles' fortified castles and insisted that they live at the Versailles Palace. Peter the Great crushed the nobility and tortured or executed anyone who opposed his rule. Suleiman the Magnificent ran a powerful and complex military state that required a strong, powerful army that would not tolerate anyone building secure castles against the authority of the ruler.

(3) None of these rulers instituted programs that provided more power to their parliament. Louis XIV never convened the Estates General, the French Parliament, during his 72-year reign. Peter the Great ruled without Parliament. Suleiman the Magnificent ruled with the help of a grand council but was the absolute ruler who made all decisions.

24. **1** One way in which the Scientific Revolution and the Enlightenment were similar is that they encouraged the spread of new ideas. The Scientific Revolution of the 16th and 17th centuries was a period in which scientists challenged traditional authority and used observations and reason to reach conclusions. The Scientific Revolution changed the way educated people looked at the world. Medieval scientists believed that the earth was the center of the universe. However, the new scientific approach of Nicholas Copernicus and Galileo Galilei showed that the sun was the center of the universe. The Scientific Revolution moved Europe from a world view that was primarily religious to one in which the secular world or the present world was more important. The new scientific approach promoted critical thinking and the rise of learned societies like the French Academy of Science, which fostered the growth of the ideas. The Enlightenment, the period also known as the Age of Reason, was an intellectual and cultural movement of the 18th century tying together the ideas of the Scientific Revolution. Enlightenment thinkers believed that just as one could use reason to explain why things happened in the physical universe, there must be natural laws to govern society. They claimed that through reason and logic one could explain the law of society and also solve the problems of society. These philosophers, such as Voltaire and Rousseau, criticized the abuse of government and proposed ways to correct it. The writers of the Enlightenment created a new way of looking at power and authority, as well as what makes up good and lawful government.

WRONG CHOICES EXPLAINED:

(2) The leaders of the Scientific Revolution and the Enlightenment challenged and attacked traditional authority. Copernicus rejected the medieval view of earth as the center of the universe and proposed the heliocentric view

of the sun as the center of the universe. In his book, *Candide,* Voltaire wrote against organized religion and denounced it because he felt that it exploited the people.

(3) The Scientific Revolution and the Enlightenment did not lead to the Protestant Revolution. Church abuses, such as the selling of indulgences, led Martin Luther to attack the authority of the Church. The Scientific Revolution, like the Enlightenment, was concerned with promoting a critical analysis of everything in society from politics to organized religion.

(4) The Scientific Revolution and the Enlightenment did not reject Renaissance individualism. Both of these movements stressed the importance of individuals to understand the world around them.

25. **1** The principle of the Enlightenment philosophers, which is expressed in this quotation from the French Revolution, is natural law. The philosophers of the Enlightenment believed that there were universal rules of behavior, which was the natural law based on reason, and an inborn sense of morality. The French philosophers, Voltaire and Rousseau, believed that as reasonable human beings individuals had the natural ability to govern and look after themselves. Rousseau believed that the only good government was one that was freely formed by the people and guided by the general will of society. In his book *The Social Contract,* published in 1762, Rousseau argued that legitimate government comes from the consent of the people and that the purpose of government was to protect the rights of the people and the common good. These ideas influenced the writing of the Declaration of the Rights of Man and of the Citizen in 1789. The first article of the Declaration of the Rights of Man and of the Citizen declared that men are born free and equal in rights and that all men enjoy the right to liberty, security, property, and resistance to oppression. Like the philosophers of the Enlightenment, the Declaration insisted that the government existed to protect the rights of citizens. The Declaration also proclaimed that all citizens were equal before the law and those social distinctions should be based on talent and virtues that were good for those in society. These ideas reflect the belief of philosophers like Rousseau and Voltaire, that all people were equal. Rousseau even proposed that the titles of nobility should be abolished. Although the philosophers promoted the idea of natural law of equality for all people, they took a traditional view about the equality of women in society.

WRONG CHOICES EXPLAINED:

(2) Nationalism is a feeling of pride and loyalty to one's nation and the belief that each group is entitled to its own nation or government.

(3) Free trade is the removal of trade restrictions or barriers between nations such as tariffs.

(4) Socialism is an economic system in which the government owns and operates all the essential means of production.

26. **2** All the elements identified in the illustration contributed to German unification. Germany was the last of the great European powers to achieve complete political unity. Beginning in the early 19th century, some Germans began to think of a unified fatherland or country. This nationalist awakening reflected the efforts of German educators, poets, writers, historians, and philosophers, who stressed the factors that united Germans, such as customs, race, language, and historic tradition. Napoleon aroused nationalist feelings and reduced the number of small German states from 300 to 100. In 1819, Prussia formed the Zollverein, a German custom union. By the 1840s, it included most of the German states except Austria. The Zollverein ended trade barriers between states but maintained high tariffs against nonmembers. The Zollverein promoted economic unity but, more importantly, established Prussia as a leader among the states. In 1862, Otto von Bismarck was appointed Chancellor of Prussia. Over the next decade, he would be the leading force behind the drive to unify Germany. Bismarck believed that the only way to unify Germany was through a policy of "Blood and Iron." He believed that the only way to unite German states was through war. From 1864–1871, Bismarck would lead Prussia into three wars, which would unite Germany and increase the prestige of Prussia as the dominant power of the new German states. In the Danish War of 1864, Bismarck provoked a war with Denmark over the provinces of Schleswig-Holstein. Prussia, joined by Austria, easily defeated Denmark and compelled it to cede Schleswig-Holstein. Prussia and Austria became joint owners of the border provinces of Schleswig and Holstein. In 1866, Bismarck deliberately quarreled with Austria regarding these two provinces; Prussia defeated Austria in just seven weeks. This was known as the Austro-Prussian War. The Prussians used their superior training and equipment to win a smashing victory. The Austrians had to accept Prussian annexation of more Austrian territory. Following the Austro-Prussian war, Prussia took control of northern Germany. For the first time, the eastern and western parts of the Prussian kingdom were joined. In 1867, the remaining northern states joined a North German Confederation that Prussia dominated completely. Only four southern German states remained outside the Confederation. In 1870, Bismarck reasoned that he would win the support of the southern states if they faced a threat from the outside. He used nationalism and the bitter memories of Napoleon's conquests to stir up support for a war against France. He manufactured an incident with Napoleon III, who was Napoleon I's nephew. When the French leader opposed Prussia's efforts to have one of their ruling family members be considered as a candidate for the Spanish throne, Bismarck published an altered telegram of a meeting between the Prussian King Wilhelm I and the French ambassador. The telegram seemed to insult the French and intensified bitter feelings toward Prussia. Napoleon III declared war on Prussia. On July 19, 1870, Prussia and German allies easily defeated France. During the war, the four southern German states agreed to unite with Prussia. The Franco-Prussian War of 1870 was the final stage in German unification. On January 18, 1871, William I was crowned Kaiser, or emperor. Germans called

their empire the Second Reich. Bismarck had achieved Prussian dominance over Germany and had united the country.

WRONG CHOICES EXPLAINED:

(1) Interdependence is the mutual way in which the economies of countries are dependent on the goods, services, and knowledge from other parts of the world.

(3) Imperialism is a policy whereby one nation dominates, by direct or indirect rule, the political, economic, and social life of an area, region, or country.

(4) Apathy is a term used to describe someone who is not involved or has very little interest in any events.

27. **4** The graph supports the statement that most enslaved Africans were sent to the Caribbean and Spanish America. From the 16th to the late 19th centuries, over 9.5 million Africans were enslaved and transported to several different destinations where they were sold and used to make high profits. The pie graph clearly indicates that 57 percent of enslaved Africans were transported to countries in the Caribbean and Spanish America.

WRONG CHOICES EXPLAINED:

(1), (2), and (3) All of these choices are incorrect. The graph does not provide any information about the slave trade before 1500. Only 6 percent of the slaves were imported to Sweden, Denmark, and Holland. The graph does not provide the conditions of slavery in Brazil versus the United States.

28. **3** The Industrial Revolution had the greatest influence on the development of laissez-faire capitalism. The Industrial Revolution brought many economic changes, of which the most important was the increase in the production and availability of goods. With the coming of the Industrial Revolution, the new production methods required large amounts of capital or money to build factories, purchase machines, secure raw materials, and pay workers before any goods were sold. Capitalists urged that the government should abandon mercantilism, which called for government regulation to achieve a favorable balance of trade. Opposed to restrictions on trade and production, capitalists wanted to manufacture and sell their goods free from government interference. This approach became known as laissez-faire. According to this theory, businesses should operate with little or no government interference. In 1776, Adam Smith, the Scottish economist, published *The Wealth of Nations*, which promoted the idea of a laissez-faire government. According to Smith, the government should act as an agency to ensure that everyone is following the laws of society and should allow the invisible hand of competition to promote the best interests of society. In the 19th century, Smith's ideas greatly influenced Britain and other industrialized nations and became the basis of the economic system of capitalism during the Industrial Revolution.

WRONG CHOICES EXPLAINED:

(1) and (2) The fall of the Roman Empire and the invention of the printing press had no influence on the development of laissez-faire capitalism that began to develop in the 18th century. The Roman Empire fell in 476 A.D. and the printing press was invented in 1440.

(4) The Green Revolution refers to 20th-century technological advances in agriculture that have led to increased production on a limited parcel of land.

29. **4** In the late 1800s, one response of workers in England to unsafe working conditions was to form labor unions. At the beginning of the Industrial Revolution, workers spent more than 14 hours a day at the job, 6 days a week, for wages of $4 or $5 a week. Women and children were employed in factories. Children were often beaten because factory owners thought they did not work hard enough and wanted to keep them awake. Factories also posed safety issues. Factories were seldom lit or clean. To press for reforms, working people began to form unions. Unions are organizations that carry on collective, or group, bargaining with the employer to gain better wages and working conditions for the workers. Early unions were vigorously opposed in England where they were first organized. Unions were outlawed as conspiracies and strikers were often imprisoned. The government saw unions as a threat to social order and stability. However, constant pressure by the unions forced the government to repeal the Combination Laws of 1799, 1800, and 1824, which outlawed strikes and unions. After 1825, the government tolerated unions. Under pressure from the unions and reformers, the British Parliament passed the Factory Act of 1833, which limited the workday to 12 hours for persons under 18 years of age. In 1847, Parliament passed legislation that limited the workday of women and children to 10 hours a day. Through the efforts of the unions, laws were passed requiring safety devices on dangerous machinery and establishing standards of factory sanitation. All of these laws improved the conditions of the British factory workers by the end of the 19th century.

WRONG CHOICES EXPLAINED:

(1) The workers in England never took control of the government. In 1901, the British trade unions joined with other organizations to form the Labor Party. This organization became a major political force in England and worked to secure legislation that was favorable to workers.

(2) Unsafe working conditions did not lead workers to return to farming. Workers had migrated from the farms to cities because the Agricultural Revolution had displaced many of them and they were forced to leave to find work.

(3) Before workers could set minimum wages, they had to form unions. Once workers became organized, unions fought for improvements in the basic working conditions of their members. The drive for minimum wages would not develop until the 20th century.

30. **4** When Koreans call their land "a shrimp among whales," they are referring to their location between powerful neighbors: Russia, China, and Japan. Throughout its history, Korea has been subjected to the interests of its more powerful neighbors and rarely, if ever, flexed its influence on its neighbors. Korea is a peninsula attached to the eastern mainland of Asia between China and Japan. Because of its location, Korea has served as a cultural bridge between China and Japan. As early as 100 B.C., Chinese civilization began to spread to Korea. The Koreans transformed Chinese traditions and passed them on to Japan. This peaceful transmission of Chinese traditions had a major influence on Korean culture. Location has also made Korea a battleground for forces seeking control of East Asia. The Mongols occupied Korea from the early 1200s until the 1350s. In the 1500s, Korea, with the help of the Chinese, was able to defeat a Japanese effort to conquer the country. In 1636, before they came to power in China, the Manchus conquered Korea and made it a vassal state. Under the Manchus, Korea was China's little brother. Korea adopted Chinese culture and its policy of isolation. During the Age of Imperialism, Japan competed with China and Russia for control of Korea. By 1905, the Japanese defeated their rivals and won control of Korea. In 1945, Koreans celebrated the Japanese defeat in World War II. However, Korea once again became a battleground between two great powers, the United States and Russia. The United States and Russia agreed that Korea should regain its independence. Both countries sent troops to Korea. The Soviet troops occupied the region north of the 28th parallel and the Americans occupied the southern part of Korea. The occupation was to last only until elections could be held. However, Cold War rivalries and the outbreak of the Korean War in 1950 led to the permanent division of Korea, which has lasted for the past 54 years.

WRONG CHOICES EXPLAINED:
(1) This statement does not refer to the mountains that cover much of Korea. Mountains cover about 70 percent of the Korean peninsula. However, this statement describes how Korea's proximity to powerful neighbors influenced the country.

(2) There is no connection between this statement and the environmental damage caused by overfishing in the Pacific. South Korea has the world's third-largest fishing industry after Japan and China. Neither country has made any serious attempt to limit their fishing rights in the waters between the two nations.

(3) The saying that Korea is "a shrimp among whales" does not indicate anything about Korea's traditional respect for the sea. Although many Koreans make their living from the sea by fishing, this saying describes how Korea was influenced for many years by its proximity to powerful countries.

31. **3** This late 19th-century Japanese print illustrates cultural diffusion. Cultural diffusion is the spread of ideas and customs from one group or region to another culture. This illustration shows how Japanese women were

influenced by ideas from the West. After Commodore Perry of the United States forced the Japanese to open up their ports for traders in 1854, other European countries such as France and England demanded and won similar rights. The Japanese realized that the best way to oppose Western Imperialism was to adopt new ways to avoid being carved up like China. Japanese leaders began to encourage young statesmen to study in Europe and the United States. They traveled abroad and chose what they believed to be the best Western civilization had to offer and adapted to its culture. This print shows that some Japanese began to dress like European women of the 19th century and to play the piano, a Western musical instrument.

WRONG CHOICES EXPLAINED:

(1) Isolationism is a policy of avoiding or limiting involvement in the affairs or conflicts of other nations.

(2) Ethnocentrism is a belief that one's culture or standards are superior to other societies.

(4) Democracy is a system of government in which the citizens rule or hold power.

32. **2** This print was most likely created during the period of Japanese history known as the Meiji Restoration. During the Meiji Period, the Japanese adapted Western models of industrialization. During the Meiji Period, from 1862 to 1912, Japan ended feudalism and began to modernize by selectively borrowing from the West. Meiji means enlightened ruler. These reformers rallied around the emperor and unseated the shoguns, who they claimed had weakened the power of Japan. The goal of the Meiji leader, or enlightened ruler, was "a rich country, a strong military." The new leaders sent Japanese students abroad to learn Western government, economics, technology, and customs. In 1889, Japan adopted a written constitution implementing a parliamentary government with the emperor as its head. The Meiji government set up a banking system, improved ports, and organized a telegraph and postal system. The leaders also built a modern army based on a draft and constructed a fleet of steam-powered iron ships. A broad-based program of public education was instituted. As a result of these reforms, Japan avoided falling victim to Western imperialism in the late 1800s.

WRONG CHOICES EXPLAINED:

(1) The Tokugawa shogunate ruled Japan from 1603 until 1867. These shogunates unified Japan and brought stability to the country. The shogun leaders would be forced to step down when Meiji Restoration began in the late 19th century.

(3) The Russo-Japanese War was the conflict between Russia and Japan, sparked by the two countries' efforts to dominate Manchuria and Korea.

(4) The post-World War II occupation refers to America's effort in 1945 to rebuild the economic and political structure of Japan after its defeat.

33.   **4** During World War I, the Armenians in the Ottoman Empire were the victims of genocide. Genocide is a deliberate attempt to destroy an entire religious or ethnic group. From the 16th century until World War I, a major portion of Armenia was controlled by the Ottoman Turks under whom the Armenians experienced discrimination, religious persecution, and heavy taxation. By the 1880s, there were roughly two million Christian Armenians in the Ottoman Empire, who began to demand their freedom. Muslim Turks distrusted the Armenians and believed they were supporting Russian plans against the Ottoman Empire. Throughout the 1890s, Turkish troops killed tens of thousands of Armenians in response to their nationalist stirrings. When World War I erupted in 1914, the Armenians pledged their support to the Turk's enemies. In April 1915, the Turks ordered the deportation of the nearly 2 million Armenian population to the deserts of Syria and Mesopotamia. Along the way, more than 600,000 died of starvation or were killed by Turkish soldiers. The Armenian massacre is considered the first genocide in the 20th century.

WRONG CHOICES EXPLAINED:

(1), (2), and (3) None of these groups were victims of genocide. At the end of World War I, the British and French signed the Treaty of Sevres in 1920 with the Ottoman Empire. The Ottoman Empire was liquidated and the British took control of the Middle East, Mesopotamia (Iraq), and Palestine, including Trans-Jordon, which became a British mandate. The French gained control of Algeria in 1830, and there were few Algerians living in France at the end of World War I. The groups living in these areas were victims of colonialism, not genocide.

34.   **1** The Treaty of Versailles punished Germany for its role in World War I by forcing Germany to accept blame for the war and to pay reparations. In Article 231 of the Versailles Treaty, Germany was forced to accept sole responsibility for the war. By signing the war guilt clause, the Germans were also required to pay all the costs of the war, including civilian damages to widows and others in Allied countries. The total cost was expected to be spread over a 30-year period and would eventually cost Germany more than $30 billion. To pay for the reparations to the Allied countries, the German government had to print more money, resulting in the fall of the German mark. Rampant inflation set in and made the mark worthless. It was reported that in 1923 a loaf of bread cost 200 billion marks and that 4 trillion marks were the equivalent of one dollar. Many Germans blamed their economic problems on the harshness of the Versailles Treaty, which they believed not only forced the country to pay for the war but made it impossible to rebuild. By forcing the country to disarm, it was robbing it of its European territories and overseas colonies. Despite a brief recovery in the mid-1920s, the Great Depression of 1929 destroyed any hope of recovery. Hitler and the Nazi Party exploited German bitterness about the Versailles Treaty and focused on nationalists who were unable to accept their defeat in World War I. Hitler

promised to tear up the Treaty of Versailles and denounced the war guilt clause. He claimed that the Versailles Treaty had stabbed Germany in the back and was responsible for the economic chaos in Germany.

WRONG CHOICES EXPLAINED:

(2) Germany was divided into four occupied zones at the end of World War II in 1945.

(3) There were no economic sanctions against Germany at the end of World War I. The League of Nations was formed in 1920 and the United Nations was formed in 1945.

(4) Germany did not have any territory in Spain. The Austrian-Hungarian Empire lost territory in the Balkans. Germany did lose German-speaking regions, such as the Sudetenland in Czechoslovakia and the former German port of Danzig, which had been given to Poland at the end of World War I.

35. **2** The main reason Japan invaded Southeast Asia during World War II was to acquire supplies of oil and rubber. As a small island nation, Japan lacked many basic resources necessary to ensure its growth as an industrial nation. Japan's late 19th-century industrialization created the need for raw materials, especially cotton, iron ore, coal, and oil. It wanted to gain markets for its manufactured goods. Japanese nationalists also wanted to replace European imperialism with Asian imperialism. In 1895, Japan defeated China in a war and forced the Chinese to give up their claims to Korea. They also gained Taiwan and won special trading privileges. In 1910, Japan annexed Korea and forced its people to build railroads and roads for Japan's benefit. The Japanese took half of Korea's yearly rice crops to support Japanese expansion. In the 1920s and 1930s, the Japanese leaders developed the East Asia Co-Prosperity Sphere. Its aim was to conquer East Asia by taking raw materials. In 1931, Japan invaded Manchuria, a northern province of China, which was rich in coal, iron, and fertile soil. The Japanese argued that they had won Manchuria in the same way the Western nations had gained their colonies. By 1932, they gained control of the area, began to build hydroelectric plants, and created a sizable iron and steel industry, thereby increasing Japan's economy and military power. During World War II, the Japanese invaded French Indochina as well as the former Dutch East Indies (Indonesia). These areas provided the Japanese military with the important natural resources of rubber and oil. Japanese foreign policy led to conflict with Great Britain and the United States.

WRONG CHOICES EXPLAINED:

(1) The Japanese did not invade Southeast Asia during World War II to recruit more men for its army. The Japanese government never had any difficulty recruiting men for its army. The government was a military dictatorship and no one questioned its authority.

(3) The Japanese people did not have any need for spices. The Japanese needed necessary natural resources such as oil and rubber in order to continue its quest for domination in Asia.

(4) Japanese foreign policy did not prevent the United States from entering the war. The Japanese attack on Pearl Harbor on December 7, 1941, led to World War II with the United States.

36. **1** This passage described the Munich Conference. The policy that France, Britain, and Italy chose to follow at this meeting is known as appeasement. Appeasement was a policy followed by several European leaders in the 1930s. These European leaders agreed to the demands of an aggressor to preserve peace at any cost. In September 1938, Hitler demanded that the Sudetenland, a region in Czechoslovakia bordering on Germany and inhabited by about three million German-speaking people, be given to Germany. The Czech government, a democracy under President Edward Benes, refused to yield. They asked for help from France. The Munich Conference, held on September 29, 1938, tried to resolve the problem. Germany, France, Britain, and Italy attended, but the Czechs were not invited. British Prime Minister Neville Chamberlain believed that he could preserve peace by giving into Hitler's demands. The Western democracies agreed that Germany would seize control of the Sudetenland, and in exchange Hitler pledged to respect Czechoslovakia's new borders. Less than six months after the Munich meeting, Hitler's troops took over the rest of Czechoslovakia and Mussolini seized Albania. In August 1939, England and France refused to give in to Hitler's demand that Poland return the former German port of Danzig. But appeasement had convinced Hitler that neither nation would risk war. On September 1, 1939, Hitler invaded Poland. Two days later, Britain and France honored their guarantee to Poland and declared war on Germany. World War II had started. Appeasement had failed to keep peace.

WRONG CHOICES EXPLAINED:

(2) Self-determination is the right of people to make their own decisions about their political and economic development.

(3) Liberation describes the efforts of people or nations to gain political and economic freedom.

(4) Pacification is a term used to show how a government tries to establish peace and security in their own country.

37. **3** The political climate of the Cold War caused the world's two superpowers to compete economically and militarily. The Cold War was an ideological and economic struggle between the Untied States and the Soviet Union. The Cold War began in 1945 and ended with the collapse of the Soviet Union in 1991. The United States represented the forces of democracy and the Soviet Union represented the forces of communism. The Cold War was a war of words, which was fought by the use of military alliances and economic rivalry to show which system was superior. In 1947, the United States began the Truman Doctrine to stop the spread of communism in Greece and Turkey. Later, the United States organized the European Economic

Recovery, which gave Western European countries more than $17 billion in aid from 1947 to 1951. The purpose of the Marshall Plan, named after the United States Secretary of State, was to rebuild the economies of Europe as a way to strengthen democracy against communism. Although the United States offered economic aid to Eastern European countries, Stalin did not allow these countries to accept any form of aid. He was determined to make these Soviet satellites dependent upon Russia for economic and military aid. In 1949, the United States, Canada, and nine Western European countries formed NATO, a defensive alliance designed to protect European countries from communism. In 1955, the Soviet Union formed the Warsaw Pact with seven of its satellites in Eastern Europe. This was also a defensive alliance, promising mutual cooperation. Throughout the Cold War, the United States and the Soviets competed with each other in Asia, the Middle East, Africa, and Latin America. Cold War tensions grew bitter in Asia during the Korean War in the 1950s and in Vietnam in the 1960s. In each case the superpowers supported opposing sides with economic aid, advisors, and troops. In the Middle East, the Soviet Union and the United States struggled with each other over ways to resolve the conflict between Israel and Arab nations. In Africa, there was tension over the Belgian Congo in the 1960s, and with Angola and South Africa in the 1970s. In Latin and Central America, Soviet Union support of Castro in Cuba led to tensions with the United States throughout the 1960s and the struggle in Nicaragua and El Salvador in the 1980s added to rivalry between the two superpowers. Throughout the Cold War, the United States and the Soviet Union competed for worldwide influence without any actual armed conflict between the two nations.

WRONG CHOICES EXPLAINED:

(1) There was no cooperation between the United States and the Soviet Union about communism. The United States wanted to contain communism and the Soviet Union wanted to spread its influence to other countries.

(2) The Cold War did not cause the United States or the Soviet Union to colonize Africa and Asia. Both of these countries supported nationalist movements for freedom. They based their support of national political leaders on whether these leaders were pro democracy or communism.

(4) The Cold War did not cause either of the two superpowers to protect human rights. The United States supported dictatorial regimes in many parts of the world as long as they were opposed to communism. In 1956, the Soviet Union crushed the Hungarian rebellion, and in 1965 invaded Czechoslovakia to end liberal reforms in the country. These incidents showed that the Soviet Union would use whatever force necessary to ensure its domination in Eastern Europe.

38. **4** The political ideas of Ho Chi Minh, Fidel Castro, and Pol Pot were strongly influenced by the writings of Karl Marx. Karl Marx wrote the *Communist Manifesto* in 1848, outlining the abuses of capitalism and predicting the inevitability of communism because of the laws of history. Marx

claimed that the workers of the world would unite in a worldwide revolution that would lead to the overthrow of the capitalistic system. The *Communist Manifesto* inspired revolutionary leaders in their struggle against capitalist countries. Ho Chi Minh (1890–1969) was a communist leader who sought independence for Vietnam. He fought against French colonialism in Vietnam. Ho Chi Minh (which means "He Who Enlightens") turned to the communists for help in his struggle. During the 1930s, Ho's Indo-Chinese Communist Party led revolts and strikes against the French, who jailed Vietnamese protesters and sentenced Ho, the party leader, to death. Ho fled his death sentence, and continued to lead the nationalist movement from exile. He returned to Vietnam in 1941, a year after the Japanese seized control of the country. He and other nationalists founded the Vietminh (Independence League). The Japanese left in 1945, but the French wanted to retain their former colony. However, in 1945, Ho announced Vietnam's independence from the French. He joined together with Vietnamese nationalists and communists to fight the French. After the French were defeated in 1954, he continued his struggle against the United States, which wanted to prevent the communists from taking over South Vietnam. In 1975, the communist forces took over Saigon, the capital of South Vietnam and renamed it Ho Chi Minh City. Vietnam was finally united. Fidel Castro, who was born in 1927, was the son of a wealthy Spanish Cuban farmer. He became involved in politics while studying law at the University of Havana. In 1959, Fidel Castro overthrew the dictatorship of Fulgencia Batista and seized power in Cuba. Throughout the 1950s the United States had supported the unpopular dictator Batista. Castro denounced the United States as an imperialist, forbade elections, and nationalized American investments in Cuba without compensation. In 1961, Castro proclaimed his intention to transform Cuba into a communist state and threatened to export communism to other Latin American countries. He also established close ties with the Soviet Union, which had established a communist government in Russia in 1917. The close ties between Cuba and the Soviet Union ended in 1991 with the collapse of the Soviet Union. Castro's government is one of the last communist governments in the world. The aging Castro has refused either to change his communist system of government or give up power after 55 years in office. In 1975, Cambodian communist guerrillas, under the leadership of Pol Pot took control of the government. His guerrilla movement was known as the Khmer Rouge. Pol Pot renamed the country Kamphuchea. Under the leadership of Pol Pot, they began a reign of terror to remove all Western influence from Cambodia. It is estimated that the government killed more than 3 million people, nearly one-third of the population. From 1975 to 1979, he tried to establish a purely agrarian society. The government forced people out of the cities and resettled them in the country. He and his followers killed off the educated classes of the country, its monks, minority groups, technicians, and artists. Their goal was to create a classless society. In the early 1990s, the United Nations intervened in Cambodia to supervise general elections. Pol

Pot died in the jungles of Cambodia in 1998. These three revolutionary leaders adapted Marx's beliefs and ideas to their own countries.

WRONG CHOICES EXPLAINED:

(1) Confucius was a Chinese philosopher who founded Confucianism, a system of ethical conduct stressing the importance of tradition and respect and reverence to family and authority.

(2) Mohandas Gandhi was a Hindu nationalist leader who led the independence movement from Great Britain. He preached a philosophy of nonviolence to achieve his goals.

(3) Desmond Tutu is an Anglican Archbishop in South Africa who won the Nobel Peace Prize in 1984 for his opposition to apartheid. Apartheid was the official policy of strict segregation of the races practiced in South Africa from 1945 until it was repealed in 1991.

39. **3** In India, urbanization affected society by weakening the traditional caste system. In India, the population movement from rural to urban areas has resulted in a decrease in rigid class distinctions. The industrialization of India's economy has contributed to the growth of large cities or urban areas. In 1900, Bombay (Mumbail) had a population of 1.5 million. At the end of this century, the population had grown to more than 10 million. It is the third-largest city in the world. New Delhi, the capital of India, has a population of more than 7.5 million. Urbanization weakens rigid class distinctions. In rural areas, individuals are separated from each other by the caste system, which laid down specific guidelines for each class of people. Since one group did only one kind of work, it gave its members a chance to live more or less apart from other people. City dwellers do not always know the backgrounds of their neighbors. In the city, Indians from the lower caste system are free to move up in society. In offices and factories, caste or class rules are hard to maintain. Workers come from many different backgrounds. They all have to live and work together, and gradually social distinctions become less important.

WRONG CHOICES EXPLAINED:

(1) Urbanization does not reinforce Hindu beliefs. As people move into the cities to work, they encounter workers from many different backgrounds and approaches to religion. In many cases, urbanization weakened religious beliefs.

(2) As people move to the city, they tend to lose contact with their native arts and crafts. Urbanization forces people to abandon their traditional crafts in order to survive in their new environment.

(4) Urbanization has led to the decrease, not the increase, in the number of farmers. Most people who come to urban areas are farmers who have been displaced by new technology in agriculture.

40. **2** The main purpose of the North American Free Trade Agreement (NAFTA) and the European Union (EU) is to encourage increased economic

development. In 1993, Mexico, the United States, and Canada signed the North American Free Trade Agreement. Under NAFTA, these three countries have pledged to gradually reduce tariffs on one another's goods within 15 years. The treaty created one huge regional market of more than 380 billion people. The European Economic Community, now known as the European Union, was formed in 1958 by six industrialized Western nations to expand trade and end trade restriction among nations. By 1993, it combined with other European nations to become the European Union, and increased its membership to 15. Its goal has been to end all tariff barriers and ensure the free movement of manufactured goods, farm products, and people among member nations. The European Union has a common banking system, and in 2000 introduced the Euro dollars. The Euro has become the common currency of 12 out of the 15 member nations. Also, European travelers no longer need visas from each individual nation to travel and can use a common passport. In May 2004, the European Union expanded to 25 nations. Eight of these nations were former Russian satellites. The European Union now includes 45 million people speaking 20 different languages. The EU represents the largest market for a variety of United States products, including toys, precious metals, software, fighter jets, and bananas. The European Union is the second-largest provider of goods and services (after Canada) to the United States. The European Union is also working on a unified law on immigration and asylum, as Europe has admitted new nations from Eastern Europe. The goal is to insure that these new nations from Eastern Europe will not take jobs away from Western Europe.

WRONG CHOICES EXPLAINED:

(1) Neither NAFTA nor the European Union was formed to increase the authority of the United Nations. These agreements are designed to promote economic cooperation.

(3) NAFTA and the European Union do not address the issues of peace between nations. Their purpose is purely economic.

(4) NAFTA and the European Union are not designed as military alliances.

41. **4** These statements are examples of the efforts of different peoples to achieve self-determination. Self-determination is the freedom of the people to determine what form of government they wish to establish. Since the partition of 1947, India, which is predominantly Hindu, and Pakistan, which is mostly Muslim, have been at odds over Kashmir, located on India's northwest frontier. In 1947, Kashmir's Hindu prince signed it over to India. However, its majority Muslim population wanted to be part of Pakistan. Although most of the people are Muslim, two-thirds of the territory is governed by India. In 1948, the UN Security Council called for a vote of the people of Kashmir to choose which country they wanted to join. A vote was never taken. In Indian-held regions, Muslim guerrillas have been fighting against Indian rule, leading to frequent flare-ups and border wars between

Pakistan and India. In 1975, Indonesia seized the Portuguese colony of East Timor. Indonesia is the largest Muslim nation in the world but East Timor is predominantly Catholic. Even before Indonesia took East Timor away from Portugal, a pro-independence rebellion was under way. Indonesia used military force to deal with this independence movement. More than 200,000 citizens of East Timor died as a result of their efforts to gain independence. In 1996, two activists from East Timor, Bishop Carlos Ximenes Beto and Jose Ramos-Horta, won the Nobel Peace Prize for their efforts to gain independence for their country. In 1999, Indonesia agreed to let the people of East Timor vote for or against independence. The vote was held under UN supervision and more than 80 percent of the voters chose independence. The pro-Indonesian militias went on a rampage. The soldiers destroyed East Timor's main cities. Many of the territory's 600,000 people fled into West Timor, still part of Indonesia. An Australian-led peacekeeping force helped restore order. Then, UN administrators came to help rebuild East Timor and prepare for independence. East Timor became an independent country in 2002. Tibet is a mountainous region in the southwestern part of China. Tibet was an independent Buddhist kingdom with its own culture, language, and religion. In 1950, China seized Tibet, which they called Xizang, setting up collective farms and factories and suppressing Buddhism. Since an unsuccessful Tibetan rebellion in 1959, the Dalai Lama, the spiritual leader of Tibet, has led the movement to restore freedom for his country. From his place of exile in India, the Dalai Lama has become an international symbol of peace and his intent to reclaim a free Tibet a cause for many. Since 1950, it is estimated 1.2 million Tibetans have been killed by the Chinese. In 1988, the Dalai Lama put forward the "Strasbourg Proposal," which called for autonomy for Tibet rather than independence. Although it was rejected by the Chinese, the Dalai Lama received the Nobel Peace Prize. Tibet remains an occupied country and liberation is a dim hope. The Kurds are the largest ethnic group in the Middle East without their own homeland. There are 12 million Kurds living in Turkey, five million in Iran, four million in Iraq, and 500,000 in Syria, Azerbaijan, Armenia, and Georgia. Throughout the 20th century, their struggle for political and cultural autonomy was opposed by the countries to which they have been scattered. The Turks have responded to Kurdish nationalism by forbidding Kurds to speak their native language. The Iranians have also persecuted the Kurds, attacking them over religious issues. In the 1980s, Iraqis dropped poison gas on the Kurds killing 5,000 people. After the Persian Gulf War of 1991, Iraqi Kurds revolted against Saddam Hussein but the revolt was crushed. Thousands of Kurdish rebels and civilians fled to the border areas of Iran and Turkey. Many refugees died of starvation and exposure in the snowbound mountains. The United States responded by establishing in Northern Iraq a safe haven for Kurds and a Kurdish control zone of four to five million refugees. The Kurds hoped that the zone would eventually become the core of a self-governing Kurdistan. The American invasion of Iraq in 2003 and the end of Saddam Hussein's government has renewed the issue of a separate independent Kurdistan.

WRONG CHOICES EXPLAINED:

(1) The free market systems are economic systems based on supply and demand and do not address the issue of self-determination.

(2) These statements are examples of struggles for independence, not for democratic governments.

(3) These statements deal with the struggle for political freedom. Social Equality tries to promote equal opportunities for everyone.

42. **3** The concern expressed in this cartoon is most closely related to the consequences of industrialization and the burning of fossil fuels. One of the main problems created by industrialization is global warming. Global warming, or the gradual rise in the earth's temperature, has caused the greenhouse effect. The burning of fossil fuels, such as oil, coal, and natural gas, releases large amounts of carbon dioxide into the earth's environment. The excess carbon dioxide traps more heat near the earth, a process that creates the greenhouse effect. Overall warming can adversely affect agriculture and upset the delicate ecological balance in nature. During the 1990s, scientists noticed that a large hole developed seasonally in the ozone layer over Antarctica. Many are concerned that the hole will spread to other parts of the globe. Experts fear that a temperature rise of only two or three degrees over the next century would have disastrous consequences, altering ocean currents and climate patterns, changing shorelines, and threatening the lives of humans, animals, and plants.

WRONG CHOICES EXPLAINED:

(1) The cartoon does not deal with the rapid migration of animals to the Northern Hemisphere. Polar bears live in the North Pole.

(2) and (4) Neither of these concerns—further exploration of the Arctic Ocean and the slow economic growth in developing nations—is expressed in this cartoon.

43. **4** The late 20th-century conflicts in Rwanda, Yugoslavia, and India were similar in that each was caused by the rivalries between ethnic groups. In 1994, the small African country of Rwanda was the scene of one of Africa's most vicious civil wars. Before the killing began in 1994, Rwanda had a population of about seven million: 85 percent were Hutu and 24 percent were Tutsis. At least 500,000 people lost their lives in massacres sparked by the animosities between the two rival ethnic groups. Hutu extremists, supported by the government, launched a murderous campaign against the minority Tutsis. In one day, 250,000 people poured into Tanzania. More than one million fled to the Congo, where tens of thousands died of cholera. The genocide was stopped when the Rwandan patriotic, Tutsi-led rebel army seized control of the government. It established a new government that included both Tutsis and Hutus; however, Rwanda's troubles were not over. Armed Hutus used the Congo as a basis for attacks into Rwanda. Accusing the government of supporting the Hutus, Rwanda sent its own troops into the Congo, where

they became entangled in a widening war. Eventually, Hutu attacks into Rwanda began to die down. In the election of April 2000, a Tutsi was elected president. The breakup of Yugoslavia in 1991 and 1992 sparked ethnic violence. In Bosnia, fighting erupted between Serbs and Muslims. Serbs began a campaign of ethnic cleansing that was designed to drive Muslims out of the parts of Bosnia that Serbia claimed. Many Bosnians became refugees and were either brutalized or killed. In 1995, representatives from all warring sides met in the United States and agreed to a peace settlement. NATO troops were sent into Bosnia to enforce the peace. In 1997, violence broke out between Serbians and Albanians living in the Kosovo region of Serbia. Albanians resented Serbian control and wanted to unite with Albania. Serbians began a systematic mass murder of the Albanians living in Kosovo. In March 1999, NATO forces began air attacks on the Yugoslavian troops in Kosovo and on other Serbian cities. After 72 days, President Slobodan Milosevic of Serbia was forced to pull his troops out of Kosovo. While NATO agreed that Kosovo would remain part of Serbia, UN administrators and 35,000 NATO-led peacekeeping troops (which included some 5,000 U.S. troops) entered Kosovo to maintain peace. Rivalries between different groups also led to conflicts in India. In northeast India, the Naga people claimed the right to a separate state. They formed a small army and waged bloody battles with government forces. In 1960, the government decided that Nagaland should become a separate state of India. The Sikhs are a religious group that began blending elements of Islam and Hinduism in the early 1500s. They make up 2 percent of the population and believe that the government does not provide them with enough aid and resources. Sikh separatists want to break away and form a separate country. In the state of Punjab, where Sikhs form a majority, they have led many protests. In 1984, they occupied the Golden Temple in Amristar and the government was forced to use violence to remove them. Thousands of Sikhs were killed. The conflict between Muslims and Hindus also continues to exist. Although many Muslims fled to Pakistan, about 100 million still live in India. In 1992, Hindu fundamentalists called for the destruction of a mosque in Ayodhya. This conflict touched off rioting and the mosque was destroyed.

WRONG CHOICES EXPLAINED:

(1) Deforestation describes the destruction of the rain forests. These conflicts were civil wars among different groups living in their countries

(2) The collapse of communism led to ethnic conflicts in Yugoslavia but did not cause conflicts in either Rwanda or India.

(3) United Nations peacekeeping forces intervened in Yugoslavia and Rwanda but not in India.

44. **3** The Twelve Tables, Justinian's Code, and the English Bill of Rights are similar in that each addresses the issue of the individual and the state. In 450 B.C., the plebeians (farmers, merchants, and traders), who made up the majority of the population of ancient Rome, forced the patricians (the

wealthy class) to have all the laws written down in what became known as the law of the Twelve Tables. These laws were displayed in the market and for the first time made it possible for plebeians to appeal a judgment handed down by a patrician judge. The Justinian Code was developed by Emperor Justinian of the Byzantine Empire, who ruled from 565 to 527 B.C. Between 534 and 528 B.C., Justinian assigned a group of legal scholars to gather and organize the ancient laws of Rome. This collection of laws, known as the Justinian Code, presented nearly 5,000 laws from the Roman Empire, as well as legal writings and a handbook for students. The English Bill of Rights was a series of acts passed by the British Parliament to ensure its superiority over the monarchy. In 1689, the Parliament forced James II to abdicate because of his Catholicism and his wish to become an absolute ruler. The English Bill of Rights limited the power of kings to repeal any laws or raise an army or taxes without the consent of Parliament.

WRONG CHOICES EXPLAINED:
(1) The Twelve Tables, Justinian's Code, and the English Bill of Rights are principles of law and government and not of social mobility.
(2) and (4) The Twelve Tables, Justinian's Code, and the English Bill of Rights do not address either economic development or the importance of religion. The Twelve Tables and Justinian's Code were designed to ensure that everyone knew the laws of their society. The English Bill of Rights was signed to limit the power of the monarchs in England.

45. **2** The statement that best describes the main point of the cartoon is that the actions of one nation often affect other nations. The cartoon describes nuclear proliferation or the spread of nuclear weapons. In May 1998, India set off five nuclear tests, surprising the international community, which widely condemned India's pro-nuclear stance. Despite international urgings for restraints, Pakistan responded by conducting several nuclear tests of its own. Both of these nations have refused to sign the Nuclear Non-Proliferation Treaty. The United Sates imposed sanctions on both countries. However, many people in India and Pakistan were jubilant because they believe that the possession of nuclear weapons makes them part of the elite nuclear club that is composed of the Unites States, England, France, Russia, and China. The international community is fearful that India and Pakistan will rely entirely on nuclear weapons to maintain their security. It is also believed that Iran has developed nuclear weapons. In November 2003, Iranian officials admitted to the United Nations International Atomic Energy Agency that they had been secretly developing a broad range of nuclear capabilities for the past 18 years. Iran, however, agreed to unannounced weapon inspections and to temporarily halt its uranium enrichment program. Later, in March 2004, Iran barred nuclear inspections by the International Atomic Energy Agency. The United States, which labeled Iran as one of the three nations in the Axis of Evil, is concerned that a nuclear-armed Iran would further destabilize the Persian Gulf and possibly give terrorists access to weapons

of mass destruction. India, Pakistan, and Iran believe that they must develop nuclear weapons or begin a nuclear program because they feel threatened by their neighbors.

WRONG CHOICES EXPLAINED:

(1) While nuclear proliferation occurred in nations such as India, Pakistan, and Iran, this cartoon does not indicate that nuclear proliferation occurs in all societies.

(3) This cartoon does not claim that nuclear proliferation should be limited to the global superpowers. The cartoon makes no reference to global superpowers.

(4) This cartoon does not indicate or explicitly show that most governments are critical of India's nuclear tests. It makes no reference to any criticisms by other nations.

46. **1** The heading that best completes the partial outline is Empires of India. In 321 B.C., Chandragupta founded the Maurya Dynasty or ruling family. The Maurya Dynasty ruled India for 140 years. Chandragupta established the first united empire. His empire stretched across the northern plains from the Bay of Bengal to the Hindu Kush. The Maurya Dynasty set up an efficient bureaucracy modeled after the Persians. Asoka, Chandragupta's grandson who ruled from 273–232 B.C., continued the Maurya conquest eastward until he ruled over two-thirds of India. Disturbed by the bloodshed of warfare, Asoka converted to Buddhism. He promoted Buddhism within India and sent Buddhist religious teachers to convert people of Southeast Asia and China. His efforts helped to make Buddhism a major religion and spread Indian culture throughout India. Asoka's rule united his diverse people and brought peace and prosperity. The capital at Pataliputra was one of the largest and richest cities of its time. After Asoka's death, the Maurya Empire declined. It was followed by five centuries of invasion, war, and disorder. In the 4th century A.D., the Gupta Empire, another native Indian family, established an empire embracing northern India. The Gupta Empire lasted from 320 to 535 A.D. The two centuries of Guptan rule are sometimes referred to as the Golden Age of India. Arts and literature flourished in the Gupta Empire. Artists painted colorful murals while writers created poems and plays in Sanskrit that are still recited and performed today. The best-known playwright was Kalidasa. His play *Shakuntali* is still performed today. In mathematics, Indian scholars developed the decimal system and the concept of zero. In the 6th century, the Gupta invaders from Central Asia, the Huns, overthrew the government. Around 1200, Muslim rulers set up a capital at Delhi. For 300 years, the Delhi sultanate or rulers governed much of northern and central India. The Delhi sultans generally did not force their Hindu subjects to adopt Islam. Instead, non-Muslims had to pay special taxes. Taxes on non-Muslims helped to support a lavish court. The Delhi sultans introduced Persian culture into Southeast Asia. Sultan Firuz Tughlak was a great builder. During his reign from 1351 to 1388, he supervised the building of 30

colleges, 50 dams and reservoirs, 100 hospitals, and 20 new towns. After the death of Firuz Tughlak, the Delhi sultanate declined. The Mongols from Central Asia descended into India and destroyed Delhi. The Mongols enslaved the entire population of the city and carried off the treasures. After the Mongols left to conquer other parts of India, the Delhi sultans were restored but never regained their former power and greatness.

WRONG CHOICES EXPLAINED:
(2), (3), and (4) None of these headings can be used for the partial outline. Latin American Civilizations would include the Aztecs, Mayans, or Incas. The Empire of the Fertile Crescent refers to the civilizations near the Tigris-Euphrates, such as the Sumerians and Assyrians. The Dynasties of China include ruling families such as the Chin or Han Dynasties.

47. **2** The set of events in the correct chronological order is the Treaty of Versailles in 1920, World War II in 1939, and the Korean War in 1950.

WRONG CHOICES EXPLAINED:
(1), (3), and (4) None of these sets of events are in correct chronological order. They should be as follows: The Roman Empire (27 B.C.–476 A.D.), the Middle Ages (6th–14th centuries) and the Renaissance (15th–16th centuries); The Crusades (1095–1291), the European exploration of the Americas (1492) and the Reformation (1517); The American Revolution (1776), the French Revolution (1789), and the Bolshevik Revolution (1917).

48. **2** The cartoon illustrates the tension that led to World War I. From 1815 to the beginning of the 20th century, Europe had experienced a long period of peace and growth. The Franco-Prussian War and the establishment of the German Empire in 1871 led to a new era of international relations. By 1914, Europe had come to be divided into two large camps of secret alliances. On one side was the Triple Alliance, consisting of Austria-Hungary, Germany, and Italy, and on the other side were Great Britain, France, and Russia, who joined together in an alliance of their own. Although these alliances sought to preserve the balance of power, disputes involving any two of these countries threatened to involve all the others. The excessive nationalism preceding World War I created jealously and hatred among the people of Europe. The Balkans were a hotbed of nationalistic rivalries. The spread of nationalism had led some groups to break away from the Ottoman Empire and form new nations including Bulgaria, Rumania, and Serbia. Each of these groups wanted to extend their borders. Serbia, which declared its independence in 1878, had a large Slavic population and hoped to absorb the Slavs of the Baltic Peninsula. Austria-Hungary opposed Serbian expansion because it feared rebellion among its own multiethnic empire and felt threatened by Serbia's growth. Serbia, for example, wanted to annex Bosnia-Herzegovina, which had a large Serbian population. Russia, the largest Slavic country, defended the rights of people of similar backgrounds to unite. Russia's big

brother policy became known as Pan-Slavism. Thus, by 1914, Russia was ready to support Serbia, its Slavic brother, against any threats. European powers such as Great Britain, France, and Germany, competed with each other over imperialistic interests in areas of Asia and Africa. Economic and military competition also led to tension among the European nations. Germany's growing economic and military strength threatened the balance of power in Europe. By 1912, Great Britain began to increase its military spending to compete with the Germans. The explosion that led to World War I was the assassination of Archduke Ferdinand of Austria-Hungary on June 28, 1914, by a Serbian nationalist, Gavriol Princip, who was a member of a secret group known as the Black Hand. The assassination set off a chain reaction that broke the peace of Europe. Austria-Hungary, supported by Germany, was determined to teach Serbia a lesson. Serbia was encouraged by its Slavic brother, Russia, to stand tough against Austrian demands. Russia turned to France, which promised its support against Germany and Austria. On July 28 Austria-Hungary invaded Serbia, and by July 30 Russia came to the aid of Serbia. As an ally of Austria-Hungary, Germany declared war on Russia and later on France. When Germany invaded Belgium on August 3 so that German forces could enter France more easily, Great Britain declared war on Germany. Thus, Russia, Germany, Austria-Hungary and France were at war with each other.

WRONG CHOICES EXPLAINED:

(1) This cartoon does not refer to the Franco-Prussian War, a conflict between France and Prussia that took place in 1870.

(3) This cartoon does not refer to World War II, a conflict started by Germany's attack on Poland in 1939.

(4) This cartoon does not refer to the Cold War, an ideological conflict between Russia and the United States, as well as a conflict between democracy and communism.

49. **1** The Panama Canal and the Suez Canal are similar in that both shortened shipping routes between major bodies of water. The Panama Canal is a man-made waterway connecting the Atlantic and Pacific Oceans. The canal was built in Panama by the United States in 1914. It allowed American fleets to move quickly between the Atlantic and Pacific Oceans and protected the coastlines on either side of the continent. The Panama Canal also greatly reduced the time of travel and the cost of trade between the two oceans. The Panama Canal, which took ten years to build, eliminated 7,800 miles from the sea voyages between New York and San Francisco. The canal cost $387 million to build. President Theodore Roosevelt, who strongly promoted the building of the Panama Canal, thought that the canal was necessary to boost American power in order for the United States to compete more effectively with the imperial powers of Europe and Japan. The Suez Canal is a man-made waterway that cuts through the Isthmus of Suez and connects the Red Sea and the Mediterranean Sea. It was opened in 1869. A French company

headed by Ferdinand de Lesseps built the Suez Canal, but the money and labor for the project came mostly from Egypt. The canal became a vital shortcut between Europe and Asia. The canal cut the distance between Europe and the East by thousands of miles and placed Egypt at the center of world trade. To Britain, the Suez Canal was the lifeline to India, the jewel of the British colonies. In 1875, Great Britain assumed control of the canal when Egypt was unable to repay loans that it had contracted for the canal and other modernization projects.

WRONG CHOICES EXPLAINED:

(2) Neither of these canals was built to expand the British Empire. These canals shortened the trading routes between major bodies of water. Furthermore, the French built the Suez Canal and the United States built the Panama Canal.

(3) The Silk Road was a system of ancient caravan routes across Central Asia, which carried silk and other trade goods.

(4) The Panama Canal connected the Atlantic and Pacific Oceans, but the Suez Canal connected the Red Sea with the Mediterranean Sea.

50. **1** The action taken by both Hitler and Napoleon considered by historians to be a strategic military error is invading Russia with limited supply lines. The goal of the Russian invasion was to gain control of the Ukraine's vast wheat fields and the Caucasus's oil fields. Hitler ordered a massive Blitzkrieg of three million men along a 2,000-mile border. By October 1941, German troops surrounded Leningrad in the north, which was within 25 miles of Moscow, and had conquered most of the Ukraine. Hitler's propaganda machine proclaimed the war to be over, but it was mistaken. Russia did not collapse; instead, history repeated itself. The German invaders were not prepared for the cold Russian winter; Germans, in summer uniform, froze to death as the temperature plunged to −20 degrees Fahrenheit. Their fuel and oil froze as trucks and weapons became useless. At the Siege of Leningrad, which lasted 900 days, the Russians fought valiantly. More than 1.5 million citizens died during this siege and some inhabitants even resorted to cannibalism to survive. Hitler's failure to conquer Russia drained Germany's resources and ultimately contributed to Germany's defeat. In June 1812, Napoleon decided to invade Russia when Czar Alexander I withdrew from the Continental System that forbade European countries to trade with England. Alexander I refused to stop selling grain to Britain. Leading a huge army of 600,000 men, Napoleon marched into Russia. Czar Alexander pulled back his troops and refused to be trapped in a battle, causing Napoleon to overextend his supply lines. As the Russians retreated, they adopted a scorched earth policy of burning crops and villages. Desperate soldiers deserted the French army to search for scraps of food. When Napoleon captured Moscow in September, he found the city in ashes. Russian patriots destroyed most of the city. By October, when the Czar did not make a peace offer, Napoleon was too late to advance and perhaps too late even to retreat.

He could not feed and supply his army through the long Russian winter. In October, he ordered his starving army to retreat. The 1,000-mile retreat from Moscow turned into a desperate battle. Russian raiders attacked Napoleon's ragged army. Soldiers staggered through the snow and dropped in their tracks as the temperatures fell to 35 degrees below zero. Napoleon lost three-fourths of his army. The failure of Hitler and Napoleon to plan for the size and weather of Russia contributed to their defeat.

WRONG CHOICES EXPLAINED:

(2) Hitler and Napoleon did not use any naval assaults with the invasion of Russia.

(3) Hitler and Napoleon never invaded Great Britain by land. Napoleon's navy was not strong enough to invade Great Britain. Hitler sought to defeat Great Britain by the use of the German Air Force.

(4) Hitler and Napoleon did not use conquered peoples as slave laborers during the invasion of Russia. Napoleon and Hitler were never able to enslave the people of Russia.

THEMATIC ESSAY: GENERIC SCORING RUBRIC

Score of 5:
- Shows a thorough understanding of the theme or problem
- Addresses all aspects of the task
- Shows an ability to analyze, evaluate, compare and/or contrast issues and events
- Richly supports the theme or problem with relevant facts, examples, and details
- Is a well-developed essay, consistently demonstrating a logical and clear plan of organization
- Introduces the theme or problem by establishing a framework that is beyond a simple restatement of the task and concludes with a summation of the theme or problem

Score of 4:
- Shows a good understanding of the theme or problem
- Addresses all aspects of the task
- Shows an ability to analyze, evaluate, compare and/or contrast issues and events
- Includes relevant facts, examples, and details, but may not support all aspects of the theme or problem evenly
- Is a well-developed essay, demonstrating a logical and clear plan of organization
- Introduces the theme or problem by establishing a framework that is beyond a simple restatement of the task and concludes with a summation of the theme or problem

Score of 3:
- Shows a satisfactory understanding of the theme or problem
- Addresses most aspects of the task or addresses all aspects in a limited way
- Shows an ability to analyze or evaluate issues and events, but not in any depth
- Includes some facts, examples, and details
- Is a satisfactorily developed essay, demonstrating a general plan of organization
- Introduces the theme or problem by repeating the task and concludes by repeating the theme or problem

Score of 2:
- Shows limited understanding of the theme or problem
- Attempts to address the task
- Develops a faulty analysis or evaluation of issues and events
- Includes few facts, examples, and details, and may include information that contains inaccuracies
- Is a poorly organized essay, lacking focus
- Fails to introduce or summarize the theme or problem

Score of 1:
- Shows very limited understanding of the theme or problem
- Lacks an analysis of evaluation of the issues and events
- Includes little or no accurate or relevant facts, examples, or details

• Attempts to complete the task, but demonstrates a major weakness in organization
• Fails to introduce or summarize the theme or problem

Score of 0: Fails to address the task, is illegible, or is a blank paper

PART II: THEMATIC ESSAY QUESTION

Throughout history, developments have occurred that have changed the world. These changes have had a lasting impact on society. Two of these turning points were the Renaissance and the Russian Revolution. Both of these events have altered the course of history.

The Renaissance, which means rebirth in French, was a period of artistic achievements and changes in Europe from the 1300s to 1500s. The Renaissance was a rebirth in the sense that it changed the way people looked at the world. Beginning in Italy in the 1300s and spreading northward, Italy had three advantages that helped to foster the Renaissance spirit: thriving cities, a wealthy merchant class, and the classical heritage of Greece and Rome. Unlike other areas of Europe, the Italian city-states had survived the Bubonic Plague and the wars of the Middle Ages. Overseas, trade, spurred by the Crusades, led to the growth of large city-states in northern Italy. Thus, northern Italy was urban while the rest of Europe was still mostly rural. These city-states became the breeding grounds for the intellectual revolution of the Renaissance.

The revival of trade in northern Italy contributed to the rise of a wealthy merchant class that had not inherited wealth like the nobles but depended on their own abilities to survive. Many of these successful merchants believed they deserved power and wealth because of their individual merit. The importance of individualism was a major theme of the Renaissance. These wealthy merchants, such as the Medici family in Florence and the Sforza family in Milan, became leading patrons of literature, art, and society.

Italian artists and scholars were also at an advantage because they drew their inspiration from the ruins of Ancient Rome, which surrounded them. Italy had once been at the center of the Roman Empire. Architectural remains, statues, and amphitheaters were visible reminders to Italians of the Glory of Rome. The Renaissance looked to the ancient civilizations of Greece and Rome, not to the Middle Ages, as a guide for their work.

The Renaissance changed the way people looked at the world. During the Middle Ages, the people were concerned with faith, authority, and tradition. The Renaissance emphasized reason and experimentation, glorified the individual, and viewed life as worthwhile for its own sake. While the Middle Ages focused on life as a preparation for the afterlife, the Renaissance stressed the secular world rather than the medieval preoccupation with religion and the Roman Catholic Church.

The new way of thinking led to the spirit of Humanism. The Humanist writers were more curious about life in the present rather than life after death. Humanism was a distinct literary movement that broke from the medieval tradition of writing literature that just had pious or religious themes. The Humanists examined world subjects that the Ancient Greeks had studied. They hoped to use ancient learning to increase their knowledge about their own times. Petrarch, who is considered the Father of Humanism, wrote sonnets about his love for the beautiful Laura. Humanist interest in the world was also expressed in the literature of the day. They wrote in the vernacular, the native language of ordinary people. Instead of Latin and Greek, they used Italian, French, English, and other languages.

The Renaissance also produced some of the greatest paintings, sculptures, and architecture in the history of the world. Renaissance architects rejected medieval forms of architecture. They returned to Greek and Roman styles for columns, arches, and domes. The art of the Renaissance reflected human concerns. Many paintings still had religious themes but were more realistic in recreating biblical events. Michelangelo's *Pietà*, showing Mary grieving over the dead Jesus, expresses this more realistic approach to art. Da Vinci's *Mona Lisa*, which is one of the best-known paintings in the world, expresses the realism of Renaissance art. The woman in the portrait seems so real that many writers have tried to explain the thoughts behind the smile.

Renaissance sculptors, such as Donatello and Michelangelo, demonstrated their realism and belief in the importance of the individual. These sculptors studied the human anatomy and often worked from live models so that they could portray the body in amazing detail. Donatello's *David* was the first European sculpture of a free-standing nude since classical times. Michelangelo's *David* glorifies the power of the individual. The 18-foot tall biblical figure in the city of Florence conveys power and a sense of inspiration to the people of Florence in their struggle against the rival city-state of Milan.

The Renaissance spirit also changed the way scientists looked at the world. Renaissance scientists began to challenge the Church's teaching that the earth was the center of the universe. They challenged other theories and medieval superstitions based on Aristotle's view of the world. Their approach was based on observation and experimentation, not faith. This approach laid the foundation for the Scientific Revolution and the Enlightenment in the next centuries.

The Renaissance's distinctive ideas about life, with a focus on individualism, the secular world, and the importance of reason, altered Europe and the world for generations to come.

Another major turning point in the world was the Russian or Bolshevik Revolution of 1917. An underlying cause of the Russian Revolution was that compared to Western Europe, Russia was an undeveloped nation. The Romanov czars who had ruled Russia for close to 300 years were absolute rulers. Through the secret police, the czars vigorously suppressed demands for reform and punished reformers by imprisonment, execution, or exile to Siberia. Economically, Russia had not been industrialized. Serfs or farmers made up more than 75 percent of the population. They were still bound to the land like the serfs of the Middle Ages.

In the late 19th century, Alexander III and his son, Nicholas II, began the process of industrializing Russia. The landless peasants provided the cheap labor and French investors provided the resources. The Russians constructed iron and steel mills, textile factories, and railroads. Russia's Industrial Revolution created two new economic classes: workers and capitalists. The workers and the middle-class business owners began to demand more rights. Both groups desired a voice in the government and opposed Czarist absolutism.

The immediate cause of the Russian Revolution was Russia's involvement in World War I. The country was unprepared for war. Russian industries were not developed enough to meet the demands for war supplies. The transportation system could not supply the armies at the front. At one time, only one out of three soldiers had a rifle. Poorly equipped troops suffered enormous losses. Due to the war, people faced shortages of food and other goods, especially in the cities. Nicholas II ignored demands to withdraw from the war and did nothing to improve these conditions. In March 1917, riots and strikes erupted in Petrograd, the Russian capital. Angry crowds protested the war and shortages of food. When Czar Nicholas II's troops refused to fire on the striking city workers and some joined the protest, the Russian Revolution had officially begun. Nicholas II abdicated and a new provisional government headed by Alexander Kerensky was established. This new government guaranteed civil liberties, but refused to withdraw from the war. When the Kerensky government was unable to solve the food crisis and refused to support the land seizures by the peasants, the Bolsheviks, under the leadership of Nikolai Lenin, began to gain supporters using the slogan of Peace, Land, and Bread. The Bolsheviks gained followers because they promised to end the war, provide food for the people, and obtain land for the peasants. On November 7, 1917, armed Bolsheviks seized power and set up a communist government.

The Revolution turned Russia into a communist country, which affected Europe, as well as the rest of the world. In 1922, the communists reorganized Russia into a union of four republics. They renamed the country the Union of Soviet Socialist Republics (USSR), or the Soviet Union.

The Russian Revolution also created the fear that communism would spread to other countries. The fear of communism contributed to the rise of fascism in Italy and Nazism in Germany. The ideas of communism led to the rise of Mao Zedong in China and Fidel Castro in Cuba. The Communist Revolution also led to tensions with the United States. The Cold War, which lasted from 1945 to 1989, has often been described as a struggle between the forces of democracy and communism. The Cold War also led to the development of nuclear arsenals that threatened the safety of the universe.

Although the Soviet Union collapsed in 1990, communism still exists in Cuba and China. The fall of communism in Russia has left the country with unresolved economic, social, and political issues. Poverty is still a problem in Russia, and the quality of life continues to decline.

Both the Renaissance and the Russian Revolution impacted their own era and continue to influence us today. The Renaissance not only changed our view from the religious to the secular world but also stressed the role of the individual in society. The focus of the creative individual has been an underlying theme of Western society. In Russia, the aftermath of communism still affects the country. There is concern whether Russia can solve its economic problems and whether it can ever become a democratic nation. European nations and the United States realize that the stability of the continent and the world is dependent upon Russia's playing a constructive role in the coming years.

PART III: DOCUMENT-BASED QUESTION

Part A: Short Answers

Document 1

Two reasons that help from Britain was needed in the Malay States are

(1) Trained British civil servants organized a system of government that established order and trained civil servants to help advise rulers.
(2) The British provided sufficient revenue to meet all the charges of a government.

Note: This response receives full credit because it correctly states two reasons why British help was needed in the Malay States.

Document 2

One effect of British colonial rule on Africa was that the Africans were Christianized and also lost their land.

Note: This response receives full credit because it correctly identifies an effect of British rule on Africa.

Documents 3a and 3b

Two reasons for imperialism were

(1) The demands of giant industries for colonial raw materials.
(2) Industrial nations needed markets for their manufactured goods as part of a worldwide rivalry for markets.

Note: This response receives full credit because it cites two specific reasons for imperialism.

Document 4a

This advertisement shows that the British had interests in Ceylon because they could make a profit from their tea.

Note: This response receives full credit because it shows the reason for British interests in Ceylon.

Document 4b

The cartoon shows that the British were interested in Africa because they wanted to gain gold.

Note: This response receives full credit because it correctly states why the British were interested in Africa.

Document 5

Two ways that India changed under British rule are

(1) The British improved sanitation and raised the standard of living for India.
(2) The British developed means of communication and built more than 40,000 miles of railway.

Note: This response receives full credit because it cites the ways in which India changed under British rule.

Document 6

According to Lord Lugard, two ways the British helped Africa are

(1) They put an end to slavery.

(2) They established a Court of Law and system of education that produced happiness and progress.

Note: This response receives full credit because it identifies the ways the British helped Africa.

Document 7

Based on this document, two reasons Gandhi wanted to drive away the English are

(1) The British kept the Indians in a state of slavery.

(2) The British took away their money and disregarded their feelings.

Note: This response receives full credit because it quotes a portion of the document to identify why Gandhi wanted to drive away the British.

Document 8

Based on this document, two ways British colonialism harmed Africa are

(1) Education was limited to the privileged and hospitals were available only to a small minority.

(2) Racial segregation and discrimination made it difficult for Africans to develop full personalities.

Note: This response receives full credit because it cites specific ways in which British colonialism harmed Africa.

DOCUMENT-BASED QUESTION:
GENERIC SCORING RUBRIC

Score of 5:
- Thoroughly addresses all aspects of the *Task* by accurately analyzing and interpreting at least **four** documents
- Incorporates information from the documents in the body of the essay
- Incorporates relevant outside information
- Richly supports the theme or problem with relevant facts, examples, and details
- Is a well-developed essay, consistently demonstrating a logical and clear plan of organization
- Introduces the theme or problem by establishing a framework that is beyond a simple restatement of the *Task* or *Historical Context* and concludes with a summation of the theme or problem

Score of 4:
- Addresses all aspects of the *Task* by accurately analyzing and interpreting at least **four** documents
- Incorporates information from the documents in the body of the essay
- Incorporates relevant outside information
- Includes relevant facts, examples, and details, but discussion may be more descriptive than analytical
- Is a well-developed essay, demonstrating a logical and clear plan of organization
- Introduces the theme or problem by establishing a framework that is beyond a simple restatement of the *Task* or *Historical Context* and concludes with a summation of the theme or problem

Score of 3:
- Addresses most aspects of the *Task* or addresses all aspects of the *Task* in a limited way, using some of the documents
- Incorporates some information from the documents in the body of the essay
- Incorporates limited or no relevant outside information
- Includes some facts, examples, and details, but discussion is more descriptive than analytical
- Is a satisfactorily developed essay, demonstrating a general plan of organization
- Introduces the theme or problem by repeating the *Task* or *Historical Context* and concludes by simply repeating the theme or problem

Score of 2:
- Attempts to address some aspects of the *Task*, making limited use of the documents
- Presents no relevant outside information
- Includes few facts, examples, and details; discussion restates contents of the documents

- Is a poorly organized essay, lacking focus
- Fails to introduce or summarize the theme or problem

Score of 1:
- Shows limited understanding of the *Task* with vague, unclear references to the documents
- Presents no relevant outside information
- Includes little or no accurate or relevant facts, details, or examples
- Attempts to complete the *Task*, but demonstrates a major weakness in organization
- Fails to introduce or summarize the theme or problem

Score of 0: Fails to address the *Task*, is illegible, or is a blank paper

Part B: Essay

The British Empire expanded in the 1800s to include territories that spread over several continents. Economic, political, and social causes influenced British Imperialism. The New Imperialism of the late 19th century refers to the renewed expansion of British Imperialism in India, Africa, and Asia. Imperialism allowed the British to extend political and economic control over these areas. While British Imperialism had some positive benefits for the colonial people, it also left a negative legacy that continues to affect these areas today.

At the beginning of the 19th century, the British controlled India, South Africa, and parts of East Asia. While Britain was expanding in its early years, many British people thought the colonies were more trouble than they were worth. Economist Adam Smith argued that the burdens of colonialism outweighed the benefits. As late as 1868, British Prime Minister Benjamin Disraeli called the colonies "a millstone around our necks." However, by the 1880s, economic factors contributed to the growth of the British Empire. The Industrial Revolution created the need for Great Britain to expand its markets globally in order to sell those products that could not be sold domestically on the continent. The British needed colonies because they could sell cotton and iron goods to their subjugated people (Doc. 3a). British industries also needed a steady supply of raw materials, such as rubber, petroleum, iron, coal, and cotton, to keep operating (Doc. 3b). Only by directly controlling these regions could the industrial economy work effectively.

Britain looked at other areas for other specific needs. The British were interested in Ceylon, an island off the coast of India, for their tea and in Africa for their gold (Doc. 4a and 4b). The acquisition of these areas allowed the British to extend their economic dominance and increased the wealth of the empire. Businessmen and bankers also had excess capital and invested in colonies and colonial companies in the hope of making even greater profits.

The struggle for colonies increased competition among the European nations of Great Britain, France, Germany, and Italy. In 1884–1885, 14

European nations met at the Berlin Conference to outline the rules for the division of Africa. The Berlin Conference was designed to prevent fighting over colonial territory in Africa and insure that one power did not dominate the continent. The Berlin Conference began the "Scramble for Africa," with little regard for the rights of the colonial people. The colonies became important for political as well as economic reasons. Great Britain, Germany, and other European nations began to believe that the colonies were crucial to military power and national security. In order to satisfy these needs, colonies were used as military bases for resupplying ships for defense as well as for economic benefits.

There were also social and humanitarian reasons behind Britain's expansion. Cecil Rhodes, a believer in Social Darwinism, claimed that the British were the superior race and it was their obligation to educate and civilize other people. Rudyard Kipling expressed this mission in the 1890s when he proclaimed that it was "The White Man's Burden" to civilize the uncivilized people of Africa and Asia. The British also believed that they were needed to set up order and government in colonies, such as Malay (Doc. 1). Lord Lugard reinforced this belief when he asserted that it was the task of British civilization to promote freedom and justice (Doc. 6).

The British control of its vast empire had positive and negative effects on those living in the colonies. In Malay, British officials taught the Malaysians how to effectively administrate a government. They brought justice and freedom and provided revenue to the country so that the government could use the money to build railroads and hospitals to improve the lives of the people (Doc. 1). Clearly, the British helped to stabilize Malay.

The British helped India by increasing British exports to India (Doc. 3). The British, who controlled India from 1763, tried to make it the "Jewel of the British Crown." They improved India by building more than 40,000 miles of railways and 70,000 miles of metalled roads. They added to the agricultural wealth of the country by bringing 30,000,000 acres under cultivation (Doc. 5). The British also helped India by adding canals to improve transportation and improved irrigation and sanitation, thus raising the standard of living for the people in India (Doc. 5). These improvements helped India to conquer the problem of famine (Doc. 3). The introduction of Western medicine also helped to save lives and to improve infant mortality rates.

The introduction of Western ideas also forced colonies in India to reevaluate their traditions, such as Sati. Sati was the custom in which virtuous women (*sati*) threw themselves on their husbands' funeral fire in the hope that the sacrificial act would wipe away the sins of their husbands and themselves.

Great Britain's imperial power over India also had a negative effect. According to Gandhi, the British impoverished India, controlled the Indian government instead of letting the Indians rule, and disregarded the interests of India in most instances (Doc. 7). The British became rich from Ceylon's tea (Doc. 4) and Indian industries had to compete with British manufacturers, which contributed to the poverty of India (Doc. 5).

British rule in India also brought cultural confrontations between the two cultures. The British insulted the Indian culture (Doc. 7). They were insolent to the Hindus and Muslims in 1857 when they issued new rifles and cartridges to the Sepoys (native Indian soldiers). The troops were told to bite off the tips of cartridges before loading them into their rifles. The cartridges were greased with animal fat, either from cows, which the Hindus considered sacred, or from pigs, which was forbidden to the Muslims. The troops' refusal to load their rifles led to the Sepoy Rebellion, which swept across northern and central India. The British brutally crushed the rebellion.

The British Empire also had a positive effect in Africa. The British brought the Bible because they felt that it was their duty to bring religion and civilization to the people of Africa (Doc. 2) as part of the "White Man's Burden." The British believed that religion would improve conditions for the colonial people of Africa. The British also brought about the end of slavery, established courts of law, and applied the British principle of freedom and impartial justice (Doc. 6). They also taught the people a sense of individual responsibility of liberty and justice and taught them how to apply these ideas to their government. Finally, the British introduced a system of education that improved the quality of life for Africans.

Although the British brought many positive changes to Africa, their colonial rule had many negative effects. In Africa, British missionaries used religion to steal their lands. As Desmond Tutu said, "They had the Bible and we had the land" (Doc. 2). The British destroyed African native customs and tribal religions. The British also tolerated racial segregation, known as apartheid, which plagued South Africa until the end of the 20th century.

In Nigeria, the benefits of British rule, such as hospitals and educational opportunities, were available to only a small minority of the people (Doc. 8). The penal system was oppressive in Africa, and there was a lack of basic services, such as water, postal, and transportation. Religious freedom, like other so-called benefits, was limited to a small minority (Doc. 8). British rule and racial discrimination stifled the development of the African continent. The British also contributed to ethnic violence in the 20th century in such countries as Nigeria and Rwanda. Britain, like other imperial European countries, drew boundary lines for many nations disregarding the ethnicities of the people living in these areas.

During the 1800s, the British expanded to become the largest empire in the world. By 1914, the British Empire covered an area nearly 100 times larger than Britain. About one-fourth of the world's population was under British rule. The British controlled territories on every continent except Antarctica and boasted that the "Sun never set on the British Empire." This vast empire was an outgrowth of the economic thrust of the Industrial Revolution, which created the need for markets and raw materials. The competitive pressure among the European nations and the belief that the British thought it was their duty to spread the benefits of their superior culture further contributed to their overseas expansion. British colonial rule brought positive benefits, such as better transportation systems, stable government, and improved sanitation. However, colonial rule also oppressed the governed people and destroyed native culture and their economies.

The consequences of British rule and imperialism in different parts of the world is difficult to assess. However, there is little doubt that both the West and the colonial areas have been altered by the spread of the British Empire.

Topic	Question Numbers	Total Number of Questions	Number Wrong	*Reason for Wrong Answer
U.S. AND N.Y. HISTORY				
WORLD HISTORY	1, 5, 8, 10, 12, 15, 16, 17, 18, 24, 26, 31, 32, 33, 36, 37, 38, 40, 43, 45, 46, 47, 48, 50	24		
GEOGRAPHY	3, 7, 9, 11, 19, 20, 21, 27, 30, 35, 39, 42, 49	13		
ECONOMICS	4, 14, 22, 28, 29, 34	6		
CIVICS, CITIZENSHIP, AND GOVERNMENT	2, 6, 13, 23, 25, 41, 44	7		

*Your reason for answering the question incorrectly might be (a) lack of knowledge, (b) misunderstanding the question, or (c) careless error.

Actual Items by Standard and Unit

	1 U.S. and N.Y. History	2 World History	3 Geography	4 Economics	5 Civics, Citizenship, and Gov't	Number
Methodology of Global History and Geography		1				1
UNIT ONE Ancient World		5, 10, 12	3, 7	4	6	7
UNIT TWO Expanding Zones of Exchange		8				1
UNIT THREE Global Interactions		15	9, 19, 20	14	13	6
UNIT FOUR First Global Age		16, 17, 18	21, 27	22		6
UNIT FIVE Age of Revolution		24, 26, 31, 32	11, 30	28, 29	25	9
UNIT SIX Crisis and Achievement (1900–1945)		33, 36, 48	35	34	2	6
UNIT SEVEN 20th Century Since 1945		37				1
UNIT EIGHT Global Connections and Interactions		45	39, 42			3
Cross topical		38, 40, 43, 46, 47, 50	49		23, 41, 44	10
Total # of Questions		24	13	6	7	50
% of Items by Standard		48%	26%	12%	14%	100%

Examination
August 2004
Global History and Geography

PART I: MULTIPLE CHOICE

Directions (1–50): For each statement or question, write in the space provided, the *number* of the word or expression that, of those given, best completes the statement or answers the question.

1 Which geographic feature had the greatest influence on the development of ancient civilizations?

 1 dense forests 3 smooth coastlines
 2 mountain passes 4 river valleys 1 ____

2 What is one characteristic of a society that practices subsistence agriculture?

 1 growth of surplus crops for export
 2 production of crops mainly for its own use
 3 establishment of large state-owned farms
 4 dependence on the use of slave labor for the production of crops 2 ____

3 What was one cause of the development of many small independent city-states in ancient Greece?

1 Greece and Rome were often at war.
2 The mountainous terrain of Greece resulted in widely scattered settlements.
3 Military leaders found small Greek settlements easy to control.
4 The Greek people had many different languages and religions. 3____

4 In India, Bangladesh, and much of Southeast Asia, agricultural productivity is most affected by the

1 seasonal monsoons   3 numerous deserts
2 unnavigable rivers   4 cold climate   4____

5 Which belief is shared by Hindus and Buddhists?

1 Everyone should have the same social status.
2 People should pray five times a day.
3 The soul can be reincarnated.
4 Material wealth is a sign of the blessing of the gods. 5____

Base your answer to question 6 on the passage below and on your knowledge of social studies.

... Muslims, Christians, and Jews lived together in peace. Because several Christian and Jewish prophets, including Adam, Abraham, and Moses, are named in the Qur'an and because the Jewish Torah and Christian gospels are recognized as revelations from Allah, the Muslim rulers called Christians and Jews "people of the Book" and permitted them much religious and personal freedom. Jews, especially, enjoyed many liberties, and many Jews distinguished themselves in science, the arts, and government. *Convivencia*, a Spanish word meaning "living together," helped make tenth-century al-Andalus the most civilized country in Europe. ...

—Lawrence Houghteling, "Al-Andalus: Islamic Spain," *Calliope*, Nov.–Dec. 1995

6 What is the main idea of this passage?

1 The Torah and the Bible were rejected in Muslim Spain.
2 Arabs, Jews, and Christians shared houses and places of worship in Muslim Spain.
3 Religious tolerance in Muslim Spain encouraged the growth of a rich and diverse culture.
4 Spain was troubled by deep-rooted religious conflicts.   6____

_____

7 Some historians suggest that as a result of the Mongol invasions of Russia, the Russian people were

1 united with the Ottomans
2 converted to Christianity
3 freed from serfdom
4 cut off from most of western Europe   7____

Base your answers to questions 8 and 9 on the map below and on your knowledge of social studies.

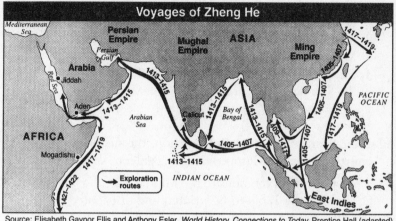

Source: Elisabeth Gaynor Ellis and Anthony Esler, *World History, Connections to Today,* Prentice Hall (adapted)

8 The map shows that on his voyages, Zheng He explored

  1 both the Pacific and the Atlantic Oceans
  2 at the same time as the Spanish explorers
  3 lands in the Western Hemisphere
  4 Arabia and the east coast of Africa   8 _____

9 One result of the voyages of Zheng He was that

  1 Chinese merchants began trading with Africa
  2 Christian missionaries arrived in China
  3 Indian artisans showed the Chinese how to make Ming porcelain
  4 China set up colonies in Europe   9 _____

10 Many achievements of Islamic civilization reached European society by way of the

  1 Crusades and eastern Mediterranean trading networks

  2 merchant guilds and the Industrial Revolution

  3 Middle Passage and the Columbian Exchange

  4 conquests of the Germanic tribes and trade along the Silk Road   10____

11 Prior to the Protestant Reformation, the medieval church in western Europe was criticized for

  1 sponsoring explorations to the Middle East

  2 allowing the Bible to be printed and distributed to the people

  3 being too concerned with worldly power and riches

  4 refusing to sell indulgences to peasants   11____

Base your answer to question 12 on the map below and on your knowledge of social studies.

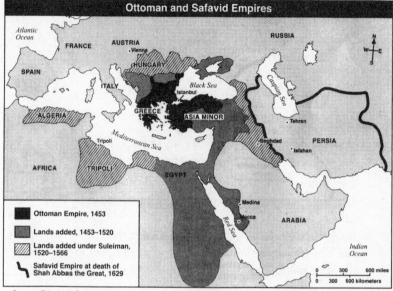

Source: Elisabeth Gaynor Ellis and Anthony Esler, *World History: Connections to Today*, Prentice Hall (adapted)

12 Which generalization is best supported by the information in this map?

  1 The Ottoman Empire controlled the largest amount of territory by 1453.

  2 The Safavid Empire controlled parts of western Europe by 1629.

  3 By the 1500s, the Ottoman Empire controlled parts of the Middle East, North Africa, and eastern Europe.

  4 The Mediterranean Sea served as a cultural barrier between Asia Minor and North Africa.   12 ____

13 Which statement about the geography of Africa is most accurate?

1 Much of the land in Africa is below sea level.
2 The variety of geographic barriers has served to promote cultural diversity.
3 Africa has an irregular coastline with many natural harbors.
4 Much of the land in Africa is tundra and forest. 13 _____

14 Which statement best describes an impact of geography on the history of the Korean peninsula?

1 Large deserts have led to isolation.
2 Location has led to invasion and occupation by other nations.
3 Lack of rivers has limited food production.
4 Lack of natural resources has prevented development of manufacturing. 14 _____

15 ". . . If from now on the King starts by rising early and going to bed late, and if the ministers take oaths among themselves to cut out the evils of parties and merriment, be diligent in cultivating frugality and virtue, do not allow private considerations from taking root in their minds, and do not use artifice as a method of operation in government affairs, then the officials and common people will all cleanse and purify their minds and be in great accord with his will. . . ."

—Yi Hang-no, Korean Royal Adviser

Which Confucian principle is reflected in this statement?

1 The ruler must set an example for the people.
2 Respect for elders is the foundation of civilization.
3 Virtue increases with education.
4 Compassion and sympathy for others is important.   15____

16 Which action would best complete this partial outline?

I. Byzantine Heritage
  A. Blended Christian beliefs with Greek art and philosophy
  B. Extended Roman engineering achievements
  C. Preserved literature and science textbooks
  D. _____

1 Adapted the Roman principles of justice
2 Used a senate as the chief governing body
3 Led crusades to capture Rome from the Huns
4 Helped maintain Roman rule over western Europe   16____

17 The expeditions of Hernán Cortés and Francisco Pizarro resulted in the

1 destruction of the Aztec and Inca empires
2 capture of Brazil by Portugal
3 colonization of North America by Portugal
4 exploration of the Philippines and East Indies   17 _____

18 Which statement best describes a result of the Glorious Revolution in England (1688)?

1 England formed an alliance with France.
2 The power of the monarchy was increased.
3 Principles of limited government were strengthened.
4 England lost its colonial possessions.   18 _____

19 One reason Italy and Germany were not major colonial powers in the 16th and 17th centuries was that they

1 had self-sufficient economies
2 lacked political unity
3 rejected the practice of imperialism
4 belonged to opposing alliances   19 _____

20 The ideas of Rousseau, Voltaire, and Montesquieu most influenced

1 the growing power of priests in the Roman Catholic Church
2 improvements in the working conditions of factory workers
3 the rise of industrial capitalism
4 movements for political reform   20 _____

21 During the late 19th century, which geographic factor helped attract European investors to southern Africa and southeast Asia?

  1 smooth coastlines
  2 navigable rivers
  3 natural resources
  4 temperate climates

21 _____

22 One result of the Opium War was that China

  1 adopted democratic reforms
  2 gained control of Hong Kong
  3 regained control of Manchuria
  4 was divided into spheres of influence

22 _____

Base your answers to questions 23 and 24 on the maps below and on your knowledge of social studies.

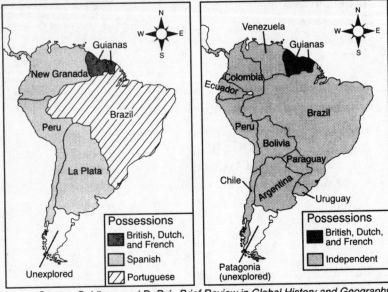

South America, 1790

South America, 1828

Source: Goldberg and DuPré, *Brief Review in Global History and Geography,* Prentice Hall (adapted)

23 Based on a comparison of these maps of South America, which conclusion is accurate?

1 Many regions of South America gained their independence between 1790 and 1828.

2 All of South America was independent by 1828.

3 Spain continued to gain South American colonies in the 19th century.

4 Between 1790 and 1828, South American political boundaries remained unchanged except for Brazil.   23 ____

24 Which individual is most closely associated with the changes indicated on these maps?

1 Emiliano Zapata
2 Simón Bolívar
3 Porfirio Díaz
4 Pancho Villa

24____

25 "... The replacement of the bourgeois by the proletarian state is impossible without a violent revolution. The abolition of the proletarian state, i.e., of all states, is only possible through 'withering away.' ..."

—V.I. Lenin, *State and Revolution*, 1917

This quotation is associated with the principles of
1 imperialism   3 communism
2 capitalism   4 militarism

25____

26 In Europe during the 1920s and 1930s, severe inflation, high unemployment, and fear of communism all contributed to the

1 overthrow of monarchies in Italy and Germany
2 rise of Fascist governments in Italy, Germany, and Spain
3 formation of the Common Market in Italy and Spain
4 growth of democratic institutions

26____

Base your answer to question 27 on the cartoon below and on your knowledge of social studies.

THE WORLD'S PLUNDERERS.
"It's English, you know."

Source: Thomas Nast, *Harper's Weekly*, June 20, 1885
(adapted)

27 This Thomas Nast cartoon shows the

1 competition between European nations for over-seas territories after the Berlin Conference
2 aggressive action of the Triple Alliance before World War I
3 spread of communism throughout the world during the 19th century
4 concern of European nations for the welfare of developing nations at the end of the 19th century

27 _____

28 **"Gandhi Calls for Boycott of British Textiles"**
"Gandhi and Followers Complete March to the Sea"
"Gandhi Begins Hunger Fast"

These headlines reflect Gandhi's belief in

1 nonalignment   3 appeasement
2 isolationism   4 nonviolence   28____

Base your answers to questions 29 and 30 on the passage below and on your knowledge of social studies.

. . . "From the beginning," says Marquis Ito, "we realized fully how necessary it was that the Japanese people should not only adopt Western methods, but should also speedily become competent to do without the aid of foreign instruction and supervision. In the early days we brought many foreigners to Japan to help to introduce modern methods, but we always did it in such a way as to enable the Japanese students to take their rightful place in the nation after they had been educated.". . .

—Alfred Stead, *Great Japan: A Study of National Efficiency*, John Lane Co., 1906

29 Which occurrence in Japanese history is described in the passage?

1 Meiji Restoration
2 Tokugawa shogunate
3 assimilation of Buddhism
4 adoption of Confucian practices   29____

30 The author of the passage suggests that Japan

1 remained isolated
2 accepted new technologies in order to modernize
3 became dependent on foreign nations
4 became militaristic   30____

31 • Japan resigns from the League of Nations, 1933
   • Rome-Berlin-Tokyo Axis formed, 1936
   • Japan invades China, 1937
   • United States places embargo on scrap iron, steel, and oil exports to Japan, 1941

Which event occurred immediately after this series of developments?

1 Manchuria became a Japanese protectorate.
2 Pearl Harbor was attacked.
3 The Japanese fleet was destroyed.
4 The atomic bomb was dropped on Hiroshima.   31 _____

Base your answer to question 32 on the maps below and on your knowledge of social studies.

Source: Henry Abraham and Irwin Pfeffer, *Enjoying World History*, AMSCO (adapted)

32 Which factor was the most significant force in causing the changes between 1914 and 1919 as shown on the two maps?

1 worldwide depression
2 treaties signed at the end of World War I
3 rise of Mussolini
4 dissatisfaction of the German people   32 _____

Base your answer to question 33 on the excerpt below and on your knowledge of social studies. This excerpt is taken from a poem written about World War I.

"If I should die, think only this of me:
That there's some corner of a foreign field
That is for ever England. There shall be
In that rich earth a richer dust concealed;
A dust whom England bore, shaped, made aware,
Gave, once, her flowers to love, her ways to roam,
A body of England's, breathing English air,
Washed by the rivers, blest by suns of home. . . .

—Rupert Brooke, "The Soldier"

33 Which idea is expressed in this excerpt from Brooke's poem?

1 pacifism
2 neutrality
3 nationalism
4 anarchy

33 _____

34 A major result of the Nuremberg trials after World War II was that

1 Germany was divided into four zones of occupation
2 the United Nations was formed to prevent future acts of genocide
3 the North Atlantic Treaty Organization (NATO) was established to stop the spread of communism
4 Nazi political and military leaders were held accountable for their actions

34 _____

35 The continued importance of the Middle East to the global economy is based on its

1 research facilities
2 exports of manufactured goods
3 semiarid climate
4 quantity of oil reserves

35 _____

Base your answer to question 36 on the chart below and on your knowledge of social studies.

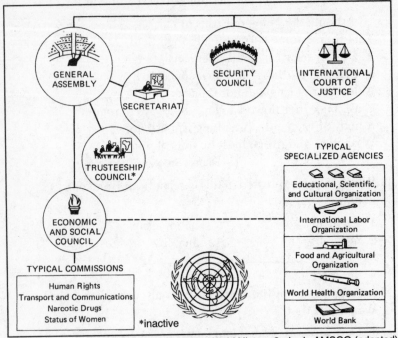

Source: Irving L. Gordon, *World History*, 2nd ed., AMSCO (adapted)

36 This chart shows the organization of the

1 United Nations (UN)
2 North Atlantic Treaty Organization (NATO)
3 European Union (EU)
4 Organization of American States (OAS)   36 _____

37 ". . . The Nazi holocaust, which engulfed millions of Jews in Europe, proved anew the urgency of the re-establishment of the Jewish state, which would solve the problem of Jewish homelessness by opening the gates to all Jews and lifting the Jewish people to equality in the family of nations. . . ."

This statement is referring to the establishment of which nation?

1 Jordan   3 Israel
2 Poland   4 Ethiopia   37____

38 Which statement related to the recent history of Pakistan is an opinion?

1 Pakistan gained its independence from Britain in 1947.
2 The majority of the people who live in Pakistan are Muslims.
3 Pakistan would be better off if it was still part of India.
4 Mohammed Ali Jinnah was a major leader in Pakistan's independence movement.   38____

39 The caste system in India and the feudal system in Europe were similar in that both

1 provided structure for society
2 developed concepts of natural rights
3 established totalitarian governments
4 promoted peace and prosperity   39____

Base your answer to question 40 on the cartoon below and on your knowledge of social studies.

Source: Cummings, *Winnipeg Free Press,*
Cartoonists and Writers Syndicate

40 What is the cartoonist's view about democracy in India since 1947?

1 India has become a democratic nation after fifty years.
2 India has led Asia in democratic reforms.
3 India is not a democratic nation and has not been for the last five decades.
4 India's progress in becoming a democratic nation has been slow.

40 _____

41 Which problem has faced both Cuba and North Korea under communist rule?

1 Their monarchs have been ineffective rulers.
2 Their governments have played a limited role in the economy.
3 Their workers have called many strikes.
4 Their command economies have been inefficient.

41 _____

42 Which set of historical periods in European history is in the correct chronological order?

A. Medieval Europe
B. Italian Renaissance
C. Golden Age of Greece
D. Enlightenment

1 $C \rightarrow A \rightarrow B \rightarrow D$
2 $A \rightarrow B \rightarrow D \rightarrow C$
3 $C \rightarrow B \rightarrow D \rightarrow A$
4 $B \rightarrow A \rightarrow G \rightarrow D$

42____

43 ". . . I have walked that long road to freedom. I have tried not to falter; I have made missteps along the way. But I have discovered the secret that after climbing a great hill, one only finds that there are many more hills to climb. I have taken a moment here to rest, to steal a view of the glorious vista that surrounds me, to look back on the distance I have come. But I can rest only for a moment, for with freedom comes responsibilities, and I dare not linger, for my long walk is not yet ended."

—Nelson Mandela, *Long Walk to Freedom*,
Little, Brown and Co., 1994

When Mandela referred to "climbing a great hill," he was referring to the struggle to

1 end apartheid in South Africa
2 modernize South Africa's economy
3 end economic sanctions against South Africa
4 stop majority rule in South Africa

43____

44 Which statement best describes an impact of the computer on the global economy?

1 Countries can increase tariffs on imports.
2 Companies now market more products worldwide.
3 Wages have risen dramatically for most people in developing nations.
4 Prices of oil and other resources have declined worldwide.

44 _____

45 Which belief is shared by an African who practices animism and a Japanese who practices Shinto?

1 Only one God rules the universe.
2 Periodic fasting is essential to spiritual purity.
3 Spirits exist in both living and nonliving things.
4 All suffering is caused by desire and selfishness.

45 _____

46 Which headline would most likely have appeared in a pamphlet during the Industrial Revolution?

1 **"Michelangelo Completes Sistine Chapel"**
2 **"Karl Marx Attacks Capitalism"**
3 **"Martin Luther Speaks Out Against Sale of Indulgences"**
4 **"John Locke Calls for the People to Choose the King"**

46 _____

Base your answer to question 47 on the cartoon below and on your knowledge of social studies.

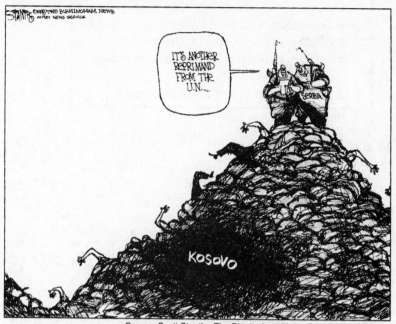

Source: Scott Stantis, *The Birmingham News,* Copley News Service

47 What is the main idea of this 1995 cartoon?

  1 The United Nations supported the Serbians in Kosovo.
  2 The United Nations was ineffective in its attempt to end genocide in Kosovo.
  3 Killing in Kosovo stopped because of United Nations reprimands.
  4 The Serbians lost the battle for Kosovo.

47 _____

48 Which title would best complete this partial outline?

> I. _____
>
> A. Formation of secret alliances
> B. Conflict over colonies in Africa
> C. Military buildup of European armies and navies
> D. Assassination of Archduke Ferdinand

1 Scramble for Africa
2 Causes of World War I
3 Results of World War II
4 Reasons for the United Nations　　　　　48 _____

49 • Many of Africa's traditional musical instruments are made of gourds and shells.
   • Ancient Egyptians wrote on papyrus, a reed found growing near the Nile River.
   • A major feature of Japanese art is the relationship between humans and nature.

Which concept is illustrated in these statements?

1 role of education in the ancient world
2 development of traditional government
3 effect of artistic expression on religion
4 impact of geography on cultural development　　　49 _____

Base your answer to question 50 on the statements below and on your knowledge of social studies.

> Article 4: "No one shall be held in slavery or servitude; slavery and the slave trade shall be prohibited in all their forms."
>
> —Universal Declaration of Human Rights,
> United Nations, 1948

> . . . My best estimate of the number of slaves in the world today is 27 million. . . .
>
> —Kevin Bales, *Disposable People*,
> University of California Press, 1999

50 Based on an analysis of these statements, which conclusion is accurate?

1 All governments have taken active steps to end slavery.
2 The United Nations has solved the problem of slavery.
3 The number of enslaved persons has increased dramatically since 1948.
4 Slavery remains a problem in the modern era.   50 ____

In developing your answer to Part II, be sure to keep these general definitions in mind:

(a) <u>discuss</u> means "to make observations about something using facts, reasoning, and argument; to present in some detail"

(b) <u>describe</u> means "to illustrate something in words or tell about it"

(c) <u>evaluate</u> means "to examine and judge the significance, worth, or condition of; to determine the value of"

PART II: THEMATIC ESSAY QUESTION

Directions: Write a well-organized essay that includes an introduction, several paragraphs addressing the task below, and a conclusion.

Theme: Economic Systems

> Societies have developed different economic systems for many reasons. Some of these economic systems include manorialism, capitalism, and communism.

Task:

> Identify *one* society and *one* economic system that has been used or is being used in that society and
> - Discuss the historical circumstances surrounding the development of that economic system
> - Describe *two* features of the economic system
> - Evaluate the impact the economic system had on this society during a specific historical period

You may use any society from your study of global history. Some suggestions you might wish to consider include western Europe during the Middle Ages, western Europe during the Industrial Revolution, the Soviet Union between 1917 and 1990, Japan after World War II, China since 1949, and Cuba since 1959.

You are *not* limited to these suggestions.
Do *not* use the United States as the example
of a society in your answer.

Guidelines:

In your essay, be sure to:

- Develop all aspects of the task
- Support the theme with relevant facts, examples, and details
- Use a logical and clear plan of organization, including an introduction and a conclusion that are beyond a restatement of the theme

In developing your answer to Part III, be sure to keep these general definitions in mind:

    (a) <u>explain</u> means "to make plain or understandable; to give reasons for or causes of; to show the logical development or relationships of"

    (b) <u>discuss</u> means "to make observations about something using facts, reasoning, and argument; to present in some detail"

PART III: DOCUMENT-BASED QUESTION

This question is based on the accompanying documents (1–9). The question is designed to test your ability to work with historical documents. Some of the documents have been edited for the purpose of this question. As you analyze the documents, take into account both the source of each document and any point of view that may be presented in the document.

    Historical Context:

        Throughout global history, rapidly spreading diseases have had an impact on many societies. Epidemics such as the Black Death in the 14th century, smallpox in the 16th century, and AIDS in the 20th and 21st centuries have had significant effects on societies.

    Task:

        Using information from the documents and your knowledge of global history, answer the questions that follow each document in Part A. Your answers to the questions will help you write the Part B essay, in which you will be asked to

Choose *two* epidemics and for *each*
- Explain why the epidemic spread
- Discuss the effects of the epidemic on a specific society or societies

You may *not* use the United States as one of the societies.

Part A: Short-Answer Questions

Directions: Analyze the documents and answer the short-answer questions that follow each document in the space provided.

Document 1

... The late-medieval depression began well before the coming of the Black Death (1348–1349). The fundamental trends of demographic and economic decline were not set off by the plague, but they were enormously aggravated by it. Carried by fleas that infested black rats, the bubonic plague entered Europe along trade routes from the East and spread with frightening speed. The death toll cannot be determined with any precision. The best estimate would probably be $\frac{1}{4}$ to $\frac{1}{3}$ of Europe's population. In many crowded towns the mortality rate may well have exceeded 50 percent, whereas isolated rural areas tended to be spared. Consequently, the most progressive, most enterprising, and best-trained Europeans were hit the hardest. Few urban families can have been spared altogether. Those who survived the terrible years 1348–1349 were subjected to periodic recurrences of the plague over the next three centuries. Fourteenth-century medical science was at a loss to explain the process of infection, and fourteenth-century urban sanitation was so primitive as to only encourage its spread. Some people fled their cities, some gave way to religious frenzy or stark hedonism [lack of moderation], and some remained faithfully at their posts, hoping for divine protection against the pestilence [disease]. But none can have emerged from the ordeal unaffected. ...

Source: C. Warren Hollister, *Medieval Europe: A Short History*, Second Edition, John Wiley & Sons, 1968

1 Based on this document, identify *two* ways the Black Death spread throughout Europe. [2]

(1) _____

_____

(2) _____

_____

Document 2

. . . The plight of the lower and most of the middle classes was even more pitiful to behold. Most of them remained in their houses, either through poverty or in hopes of safety, and fell sick by thousands. Since they received no care and attention, almost all of them died. Many ended their lives in the streets both at night and during the day; and many others who died in their houses were only known to be dead because the neighbours smelled their decaying bodies. Dead bodies filled every corner. Most of them were treated in the same manner by the survivors, who were more concerned to get rid of their rotting bodies than moved by charity towards the dead. With the aid of porters, if they could get them, they carried the bodies out of the houses and laid them at the doors, where every morning quantities of the dead might be seen. They then were laid on biers [coffin stands], or, as these were often lacking, on tables. . . .

Not to pry any further into all the details of the miseries which afflicted [struck] our city, I shall add that the surrounding country was spared nothing of what befell Florence. The villages on a smaller scale were like the city; in the fields and isolated farms the poor wretched peasants and their families were without doctors and any assistance, and perished in the highways, in their fields and houses, night and day, more like beasts than men. Just as the townsmen became dissolute and indifferent to their work and property, so the peasants, when they saw that death was upon them, entirely neglected the future fruits of their past labours both from the earth and from cattle, and thought only of enjoying what they had. Thus it happened that cows, asses, sheep, goats, pigs, fowls and even dogs, those faithful companions of man, left the farms and wandered at their will through the fields, where the wheat crops stood abandoned, unreaped and ungarnered [not gathered]. Many of these animals seemed endowed with reason, for, after they had pastured all day, they returned to the farms for the night of their own free will, without being driven. . . .

Oh, what great palaces, how many fair houses and noble dwellings, once filled with attendants and nobles and ladies, were emptied to the meanest servant! How many famous names and vast possessions and renowned estates were left without an heir! How many gallant men and fair ladies and handsome youths, whom Galen, Hippocrates and Æsculapius themselves would have said were in perfect health, at noon dined with their relatives and friends, and at night supped with their ancestors in the next world! . . .

— Giovanni Boccaccio, *The Decameron*

2 According to this document, what was **one** impact of the Black Death on European society? [1]

_____

_____

Document 3

Henry Knighton, a 14th-century author, wrote about the effects of the Black Death in England between 1348–1350.

> . . . Ox hides fell to a wretched price, namely 12*d*., and yet a pair of gloves would cost 10*d*., 12*d*., or 14*d*., and a pair of breeches 3*s*. or 4*s*. In the mean time the king sent word into every shire [county] that mowers and other workmen should take no more than they had before [the outbreak of the plague], under the penalties laid down in the order, and thereupon made a statute. Nevertheless the workmen were so puffed up and contrary-minded that they did not heed the king's decree, and if anyone wanted to hire them he had to pay what they asked: either his fruit and crops rotted, or he had to give in to the workmen's arrogant and greedy demands. . . .
>
> In the following winter there was such a want of hands, for every kind of work, that people believed that the like shortage had never been known at any time in the past, for cattle and such livestock as a man might have wandered about without a keeper, and there was no one to look after people's possessions. And thus the necessities of life became so dear, that what in previous times was worth 1*d*. now cost 4*d*. or 5*d*. . . .

Source: G. H. Martin, ed., *Knighton's Chronicle 1337–1396*,
Oxford University Press, 1995

3 Based on this document, state **two** effects of the Black Death on the economy of England. [2]

(1) _____

_____

(2) _____

_____

Document 4

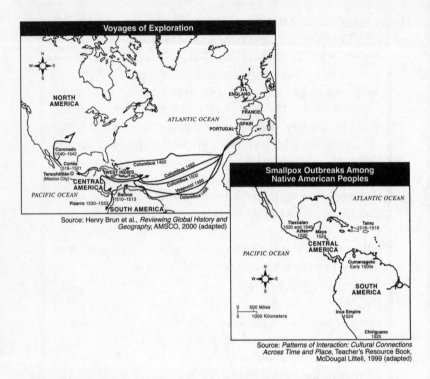

Source: Henry Brun et al., *Reviewing Global History and Geography*, AMSCO, 2000 (adapted)

Source: *Patterns of Interaction: Cultural Connections Across Time and Place*, Teacher's Resource Book, McDougal Littell, 1999 (adapted)

4 After studying these two maps, state *one* way smallpox was introduced to Central and South America. [1]

_____

_____

Document 5

... The first was a plague of smallpox, and it began in this manner. When Hernando Cortés was captain and governor, at the time that Captain Pánfilo de Narváez landed in this country, there was in one of his ships a negro stricken with smallpox, a disease which had never been seen here. At this time New Spain was extremely full of people, and when the smallpox began to attack the Indians it became so great a pestilence [disease] among them throughout the land that in most provinces more than half the population died; in others the proportion was little less. For as the Indians did not know the remedy for the disease and were very much in the habit of bathing frequently, whether well or ill, and continued to do so even when suffering from smallpox, they died in heaps, like bedbugs. Many others died of starvation, because, as they were all taken sick at once, they could not care for each other, nor was there anyone to give them bread or anything else. In many places it happened that everyone in a house died, and, as it was impossible to bury the great number of dead, they pulled down the houses over them in order to check the stench that rose from the dead bodies so that their homes became their tombs. This disease was called by the Indians 'the great leprosy' because the victims were so covered with pustules [pimples] that they looked like lepers. Even today one can see obvious evidences of it in some individuals who escaped death, for they were left covered with pockmarks. ...

Source: Elizabeth A. Foster, ed., *Motolinía's History of the Indians of New Spain*, Greenwood Press, 1977

5 According to this document, what were *two* results of the smallpox epidemic in Latin America? [2]

(1) _____

_____

(2) _____

_____

Document 6

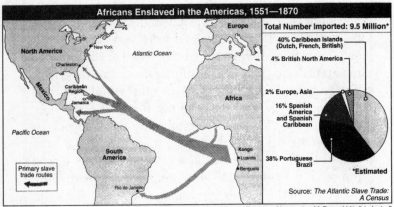

Source: Roger B. Beck et al., *World History: Patterns of Interaction*, McDougal Littell (adapted)

6 According to the information provided by this document, how did the decline in Latin America's native populations affect the population of Africa? [1]

_____

_____

Document 7

. . . In Donghu, residents estimate that more than 80 percent of adults carry H.I.V., and more than 60 percent are already suffering debilitating [disabling] symptoms. That would give this village, and the others like it, localized rates that are the highest in the world.

They add that local governments are in part responsible. Often encouraged by local officials, many farmers here in Henan contracted H.I.V. in the 1990s after selling blood at government-owned collection stations, under a procedure that could return pooled and infected blood to donors. From that point, the virus has continued to spread through other routes because those officials have blocked research and education campaigns about H.I.V., which they consider an embarrassment. . . .

"I do not know how many villages have a very grave problem, but I know that it's a lot more than just a handful," said a Chinese doctor who works in the province. "I've been a doctor for many decades, but I've never cried until I saw these villages. Even in villages where there was no blood selling, you now can find cases." Such transmission occurred through migration, marriage and sexual contact. . . .

Source: Elisabeth Rosenthal, "Deadly Shadow Darkens Remote Chinese Village," *New York Times*, May 28, 2001

7 According to this document, what is *one* way HIV has spread in China? [1]

_____

_____

Document 8

> . . . Like many countries before it, China has been slow in facing up to AIDS. Misconceptions, taboos and outright deceit have fostered denial among both officials and the broader population. This reluctance to be open and realistic is dangerous, as the experience of other countries shows.
>
> In India, for example, deeply rooted cultural norms and taboos still thwart [hinder] frank assessments and effective preventive measures, even though the United Nations estimates that if the disease is not checked, a mind-boggling 37 million people in India could be infected over the next 10 to 15 years. South Africa, where AIDS was barely acknowledged for years and whose president remains doubtful even now about its cause, today holds the dismal distinction of having the world's largest caseload of H.I.V infection and AIDS, 4.5 million. And even in industrialized nations, like the United States, lingering social stigmas [disgrace] can still create substantial hurdles to combating the spread of H.I.V. . . .

Source: Bates Gill and Sarah Palmer, "The Coming AIDS Crisis in China," Op-Ed page, *New York Times*, July 16, 2001

8 Based on this document, identify *one* factor that has contributed to the spread of AIDS. [1]

_____

_____

Document 9

> . . . Across the [African] continent, AIDS has robbed schools of their teachers, hospitals of their doctors and nurses, and children of their parents. Until recently, orphanages have been relatively rare, because in Africa families take in the children of relatives. But AIDS has created some 12 million orphans. Orphanages have sprung up everywhere, and in rural villages, one can find huts where one big sister or one grandmother is trying to find food for 10 or more children. On a poor continent, the disease is overwhelming family love.
>
> At this stage of the epidemic, health authorities say preventing new cases—by distributing condoms, for example—is not enough. In order to spare the continent from complete collapse, something must be done for the millions already infected. But in a region where most people live on less than $2 a day, drugs that cost more than $10,000 a year are not an option. Of the 26 million HIV-infected Africans only 10,000 have access to the drugs. . . .

Source: Donald G. McNeil, Jr., "A Continent at Risk,"
New York Times Upfront, May 14, 2001

9 Based on this document, state *two* ways AIDS has affected Africa. [2]

(1) _____

_____

(2) _____

_____

Part B: Essay

Directions: Write a well-organized essay that includes an introduction, several paragraphs, and a conclusion. Use evidence from at least *four* documents in your essay. Support your response with relevant facts, examples, and details. Include additional outside information.

Historical Context:

> Throughout global history, rapidly spreading diseases have had an impact on many societies. Epidemics such as the Black Death in the 14th century, smallpox in the 16th century, and AIDS in the 20th and 21st centuries have had significant effects on societies.

Task:

> Using information from the documents and your knowledge of global history, write an essay in which you

> Choose *two* epidemics and for *each*
> - Explain why the epidemic spread
> - Discuss the effects of the epidemic on a specific society or societies

You may *not* use the United States as one of the societies.

Guidelines:

In your essay, be sure to
- Develop all aspects of the task
- Incorporate information from at *least four* documents
- Incorporate relevant outside information
- Support the theme with relevant facts, examples, and details
- Use a logical and clear plan of organization; including an introduction and conclusion that are beyond a restatement of the theme

Answers
August 2004
Global History and Geography

Answer Key

PART I (1–50)

1. 4	**14.** 2	**27.** 1	**40.** 4
2. 2	**15.** 1	**28.** 4	**41.** 4
3. 2	**16.** 1	**29.** 1	**42.** 1
4. 1	**17.** 1	**30.** 2	**43.** 1
5. 3	**18.** 3	**31.** 2	**44.** 2
6. 3	**19.** 2	**32.** 2	**45.** 3
7. 4	**20.** 4	**33.** 3	**46.** 2
8. 4	**21.** 3	**34.** 4	**47.** 2
9. 1	**22.** 4	**35.** 4	**48.** 2
10. 1	**23.** 1	**36.** 1	**49.** 4
11. 3	**24.** 2	**37.** 3	**50.** 4
12. 3	**25.** 3	**38.** 3	
13. 2	**26.** 2	**39.** 1	

PART II: Thematic Essay   See answers explained section.

PART III: Document-Based Essay   See answers explained section.

Answers Explained

PART I

1. **4** The geographic feature that had the greatest influence on the development of ancient civilizations was river valleys. The fertile soil along the river valleys influenced the development of ancient civilizations. The first river valley civilization developed in Mesopotamia in the regions located along the Tigris and Euphrates Rivers. Although the area was hot and dry, people learned how to irrigate the land by diverting water from these rivers. The irrigation allowed settlements to grow and increase food supplies. In Egypt, the land would be a desert without the Nile River. Each year the overflowing of the Nile River deposited fertile soil that enabled farmers to grow large amounts of food and required a strong government to control the flooding of the Nile. Like the Tigris and Euphrates in Mesopotamia, the Nile River in Egypt, the Indus River in India, and the Huang He (Yellow River) in China fostered the development of civilization. The overflowing of these rivers created a rich deposit of fertile soil that encouraged permanent settlements, ultimately fostering the development of civilization.

WRONG CHOICES EXPLAINED:
(1) The civilizations of the Americas (Mayans, Incas, and Aztecs) developed near dense forests.
(2) There were no mountain passes that influenced the development of ancient civilizations. Egypt and Mesopotamia had large desert areas, not mountains. The mountain ranges of India and China contributed to their isolation rather than the development of their civilizations.
(3) Smooth coastlines influenced the development of Africa. Africa's smooth coastlines with few natural harbors made exploration of the interior very difficult. Africa was known as the Dark Continent until the mid-19th century because Europeans were unable to explore the continent.

2. **2** One characteristic of a society that practices subsistence agriculture is the production of crops mainly for its own use. Subsistence agriculture is a type of farming in which the farmer and his family can barely make a living. A subsistence farmer is one who grows only enough to supply a family or a village, with little or no surplus.

WRONG CHOICES EXPLAINED:
(1) Cash crop refers to the growth of surplus crops for export. Under colonial rule, the colonized people in Asia, Africa, and Latin America worked on plantations that produced cash crops grown for profit and export.

(3) The establishment of large state-owned farms is characteristic of collective farms. Collective farms were farms operated and managed under government direction.

(4) Plantation farming depended on the use of slave labor for the production of crops. Colonial powers in Africa, Asia, and Latin America set up plantations, or large farms, that employed native workers as slave labor to grow cash crops, such as sugar and rubber, for export. In Latin America, the Spanish replaced Native Americans with African slaves to work on their plantations.

3. **2** One cause of the development of many small independent city-states in ancient Greece was the mountainous terrain of Greece, which resulted in widely scattered settlements. The Greek mainland is a mountainous peninsula. Low-lying mountains make up about three-fourths of the Greek mainland. The mountains both protected and isolated Greeks on the mainland. Besides making attacks by foreigners difficult, the mountains limited travel and communication between communities. For example, the city-state of Sparta was only 60 miles from Olympia, the site of the Olympic Games, but it took Spartans nearly a week to travel that distance. These mountain barriers also led the Greeks to organize small independent communities rather than a large empire like the Egyptians. In time, these communities grew into city-states. Although they spoke one language and practiced the same religion, the Greeks never united under one government. Each city-state prized its freedom and resisted outside interference. The mountainous regions helped to create political disunity because the first loyalty of the people was not to Greece as a nation but to their own city-states that were scattered throughout Ancient Greece.

WRONG CHOICES EXPLAINED:
(1) City-states, such as Athens and Sparta, existed because of geographic mountain barriers, not because of war between the Greeks and Romans. Because of their stronger army, the Romans conquered the Greeks.

(3) Military generals did not find the small Greek settlements easy to control. Throughout Greek history, the city-states of Athens and Sparta competed with each other in a series of wars known as the Peloponnesian Wars. The Greeks also effectively turned back the efforts of the Persian Empire to crush them.

(4) The Greek people did not have many different languages and religions. The Greeks shared a common culture based on a common language and religious beliefs. For example, Greeks from all city-states participated in the Olympic Games in honor of Zeus and other Greek gods.

4. **1** In India, Bangladesh, and much of Southeast Asia, agricultural productivity is most affected by the seasonal monsoons. The monsoons are the seasonal winds that dominate the climate of South Asia. The word monsoon means "seasons" in Arabic. Two monsoons define the seasons of South Asia,

the wet season of summer and the hot, dry weather of winter. The wet monsoons arrive in late May or early June. At this time, temperatures may reach as high as 120°F (45°C) in India, or Bangladesh. Little or no rain falls for eight or nine months and the ground is parched and cracked. The land heats the air, causing it to rise. Cool, moist air from the sea flows across the land, bringing the hope for rain. By October, the cool masses from the northern mountains sink, creating winds that blow back toward the sea. These monsoons carry dry air across the subcontinent. They bring a season of clear skies, mild temperatures, and low humidity. In March, however, the temperature rises. The cycle that leads to the wet monsoon begins again. The monsoons are the key to the life of the farmers in South Asia. In the months before the wet season, farmers plant seeds in the dry, sun-baked earth. The seeds must take root before the summer downpours. If the monsoon is late, the plants will die and famine results. On the other hand, if the monsoon brings too much rain, the rivers can overflow and wash away the crops. In both cases, the monsoons can directly affect the productivity of the farmers and what they are able to produce.

WRONG CHOICES EXPLAINED:

(2) Unnavigable rivers have not affected the agricultural productivity of the farmers in India, Bangladesh, and much of Southeast Asia. The Indus and Ganges Rivers have helped to create an enormous delta on the Bay of Bengal. The delta region located in Bangladesh has fertile soil but is subject to flooding. The Indus, which means river, is the source of the name of India, and was the center of the region's earliest civilization.

(3) The only major desert near India, Bangladesh, and much of Southeast Asia is the Thar Desert. This vast desert covers about 100,000 square miles and is about the size of Colorado. This desert does not affect the agricultural economy of Southeast Asia.

(4) Much of Southeast Asia has a tropical, not a cold, climate with warm temperatures year-round.

5. **3** A belief shared by Hindus and Buddhists is that the soul is reincarnated. Reincarnation is the rebirth of the soul in various forms. Hindus believe that after the body dies, the soul may be reborn as anything from a god to a flower or a snake. Those who follow Hindu practices in previous existences are rewarded by reincarnation into a higher state, allowing them to continue their journey toward union with Brahman, the creator or unifying spirit. People get closer to this union by being born into higher and higher levels of existence. The soul will eventually be completely purified from further rebirth and unite with the all-embracing spirit. Buddhism accepts the concept of reincarnation and believes that salvation is achieved when the individual self escapes the body. However, the Buddhists believe a person can escape endless reincarnations by following the Eightfold Path of Righteous Living, renouncing material pleasures, controlling emotions, respecting all living creatures, acquiring knowledge, cultivating goodness, speaking truths,

and acting generously. Buddhists also accept the Hindu concept of Karma, which is the belief that every deed in this life affects a person's fate in the future, and Dharma, which includes the moral and religious duties expected of an individual.

WRONG CHOICES EXPLAINED:

(1) The Hindus reject the idea that everyone should have the same social status. The caste system is an important part of Hinduism. The caste system is the division of society into four major groups based on occupation or birth. The Buddhists rejected the caste system.

(2) Muslims believe that people should pray five times a day.

(4) The Buddhists reject the idea that material wealth is a sign of the blessings of the gods. Siddhartha Gautama, the founder of Buddhism, left his wealthy home and family in search of the truth. Buddhism is based on a philosophy of self-denial and meditation. The caste system, which is a central part of Hinduism, is based upon the idea that one's social status is determined by birth and wealth.

6. **3** The main idea of this passage is that religious tolerance in Muslim Spain encouraged the growth of a rich and diverse culture. Al-Andalus, which means "to become green at the end of the summer," refers to the territory occupied by the Muslim Empire in southern Spain. The Muslim Empire in Spain spanned from the 8th to the 15th century. Throughout the period of Islamic rule, al-Andalus was an example of tolerance. Jews and Christians were allowed to maintain their beliefs and live their lives as they desired as long as they respected their Muslim rulers. Although the Muslim rulers allowed Christians and Jews to practice their own faiths, they did impose a special tax on non-Muslims. At the great centers of learning, such as the city of Cordoba, rulers employed Jewish officials and welcomed Christian students to absorb Greek ideas from Muslim teachers. Jewish poets, such as Abraham Ibn Ezra, Shlomo Ibn Gabirol, and Yehuda HaLevi, wrote some of the finest poetry during this period of Muslim dominance. In their poetry, they described culinary feasts at which Muslim and Jewish poets and musicians entertained guests with their artistic productions. Yehuda HaLevi was the first to write in Castilian as well as Hebrew and Latin for Jews and Christians. Moses Ben Marmon (Maimonides), a Jewish physician and philosopher, was born in Cordoba and lived in Egypt. Although he spent most of his life outside Spain, his philosophical works influenced the people of the Middle Ages. In 1190, he wrote *The Guide for the Perplexed*, which blended philosophy, religion, and science. In 1492, Queen Isabella of Castillo and King Ferdinand of Aragon exiled the Jews and the Arabs from Spain.

WRONG CHOICES EXPLAINED:

(1), (2), and (4) None of these statements are supported by this passage. The reading does not refer to the Muslims rejecting the Torah and the Bible. There is no mention of Arabs, Jews, and Christians sharing houses of worship in Muslim Spain. There is also no reference to deep-rooted religious conflicts that developed during the Reconquista. The Reconquista represented Spain's efforts to expel Arabs and Jews and unite the country under Catholicism.

7. **4** Some historians suggest that as a result of the Mongol invasions of Russia, the Russian people were cut off from most of western Europe. In 1240, Russia was conquered by Asian warriors, the Mongols (or Tartars). For nearly 250 years, the Mongols controlled Russia. Under Mongol rule, the Russians could follow all their usual customs as long as they showed no sign of rebellion. Although the Mongols were fierce conquerors, they were tolerant rulers. The Mongols demanded just two things from the Russians: slavish obedience to their Mongol overlords, and massive amounts of tribute. The absolute power of the Mongols served as a model for later Russian rulers. Russian princes came to develop a strong desire to centralize their own power without interference from nobles, the clergy, or wealthy merchants. Mongol rule also reduced Russia's ties with the Byzantine Empire and western Europe. Mongol rule isolated Russia from western Europe and cut them off from many new ideas and inventions. In the 1700s, Peter the Great, the outstanding Romanov ruler of Russia, tried to westernize Russia. He tried to model Russia after European culture rather than the Asian culture. Peter's efforts, however, had little lasting impression on the Russian people.

WRONG CHOICES EXPLAINED:
(1) The Russians never united with the Ottomans. Russia fought several wars against the Ottomans. Russia pushed southward toward the Black Sea and Istanbul, which the Russians called Constantinople. Russia was eager to divide up Ottoman lands.

(2) The Mongols did convert the Russians to Christianity. In the 9th century, Cyril and his brother Methodius, Byzantine Christian missionaries, introduced Christianity to Russia.

(3) Czar Alexander II of Russia, not the Mongols, ended serfdom in 1861.

8. **4** The map shows that on his voyages, Zheng He explored Arabia and the east coast of Africa. Between 1405 and 1433, the Ming emperor sent Admiral Zheng on seven voyages to promote trade. His earliest voyages were to southeast Asia and India. Later, he traveled as far as Arabia and eastern Africa. After the Mongols were overthrown in 1368, the emperor of the new Ming Dynasty wanted to assert Chinese power. The emperor thought that China needed to renew trade with the outside world to demonstrate his nation's supremacy over other nations. After Zheng's death in 1453, the Ming emperor halted voyages of exploration.

WRONG CHOICES EXPLAINED:
(1) Zheng He never explored the Atlantic Ocean. He traveled the Pacific Ocean in his voyages to the East Indies.

(2) The map provides no information about the Spanish explorers.

(3) Zheng He never explored land in the Western Hemisphere. The map shows voyages of Zheng He in Africa and Asia. Furthermore, Spanish

exploration of the Western Hemisphere began in the 16th century after Zheng He's death.

9. **1** One result of the voyages of Zheng He was that Chinese merchants began trading with Africa. The purpose of Zheng He's voyages of exploration was to expand China's tribute system. The ships of his grand fleet carried silk, porcelain, and art in exchange for ivory, pearls, and other jewels. When Zheng He was in Africa, he returned home with new and unfamiliar animals for the imperial zoo. One of these creatures was a 15-foot-tall creature—a giraffe. The Chinese interpreted the giraffe as the legendary beast that had played an important part in the birth of Confucius and considered it a sign of Heaven's favor on the Ming Dynasty. In the wake of Zheng He's voyages, the Chinese set up trading posts in East Africa as well as Southeast Asia and India. These voyages spread the glory and supremacy of the Chinese society to Africa and other countries, which now sent tributes and ambassadors to the Ming Court.

WRONG CHOICES EXPLAINED:
(2) Christian missionaries first arrived in China in 635 A.D. and the second time during the Mongol Dynasty (1271–1368). These events took place before Zheng He's voyage in the 15th century.
(3) Indian artisans did not show the Chinese how to make Ming porcelain. The Chinese developed porcelain during the Tang Dynasty that lasted from 618–907 and the Song Dynasty (960–1279). In the Ming Dynasty, blue and white porcelain was developed by Chinese artisans, not Indian artisans.
(4) The Chinese never set up colonies in Europe. After the death of Zheng He, Chinese emperors returned to a policy of isolation from the West.

10. **1** Many achievements of Islamic civilization reached European society by way of the Crusades and eastern Mediterranean trading networks. The Crusades were religious wars between Christian Europe and Muslims for control of the Holy Lands and lasted from 1096 until 1291. The Crusaders failed to capture the Holy Land but had a major impact on the world. European contacts during the Crusades with the more advanced Muslim and Byzantine civilizations helped to bring back classical texts of Plato and Aristotle to the West. The increased contact led to a renewed interest in learning. Returning Crusaders brought back new products, spices, and perfumes. Trade increased during the Crusades; Italian merchants who had built fleets to transport the Crusaders used these same transports to keep trade open. European cities, especially Venice and Genoa, became prosperous and powerful due to increased trading in the Mediterranean. Contact with the East spurred new demand for luxury items, such as spices, sugar, melon, silks, and other items that Europe had been unable to obtain. From the Muslims, the Crusaders learned how to build better ships and to make more accurate maps. They began to use the magnetic compass to tell direction. They also learned new military skills, especially siege techniques.

WRONG CHOICES EXPLAINED:

(2) Merchant guilds and the Industrial Revolution did not provide European society with the achievements of Islamic civilization. Merchant guilds were formed in the Middle Ages to protect their common interests. The Industrial Revolution dealt with the transformation of society from handmade items to machine-made goods.

(3) The Middle Passage is the voyage that brought captured Africans to the West Indies and later to North and South America. The Columbian Exchange refers to the global transfer of plants, animals, and diseases during the European colonization of the Americas.

(4) The conquests of the Germanic tribes by the Romans were during the 1st and 2nd centuries. Trade along the Silk Road dealt with the system of ancient caravan routes across central Asia. Neither of these events had any impact on spreading the achievements of Islamic civilization to Europe.

11. **3** Prior to the Protestant Reformation, the medieval church in western Europe was criticized for being too concerned with worldly power and riches. Critics of the church claimed that its leaders were corrupt. The popes who ruled during the Renaissance patronized the arts and sought personal pleasures. They also fought long wars to protect the Papal States against invasions from the secular world. Many church leaders violated the law of celibacy and neglected their religious duties for more worldly activities. Pope Alexander VI publicly admitted that he had several children. To finance many of their projects, such as rebuilding the Cathedral of St. Peter's at Rome, the church increased fees for religious services, such as marriages and baptism, and sold appointments to church officers. The church also began to sell indulgences as a way to reduce punishment for sins committed during one's lifetime. In the Middle Ages, the church had granted indulgences only for good deeds, for example going on a crusade. By 1400, however, an indulgence could be obtained in exchange for money. The sale of indulgences was used to raise money to finance many church projects. These conditions within the church led to the Protestant Reformation.

WRONG CHOICES EXPLAINED:

(1) The church never sponsored explorations to the Middle East. The church promoted the Crusades, which were religious wars waged against the Muslims to regain the Holy Land.

(2) In 1456, Johannes Gutenberg of Main, Germany, printed a complete edition of the Bible using movable metal type. The medieval church did not promote the printing of the Bible and its distribution to the people. The church believed that the Bible was to be interpreted by the clergy, not the people.

(4) The medieval church was not criticized for refusing to sell indulgences to peasants. Critics accused the church of selling indulgences to raise money.

12. **3** The generalization that is best supported by the information in this map is that by the 1500s, the Ottoman Empire controlled parts of the

Middle East, North Africa, and eastern Europe. The Ottomans, a nomadic group of Turkish people originally from Central Asia, emerged as rulers of the Islamic world in the 13th century. In 1453, they succeeded in capturing Constantinople, the capital of the Byzantine Empire. In 1514, the Ottoman Turks swept into Syria, Palestine, and North Africa, as well as Mecca, Medina, and Egypt. The Ottomans united the Muslim world except for Persia and Afghanistan. The Ottoman Empire reached its heights under Suleiman I, who ruled from 1520–1566. Under Suleiman, the Ottomans captured Tripoli as well as all the people along the North African coastline including Algiers. In 1525, Suleiman advanced into Hungary and the out-skirts of Vienna but the siege of Vienna failed. Although they failed to con-quer Vienna, the Ottoman Empire was the most powerful empire in both Europe and the Middle East. At its peak, the Ottoman Empire stretched from Hungary in the North, through Greece around the Black Sea, south through Syria, and across Egypt all the way west to the borders of Morocco.

WRONG CHOICES EXPLAINED:

(1) The map indicates that the Ottoman Empire did not control the largest amount of territory by 1453. The Ottoman Empire added more land from 1520 to 1566.

(2) The map shows that the Safavid Empire never controlled parts of western Europe by 1629. The Safavid Empire was centered on Persia, not western Europe.

(4) The map provides information about the territorial boundaries of the Ottoman and Safavid Empires. There is no information on the map to deter-mine whether the Mediterranean Sea served as a cultural barrier between Asia Minor and North Africa.

13. **2** The most accurate statement about the geography of Africa is that the variety of geographic barriers has served to promote cultural diversity. Africa is the second largest continent in area. The main regions of Africa are divided into North Africa, West Africa, Central Africa, and Southern Africa. Geographic features give each region its own identity. North Africa has a warm, dry climate. On its northern borders is the Mediterranean Ocean, which has allowed Africa to establish close contacts with Europe and the Middle East. However, the Sahara Desert, the world's largest desert, takes up much of North Africa. Thus, for centuries it has served as a sea barrier sepa-rating the people of the North from the South. Most of the people of North Africa are mainly of Arab descent and the followers of Islam. North Africa is more closely tied to the Middle East than to the rest of Africa. A large part of sub-Saharan Africa is savanna or grassy plains. Despite hot weather and occa-sional droughts, this area has good soil and enough rain to support farming. It is the most densely populated climate region. The southern part of West Africa and much of Central Africa consists of tropical rain forests. The area gets from 60 to 100 inches of rain a year. The area south of the Sahara Desert has a different climate and topography than North Africa and with its non-Arab

population is often considered a separate and distinct region. Africa's mountains, such as the Atlas in the northwest and the Drakensberg Mountains in the southeast, have also kept Africans apart and allowed them to develop separate cultures, languages, and traditions.

WRONG CHOICES EXPLAINED:

(1) Africa's land is not below sea level. The Equator runs almost through the middle of Africa.

(3) Africa does not have an irregular coastline. It does have few natural harbors. For centuries, Africa's Mediterranean and Atlantic coasts have been accessible to European ships.

(4) Much of Africa's land is not tundra. Tundra climate is found in northern Alaska, Canada, and Siberia; 80 percent of Africa's continent is in the tropics. Because of this tropical location, African climates are generally warm throughout the year.

14. **2** The statement that best describes an impact of geography on the history of the Korean peninsula is that location has led to invasion and occupation by other nations. Korea is located on a peninsula that juts south from the Asian mainland with its tip pointing toward Japan. Mountains and the Yalu River separate Korea from China. Korea's location on China's doorstep has played a key role in its development. Under the Shilla Dynasty that ruled Korea from 668 to 918, Korea became a tributary state, acknowledging China's lordship but preserving its independence. Later, the Mongols took control of Korea from the early 1200s until the 1350s. In the 1590s, the Japanese decided to invade Korea but with the help of the Chinese, Korea was able to turn back the Japanese invasion. In 1636, the Manchu, who ruled China until 1912, conquered Korea and made it a vassal state. When China began declining in power during the 19th century, Japan competed with China and Russia for control of the Korean peninsula. In 1894, the Japanese, after defeating China, gained a sphere of influence in Korea and annexed all of Korea. After the Japanese were defeated in World War II in 1945, the United States and Russia agreed that Korea should receive its independence. However, Korea became a battleground in the Cold War struggle between the United States and the Soviet Union. The United States sent troops to the South and the Russians sent troops to the North. Both sides agreed to withdraw their troops once elections could be held. In 1950, the Korean War broke out, leading to the permanent division of Korea at the 38th parallel for the last 54 years.

WRONG CHOICES EXPLAINED:

(1) Korea does not have any large deserts. Its mountains and seas have contributed to Korea's isolation.

(3) Lack of rivers has not limited food production. The Korean peninsula has a 6,000-mile coastline with many good harbors. Many Koreans make a living by fishing. South Korea has one of the world's largest fishing industries and is among the highest in the world for its rice production.

(4) The lack of natural resources, especially in South Korea, has not prevented the development of manufacturing. South Korea stresses manufacturing for export. Its skilled work force produces goods such as textiles and electronic equipment. Because of its reliance on exports and the need for raw materials, South Korea is interdependent with the world's economy. Although North Korea is rich in natural resources such as coal, iron, and lead, the Communist government has been unable to develop a strong industrial economy.

15. **1** The Confucian principle that is reflected in this statement is that the ruler must set an example for the people. Confucius was one of China's greatest philosophers and lived between 551 and 479 B.C. The only record of his ideas is the writings of his students. His students later collected his works in a book called *The Analects*. Confucius believed that social order, harmony, and good government should be based on family relationships. He taught that the five relationships must govern human society: the relationship between ruler and subjects; father and son; older brother and younger brother; husband and wife; friend and friend. In each, Confucius believed that the superior person must set an example for the inferior. A supporter of the Mandate of Heaven, he said that the ruler must provide good government for his subjects. To govern well, a prince must live virtuously. The people will then imitate their ruler's example and peace and order would follow. In turn, the ruler's subjects owed the ruler loyalty and obedience. Confucius created a guide to proper behavior based on ethical or moral principles. Confucianism was never a religion but an ethical system. It became the foundation of the Chinese government and social order. In addition, the ideas of Confucius spread beyond China and influenced civilizations in East Asia, such as Korea and Japan.

WRONG CHOICES EXPLAINED:
(2), (3), and (4) None of these choices is described in this passage. The importance of respect for elders, education, and compassion and sympathy for others are associated with Confucianism but these ideas are not highlighted in the passage.

16. **1** The action that would best complete this partial outline is that the Byzantine Heritage adapted the Roman principles of justice. The Byzantine Empire remained a political and cultural force for nearly 1,000 years after the fall of Rome. Byzantine culture represented a continuation of the classical knowledge, especially its Greek and Hellenistic aspects combined with orthodox Christianity. The accomplishments of Roman engineers were also preserved and extended in Byzantine architecture. Byzantine architecture combined the features of Greco-Roman and Persian architecture by devising the rectangular building topped by a round dome. The Byzantine Empire preserved Greek science, philosophy, and literature. Between 534 and 528 B.C., Emperor Justinian of the Byzantine Empire assigned a group of scholars to gather and organize the ancient laws of Rome. This collection of laws, known

as the Justinian Code, preserved nearly 5,000 laws of the Roman Empire as well as legal writings and a handbook for students. Although Justinian died in 565, the Code served the Byzantine Empire for 900 years.

WRONG CHOICES EXPLAINED:

(2) Byzantine Emperors were absolute rulers and did not use the senate as the chief governing body.

(3) The Byzantine rulers never led crusades to capture Rome from the Huns. Emperor Justinian was the only Byzantine ruler who tried to recapture Rome from the Huns in the 530s and 540s, but failed. No other attempts were made to capture Rome during the Empire's 1,000-year history.

(4) The western European part of the Roman Empire fell in 476 A.D. The Byzantine Empire was never able to help Rome maintain control over western Europe or reassert its authority again.

17. **1** The expeditions of Hernán Cortés and Francisco Pizarro resulted in the destruction of the Aztec and Inca empires. Hernán Cortés, the Spanish conquistador, landed on the coast of Mexico in 1519. When he heard the stories about the fabled riches of the Aztec Empire, he decided to conquer it. In 1521, having formed an alliance with other native groups, he was able to conquer the empire. Although he had only 600 men, 16 horses, and a few cannons, Cortés slaughtered more than 50,000 Aztec people and within a year ruled the Aztec Empire. With the advantages of horses and guns, the Spanish were able to terrorize the Indians. The soldiers' helmets protected them from the Indians' spears and arrows. The Spanish horses also frightened some Aztecs since they had never seen this type of animal. In 1532, Francisco Pizarro, another Spanish conquistador, conquered the mighty Inca Empire. Riding horses and armed with muskets, Pizarro and his army of about 200 soldiers spread terror among the Indian armies. Pizarro also used trickery to capture Atahualpa. The Inca Emperor brought several thousand unarmed men to a meeting with Pizarro. Pizzaro's army crushed the Inca forces and kidnapped Atahualpa. The Inca Emperor then offered to buy his freedom by filling a room with gold treasures. Pizarro agreed to this, but then seized the treasures and murdered Atahualpa. Without a strong leader, organized Inca resistance faltered. By 1535, Pizarro controlled the vast Inca Empire.

WRONG CHOICES EXPLAINED:

(2) Hernán Cortés and Francisco Pizarro were Spanish conquistadors whose expeditions never resulted in the capture of Brazil. Their expeditions were aimed at Mexico and Peru. Pedro Cabral explored Brazil for Portugal in 1500.

(3) Portugal never colonized North America.

(4) Cortés and Pizarro never explored the Philippines and the East Indies.

18. **3** The statement that best describes a result of the Glorious Revolution in England (1688) is that principles of limited government were strengthened. The Glorious Revolution refers to the nonviolent transfer of power from James II to William and Mary of Orange. The British Parliament

forced James II to abdicate because of his wish to become an absolute ruler and because of his Catholicism. Parliament invited William and Mary to rule, provided that they would agree to submit all legislation to Parliament for approval. As part of the Glorious Revolution, Parliament passed the Bill of Rights, a series of acts passed to ensure its superiority over the king. The Bill of Rights limited the power of the king to repeal any laws or raise an army or taxes without the consent of Parliament. The Glorious Revolution ended the absolute or divine right in England and established the principle that the power of government was limited.

WRONG CHOICES EXPLAINED:

(1) The Glorious Revolution did not result in the formation of an alliance of England with France. The English and the French were enemies with each other throughout the 17th and 18th centuries.

(2) The Glorious Revolution limited, not increased, the power of the monarchy in England.

(4) The Glorious Revolution was a political resolution and did not result in England's losing its colonial possession. During the next two centuries, England would become the world's largest colonial empire.

19. **2** One reason Italy and Germany were not major colonial powers in the 16th and 17th centuries was that they lacked political unity. For many centuries, Italy consisted of many small states. It was not a united nation before 1861. There were rivalries among the different states, such as Venice, Genoa, and Florence, as well as the Papal States. Furthermore, Austria dominated many of the northern Italian city-states and opposed Italian unity. Like Italy, Germany consisted of a number of small states and did not become unified until 1871. Germany consisted of more than 300 small states. In Germany, there was also a regional split between the northern states of Germany that were Protestant and the southern states that were primarily Catholic. The rivalry between Austria and Prussia for control of Germany also led to political disunity. Spain, England, and Portugal had become nation states during the 15th and 16th centuries. These nations were able to finance colonial ventures. Italy and Germany would become colonial powers at the end of the 19th century after they had become united nations.

WRONG CHOICES EXPLAINED:

(1) Neither of these countries had self-sufficient economies. A self-sufficient economy is one that has all the necessary resources to survive by itself. The medieval manor was a self-sufficient agricultural economy. The Italian and German states depended on trade to prosper. None of the colonial powers of the 16th and 17th centuries had self-sufficient economies.

(3) Neither Italy nor Germany rejected the practice of imperialism. Their internal division prevented them from participating in colonization.

(4) Neither of these countries joined opposing alliances against each other during the 16th and 17th centuries. Neither of these countries were major powers at this time in European history.

20. **4** The ideas of Rousseau, Voltaire, and Montesquieu most influenced movements for political reform. These men were part of an intellectual movement called the Enlightenment. The writers of the Enlightenment believed that people possessed natural rights and that society could be improved. These writers also claimed that science and reason could explain the laws of human society. They challenged traditional authority and Church authority. Rousseau criticized the abuses of society and put forth his ideas in his book, *The Social Contract*. Rousseau maintained that people in the state of nature were happy and possessed natural rights but were corrupted by the evils of society, such as the inequalities of distribution of property. People entered into a social contract to form a government, agreeing to surrender all their rights for the common good. Rousseau believed in the will of the majority, which he called the general will. If the government failed in its purpose, the people have the right to replace it. Voltaire, after living in Great Britain for a while, wrote *Letters on the English*. Voltaire praised Britain's limited monarchy and civil liberties and denounced the French government's censorship, injustices, and despotism. Montesquieu wrote *The Spirit of the Law*. To prevent despotism, he urged that those powers of the government should be separated into three branches—executive, legislative, and judicial. Each branch would check the other instead of permitting power to be concentrated into one person, the king. Montesquieu's ideas of separation of power were adapted into the United States Constitution. The ideas of these Enlightenment writers had a great impact throughout Europe in the 1700s, especially in France.

WRONG CHOICES EXPLAINED:

(1) The ideas of these writers did not influence the growing powers of the priests in the Roman Catholic Church. These men attacked the abuses of the Church and forced Church leaders to defend their institutions.

(2) These writers did not address the issue of improvements in the working conditions of factory workers. These men wrote before the beginning of the Industrial Revolution in England in the 1800s.

(3) Rousseau, Voltaire, and Montesquieu dealt with the injustices of human society, not the rise of industrial capitalism.

21. **3** During the late 19th century, the geographic factor that helped attract European investors to southern Africa and southeast Asia was natural resources. In the late 1800s, the Industrial Revolution created a tremendous demand for raw materials. European factories consumed tons of raw materials and churned out thousands of manufactured goods. The owners of these factories constantly searched for new sources of raw materials, or natural resources, as well as new markets for their products. Rubber, copper, and gold came from Africa, cotton and jute from India, and tin from Southeast Asia. Africa was also a source of palm oil for soap and gum for paper fabrics. The rain forests provided rubber, ivory, and rare hardwood. These natural resources spurred the growth of European industries and financial markets.

Businessmen and bankers had excess capital to invest and foreign investments offered the incentive for greater products. Businessmen also sought ventures in far-flung parts of the world because the need for natural resources forced nations to take direct control of those colonies, which would guarantee the constant flow of natural resources to the mother country. This approach would ensure that investments in natural resources would be profitable.

WRONG CHOICES EXPLAINED:

(1) Investors were not interested in Africa and southeast Asia because of their smooth coastlines. They sought this area for economic profits. Neither Africa nor southeast Asia has smooth coastlines and few natural harbors.

(2) Navigable rivers did not attract investors to southern Africa nor southeast Asia. The investors saw rivers only as a source of transportation to help make it easier to acquire the natural resources of these areas.

(4) Investors were not attracted to southern Africa or southeast Asia because of the temperate climates. Investors wanted these areas for economic gains.

22. **4** One result of the Opium War was that China was divided into spheres of influence. Spheres of influence are areas of a country in which foreign nations have special economic privileges, such as the right to build factories or railroads. In the late 1700s, British merchants began to trade opium in China. The use of opium was strictly controlled in India, Europe, and China. The Chinese became addicted to the drug, and in 1836, the Chinese government appealed to Queen Victoria to help them stop the opium trade. In 1839, when the Chinese tried to outlaw the drug, the British went to war. This conflict, which became known as the Opium War, demonstrated the weaknesses of the Chinese. In 1843, England and China signed the Treaty of Nanking. For the Chinese, the Treaty of Nanking marked the beginning of a century of humiliation. The British annexed Hong Kong and won the right to trade at four Chinese ports besides Canton. China was required to pay a $100 million indemnity for the opium it had destroyed. The trade in opium continued and Britain received the privilege of extraterritoriality. Extraterritoriality meant that the British did not have to obey Chinese laws and were subject only to British laws and courts. France gained a sphere of influence in southeastern China and Germany over the Shantung Peninsula in northeastern China. The Russians forced China to give up Ussuri territory where the Russians built their major Pacific naval base. The Japanese annexed Formosa. By the end of the 19th century, much of China was divided into spheres of influence under European or Japanese control.

WRONG CHOICES EXPLAINED:

(1) The Opium War did not force China to adapt democratic reforms. The Chinese Emperor ruled until 1912, when the Manchu Dynasty ended.

(2) China did not take control of Hong Kong. The British annexed Hong Kong and did not return it to China until the end of the 20th century.

(3) China did not regain control of Manchuria. Russia had established a sphere of influence over Manchuria. Japan took over the Russian sphere of influence in southeastern Manchuria as a result of Russia's defeat in the Russo-Japanese War of 1905.

23. **1** Based on a comparison of these maps of South America, an accurate conclusion is that many regions of South America gained their independence between 1790 and 1828. The maps show that in 1790, South America was controlled by either the Portuguese in Brazil, the Spanish in La Plata, Peru, and the British, Dutch, and French in Guianas. By 1828, all of South America had become independent except for Guianas. The success of the American Revolution showed that foreign rule could be overthrown. Educated Latin Americans read Thomas Jefferson's Declaration of Independence. The French Revolution also influenced South America. Between 1790 and 1828, South America struggled to gain independence.

WRONG CHOICES EXPLAINED:

(2) All of South America was not independent by 1828. Guianas was still a British, Dutch, and French possession.

(3) Spain lost its South American colonies in the 19th century.

(4) Between 1790 and 1828, South American political boundaries did not remain unchanged except for Brazil. New nations were defeated in the area near La Plata and New Granada. These nations, such as Argentina, Chile, Ecuador, and Colombia, had new political boundaries.

24. **2** The individual most closely associated with the changes indicated on these maps is Simón Bolívar. Simón Bolívar, who was born to a wealthy Venezuelan Creole family in 1783, always envisioned an independent and united Latin America, free from Spanish domination. As a young man, he studied in Europe. His love of freedom was strengthened by the ideas of the French Revolution. Before returning from Europe, Bolívar promised that he would not rest until he broke the chain put upon the people of Latin America by the Spanish. He became known as the "Liberator" for his role in the wars for independence against Spain. In 1819, he helped free Venezuela and by 1824 had secured the freedom of Colombia, Ecuador, Peru, and Bolivia.

WRONG CHOICES EXPLAINED:

(1) Emiliano Zapata led a peasant revolt against the dictatorship of Porfirio Díaz in Mexico in 1910. Zapata, an Indian, demanded land reform. "Land and Liberty" was his battle cry.

(3) Porfirio Díaz was dictator of Mexico and ruled in the late 1800s and early 1900s. Díaz was forced to resign in 1911.

(4) Pancho Villa was a rebel leader in northern Mexico who won the loyalty of a large number of peasants. Like Zapata, Villa won important victories against Porfirio's army and helped to contribute to Díaz' defeat in 1911.

25. **3** This quotation is associated with the principles of communism. Communism is a form of socialism proposed by Karl Marx and Friedrich Engels, which is characterized by a classless society. This society supports a common ownership of the means of production and equal distribution of the products of society. According to Marx, the father of communism, a class struggle was inevitable and only violent revolutions would create the classless society in which the government would win anyway. Marx predicted that a communist revolution was inevitable only in industrial societies such as those in western Europe. Lenin, who was the Father of Russian communism, thought that communism could only occur in agrarian Russia if an intellectual elite led it. Lenin believed that a small disciplined party of professional revolutionaries would prepare the groundwork by which the state would wither away and communism would be established.

WRONG CHOICES EXPLAINED:

(1) Imperialism is a policy whereby a strong nation seeks to dominate the political, economic, and social life of another country.

(2) Capitalism is an economic system in which the means of production and the distribution of goods and wealth are controlled by individuals and operated for profit.

(4) Militarism is a policy of glorifying military power and keeping a standing army always prepared for war.

26. **2** In Europe during the 1920s and 1930s, severe inflation, high unemployment, and fear of communism all contributed to the rise of Fascist governments in Italy, Germany, and Spain. The Fascist governments of Benito Mussolini in Italy, Adolf Hitler in Germany, and Francisco Franco in Spain came to power because these nations faced economic and political difficulties. After World War I, Italy and Germany faced widespread unemployment and inflation that created severe economic unrest. Mussolini and Hitler, the leaders of the Fascists, gained support among the middle class and business leaders by promising to improve the economy. In Germany, the government policy of simply printing money led to runaway inflation and destroyed the life savings of many people. The Great Depression of 1929 added to the economic unrest in these countries. The inability of the Italian government and the Weimar Republic to command a majority in their Parliament made it difficult to solve each nation's economic problems and maintain law and order. In Italy, as in Germany, the fear of communism also created support for the Fascists. By fighting Socialists and Communists, the Fascists won the support of industrialists and landowners. From these wealthy and influential people, Mussolini and Hitler secured funds for their party, arms for their private military forces, and jobs for their followers. Like Italy and Germany, Spain also suffered economic problems during the 1920s and 1930s. In 1931, King Alfonso XIII was overthrown after presiding over many years of social and economic chaos. A republic was set up that passed many controversial reforms that redistributed the land to peasants, limited

the role of the Catholic Church in education, and ended the privileges of the old ruling class. In 1936, the Fascist leader, Francisco Franco, led a revolt that touched off a bloody civil war. Conservatives, called Nationalists, supported Franco, and Loyalists consisting of Communists and supporters of democracy, fought for control of Spain. Hitler and Mussolini sent forces to help Franco. The Soviet Union supported the Loyalists. By 1939, Franco had triumphed. Once in power, he created a Fascist dictatorship like those of Hitler and Mussolini.

WRONG CHOICES EXPLAINED:

(1) In neither Italy nor Germany was the monarchy overthrown. In Italy, the king invited Mussolini to form a new government, but the king remained a figurehead. In Germany, the Kaiser had been abdicated at the end of World War I and the Weimar Republic was created to govern Germany.

(3) The Common Market was created in 1957 and not during the 1920s and 1930s. Italy joined the Common Market in 1957.

(4) In the 1920s and 1930s, there was not a growth of democratic institutions in Italy, Germany, and Spain. These countries turned to Fascism to solve their problems.

27.　**1** This Thomas Nast cartoon shows the competition between European nations for overseas territories after the Berlin Conference. This cartoon deals with the division of Africa, which began in earnest about 1880. At that time, the French began to expand from the West African coast toward western Sudan. The discoveries of diamonds and gold in South Africa in 1867 increased European interest in colonizing the land. No European power wanted to be left out of the race. Otto von Bismarck of Germany and Jules Ferry of France arranged for an international conference in Berlin to lay down the rules for colonizing Africa. Fourteen European nations, including Russia, Germany, England, and France, attended. The Congress of Berlin established the principle that European occupation of African territory had to be based on effective occupation that was recognized by other states and that no single European power could claim Africa. The Berlin Conference led to the "Scramble for Africa." The Germans took over lands in Eastern and Southeastern Africa. Great Britain established colonies in West Africa along the length of East Africa down to South Africa. Russia did not acquire territory in Africa but sought to extend its control over the decaying Chinese Empire. Although no African ruler attended these meetings, the conference sealed Africa's fate. By 1914, only Liberia and Ethiopia remained free from European control.

WRONG CHOICES EXPLAINED:

(2), (3), and (4) None of these events are represented in this cartoon.

28.　**4** These headlines reflect Gandhi's belief in nonviolence. In the 1920s and the 1930s, Mohandas Gandhi, called the Saintly One or Mahatma, was the leader of the Indian Nationalist Movement that sought independence from Great Britain. Gandhi preached that by using nonviolent means, such as boycotting or refusing to buy British goods, India could gain its freedom. He believed that nonviolent resistance and civil disobedience, which was the refusal to obey unjust laws, were ways to gain political freedom. In 1930, Gandhi set out to end the British salt monopoly. The Indians were forbidden to touch salt and could buy salt sold only by the British government. Gandhi claimed that the intention of his 240-mile Salt March was to break the law and condemn British rule as a curse. Gandhi's nonviolent protests, as well as his hunger strike after his arrest for the Salt March, were also designed to embarrass the British around the world. India gained its independence in 1947, one year before Gandhi's death.

WRONG CHOICES EXPLAINED:

(1) Nonalignment is a policy that Third World nations followed during the Cold War of not supporting either the United States or the Soviet Union.

(2) Isolationism is a policy of avoiding or limiting involvement in the affairs or conflicts of other nations.

(3) Appeasement is a policy used by England and France to satisfy Hitler's demands for lands during the 1930s. The purpose of these concessions was to avoid war.

29. **1** The Meiji Restoration is the occurrence in Japanese history being described in the passage. In the Meiji Period from 1862 to 1912, Japan ended feudalism and began to modernize by selectively borrowing from the West. Meiji means enlightened ruler. These reformers rallied around the emperor and unseated the shoguns, who they claimed had weakened the power of Japan. The goal of the Meiji leader was "a rich country, strong military." The new leaders sent Japanese students abroad to learn Western government, economics, technology, and customs. In 1889, Japan adapted a written constitution implementing a parliamentary government with the emperor as its head. The Meiji government set up a banking system, improved ports, and organized a telegraph and postal system. The leaders also built a modern army based on a draft and constructed a fleet of steam-powered iron ships. A broad-based program of public education was instituted.

WRONG CHOICES EXPLAINED:

(2) There is no reference to Tokugawa shogunates. Tokugawa shogunates came to power in Japan in 1603 and brought peace and stability to Japan for more than 200 years. However, the shogunates were hostile to foreigners and followed a policy of strict isolation.

(3) and (4) Neither of these statements is described in the passage. There is no reference to Buddhism or Confucianism.

30. **2** The author of the passage suggests that Japan accepted new technologies in order to modernize. During the Meiji Restoration, Japanese leaders

focused on modernizing Japan's economy to compete with western nations. During the Meiji Restoration, Japan reversed its policy of isolation and began to modernize by copying the technology of the West. The Meiji Emperor realized that the nation had to modernize in order to avoid becoming a victim of imperialism. The Japanese also brought foreign exports to Japan to improve industry. The Japanese adopted a constitution based on the model of Prussia with the emperor as the head. The Japanese were sent abroad to study western ways and to implement them in their country. However, the Japanese also wanted to become competent in western technology so that they could modernize their nation without depending on foreign powers. As a result of these efforts, the Japanese avoided becoming a victim of imperialism and became a strong industrialized nation.

WRONG CHOICES EXPLAINED:

(1), (3), and (4) None of these statements are suggested by the author in this passage. The author does not encourage them to remain isolated. He encourages Japan to become less dependent on foreign nations and does not write about Japan's becoming militaristic.

31. **2** The event that occurred immediately after this series of developments is the Japanese attack on Pearl Harbor. The Japanese attacked the American naval fleet on December 7, 1941. They damaged or destroyed 19 ships and killed more than 2,400 people. On December 8, 1941, President Franklin D. Roosevelt asked Congress to declare war on Japan.

WRONG CHOICES EXPLAINED:

(1) Manchuria became a Japanese protectorate in 1931.

(3) The Japanese fleet was destroyed at the Battle of Midway in 1942.

(4) The atomic bomb was dropped on Hiroshima on August 6, 1945.

32. **2** The factor that was the most significant force in causing the changes between 1914 and 1919 as shown on the two maps was the signing of the treaties at the end of World War I. The Versailles Treaty signed between the Allied nations and Germany contributed to the changes on the map. Poland became an independent nation for the first time in the century. The Treaty of St. Germain with Austria (1919) and the Treaty of Trianon (1920) with Hungary ended the Hapsburg Empire. Austria and Hungary became independent. Czechoslovakia, a new republic, was also created out of the Austro-Hungarian territories. In the Balkans a new South Slav state, Yugoslavia, was created. When the Communists gained control of Russia in 1918, they changed the name to the Union of the Soviet Socialist Republic. Where the Russian Empire had ruled the Baltic States, the new independent nations of Lithuania, Latvia, and Estonia emerged. The Treaty of Serves (August 1920) forced the Ottoman Turks to give up almost all their former empire. They retained only the territory that is today the country of Turkey.

WRONG CHOICES EXPLAINED:

(1) Worldwide depression began in 1929. These maps provide information about territorial changes in Europe between 1914 and 1919.

(3) and (4) These maps do not provide any data about the rise of Mussolini or the dissatisfaction of the German people. The maps show the new nations created between 1914 and 1919.

33.   **3**   The idea of nationalism is expressed in this excerpt from Brooke's poem. Rupert Brooke was an English poet who lived from 1887 to 1915. At the outbreak of World War I, he joined the Royal Naval Division. Brooke saw little combat during the war. He contracted blood poisoning from a small neglected injury and died in April 1915. Brooke is remembered as a "war poet," who inspired patriotism in the early months of World War I. "The Soldier," which is from his collection of poems entitled *War Sonnets of 1914* reflect the romantic enthusiasm and national pride that many people felt at the outbreak of World War I.

WRONG CHOICES EXPLAINED:

(1) Pacifism is an opposition to all war.

(2) Neutrality is a policy of not supporting any one side in a conflict.

(4) Anarchy is a condition in which lawlessness, confusion, and political disorder exist.

34.   **4**   A major result of the Nuremberg trials after World War II was that Nazi political and military leaders were held accountable for their actions. At the wartime meetings, the Allies had agreed that war criminals were to be brought to trial. The discovery of Hitler's death camps at the end of World War II led the Allies to put 22 surviving Nazi leaders on trial for "crimes against humanity," the murder of 11 million people. An International Military Tribunal met in 1946 at Nuremberg, a town in southern Germany. Twelve Nazis were sentenced to death, seven received long sentences, and three were acquitted. These trials showed that political and military leaders could be held accountable for their actions in wartime. The trials also exposed the evils of Nazism.

WRONG CHOICES EXPLAINED:

(1) Germany was not divided into four zones as a result of the Nuremberg trials. Germany's postwar fate was decided at the Yalta Conference in 1945.

(2) The United Nations was formed in April 1945 as an international police force and to protect the human rights of all people. The Nuremberg trials of 1946 did not result in using the United Nations to prevent future acts of genocide. The charter of the United Nations stressed the importance of human rights.

(3) The Nuremberg trials were established to address the injustices of Nazi tyranny. The Nuremberg trials did not have any impact on the formation of the North Atlantic Treaty Organization (NATO), which was formed to stop the spread of communism.

35. **4** The continued importance of the Middle East to the global economy is based on its quantity of oil reserves. Current proven oil reserves located in the Middle East nations of Saudi Arabia, Iran, Kuwait, Iraq, the United Arab Emirates, Qatar, and Oman are estimated at 367.3 billion barrels of oil. These Middle East countries have about 67 percent of the total proven oil reserves. Saudi Arabia's oil reserves, which are estimated at over 151 billion barrels, are the largest in any single country. Studies also show that the Middle East provides 30 percent of the world's oil production and has 55 percent of the world's oil reserves. Dependence on oil is a major reason why countries around the world take an active interest in the Middle East.

WRONG CHOICES EXPLAINED:
(1) The Middle East does not have research facilities to make it an important part of the world.
(2) The Middle East is not an important exporter of manufactured goods. Most nations of the Middle East import manufactured goods.
(3) The semiarid climate does not contribute to the importance of the Middle East. The semiarid climate has made the question of water rights a problem in the Middle East.

36. **1** This chart shows the organization of the United Nations (UN). The purpose of the United Nations is to maintain international peace by using collective action to remove threats to peace. The role of the UN is also to promote respect for human rights and to encourage international cooperation to solve economic, social, cultural, and humanitarian problems. The United Nations has five major bodies. Until 1995, the UN had a sixth body, the Trusteeship Council. The General Assembly, which is composed of all UN member nations, has the power to discuss all international problems and to make recommendations to the member nations. The General Assembly also makes recommendations to the Trusteeship Council and the Economic and Social Councils. The Trusteeship Council was established to supervise and safeguard the rights of colonial people. It is no longer active since colonial powers have given up all their possessions. The Economic and Social Councils (ECOSOC) were formed to protect humanity's welfare. The members of these councils are chosen by the General Assembly and elected for three years. The commission deals with human rights issues as well as social problems created by the trafficking of drugs. The Security Council, which consists of the five permanent members: United States; Great Britain; France; Russia; China; and 10 nonpermanent members, has the primary responsibility of maintaining peace and security. The Security Council has the power to call up UN member nations to take economic or military action against aggressor nations. All important decisions require the vote of nine members, including the five permanent members. If any one of the Big Five vetoes a Security Council resolution, the resolution fails. The Secretariat performs the administrative work of the United Nations and brings to the attention of the Security Council any matter threatening world peace. The

Secretary General is in charge of this body. The International Court of Justice consists of 15 judges who decide cases by majority rule. The Court settles legal disputes between nations. Nations submitting disputes to the Court agree in advance to accept its decision. The UN has a number of specialized agencies, such as the Food and Agricultural Organization (FAO), which fights hunger through agricultural improvement. The other agencies deal with problems of health, labor, and economics. These agencies are independent of the United Nations. The efforts of all these agencies are coordinated with the UN through the Economic and Social Councils.

WRONG CHOICES EXPLAINED:

(2), (3), and (4) None of these choices are shown on the chart. The chart does not outline the structure of the North Atlantic Treaty Organization (NATO), the European Union (EU), and the Organization of American States (OAS).

37. **3** This statement is referring to the establishment of the nation of Israel. In 1917, the British issued the Balfour Declaration, promising to support the establishment of a national homeland for the Jewish people in Palestine. However, the declaration also noted that nothing should be done to injure the civil and religious rights of the existing non-Jewish communities in Palestine. These communities were Arab. During the 1930s, Jewish immigration increased as anti-Semitism worsened in Europe and Jews sought safety in Palestine. By 1938, more than 500,000 Jews had migrated to Palestine. At the end of World War II, thousands of Jewish refugees left Europe for Palestine. Most of the Jewish settlers were survivors of Hitler's death camps. To both Jews and non-Jews, Hitler's murder of 6 million European Jews showed the need for a homeland where the Jews could live in safety. Together with the earliest settlers, these Jewish refugees were determined to set up a Jewish state. In 1947, the United Nations drew up a plan to divide Palestine, which was under British rule, into an Arab and Jewish state. In 1948, thirty one years after the issuance of the Balfour Declaration, Israel proclaimed its independence and the nation of Israel was established.

WRONG CHOICES EXPLAINED:

(1) Jordan was taken from the Turks by the British in World War I. Jordan, formerly known as Transjordan, was separated from the Palestine state in 1921. In 1923, Britain recognized Jordan's independence and subjected it to a mandate, which put it under British control. In 1946, Britain abolished the mandate.

(2) Poland became an independent nation in 1918 at the end of World War I.

(4) Modern Ethiopia was established in 1896.

38. **3** A statement related to the recent history of Pakistan that is an opinion is that Pakistan would be better off if it was still part of India. There

is no specific data or concrete information to support the belief that Pakistan would have been better off as part of India or as an independent Muslim nation.

WRONG CHOICES EXPLAINED:

(1) It is a fact that Pakistan gained its independence from Britain in 1947. The British passed the Indian Independence Act in 1947, dividing the Indian subcontinent into two separate states, India and Pakistan.

(2) The majority of the people who live in Pakistan are Muslims. It is a fact that 97 percent of the population is Muslim.

(4) Mohammed Ali Jinnah was a major leader in Pakistan's independence movement. In 1906, Muslim leader Mohammed Ali Jinnah formed the Muslim League to promote a separate Muslim state. In 1947, Ali Jinnah became the governor-general of an independent Pakistan.

39. **1** The caste system in India and the feudal system in Europe were similar in that both provided structure for society. The caste system in India divided society into four main groups based on occupation or birth. About 1500 B.C., India developed a complex social and economic division called castes. The four castes were scholars and priests (Brahmans); rulers and warriors; landowners and merchants; peasants and artisans. Below the castes were the Untouchables, who performed the lowest of tasks such as handling dead bodies or sweeping the streets. They were considered the outcasts of society. Caste lines were rigid and people were not permitted to marry outside their caste. The outstanding feature of the caste system was strict segregation. Feudalism was a political, economic, and social system that developed in Europe during the 1100s. A major characteristic of feudalism was the establishment of a strict class structure based on control of land and military power. Feudal society was divided into landholding nobles, or the upper class, and the peasants (serfs) who made up the majority of the people. People were born as serfs, knights, or lords, and could not change their position. Positions were determined by birth. Despite ability or hard work, the serf could not advance to a higher social status. Local nobles or lords were given lands by their rulers or kings in exchange for military service. The lords had small armies of their own made up of knights. The knights were the lowest group of nobles and constituted the bulk of the feudal armies. Most people in medieval Europe lived on the manor, which was the noble's estate, and serfs gave their lord part of their harvest in return for the use of the land. The lords provided protection for the serfs from outsiders. The feudal system, like the caste system, provided a structure for society in which social stability was established for everyone in society.

WRONG CHOICES EXPLAINED:

(2) The caste and feudal systems did not develop the concept of natural rights. Natural rights are those rights that people have from birth, such as liberty. Neither the caste system nor the feudal system assumed that individuals had any basic rights.

(3) Neither the caste system nor the feudal system established totalitarian government. Totalitarian governments are forms of government in which the state controls all aspects of a person's life. The caste system is a social system and the feudal system did not create a strong central government.

(4) The caste system and feudal system did not promote peace and prosperity. The caste system was designed to provide social peace, not economic prosperity. The feudal system could not prevent rival nobles from fighting with each other for additional lands in their kingdoms.

40.   **4** The cartoonist's view about democracy in India since 1947 is that India's progress in becoming a democratic nation has been slow. In 1947, India finally gained independence from Britain and became its own nation. No longer under colonial rule, India was left to form its own government. The country consisted of many different principalities, each of which had its own prince or ruler. This structure, along with India's rigid caste system, as well as India's religious and ethnic conflicts among the Hindus, Muslims, and Sikhs, have made it very difficult for India to adapt to a democratic system of government. The first prime minister, Nehru, helped the country adopt a federal constitution and in 1950, India became known as the "largest democracy on earth." However, it has been a slow process for India and democracy has not come easily for the country. In many ways, India's caste system—based solely on class—is counter to the idea of democracy, which puts forth that the will of the majority, regardless of class, has the power to make governmental decisions. In a caste system, the wealthier people had the biggest say in decisions about the country. Under Nehru's new system of government, universities, jobs, and positions in the army were open to all Indian citizens, regardless of the caste to which they belonged. It has been difficult for India to adjust to this shifting way of life. Furthermore, one party, the Indian National Congress, dominated the national government. Indians voted for it as the party that led them to independence. In 1996, the Bharata Janata Party gained control of the government and ended the Congress Party's domination of the government. The Congress Party returned to power after the 2004 elections. In May 2004, Dr. Manmohah Singh was sworn in as prime minister. Singh was the first non-Hindu to lead the country.

WRONG CHOICES EXPLAINED:

(1) This cartoon does not show that India has become a democratic nation after fifty years. Instead, it alludes to the difficulty that India has had in adopting a democratic system of government due to ethnic, religious, and historical trends.

(2) This cartoon does not show that India has led Asia in democratic reforms. The cartoon makes no comparison to any other Asian nation and shows only India's difficulty in dealing with democracy.

(3) This cartoon does not show that India is not—or never has been—a democratic nation. Instead, it shows the slow progress India has faced in the past fifty years.

41. **4** A problem that has faced both Cuba and North Korea under communist rule is that their command economies have been inefficient. A command economy is one in which the government makes all production decisions on what to and how to produce goods. Under the dictatorship of Fidel Castro, who has ruled Cuba since 1959, the economy of the country has declined. Although Cuba's infant mortality and literacy rates are among the best in the world, economic and social indicators have declined since the 1959 revolution. Overall, Cuban per capita food consumption declined by 11.5 percent and the number of automobiles produced has fallen since the 1950s. Cuba is the only country in Latin America in which automobile production has declined. The number of telephone lines has been virtually frozen at the 1950 level. Cuba, which ranked first in Latin America in television sets per capita, now ranks ninth in Latin America. Cuba's rate of development of electrical power since the 1950s also ranks behind every other country in Latin America, including Haiti. The per capita income for Cuba was estimated at $2,800 based on 2003 figures. The average Cuban standard of living remains at a lower level in 2003 than before the depression of the 1990s, which was caused by the loss of Soviet aid and domestic inefficiencies. Kim Jong Il has ruled North Korea since his father and the country's founder president Kim Il Sung died in 1994. North Korea is one of the world's most centrally planned and isolated economies. As a result of years of underinvestment and spare parts shortages, industrial capital stock is nearly beyond repair. Industrial and power outputs have declined greatly. Despite some good harvests recently, the nation still faces food shortages because of a lack of arable land and weather-related problems, including a major drought in 2000. North Korea also faces a chronic shortage of fertilizer and fuel, which contributes to its problems. Massive international food deliveries have allowed the regime to escape mass starvation since 1995–1996, but the population remains vulnerable to prolonged malnutrition and deteriorating living conditions. Large-scale military spending continues to eat up the resources needed for investment and civilian consumption. Heightened political tensions, especially with the United States and South Korea, have also held down the flow of desperately needed food, thus adding to the difficulties of life in North Korea.

WRONG CHOICES EXPLAINED:

(1) Cuba and North Korea are ruled by communist dictatorships, not monarchs. A monarchy is a government that is headed by a king, not a dictator.

(2) The governments of Cuba and North Korea have played an active, not a limited role, in the economy. Both governments have dominant control over what is produced in the country.

(3) In Cuba and North Korea, workers have not called many strikes. Strikes are not allowed in these communist countries.

42. **1** The correct chronological order for historical periods in European history is the Golden Age of Greece (5th century B.C.), Medieval Europe

(500–1200 A.D.), the Italian Renaissance (1300–1500), and the Enlightenment (late 1600s to 1760s).

WRONG CHOICES EXPLAINED:

(2) and (4) The Golden Age of Greece must be first in any correct chronological sequence of events.

(3) The Golden Age of Greece was followed by Medieval Europe, not the period of the Italian Renaissance.

43. **1** When Mandela referred to "climbing a great hill," he was referring to the struggle to end apartheid in South Africa. Europeans ruled South Africa for nearly 300 years. In 1919, South Africa won self-rule from Britain. However, freedom was limited to whites and the black majority was denied these rights. In 1948, the Nationalist Party in South Africa instituted a policy of apartheid. Apartheid was a policy of complete separation of the races. The government banned social contact between whites and blacks, and established segregated schools, hospitals, and neighborhoods. The African National Congress (ANC), which had been formed in 1912 to fight for the rights of blacks, organized strikes to protest these policies. In 1964, Nelson Mandela, the leader of the ANC, was arrested for his opposition to apartheid. He was imprisoned for 27 years. In 1990, Nelson Mandela was released from prison. By 1991, the South African Parliament repealed the apartheid laws. The end of apartheid was the first step toward political equality for all men. In 1994, the ANC won 62 percent of the vote in the nation's first multicultural election; Mandela was also elected the first South African black president.

WRONG CHOICES EXPLAINED:

(2) In 1994, Mandela was not referring to the struggle to modernize South Africa's economy. After his election in 1994, Mandela was faced with raising the standard of living for many disadvantaged South Africans. However, the economy of South Africa was not undeveloped. The country's large deposits of gold, diamonds, and uranium had contributed to the country's prosperity.

(3) Economic sanctions against South Africa ended in 1991, when the government ended its policy of apartheid.

(4) Mandela's struggle was not to stop majority rule in South Africa. The struggle against apartheid would give the majority of Africans eventual control of the government, which had been run by minority Europeans for more than three centuries.

44. **2** The statement that best describes an impact of the computer on the global economy is that companies now market more products worldwide. In the early 21st century, the volume of international trade stood at an all-time high. Just after World War II, its total amounted to 57 billion; by the end of the century this total was a staggering 6,890 billion. The advent of the Computer Revolution has helped to contribute to the growth of trade. Personal computers have become essential in most offices. Millions of people

around the globe can be connected through computers. A variety of consumer products, such as microwave ovens, mobile phones, digital music players, and cars, use computer chips. Starting in 1990, businesses and individuals began using the Internet. The Internet is the voluntary linkage of computer networks around the world. Corporations have been competing to offer services across the world. People use the Internet to shop for hard-to-find products. Business firms and other types of organizations have expanded their normal operations by developing web sites on the Internet. A web site provides information about a company, its products, and services. This information makes more products available to people around the world.

WRONG CHOICES EXPLAINED:

(1) Computers have not increased tariffs on imports. Computers have helped to create an interdependent economy, based on the free exchange of imports among nations. Increasing tariffs or taxes on imports would hurt the global economy's prospects for growth.

(3) Wages have not risen dramatically for most people in developing countries because of the impact of the computers. Some workers in the computer and technical field have benefited, but the majority of the workers in developing countries have not seen an increase in their wages. In India, a majority of the people live on less than $2 a day, even though a small percentage of computer workers make much more money.

(4) Computers have not contributed to the decline of the price of oil and other resources worldwide. In 2004, oil prices and prices of other resources, such as lumber and steel, were very high.

45. **3** A belief that is shared by an African who practices animism and a Japanese who practices Shinto is that spirits exist in both living and nonliving things. Animism is a belief that the spirit of nature inhabits all living and nonliving objects. Africans respect nature because they believe that it created all things. For example, some Pygmy tribes in Africa believe in a Supreme Being that they identify with the forest. Animism is not one set religion because separate villages and tribes have different sets of beliefs. The one common bond in animism is the idea that spirits exist in the forces of nature and in all living and nonliving things. Shintoism in Japan, like animism in Africa, combines the notion that objects possess a living spirit and worship nature. The Japanese believe that the spirit of *kami* lives in everything from plants and animals to rocks and mountains. Spirits also control natural forces such as earthquakes and typhoons. The Japanese also believe that through prayers and offerings, you can win the favor of the spirits. Animism and Shintoism focus on the importance of spirits in their religions.

WRONG CHOICES EXPLAINED:

(1) Shintoism does not promote the belief that only one god rules the universe. Animists believe in one Supreme Being, but they also believe that a number of lesser gods or spirits help them in the universe.

(2) Neither animism nor Shintoism believes that periodic fasting is essential to spiritual purity. Animists and Shintoists do not seek spiritual purity but want to win favor with the spirits by offering prayers and offerings.

(4) Buddhists, not animists or Shintoists, believe that all suffering is caused by desire and selfishness.

46. **2** The headline that would most likely have appeared in a pamphlet during the Industrial Revolution is "Karl Marx Attacks Capitalism." The Industrial Revolution, which began in England in the 1750s, brought about many economic and social changes. The Industrial Revolution gave rise to the factory system, which relocated workers from the home to the factory. The average workday was 12 to 14 hours. Workers were subjected to unsanitary conditions and suffered from poor health. Karl Marx believed that industrial leaders, or the capitalists, were exploiting the workers. In 1848, Marx wrote *The Communist Manifesto* as a propaganda document to inspire revolutionaries in capitalistic societies. He strongly believed that all the evils of industrial society would disappear when communism was established. Karl Marx believed that history was determined by economic class struggle. Marx proposed a scientific theory of history in which economic conditions determine history. He wrote that history is a struggle between the haves and have-nots. In ancient times, the struggle was between plebeians and patricians. During the Middle Ages, the struggle was between lords and serfs. In industrial societies, the final struggle is between the factory owners, who are the haves, and the workers, who are the have-nots. Marx predicted that there would be a worldwide revolution in which the workers would rise up against the owners and form a classless society. The conflict is inevitable because workers worldwide are being oppressed by capitalist owners.

WRONG CHOICES EXPLAINED:
(1) Michelangelo completed the Sistine Chapel during the Renaissance in the 16th century.

(3) Martin Luther spoke out against the sale of indulgences during the Protestant Reformation in 1517.

(4) John Locke called for the people to choose the king during the Glorious Revolution in England in the 17th century.

47. **2** The main idea of this 1995 cartoon is that the United Nations was ineffective in its attempt to end genocide in Kosovo, a southern Serbian province. Genocide, or ethnic cleansing, describes the systematic extermination of an entire ethnic, political, religious, or national group. In the 1990s, the United Nations was ineffective in preventing Bosnian Serbs from expelling Bosnian Muslims living in Serbian-held territory. The United Nations and the European Union arranged a series of cease-fires monitored by UN peacekeeping forces. However, the UN could not stop the fighting. In 1995, the intervention of NATO led to the end of fighting but not before 200,000 were killed. In December 1995, the Dayton Accords provided for

division of Bosnia into a Muslim federation and a Bosnian Serb republic joined under a central government in Sarajevo. UN troops remained in Bosnia with 60,000 NATO troops helping to enforce the agreement. In 1997, President Milosevic, who had begun a campaign of ethnic cleansing in Serbia, set his sights on Kosovo. The Serbians in Kosovo attempted to remove, by killing, all ethnic Albanians. Hundreds of villages and thousands of homes were destroyed throughout the region. Serbian forces stole personal belongings and documents, telling the Albanians they would never return to Kosovo. NATO attempted to give ethnic Albanians self-rule in Kosovo but President Milosevic refused. Finally, in March 1999, NATO warplanes and missile attacks forced Milosevic to cease his genocide of Kosovo Albanians. The UN, as in Bosnia, was unable to stop the fighting in Kosovo. It was the intervention of NATO, not the UN, that ended the genocide.

WRONG CHOICES EXPLAINED:

(1) This cartoon does not show that the United Nations supported the Serbians in Kosovo. The man in the cartoon refers to the ineffective "reprimands" sent to the Serbians. The United Nation tried—and failed—repeatedly to cease the genocide in Kosovo.

(3) This cartoon does not show that the killing in Kosovo stopped because of United Nations reprimands. In fact, it shows two men standing on a pile of dead bodies—victims of the Kosovo genocide. The United Nations reprimands did little to stop the ethnic cleansing.

(4) This cartoon does not show that the Serbians lost the battle for Kosovo. It shows Serbians who did not pay heed to the United Nations reprimands and instead continued their campaign of ethnic cleansing in Kosovo.

48. **2** The title that best completes this partial outline is "Causes of World War I." Increased tensions and suspicions during the late 19th century led nations in Europe to form alliances to defend each other in case of attacks. By 1914, the two most important alliances were the Triple Alliance, consisting of Germany, Austria-Hungary, and Italy, and the Triple Entente, consisting of Britain, France, and Russia. Imperial rivalry over Africa also led to tensions in Europe. Britain, France, Germany, and other nations competed for colonies and economic power. France and Germany competed for colonial gains in Africa. They also clashed over Morocco. Britain and Germany, both highly industrialized nations, competed for imperialist control in Africa. There was an arms race in which the great powers competed with each other to expand their armies and navies, thus contributing to tensions in Europe. Britain, which relied heavily upon its navy for protection, considered Germany's huge naval building program a threat to its security. The spark that set off World War I was the assassination of Archduke Ferdinand and his wife on June 28, 1914 by a Serbian nationalist. Archduke Ferdinand was the heir to the Austrian throne. The assassination created a chain reaction of events. Austria-Hungary declared war on Serbia. Russia, which supported Serbia, declared war on Austria-Hungary. Germany, which was a member of

the Triple Alliance, declared war on Russia and France. France was an ally of Russia. England, as a member of the Triple Entente, declared war on Germany after it violated Belgium neutrality. By August 1914, the European continent was engulfed in a major war.

WRONG CHOICES EXPLAINED:
    (1), (3), and (4) None of these choices deal with the series of events that led to World War I.

49.   **4** These statements illustrate the concept of the impact of geography on cultural development. Gourds and hard shells are found in the tropical zone of Africa. Traditional Africa is filled with a variety of hornlike instruments, either made from gourds or with shells. These include trumpet-type horns, along with double- and single-reed oboes and clarinet snake charmers. Rattles, xylophones, which were called marimbas in Africa, and drums are made from gourds.

The Ancient Egyptians believed that it was important to record information about their religion and government. Scribes were able to preserve their beliefs on papyrus scrolls. Papyrus was the important writing material in Ancient Egypt. Our word *paper* is derived from the word papyrus. Papyrus is a triangular reed that used to grow along the banks of the Nile River. The annual flooding of the Nile River provided rich soils that enabled people to grow abundant crops that could support large populations and more advanced cultures. The mild climate along the Nile River enabled papyrus to flourish and provided the writing material used by the Egyptians to preserve their history in the form of writing known as hieroglyphics.

Japan's small size has influenced its approach to art. In their crowded cities and limited rural spaces, the Japanese created an art style in miniature. The Japanese Shinto beliefs about the forces of nature also affected their approach to art. Artists and artisans learned to suggest an idea, a thought, or a feeling with a minimum amount of detail. A few bold lines, for example, could suggest to the viewer the artist's impression of a mountain. A tiny garden could be created with sand, a single rock, or a twisted toe. The belief that beauty could be found in ordinary objects influenced such Japanese traditions as landscaping, gardening, flower arranging, and even tea ceremonies.

WRONG CHOICES EXPLAINED:
    (1), (2), and (3) None of these statements address the issue of education in the ancient world, the development of traditional government, or the effect of artistic expression on religion.

50.   **4** Based on an analysis of these statements, the conclusion that is accurate is that slavery remains a problem in the modern era. The Declaration of Human Rights was adapted in 1948 by the UN, outlining the basic rights of all individuals without regard to race, color, sex, or nationality. One of these basic rights was to end slavery or the slave trade in all forms.

Unfortunately, the slave trade still exists in the 21st century. Many workers and women are sent into bondage. The UN recently reported that people traffic is the fastest-growing business of organized crime. The UN believes that some 200 million people may now be in the hands of traffickers. Regions that suffer flooding or desertification create desperate migrants willing to go anywhere to survive. With the collapse of communism, the transition to market economies has turned millions into casualties of rapid economic change. Those who seek a better life often end up as virtual slaves in order to repay the cost of their voyage. The traffic in women and girls is also fueled by poverty and despair. Traffickers prey upon starving families in Asia who are unable to feed or provide a dowry for their daughters. According to a CIA report, traffickers can buy a female from unwitting families for less than the price of a toaster by promising to educate the child in a distant city. Like workers, the girls are held captive, permanently in debt to their owners. Within the last decade, more than 30 million women and children have been sold within and from Southeast Asia to work in sweatshops or for sexual purposes.

WRONG CHOICES EXPLAINED:

(1) These statements do not provide any information on whether governments have taken active steps to end slavery.

(2) These statements show that the United Nations has not solved the problem of slavery. Slavery still exists in the 21st century.

(3) There is no information from these statements to show the number of enslaved persons in 1948.

THEMATIC ESSAY: GENERIC SCORING RUBRIC

Score of 5:
- Shows a thorough understanding of the theme or problem
- Addresses all aspects of the task
- Shows an ability to analyze, evaluate, compare and/or contrast issues and events
- Richly supports the theme or problem with relevant facts, examples, and details
- Is a well-developed essay, consistently demonstrating a logical and clear plan of organization
- Introduces the theme or problem by establishing a framework that is beyond a simple restatement of the task and concludes with a summation of the theme or problem

Score of 4:
- Shows a good understanding of the theme or problem
- Addresses all aspects of the task
- Shows an ability to analyze, evaluate, compare and/or contrast issues and events
- Includes relevant facts, examples, and details, but may not support all aspects of the theme or problem evenly
- Is a well-developed essay, demonstrating a logical and clear plan of organization
- Introduces the theme or problem by establishing a framework that is beyond a simple restatement of the task and concludes with a summation of the theme or problem

Score of 3:
- Shows a satisfactory understanding of the theme or problem
- Addresses most aspects of the task or addresses all aspects in a limited way
- Shows an ability to analyze or evaluate issues and events, but not in any depth
- Includes some facts, examples, and details
- Is a satisfactorily developed essay, demonstrating a general plan of organization
- Introduces the theme or problem by repeating the task and concludes by repeating the theme or problem

Score of 2:
- Shows limited understanding of the theme or problem
- Attempts to address the task
- Develops a faulty analysis or evaluation of issues and events
- Includes few facts, examples, and details, and may include information that contains inaccuracies
- Is a poorly organized essay, lacking focus
- Fails to introduce or summarize the theme or problem

Score of 1:
- Shows very limited understanding of the theme or problem
- Lacks an analysis of evaluation of the issues and events
- Includes little or no accurate or relevant facts, examples, or details

- Attempts to complete the task, but demonstrates a major weakness in organization
- Fails to introduce or summarize the theme or problem

Score of 0: Fails to address the task, is illegible, or is a blank paper

PART II: THEMATIC ESSAY QUESTION

Societies have developed different economic systems to meet the conditions created during a period in history. During the Middle Ages in Europe, feudalism emerged as a political, social, and economic system to serve the needs of Medieval society. The basis of the feudal economy was manorialism, which would dominate European society until the end of the 12th century.

During the 8th, 9th, and 10th centuries, feudalism developed in western society because organized governments fell apart. Charlemagne was the most outstanding ruler of the Medieval period in western Europe. He was crowned Emperor of the Romans in 800, but his empire fell apart after his death in 814. The breakup of Charlemagne's Empire, as well as the continued raids and attacks by the Northmen in the West, the Magyar in the East, and the Muslims in the Mediterranean, weakened the existing governments. These invasions also caused widespread disorder and suffering for the people. At this time, most European nations lived in constant fear of invasions.

There was no central government and local kings were unable to protect their subjects from foreign invasions and local warfare. Cities were destroyed and communities were cut off from each other. Small farmers surrendered their lands to powerful local nobles in exchange for their promise of protection.

Feudalism was a system of holding land in exchange for military service. It was based on mutual obligations. In exchange for military protection and service, lords or landowners granted land called fiefs. The person receiving a fief was called a vassal.

In a feudal system, there was a rigid class distinction based on a person's prestige and power. Social class was usually inherited. The structure of medieval society was clearly defined. People were born into their social positions and there was little chance of moving up the social ladder. The nobility consisted of the kings and queens, greater lords, lesser lords, and knights. The powerful lords, few in number, controlled the land and power. There was a king at the top of the social ladder but he was weak and had little power beyond his own domain. The clergy was highly respected due to the dominance of the Roman Catholic Church. The vast majority of the people were peasants. The peasants, or serfs, could not leave the place where they were born. Although they were bound to the soil, serfs were not slaves. The lord could sell or buy them. The wealth of the feudal lords came from the labor of the peasants.

The basis of the medieval economy was manorialism. Manorialism was an economic system structured around a lord's manor or estate. Agriculture was the most important industry. Most people depended upon the land for a living. The manor system was also based on a set of rights and obligations between the lords and serfs. Serfs farmed the lord's land and did other work, such as repairing roads and fences. In return for the service provided by the peasants, the lord provided them with several acres of land to farm. Peasant women shared in the farm work with their husbands. All peasants, whether serfs or free, owed the lord certain duties. These included a few days' labor each week and a certain portion of their grain. The serfs also had to give the lords a share of the goods they prepared in the lord's winepress, flour mill, and baking ovens. The lords were supposed to protect the serfs during times of war.

The manor, or the estate of the land, was the center of medieval life. Manors, including farmland, usually ranged in size from 900 to 3,000 acres. On the manor were found the lord's castle, the fields in which crops were grown, and the village in which the peasants lived. Most peasants rarely traveled more than 25 miles from their manor. The manor was largely a self-sufficient community. The serfs and peasants raised crops and livestock for food, spun wool for clothing, tanned leather shoes, and cut lumber for furniture and buildings. However, some essential items, such as salt and iron for making tools, had to be secured from outside sources.

The economic system of manorialism was extremely difficult and harsh for the peasants. After meeting their obligations to their lords, the serfs had little left for themselves. They also had little personal freedom. Peasants had to pay a marriage tax. Weddings could take place only with the lord's consent. Serfs lived in crowded villages with only one or two rooms for an entire family. The estimated life expectancy of the peasants was less than 35 years of age.

In proportion to its size and labor force, the manor raised insufficient crops. Each serf family was assigned scattered strips of land rather than compact farms. The manor also followed the inefficient three field system, which meant leaving only one-third of the land uncultivated every year. Furthermore, as the manor became more self-sufficient, trade came to a virtual standstill from the 9th to the 11th centuries. Feudal wars and inadequate roads and bridges made commerce unsafe and difficult. Moreover, heavy taxes imposed by each feudal lord on goods transported across his domain raised the cost of goods. These conditions contributed to limited progress and difficulties of life during the Middle Ages.

The economic system of manorialism developed during the Middle Ages in western society in order to provide the needs of its society, which had to address the problems created by the collapse of a strong central government in western Europe. As conditions changed in Europe due to the Crusades and the growth of trade in the late 12th century, the system of manorialism would decline and disappear as society's economic needs began to change.

PART III: DOCUMENT-BASED QUESTION

Part A: Short Answers

Document 1

Two ways the Black Death spread throughout Europe are:

(1) It was carried by fleas that infested black rats that entered Europe along trade routes from the East.

(2) It was spread by the primitive 14th century urban sanitation.

Note: This response receives full credit because it cites specific ways that the Black Death spread throughout Europe.

Document 2

One impact of the Black Death on European society was the death by the thousands of the lower and most of the middle classes.

Note: This response receives full credit because it shows the impact of the Black Death on European society.

Document 3

Two effects of the Black Death on the economy of England are:

(1) Ox hides fell to wretched prices but the price of gloves rose to 10d., 12d., or 14d.

(2) Workers who had been ordered by the king not to charge more than they had before the outbreak of the plague refused to follow his orders. They demanded more and refused to work if they were not paid the wages they requested.

Note: This response receives full credit because it describes specific ways in which the Black Death affected the economy of England.

Document 4

These two maps show that one way smallpox was introduced to Central and South America was through the voyages of exploration of Cortés to the Aztec and Maya in 1520 and 1524 and Pizarro's voyage to the Inca Empire in Peru in 1532.

Note: This response receives full credit because it demonstrates how smallpox was introduced to Central and South America.

Document 5

Two results of the smallpox epidemic in Latin America are:

(1) More than half of the Native American population in most provinces died either from the disease or from starvation.

(2) Many died in heaps like bedbugs and in many places everyone in a house died.

Note: This response receives full credit because it cites specific examples from the document to show the results of the smallpox epidemic in Latin America.

Document 6

The decline in Latin America's native populations affected the population of Africa because it led to the enslavement of many Africans. The total number of Africans enslaved in the Americas was close to 95 million, of which a majority went to Latin America.

Note: This response receives full credit because it cites specific facts to show how the decline of the native American population in Latin America affected Africa.

Document 7

One way HIV has spread in China is by selling blood at government-owned collection stations under a procedure that could return pooled and infected blood to donors.

Note: This response receives full credit because it demonstrates how HIV has spread in China.

Document 8

One factor that has contributed to the spread of AIDS is through misconceptions, taboos, and outright deceit, which have fostered denial among officials and the broader population in many countries such as India and China.

Note: This response receives full credit because it identifies how various factors have contributed to the spread of AIDS.

Document 9

Two ways AIDS has affected Africa are:

(1) Schools have been robbed of their teachers, hospitals of their doctors and nurses, and children of their parents. AIDS has created some 12 million orphans.

(2) Twenty-six million Africans are HIV infected.

Note: This response receives full credit because it states how AIDS has affected Africa.

DOCUMENT-BASED QUESTION: GENERIC SCORING RUBRIC

Score of 5:
- Thoroughly addresses all aspects of the *Task* by accurately analyzing and interpreting at least **four** documents
- Incorporates information from the documents in the body of the essay
- Incorporates relevant outside information
- Richly supports the theme or problem with relevant facts, examples, and details
- Is a well-developed essay, consistently demonstrating a logical and clear plan of organization
- Introduces the theme or problem by establishing a framework that is beyond a simple restatement of the *Task* or *Historical Context* and concludes with a summation of the theme or problem

Score of 4:
- Addresses all aspects of the *Task* by accurately analyzing and interpreting at least **four** documents
- Incorporates information from the documents in the body of the essay
- Incorporates relevant outside information
- Includes relevant facts, examples, and details, but discussion may be more descriptive than analytical
- Is a well-developed essay, demonstrating a logical and clear plan of organization
- Introduces the theme or problem by establishing a framework that is beyond a simple restatement of the *Task* or *Historical Context* and concludes with a summation of the theme or problem

Score of 3:
- Addresses most aspects of the *Task* or addresses all aspects of the *Task* in a limited way, using some of the documents
- Incorporates some information from the documents in the body of the essay
- Incorporates limited or no relevant outside information
- Includes some facts, examples, and details, but discussion is more descriptive than analytical
- Is a satisfactorily developed essay, demonstrating a general plan of organization
- Introduces the theme or problem by repeating the *Task* or *Historical Context* and concludes by simply repeating the theme or problem

Score of 2:
- Attempts to address some aspects of the *Task*, making limited use of the documents
- Presents no relevant outside information
- Includes few facts, examples, and details; discussion restates contents of the documents

- Is a poorly organized essay, lacking focus
- Fails to introduce or summarize the theme or problem

Score of 1:
- Shows limited understanding of the *Task* with vague, unclear references to the documents
- Presents no relevant outside information
- Includes little or no accurate or relevant facts, details, or examples
- Attempts to complete the *Task*, but demonstrates a major weakness in organization
- Fails to introduce or summarize the theme or problem

Score of 0: Fails to address the *Task*, is illegible, or is a blank paper

Part B: Essay

Throughout global history, rapidly spreading diseases have severely impacted the fabric of a society. The heavy death toll caused by diseases destroyed a large segment of the population in both western Europe and the Americas. The Black Death in the 14th century and smallpox in the 16th century were two epidemics that had devastating effects on the people and the society in which they lived.

In 1347, four Genovese ships arrived in Sicily from the Black Sea carrying a dreaded cargo. It was the disease known as the Black Death or Bubonic Plague. The victims of this terrible plague had a raging fever. Black swellings grew at their necks and joints. The name Black Death comes from these swellings of purplish or black spots. The disease spread with frightening speed (Doc. 1). From Italy, it followed the trade routes to France, Germany, England, and other parts of Europe. The disease was spread by fleas on rats (Doc. 1). Fleas jumped from the rats to infest clothes and packs of traders traveling west. As a result, the disease spread from Asia to the Muslim world, and throughout Europe. In addition, terrible sanitary conditions in Europe's cities also promoted the spread of the Black Death (Doc. 1).

Medieval people threw their garbage and sewage into the streets. These unsanitary streets became breeding grounds for more rats. Scurrying rats spread the plague through the crowded cities. Furthermore, unaware of what a little flea bite might mean, people paid little attention until they noticed the swelling and black bruises on their skin, which led to heavy sweats, convulsive coughing, and death.

The Black Death struck with such stunning speed that frightened people did not know how to react. Many of them, such as those in Florence, remained in their houses and most of them died because they received no care or attention (Doc. 2). Normal life broke down. Dead bodies were carried out of the houses and decaying bodies filled the streets (Doc. 2). Houses were left vacant and whole villages disappeared as people either died or fled in terror (Doc. 1). Great palaces and nobles' homes were vacant as the plague destroyed these households (Doc. 2). Some people turned to magic and witchcraft for cures. Others plunged into wild pleasures (hedonism) (Doc. 1), while others saw the plague as God's punishment. Giovanni Boccaccio, the Italian Humanist, in his book *The Decameron*, describes how the plague not only destroyed the city of Florence, but also the rural areas. Peasants who saw death neglected their work and thought only of enjoying what they had (Doc. 2). They allowed their cows and other farm animals to wander at will and did nothing.

The Bubonic Plague took about four years to reach almost every corner of Europe. The estimated death toll was about one-quarter to one-third of the European population. (Doc. 1). In any given crowded town the mortality rate may have exceeded 50 percent while in rural areas it tended to be somewhat less (Doc. 1). The Black Death claimed more lives than any war until the 20th century.

The plague returned periodically in the 1300s, but never as severely as in the first outbreak. The economic effects of the plague were enormous. As workers and employers died, production declined. Prices rose as survivors demanded higher wages. In England, the price of ox hides fell but the price of gloves continued to rise (Doc. 3). Fewer people meant that workers were scarce everywhere. The English king forbade workers to ask for higher wages but they refused to follow his decree (Doc. 3.). Farmlands were abandoned or used to pasture sheep, which required less labor. Serfs, who often had been unpaid or poorly paid for their labor, left the manors in search of better wages. The old manorial system began to crumble. There was no one left on the manor to look after the cattle or other possessions of the lord (Doc 3).

In 1381, peasants in England revolted as nobles resisted their demands for higher wages. Peasants burned the manors and killed the local lords. Similar uprisings took place in France, Italy, and Belgium. In each case, nobles put down these uprisings. The Black Death and its aftermath disrupted the social structure of medieval society.

The smallpox epidemic in the 16th century severely affected the societies in the Americas. Before the Spanish voyages of exploration began in 1492, smallpox was unknown in the Americas. The Indians did not have the immunities that the Europeans had developed through long contact with these diseases. Columbus' voyages ended the Americas' isolation (Doc. 4). Indians were exposed to germs carried by European explorers and colonizers. Deadly epidemics swept over the Caribbean. Smallpox was called the great leprosy by the Indians because the victims were covered with pimples that made them look like lepers (Doc. 5). Smallpox wiped out whole villages in a matter of months. Hispaniola had an estimated population of 250,000 Indians in 1492. Twenty years later the population had fallen to 60,000.

In 1521, the Spanish Conquistador Hernándo Cortés spread the smallpox plague to Mexico and later Francisco Pizarro and his men carried the dreaded disease to the Inca Empire of Peru (Doc. 4). The Aztec Indians of Mexico did not know any remedy for the disease. They believed in bathing to help them deal with the illness and thought that it was a way to help cure them of the disease (Doc. 5). Unfortunately, they were unable to resist the devastating effects of the disease. Many died of starvation and in some provinces over half of the population was destroyed (Doc. 5). In some instances, Native Americans pulled down their houses over them in order to check the stench that rose from the dead bodies. Their houses became their tombs (Doc. 5).

The smallpox epidemic destroyed the native population of Central and South America. In 1519, when Cortés landed in Mexico, the native population of Central Mexico was 25 million, and by 1523, it was 16.8 million. It continued to decline to 8 million in 1540 and to a low of 1.5 million by 1605. In the first century of Spanish rule (1500–1600), the native populations in Central and South America died by the millions. By 1650, the population of Central Mexico had declined by 85 percent.

The loss of native life due to smallpox was incredible. One of the effects of the loss was a severe shortage of labor in the colonies. Europeans had planned to use Native Americans as a source of cheap labor. Sugar plantations and tobacco farms required a large supply of workers to make them profitable. Therefore, the Europeans in Brazil, the Caribbean, and the Americas turned to Africa for workers. Many Africans had been exposed to various European diseases and had built up immunities to them. About 40 percent of these slaves worked on the plantations in the Dutch, French, and English colonies in the Caribbean (Doc. 6). The enslaved Africans labored on the sugar, tobacco, and coffee plantations. About 30 percent of the slaves worked on the sugar plantations in Brazil and about 16 percent on the Spanish colonies in the Americas (Doc. 6). A small number of enslaved Africans eventually were imported to the British North American colonies. The overall total of Africans enslaved in the Americas from the 16th to the 19th century was over 9.5 million.

The Black Death in Europe during the 14th century and the smallpox epidemic in the Americas in the 16th century would have a lasting effect on these societies. The Black Death destroyed the medieval society of the Middle Ages in Europe and the smallpox epidemic destroyed the native population leading to the enslavement of Africans in the Americas. These biological diseases have had lasting political, economic, and social effects that still influence the world in the 21st century.

Topic	Question Numbers	Total Number of Questions	Number Wrong	*Reason for Wrong Answer
U.S. AND N.Y. HISTORY				
WORLD HISTORY	5, 6, 7, 11, 16, 17, 19, 22, 24, 27, 29, 31, 33, 34, 36, 38, 42, 43, 45, 46, 47, 48	22		
GEOGRAPHY	1, 3, 4, 8, 10, 12, 13, 14, 21, 23, 32, 35, 37, 49	14		
ECONOMICS	2, 9, 28, 30, 39, 41, 44, 50	8		
CIVICS, CITIZENSHIP, AND GOVERNMENT	15, 18, 20, 25, 26, 40	6		

*Your reason for answering the question incorrectly might be (a) lack of knowledge, (b) misunderstanding the question, or (c) careless error.

Actual Items by Standard and Unit

	1 U.S. and N.Y. History	2 World History	3 Geography	4 Economics	5 Civics, Citizenship, and Gov't	Number
Methodology of Global History and Geography						
UNIT ONE Ancient World		5, 6	1, 3, 4	2	15	7
UNIT TWO Expanding Zones of Exchange		7, 11, 16, 17	8, 10, 14	9		8
UNIT THREE Global Interactions			13			1
UNIT FOUR First Global Age			12		18	2
UNIT FIVE Age of Revolution		19, 22, 24, 27, 29	21, 23, 30		20	9
UNIT SIX Crisis and Achievement (1900–1945)		31, 33, 48	32		25, 26	6
UNIT SEVEN 20th Century Since 1945		34, 36, 38, 43	37	28, 35	40	8
UNIT EIGHT Global Connections and Interactions		47		44, 50		3
Cross topical		42, 45, 46	49	39, 41		6
Total # of Questions		22	14	8	6	50
% of Items by Standard		44%	28%	16%	12%	100%

Examination
June 2005
Global History and Geography

PART I: MULTIPLE CHOICE

Directions (1–50): For each statement or question, write in the space provided, the *number* of the word or expression that, of those given, best completes the statement or answers the question.

1 During which period did the domestication of animals and growing of crops first occur?

1 Iron Age   3 Neolithic Revolution

2 Old Stone Age   4 Scientific Revolution   1 ____

Base your answer to question 2 on the statements below and on your knowledge of social studies.

- The fertile soil of river valleys allowed early civilizations to develop and flourish.
- In the 1500s and 1600s, control of the Strait of Malacca determined who traded in the Spice Islands.
- Because Japan is an island that is mostly mountainous, people live in densely populated areas along the coast.

2 Which conclusion is best supported by these statements?

1 Major urban centers are found only along rivers.
2 The geography of a nation or region influences its development.
3 Without mountains and rivers, people cannot develop a culture.
4 The spread of new ideas is discouraged by trade and conquest.

2 ____

3 Which statement about cultural diffusion in Asia is most accurate?

1 Byzantine traders brought the Justinian Code to China.
2 Roman legions introduced Christianity to India.
3 Indian monks brought Islam to the Middle East.
4 Chinese ideas and practices spread into Korea and Japan.

3 ____

4 Which statement about Greek civilization is an opinion rather than a fact?

1 Boys in Sparta were trained to be soldiers.
2 Athens had a better culture than that of Sparta.
3 Socrates, Plato, and Aristotle were Greek philosophers.
4 Many adults in Athens did not have the right to vote.

4 ____

Base your answers to questions 5 and 6 on the diagram below and on your knowledge of social studies.

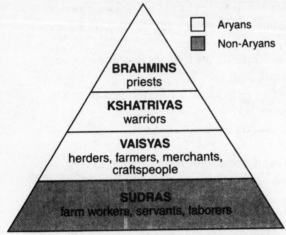

Source: *Guide to the Essentials of World History,* Prentice Hall, 1999 (adapted)

5 Which concept is illustrated in the diagram?

1 manorialism   3 caste

2 apartheid   4 encomienda   5 _____

6 Which religion or belief system is most closely associated with the social class system illustrated in the diagram?

1 Hinduism   3 Catholicism

2 Daoism   4 animism   6 _____

Base your answer to question 7 on the map below and on your knowledge of social studies.

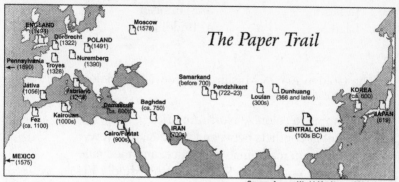

Source: *Aramco World*, May/June, 1999 (adapted)

7 The technology of papermaking traveled from China to Baghdad along the

1 Saharan caravan trails
2 Trans-Siberian Railway
3 Silk Roads
4 Suez Canal   7____

8 ". . . Let the king and his ministers labor with a mutual sympathy, saying, 'We have received the decree of Heaven and it shall be great as the long-continued years of Hsia; yea, it shall not fail of the long continued years of Yin.' I wish the king, through the attachment of the lower people, to receive the long-abiding decree of Heaven. . . ."

Clae Waltham, ed., Shu Ching, Book of History,
Henry Regnery Company

Which concept is being referred to in this passage?

1 dynastic cycle   3 natural rights
2 matriarchal society   4 monotheism   8____

9 The religious terms *Four Noble Truths*, *Eightfold Path*, and *nirvana* are most closely associated with

1 Judaism   3 Shintoism
2 Islam   4 Buddhism   9 ____

10 The Golden Age of Muslim culture was best known for its

1 attempts to colonize North America
2 frequent conflicts between Christians and Jews
3 advances in mathematics, science, and medicine
4 policies to reduce trade between the Middle East and China   10 ____

11 The Commercial Revolution helped lead to the Industrial Revolution because during the Commercial Revolution

1 the barter system was instituted
2 new forms of business were developed
3 socialism was introduced to Europe
4 subsistence agriculture was promoted   11 ____

Base your answer to question 12 on the map below and on your knowledge of social studies.

Mongol Areas of Influence

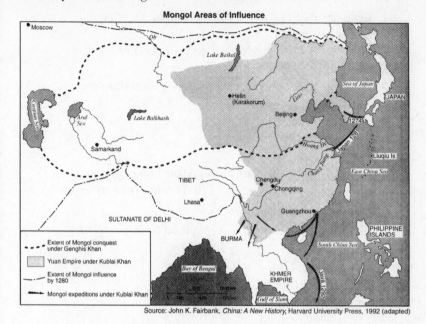

Source: John K. Fairbank, *China: A New History,* Harvard University Press, 1992 (adapted)

12 Which statement about the Mongols is supported by the information in the map?

  1 The Yuan dynasty kept China isolated from outside influence.

  2 Most of the Chinese people lived in the river valleys.

  3 Kublai Khan and Genghis Khan extended Mongol influence to other parts of Asia.

  4 The city of Samarkand was part of the Yuan Empire.

12 _____

13 What is meant by Machiavelli's belief that "the end justifies the means"?

1 Leaders may use any method to achieve what is best for the state.
2 The general public always acts in its own best interest.
3 Pleasing all of the people at any given time is possible.
4 Leaders must always act for the common good.   13____

14 Venice in Europe, Mogadishu in Africa, and Canton in China emerged during the 13th century primarily as important centers of

| 1 agriculture | 3 manufacturing |
| 2 trade | 4 mining |

14____

15 What was one influence of Mongol rule on the history of Russia?

1 Contact with kingdoms in western Europe greatly increased.
2 The Chinese writing system was introduced and adopted.
3 Most Russians converted from Orthodox Christianity to Islam.
4 Russian leaders adopted the idea of strong, centralized control of the empire.   15____

16 • Timbuktu is known as a great center of learning and trade.

  • Walls of Great Zimbabwe reveal a powerful and rich society.
  • Complex culture produces brass sculptures in Benin.

What generalization can be made on the basis of these statements?

1 Religious beliefs were the most important element in many African societies.
2 Some African societies achieved a high level of economic and cultural development.
3 North African societies were more advanced than South African societies.
4 Most African societies were hundreds of years behind Asian societies in using technology. 16 ____

17 The major reason that Portugal and Spain established water routes to Asia's spice markets was to

1 experiment with new technology such as the astrolabe and sextant
2 provide jobs for navigators, cartographers, and shipbuilders
3 avoid the overland routes that were controlled by Muslim traders
4 discover new continents, plants, and animals 17 ____

18 The Magna Carta can be described as a

1 journal about English feudal society
2 list of feudal rights that limited the power of the English monarchy
3 census of all tax-paying nobility in feudal England
4 statement of grievances of the middle class in England 18 ____

Base your answer to question 19 on the map below and on your knowledge of social studies.

Macchu Picchu: The Hidden City

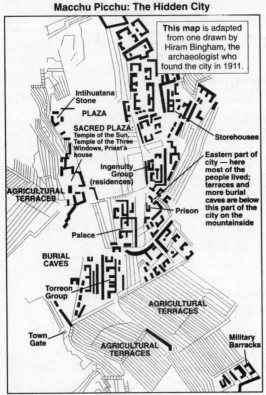

This map is adapted from one drawn by Hiram Bingham, the archaeologist who found the city in 1911.

Intihuatana Stone

PLAZA

SACRED PLAZA: Temple of the Sun, Temple of the Three Windows, Priest's house

Storehouses

Eastern part of city — here most of the people lived; terraces and more burial caves are below this part of the city on the mountainside

Ingenuity Group (residences)

AGRICULTURAL TERRACES

Prison

Palace

BURIAL CAVES

Torreon Group

AGRICULTURAL TERRACES

Town Gate

AGRICULTURAL TERRACES

Military Barracks

Source: *Latin American History on File*, Media Projects, Inc., 1996 (adapted)

19 Which conclusion about the Inca city of Macchu Picchu can be drawn from the map?

1 Religious activities were prohibited in this city.
2 The city was a ceremonial site, not a place of permanent settlement.
3 Community planning and an organized way of life are not evident in this city.
4 The city had a government with laws, leadership, and a military force.

19 _____

20 Which diagram shows the correct social hierarchy of Spain's colonial empire in the Western Hemisphere?

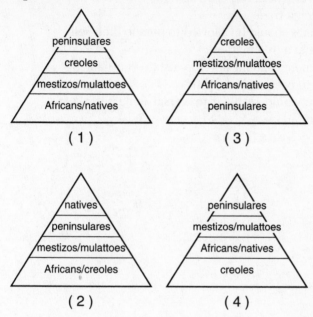

(1)
- peninsulares
- creoles
- mestizos/mulattoes
- Africans/natives

(3)
- creoles
- mestizos/mulattoes
- Africans/natives
- peninsulares

(2)
- natives
- peninsulares
- mestizos/mulattoes
- Africans/creoles

(4)
- peninsulares
- mestizos/mulattoes
- Africans/natives
- creoles

20 ____

21 Philosophers of the Enlightenment period believed that society could best be improved by

1 relying on faith and divine right
2 borrowing ideas from ancient Greece and Rome
3 applying reason and the laws of nature
4 studying the practices of successful leaders

21 ____

22 Which geographic feature made it difficult to unify South America?

1 Andes Mountains   3 Gulf of Mexico
2 Straits of Magellan   4 Argentinian pampas

22 ____

23 Laissez-faire economists of the 19th century argued that

1 the government should regulate the economy and foreign trade
2 individuals should be allowed to pursue their self-interest in a free market
3 governments should develop a state-run banking system to prevent instability
4 anarchy would result if universal male suffrage was granted
23 _____

Base your answer to question 24 on the map below and on your knowledge of social studies.

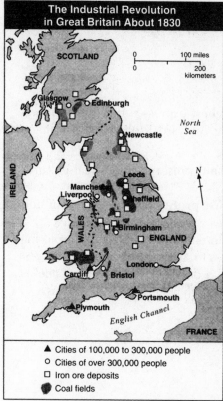

The Industrial Revolution in Great Britain About 1830

SCOTLAND

0   100 miles
0   200 kilometers

Glasgow ○ Edinburgh

North Sea

○ Newcastle

N

Leeds

Manchester
Liverpool ○   Sheffield

IRELAND

WALES

□ Birmingham

□ ENGLAND

London ○

Cardiff   Bristol

▲ Plymouth   Portsmouth

English Channel

FRANCE

▲ Cities of 100,000 to 300,000 people
○ Cities of over 300,000 people
□ Iron ore deposits
⬤ Coal fields

Source: Beers, *World History: Patterns of Civilization,*
1983 (adapted)

24 Which conclusion is best supported by the information on the map?

1 England's natural resources led to the growth of industrial cities.

2 In 1830, England had an unfavorable balance of trade.

3 Great Britain's prosperity unified the people.

4 People emigrated from Great Britain because of pollution.

24 ____

25 Where did Karl Marx predict a revolution of the proletariat would occur *first*?

1 industrial Europe
2 independent Latin America
3 colonial Africa
4 agricultural Russia

25 _____

26 Which statement best expresses the Western perspective regarding Rudyard Kipling's "white man's burden"?

1 Europeans should preserve traditional cultures in Africa and Asia.
2 Europeans must protect existing African and Asian economies.
3 Europeans suffered great hardships in exploring new trade routes to Asia.
4 Europeans had a duty to introduce the benefits of their civilization to non-European peoples.

26 _____

Base your answer to question 27 on the diagram below and on your knowledge of social studies.

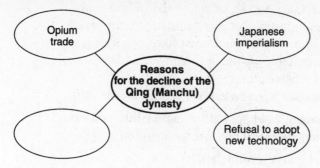

27 Which phrase correctly completes this diagram?

  1 Chinese exports of tea to Europe
  2 Spread of Confucian principles
  3 Failure of the Boxer Rebellion
  4 Expanding power of Mao Zedong   27____

28 The movement started by journalist Theodor Herzl to promote an independent Jewish state in Palestine is referred to as

  1 the Reconquista   3 Utopianism
  2 the Diaspora   4 Zionism   28____

29 The success of the women's suffrage movement in 20th-century Europe resulted in part from women

  1 holding high political offices
  2 working in factories during World War I
  3 being encouraged to have large families
  4 serving in combat positions during World War I   29____

30 ". . . A free, open-minded, and absolutely impartial adjustment of all colonial claims, based upon a strict observance of the principle that in determining all such questions of sovereignty the interests of the populations concerned must have equal weight with the equitable claims of the government whose title is to be determined. . . ."

— President Woodrow Wilson's Fourteen Points, 1918

This statement held appeal for nationalists in areas under colonial control because it suggested

1 national self-determination
2 economic development
3 a system of alliances
4 protection from terrorists   30 _____

31 In the 1920s and 1930s, Mustafa Kemal Atatürk changed the Turkish government by

1 introducing democratic reforms
2 increasing the power of the sultan
3 supporting absolutism
4 incorporating religious teachings into civil law   31 _____

32 Fascist leaders in Italy and Germany came to power in the 1920s and 1930s because they

1 supported the League of Nations
2 exploited economic hardships to gain popular support
3 resisted all forms of extreme nationalism
4 maintained political traditions   32 _____

33 How did geography affect both Napoleon's invasion and Hitler's invasion of Russia?

1 Deserts made invasion possible.
2 The climate created obstacles to success.
3 The tundra enabled the movements of troops.
4 Warm-water ports prevented the flow of supplies.   33 _____

34 The Armenian massacre, the Holocaust, and the Rape of Nanking are examples of

1 appeasement policies
2 resistance movements
3 Russification efforts
4 human rights violations   34 _____

35 During the Indian independence movement, many Muslims in India demanded a separate state of Pakistan to

1 remain under British control
2 prevent future invasions from Afghanistan and China
3 address concerns about their status as a religious minority
4 protect the sacred rivers, the Indus and the Ganges   35 _____

Base your answer to question 36 on the stamp below and on your knowledge of social studies.

Source: www.usps.com

36 This commemorative stamp was issued 50 years after the Marshall Plan. George Marshall was honored because he had

  1 insisted that Germany and the other Axis Powers pay for starting World War II

  2 proposed economic aid from the United States to rebuild the economies of European nations

  3 formed the European Union so that Western Europe could rebuild its own economy

  4 encouraged Western European nations to accept aid from the Soviet Union   36 ____

37 What was a major cause of the civil wars in many Central American nations in the 1970s and 1980s?

  1 economic differences between social classes

  2 end of slavery in the encomienda system

  3 rapid economic reform

  4 oil production policies   37 ____

38 One way in which Lech Walesa, Mikhail Gorbachev, and Nelson Mandela are similar is that each

1 led the people of his nation toward a more democratic government
2 fought for power for the black majority over the white minority
3 worked to end communism in his country
4 refused to participate in the United Nations   38____

39 • Creation of NATO (North Atlantic Treaty Organization) and the Warsaw Pact
    • Construction of the Berlin Wall
    • Cuban missile crisis

These events are most closely associated with

1 World War I   3 the Cold War
2 World War II   4 the Persian Gulf War   39____

40 The activities of Mother Teresa are most closely associated with

1 democracy and political freedom
2 industrialization and open markets
3 nationalism and independence movements
4 the needs of the poor and health care   40____

41 • Chernobyl experiences nuclear disaster.
   • Chlorofluorocarbons (CFC) deplete the ozone layer.
   • Rivers and seas are polluted throughout the world.

Which conclusion can best be drawn from these statements?

1 Modern technology can have serious negative effects.
2 Today's environment renews itself.
3 Only developing nations have environmental problems.
4 Most environmental problems originate in Europe.   41____

Base your answer to question 42 on the cartoon below and on your knowledge of social studies.

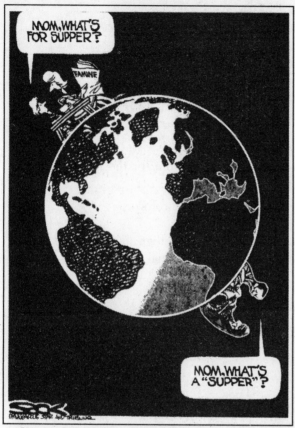

Source: Steve Sack, *Minneapolis Star and Tribune*, 1983

42 What is the main idea of this political cartoon?

1 Only the United States and Africa are affected by a lack of food.

2 Pollution is often the cause of famine.

3 The governments in Africa are unconcerned about the lack of food for their people.

4 Reading about world famine is different from experiencing it.

42 _____

43 One way in which Iran's Ayatollah Khomeini and Afghanistan's Taliban were similar is that they each

  1 established an Islamic state
  2 sponsored a United Nations Conference on Women's Rights
  3 joined the Organization of Petroleum Exporting Countries (OPEC)
  4 incorporated communist doctrine into their government   43____

44 Which factor is most responsible for the international importance of the Middle East?

  1 innovative political and social reforms
  2 superior weapons technology
  3 vital natural resources in a strategic location
  4 advanced scientific and industrial development   44____

45 ". . . A place more destitute of all interesting objects than Manchester, it is not easy to conceive. In size and population it is the second city in the kingdom, containing above fourscore thousand [80,000] inhabitants. Imagine this multitude crowded together in narrow streets, the houses all built of brick and blackened with smoke; frequent buildings among them as large as convents, without their antiquity, without their beauty, without their holiness; where you hear from within, as you pass along, the everlasting din of machinery; and where when the bell rings it is to call wretches to their work instead of their prayers, . . ."

— Robert J. Southey, *Letters from England*, 1807

The conditions described in this passage occurred during the

1 Age of Discovery   3 Industrial Revolution
2 Renaissance   4 Green Revolution   45 ____

46 Which heading best completes the partial outline below?

I. _____

  A. Fall of Constantinople
  B. Voyages of Columbus
  C. Posting of Martin Luther's Ninety-five Theses
  D. Collapse of communism in the Soviet Union

1 Importance of Revolution
2 War and Rebellion
3 Turning Points in History
4 Effects of Economic Change   46 ____

Base your answer to question 47 on the map below and on your knowledge of social studies.

Atlantic Trade Routes

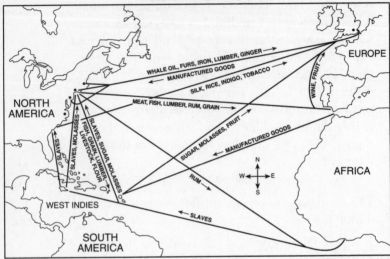

Source: Goldberg and DuPré, *Brief Review in Global History and Geography*, Prentice Hall, 2004 (adapted)

47 The routes shown on the map reflect Atlantic trade during the

    1 Hellenistic Period   3 Early Middle Ages

    2 Roman Empire   4 Age of Mercantilism   47 _____

48 A common element in the movements for German unification, Italian unification, and Indian independence was the

    1 support of the Catholic Church

    2 strength of nationalist leaders

    3 mediation of the League of Nations

    4 existence of democratic institutions   48 _____

49 Which leader is most closely associated with the use of civil disobedience in a struggle to end colonial rule?

  1 Momar Khadafi   3 Ho Chi Minh
  2 Saddam Hussein   4 Mohandas Gandhi   49____

50 One similarity between the Reign of Terror during the French Revolution and the Cultural Revolution in China was that both

  1 limited the power of absolute leaders
  2 illustrated the power of public opinion in forming national policy
  3 established social stability and economic growth
  4 used violent methods to eliminate their opponents   50____

In developing your answer to Part II, be sure to keep these general definitions in mind:

(a) <u>discuss</u> means "to make observations about something using facts, reasoning, and argument; to present in some detail"

(b) <u>describe</u> means "to illustrate something in words or tell about it"

PART II: THEMATIC ESSAY QUESTION

Directions: Write a well-organized essay that includes an introduction, several paragraphs addressing the task below, and a conclusion.

Theme: Global Problems

> Throughout history, global problems have posed major challenges for nations and regions.

Task:

> Select *two* different global problems and for *each*
> - Describe *one* major cause of the global problem
> - Discuss *one* effect of the global problem on a specific nation or region

You may use any global problem from your study of global history. Some suggestions you might wish to consider include environmental pollution, desertification, deforestation, overpopulation, refugees, spread of disease, international drug trafficking, and ethnic conflicts.

You are *not* limited to these suggestions.

**Do *not* describe problems in the United States
although the discussion of the effect of the
global problem could involve the United States.**

Guidelines:

In your essay, be sure to:

- Develop all aspects of the task
- Support the theme with relevant facts, examples, and details
- Use a logical and clear plan of organization, including an introduction and a conclusion that are beyond a restatement of the theme

In developing your answer to Part III, be sure to keep this general definition in mind:

discuss means "to make observations about something using facts, reasoning, and argument; to present in some detail"

PART III: DOCUMENT-BASED QUESTION

This question is based on the accompanying documents. It is designed to test your ability to work with historical documents. Some of the documents have been edited for the purposes of the question. As you analyze the documents, take into account the source of each document and any point of view that may be presented in the document.

Historical Context:

> Throughout history, many different reasons for wars exist. These wars have led to both expected and unexpected outcomes.

Task:

Using information from the documents and your knowledge of global history, answer the questions that follow each document in Part A. Your answers to the questions will help you write the Part B essay in which you will be asked to

> • Discuss the economic, social, **and/or** political reasons for wars
> • Discuss the expected outcomes **and** the unexpected outcomes of wars

Part A: Short-Answer Questions

Directions: Analyze the documents and answer the short-answer questions that follow each document in the space provided.

Document 1

> . . . Though the great princes were apt to remain aloof, western knights responded readily to the appeal of the holy war. Their motives were in part genuinely religious. They were ashamed to continue fighting amongst themselves; they wanted to fight for the Cross. But there was also a land-hunger to incite them, especially in northern France, where the practice of primogeniture [eldest son inherited all] was being established. As a lord grew unwilling to divide his property and its offices, now beginning to be concentrated round a stone-built castle, his younger sons had to seek their fortunes elsewhere. There was a general restlessness and taste for adventure in the knightly class in France, most marked among the Normans, who were only a few generations removed from nomadic freebooters. The opportunity for combining Christian duty with the acquisition of land in a southern climate was very attractive. The Church had reason to be pleased with the progress of the movement. Could it not be applied also to the eastern frontier of Christendom? . . .

Source: Steven Runciman, *A History of the Crusades*,
Cambridge University Press, 1951

1 According to this document, state **one** reason European knights and soldiers joined the Crusades. [1]

_____

_____

Document 2

. . . One positive, undisputed result of the Crusades was a greatly expanded knowledge of geography gained by the West. With the coming of such vast hordes of invaders from all points of Europe, the veil of the "mysterious East" had been lifted for good.

The Arab builders learned much about military masonry from the Crusaders who had brought this knowledge from Normandy and Italy. In constructing the famed Citadel of Cairo, Saladin had taken some of the features of Crusaders' castles he had observed up and down the Levant [lands of the Eastern Mediterranean]. Then, when the great cathedrals of Europe began to rise in a somewhat later period, their builders installed windows of stained glass made with a technique which had originated with the ancient Phoenicians of Syria and passed along by Syrian Arabs to Europeans living in the East. . . .

From a purely military point of view, the Crusades must be written off as a failure for the West, because, after changing hands so many times, the territory comprising the Christian Kingdom of Jerusalem reverted [returned] to the Moslems [Muslims] for good. But during that two-century struggle between East and West, it is plain now that each side made major contributions to the culture of the other. That vast interchange let in a few rays of light over a darkened Europe, and removed for good the wall of ignorance that had always existed between Europe and Asia. . . .

Source: "Legacy of the Crusades," *Aramco World*, VII, May 1956

2a According to this document, what was **one** positive, unexpected outcome of the Crusades on Western civilization? [1]

_____

_____

b According to this document, what was **one** positive, unexpected outcome of the Crusades on Muslim [Moslem] civilization? [1]

_____

_____

c Based on this document, state **one** reason the West was disappointed with the outcome of the Crusades. [1]

_____

_____

Document 3

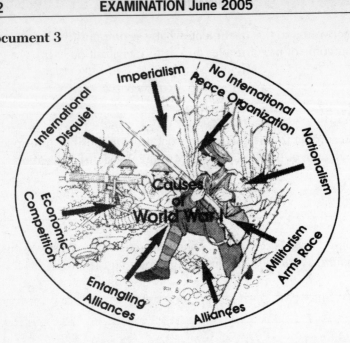

Source: Kime and Stich, *Global History and Geography STAReview*,
N & N, 2003

3 According to this diagram, what were *two* reasons for World
War I? [1]

(1) _____

(2) _____

Document 4

Selected Articles from the Treaty of Versailles
(June 28, 1919)

Article 45: As compensation for the destruction of the coal-mines in the north of France and as part payment towards the total reparation due from Germany for the damage resulting from the war, Germany cedes [gives] to France in full and absolute possession, with exclusive rights of exploitation, unencumbered and free from all debts and charges of any kind, the coal-mines situated in the Saar Basin . . .

Article 119: Germany renounces [surrenders] in favour of the Principal Allied and Associated Powers all her rights and titles over her oversea[s] possessions. . . .

Article 231: The Allied and Associated Governments affirm [acknowledge] and Germany accepts the responsibility of Germany and her allies for causing all the loss and damage [for World War I] to which the Allied and Associated Governments and their nationals have been subjected as a consequence of the war imposed upon them by the aggression of Germany and her allies. . . .

4*a* According to this document, how was France repaid for losses suffered during World War I? [1]

_____

_____

b According to this document, what was a consequence of World War I for Germany? [1]

_____

_____

Document 5

. . . State frontiers are established by human beings and may be changed by human beings.

The fact that a nation has acquired an enormous territorial area is no reason why it should hold that territory perpetually [forever]. At most, the possession of such territory is a proof of the strength of the conqueror and the weakness of those who submit to him. And in this strength alone lives the right of possession. If the German people are imprisoned within an impossible territorial area and for that reason are face to face with a miserable future, this is not by the command of Destiny, and the refusal to accept such a situation is by no means a violation of Destiny's laws. For just as no Higher Power has promised more territory to other nations than to the German, so it cannot be blamed for an unjust distribution of the soil. The soil on which we now live was not a gift bestowed by Heaven on our forefathers. But they had to conquer it by risking their lives. So also in the future our people will not obtain territory, and therewith the means of existence, as a favour from any other people, but will have to win it by the power of a triumphant sword. . . .

Source: Adolf Hitler, *Mein Kampf*, Hurst and Blackett Ltd.

5 According to this document, what was **one** reason Adolf Hitler felt war was necessary? [1]

_____

_____

Document 6

The Yalta Conference of the heads of the governments of the United States of America, the United Kingdom, and the Union of Soviet Socialist Republics (Soviet Union) which took place February 4–11, 1945 came to these conclusions.

> ### *DECLARATION ON LIBERATED EUROPE*
>
> . . . The establishment of order in Europe and the rebuilding of national economic life must be achieved by processes which will enable the liberated peoples to destroy the last vestiges [remains] of Nazism and Fascism and to create democratic institutions of their own choice. This is a principle of the Atlantic Charter—the right of all peoples to choose the form of government under which they will live—the restoration of sovereign rights and self-government to those peoples who have been forcibly deprived of them by the aggressor nations. . . .
>
> ### *POLAND*
>
> . . . A new situation has been created in Poland as a result of her complete liberation by the Red Army. This calls for the establishment of a Polish Provisional Government which can be more broadly based than was possible before the recent liberation of the Western part of Poland. The Provisional Government which is now functioning in Poland should therefore be reorganised on a broader democratic basis with the inclusion of democratic leaders from Poland itself and from Poles abroad. This new Government should then be called the Polish Provisional Government of National Unity. . . .

Source: *Protocol of the Proceedings of the Crimea* (Yalta) *Conference*, February, 1945 (adapted)

6 According to the Yalta Conference, state *two* ways Europe was expected to change as a result of World War II. [2]

(1) _____

_____

(2) _____

_____

Document 7

> . . . Our objectives in the Persian Gulf are clear, our goals defined and familiar:
>
> • Iraq must withdraw from Kuwait completely, immediately and without condition.
>
> • Kuwait's legitimate government must be restored.
>
> • The security and stability of the Persian Gulf must be assured.
>
> • American citizens abroad must be protected.
>
> These goals are not ours alone. They have been endorsed [supported] by the U.N. Security Council five times in as many weeks. Most countries share our concern for principle. And many have a stake in the stability of the Persian Gulf. This is not, as Saddam Hussein would have it, the United States against Iraq. It is Iraq against the world. . . .

Source: Speech by President George H. W. Bush, 1990

7 According to this document, what were **two** reasons President George H. W. Bush was concerned about the Persian Gulf region in 1990? [2]

(1) _____

_____

(2) _____

_____

Document 8

Throughout the 1990s and before the United States went to war with Iraq in 2003, some people were concerned about the continuing actions of Iraq and Saddam Hussein.

Source: Jimmy Margulies, *The Record*, 1998 (adapted)

8 Based on this 1998 cartoon, what was *one* unexpected outcome of the Persian Gulf War? [1]

_____

_____

Part B: Essay

Directions: Write a well-organized essay that includes an introduction, several paragraphs, and a conclusion. Use evidence from *at least five* documents in your essay. Support your response with relevant facts, examples, and details. Include additional outside information.

Historical Context:

> Throughout history, many different reasons for wars exist. These wars have led to both expected and unexpected outcomes.

Task:

> Using information from the documents and your knowledge of global history, write an essay in which you

> * Discuss the economic, social, *and/or* political reasons for wars
> * Discuss the expected outcomes *and* the unexpected outcomes of wars

Guidelines:

In your essay, be sure to:

* Develop all aspects of the task
* Incorporate information from *at least five* documents
* Incorporate relevant outside information
* Support the theme with relevant facts, examples, and details
* Use a logical and clear plan of organization, including an introduction and a conclusion that are beyond a restatement of the theme

Answers
June 2005
Global History and Geography

Answer Key

PART I (1–50)

1. 3	14. 2	27. 3	40. 4
2. 2	15. 4	28. 4	41. 1
3. 4	16. 2	29. 2	42. 4
4. 2	17. 3	30. 1	43. 1
5. 3	18. 2	31. 1	44. 3
6. 1	19. 4	32. 2	45. 3
7. 3	20. 1	33. 2	46. 3
8. 1	21. 3	34. 4	47. 4
9. 4	22. 1	35. 3	48. 2
10. 3	23. 2	36. 2	49. 4
11. 2	24. 1	37. 1	50. 4
12. 3	25. 1	38. 1	
13. 1	26. 4	39. 3	

PART II: Thematic Essay   See answers explained section.

PART III: Document-Based Essay   See answers explained section.

Answers Explained

PART I

1. **3** The domestication of animals and growing of crops first occurred during the period of the Neolithic Revolution. During the Neolithic period, which lasted from 8000 B.C. to 4000 B.C., people came out of caves and settled near lakes, rivers, and seas. People settled in small communities and secured food by farming. They learned to plow the soil, domesticate animals, and use the wheel and axle for transportation. These developments led to the Neolithic Revolution, or Agricultural Revolution, which meant that people no longer had to search for food. An abundance of food and permanent settlements were now established. The Neolithic Revolution led to organized community life, as people needed to work together to meet their basic needs.

WRONG CHOICES EXPLAINED:

(1) In the Iron Age (starting 100 B.C.), people forged iron—a harder and more durable metal than bronze. Since today's complex industrial civilization depends on iron and steel, or a mixture usually of carbon and iron, many people consider our current period of time to be part of the Iron Age.

(2) The Old Stone Age, or Paleolithic Age, began more than 2 million years ago. Paleolithic people were nomads, or people who moved from place to place, hunting and gathering their food. Their simple social structure consisted of small groups of people who traveled together.

(4) The Scientific Revolution refers to the period during the 16th and 17th centuries in which scientists challenged traditional authority. They used observation, research, and reason to find solutions to innumerable problems.

2. **2** The conclusion best supported by these statements is that the geography of a nation or region influences its development. The fertile soil of river valleys allowed early civilizations to develop and flourish. These civilizations grew in the valleys of the Tigris and Euphrates Rivers in Mesopotamia, the Nile River in Egypt, the Indus River in India, and the Huang He (Yellow River) in China. All of these civilizations developed from the farming settlements in the valleys. As the rivers overflowed, they spread silt across the land, renewed the soil, and kept it fertile, thus enabling food supplies to multiply and allowing permanent settlements to grow. The rivers also provided a regular supply of water and a means to transport goods and people. The need to regulate the flooding of these rivers and to channel the water to the fields required a strong government, which also fostered the development of civilizations. In the 1500s and 1600s, control of the Strait of Malacca determined who traded in the Spice Islands. Since ancient times, the Strait of Malacca was a virtual waterway because it offered the shortest water route between

the Pacific and Indian Oceans. At Malacca, traders exchanged goods from China, India, the Middle East, Southeast Asia, and the Mediterranean world. By the late 1400s, Europeans wanted to find a direct route to the rich Spice Islands of Southeast Asia. In 1511, the Portuguese seized the port of Malacca on the Malay Peninsula in the Indian Ocean, the most important Arab trading city. For most of the 1500s, Portugal controlled the spice trade between Europe and Asia. In the 1600s, the Dutch challenged the Portuguese domination of the Asian spice trade. By 1641, the Dutch seized Malacca from Portugal and began trading empires along these islands. The Dutch Empire did not begin to decline until the 1700s. The control of the strait enabled Portugal and later the Dutch to build large trading empires. Since the island of Japan is mostly mountainous, people live in densely populated areas along the coast. Mountainous areas account for more than 70 percent of Japan's land, so major cities are concentrated in the plains, accounting for less than 30 percent of the land. About 80 million people are concentrated in these areas. The Kanto and Nobi plains are home to Japan's largest cities and over 50 percent of the nation's people. Tokyo, which is the capital of Japan, is at the heart of the Kanto Plain. The population density of Japan is 132 persons per square mile compared with 46 persons per square mile in China and 11 persons per square mile in the United States.

WRONG CHOICES EXPLAINED:

(1) Major urban centers are not found only along river valleys. Countries such as Austria, Switzerland, Afghanistan, Uganda, and Zambia have urban centers despite being landlocked countries.

(3) People can develop a culture without mountains and rivers. Culture refers to the things that make up an entire way of life. The lack of natural barriers in the Fertile Crescent allowed frequent migration and the diversification of civilizations. In the Americas, ancient civilizations like the Incas and the Mayans developed despite the Andes Mountains, which prevented political unity. Mountains and rivers are part of different factors contributing to the culture of a society.

(4) The spread of new ideas is encouraged, not discouraged, by trade and conquest. The ancient Chinese commercial Silk Road, the Crusades, and the spread of the Mongol and British Empires led to the introduction of gunpowder, porcelain, and many of the advances of the Muslim civilization as well as the democratic ideas of the British government.

3. **4** The most accurate statement about cultural diffusion in Asia is that Chinese ideas and practices spread into Korea and Japan. Cultural diffusion is the spread of new ideas, customs, and technology from one region or culture to another. Chinese culture spread in several ways. At times, the Chinese ruled parts of northern Korea. During periods of turmoil at home, Chinese refugees fled to Korea and brought their customs with them. Buddhist missionaries carried Mahayan tradition and other Chinese ideas to Korea. Finally, many Koreans went to study in China where they learned the

Chinese language and the texts of Confucius. They brought home knowledge of Chinese achievements as well as political and social ideas. Koreans adapted Chinese traditions to their own beliefs. For example, after learning to make porcelain from the Chinese, the Koreans developed a distinctive blue-green glaze called celadon. Japanese culture features a blend of its own traditions and ideas borrowed from China. In the early 600s, Prince Shotoku, a member of the Yamato family, decided to learn about China directly instead of through Korean sources. He sent nobles to study in China. Over the next 100 years during the Tang dynasty, the Japanese upper class imported cultural traditions, ideas, and government practices directly from China. Like the Chinese emperor, Japanese rulers adopted the title Heavenly Emperor and claimed absolute power. They also set up a bureaucracy and adopted a law code similar to that of China. In 710, the Japanese emperor built a new capital at Nara, modeled on the Tang capital at Changan. Japanese courts adopted Chinese customs such as tea drinking and the tea ceremony. Chinese music and dancing as well as Chinese garden designs became popular. In addition, as Buddhism spread throughout Japan, the Japanese built Buddhist monasteries to resemble Chinese architecture. Confucian ideas and ethics also took root in Japan.

WRONG CHOICES EXPLAINED:
(1) Although the Byzantine traders commanded key trade routes linking Europe and Asia, they did not bring the Justinian Code to China. The Justinian Code had a greater impact on Western Europe and provided the basis of law for both the Roman Catholic Church and medieval rulers. Confucianism had the greatest impact on China.
(2) Roman legions did not introduce Christianity to India. The apostle Thomas introduced Christianity in A.D. 52.
(3) Muhammad, not Indian monks, brought Islam to the Middle East. In 622, Muhammad introduced the religion of Islam to the Arabian Peninsula.

4. **2** The opinion is that Athens had a better culture than did Sparta. An opinion is a conclusion or judgment based on one's personal feelings or ideas rather than on historical data. No concrete information proves that Athenian society, which promoted intellectual development and art, was better in achieving the goals of society than the Spartans, who emphasized the importance of military training. Both of these societies became important Greek city-states.

WRONG CHOICES EXPLAINED:
(1), (3), and (4) All of these statements can be supported by historical information. Spartan society did train boys to be soldiers. At the age of seven, boys were moved into barracks where they trained for the military. Socrates, Plato, and Aristotle were Greek philosophers whose ideas still influence us today. Socrates was the teacher of Plato, and Plato was the teacher of Aristotle. Although Athens had a direct democracy, it was a limited democracy.

Only male citizens were allowed to vote, and citizenship was severely restricted. Women were not allowed to vote, and slaves were not given any political rights.

5. **3** The caste system is illustrated in the diagram. The caste system is the rigid division of traditional Indian society into four major groups based on birth or occupation. Around 1500 B.C., the Aryans were a nomadic tribe who conquered the Indus Valley and controlled the area until about 500 B.C. They left very few artifacts. What we know about them comes from the Vedas, a collection of sacred writings. This period is often called the Vedic Age. From the Vedas, we learned that the Aryans divided the people by occupation or by varna (social class). At first, the Kshatriyas (warriors) were the most honored class, but eventually the Brahmins (priests) became more important. Their power grew because they claimed that they alone could make the proper sacrifices and conduct ceremonies to win the favor of the gods. Each varna had its own duties. The Brahmins performed elaborate rituals and only they could teach the Vedas. The warrior class (Kshatriyas) took charge of the army and ran the government. The Vaisyas were the common people who tended the herds, cared for the land, and traded goods. Later a separate group was created for non-Aryans. This group included the Sudras. The Sudras served other varnas and worked in the fields. Centuries later, Europeans would name the Indian system of varnas, or jati, the caste system. People were always ranked within this system. They were born into this system and could not change their position.

WRONG CHOICES EXPLAINED:
(1) Manorialism refers to the economic and social systems of Medieval Europe. The manor was a self-sufficient community consisting of a village and surrounding lands that were administered by a feudal lord. Serfs were expected to work for the lord and were bound to the land.

(2) Apartheid was an official policy of strict segregation of races that was practiced in South Africa from 1945 until it was repealed in 1991.

(4) Encomienda was a system established by the Spanish government in the Americas that enabled the colonists to tax or get labor from the Native Americans.

6. **1** The religion or belief system most closely associated with the social class system illustrated in the diagram is Hinduism. Unlike other religions, Hinduism has no single founder. However, like many religions, it serves as a guide for what people should do from birth to death. According to Hinduism, people suffer from pain and sorrow because they pursue selfish desires that separate them from the universal spirit, Brahman. Hindus believe the true goal of life is moska, freeing their soul from the body so that the soul can unite with Brahman. Most people cannot achieve this union in one lifetime. The Hindu concept of reincarnation allows people to continue their journey toward a union with Brahman. After the body dies, the soul may be reborn as anything from a god to a flower to a snake. Each form is only temporary. For

Hindus, the cycle of death continues until the individual soul achieves its union with Brahman. Whether a soul gains this release is governed by the law of Karma. Karma refers to a person's behavior in life, which Hindus believe determines that person's form in the next life. By living in a right way, a person will be reborn at a higher level or caste. Evil deeds cause people to be reborn into a lower level or caste. Good deeds involve following Dharma, the moral and religious duties that are expected of an individual. The Hindu beliefs about rebirth and Karma are closely tied to the caste system. A person's gender, class, age, and occupation affect his or her Dharma. People can improve their position in the next life by carrying out their duties in this life. To Hindus, people in different castes were different species of beings. A high-caste Brahmin, for example, was purer and therefore closer to moska than someone from a lower caste. Complex caste rules governed all aspects of life—where people lived, how they dressed, and how they earned a living. Rules even forbade marrying outside one's caste or eating with members of another caste. The lowest-ranking people, the untouchables, were at the bottom of the social system. Their life was harsh and restricted. Untouchables had to live apart and even had to sound a wooden clapper to warn of their approach. Thus, Hinduism closely allied with the caste system.

WRONG CHOICES EXPLAINED:

(2) Daoism, often spelled Taoism, sought to help people live in harmony with nature. Laos was a Chinese philosopher who founded Taoism. Followers of Laozi rejected the world and human government and often withdrew to become hermits, mystics, or poets. Taoists believe in a balance between yin and yang. The yin stands for earth, darkness, and female forces. The yang stands for heaven, light, and male forces. The peace and well-being of the universe depends upon harmony between yin and yang.

(3) Catholicism is the largest religious denomination of Christianity. It claims that it is both organizationally and doctrinally the original Christian Church founded by Jesus Christ. The Roman Catholic Church claims unbroken apostolic succession from the apostle Peter to the present.

(4) Animism is a traditional African religion. It is a belief that the spirit dwells in all living and nonliving things.

7. **3** The technology of papermaking traveled from China to Baghdad along the Silk Roads. Papermaking was invented by the Chinese, and A.D. 105 is often cited as the year in which papermaking was invented. The Silk Road, which stretched over 40,000 miles, allowed China to exchange silk and other products for goods with the Middle East and Europe. Along the Silk Road, paper was found at Loulan and Dunhuang as early as the 4th century. The technique eventually reached Tibet around A.D. 650 and then India by A.D. 645. For a long time, the Chinese closely guarded the secret of paper and tried to eliminate other centers of production to ensure a monopoly. However, around A.D. 750 the Tang army was defeated by the Ottoman Turks. Some Chinese soldiers and papermakers were brought to Samarkand.

The Arabs learned papermaking from the Chinese prisoners and built the first paper industry in Baghdad in A.D. 793. The Egyptians learned papermaking from the Arabs during the early 10th century. Eventually papermaking would spread to North Africa and arrive in Spain by 1150.

WRONG CHOICES EXPLAINED:

(1) The Saharan caravan trails refer to the vast trading networks built by Arab merchants from the 8th to the 14th centuries. The caravan routes, aided by the use of camels, revolutionized trade across the Sahara Desert.

(2) The Trans-Siberian Railway connects European Russia with its Far Eastern provinces.

(4) The Suez Canal is a Middle Eastern waterway linking the Mediterranean and the Red Seas.

8. 1 The concept being referred to in this passage is dynastic cycle. Dynastic cycle refers to the rise and fall of Chinese rulers according to the Mandate of Heaven. The Chinese believed that heaven granted a ruler a mandate, or the right to rule. In turn, the people owed the ruler complete loyalty and obedience. The Mandate of Heaven linked power to responsibility. In exchange for their loyalty, the people had the right to expect good government. If a ruler failed to maintain harmony and order, the people had the right to rebel. War, flood, and famine were signs that the ruler had lost the Mandate of Heaven.

WRONG CHOICES EXPLAINED:

(2) Matriarchal society is one in which ancestry is traced through the mother and her descendants.

(3) Natural rights are those rights that are guaranteed to all human beings from the moment of their birth.

(4) Monotheism is the belief in one God.

9. 4 The religious terms *Four Noble Truths, Eightfold Path,* and *nirvana* are most closely associated with Buddhism. The religion of Buddhism began in India around 600 B.C. Prince Siddhartha Guatama (563–487 B.C.) is considered the founder of Buddhism. Siddhartha Guatama lived his youth in comfort and luxury. Upset by the human suffering that he saw beyond the palace, he left his wealth and set out in search for truth. While meditating under a special tree, he found the answer to his questions and was therefore referred to as the Buddha, or the Enlightened One. The central philosophy of Buddhism revolves around the Four Noble Truths, which are that all of life is suffering and that suffering is caused by a desire for riches and a long life. One way to eliminate suffering is to eliminate desire. A person can eliminate desire only by following the eightfold path of righteous living. The eightfold path consists of giving up material pleasure, controlling emotions, meditating selflessly, respecting all living things, acquiring knowledge, cultivating goodness, speaking the truth, and acting generously. If Buddhists follow these

rules, they will enter into nirvana, a state in which the soul merges with the universe and is released from the endless cycles of reincarnation.

WRONG CHOICES EXPLAINED:

(1) Judaism is a monotheistic religion of the Hebrews whose spiritual and ethical principles are rooted in the Old Testament of the Bible and in the Talmud.

(2) Islam, which means submission to the will of God, is a major religion of the Middle East and was founded by Muhammad in the 7th century A.D.

(3) Shintoism is a Japanese religion that stresses the connection between people and the forces of nature. In the 18th century it became the national religion of Japan, extolling nationalism, ancestor worship, and divinity of the emperor.

10. **3** The Golden Age of Muslim culture was best known for its advances in mathematics, science, and medicine. While western European civilization declined during the early Middle Ages in the early 8th century, the Muslim world developed a flourishing civilization. The Muslims founded great universities, especially at Cairo in Egypt, Baghdad in Mesopotamia, and Cordova in Spain. These universities preserved and taught Greco-Roman culture. Classical learning provided a foundation for further advances by Muslim scholars, who were permitted to study and write with considerable freedom. In mathematics, Muslims introduced Arab numerals, which had been adopted from India to replace the Roman numbering system. The Muslim mathematician al-Khwarizimi pioneered the study of algebra. In the 800s he wrote a book that was later translated into Latin and became the standard textbook in Europe. In science, Muslim astronomers observed Earth's rotation and calculated the circumference of Earth within a few thousand feet. Muslims made remarkable advances in medicine and public health. Physicians and pharmacists had to pass tests before they could practice. Muslims used anesthetics and performed difficult surgeries, particularly progressing in eye surgery. Muslim surgeons developed a way to treat cataracts, drawing fluid out of the lenses with a hollow needle. For centuries, surgeons around the world used this method to save a patient's eyesight. The government set up hospitals, with separate facilities for women. In addition, Muhammad al-Razi, head physician at Baghdad's chief hospital, wrote a pioneering book on the study of measles and smallpox. The Persian physician Ibn Sina, known in the West as Avicenna, wrote the medical encyclopedia *Canon on Medicine*, which provided doctors with the diagnosis and treatment of diseases. These books became standard texts for doctors in Europe.

WRONG CHOICES EXPLAINED:

(1) The Muslims never made any attempt to colonize North America. The Muslim empire extended from the Middle East to North Africa, India, Southeast Asia, Spain, and Sicily.

(2) Frequent conflicts between Christians and Jews did not occur during the Muslim Golden Age. Islamic leaders imposed a special tax on non-Muslims, but they allowed people to practice their own faith. Christians and Jews often served as doctors, officials, and translators in Muslim countries.

(4) Muslim leaders did not adapt policies to reduce trade between the Middle East and China. Muslim fleets controlled the Mediterranean and sailed the Indian Ocean. Caravans carried textiles, steel, and glazed tiles from Baghdad to China. They returned with silk, paper, and porcelain. Wealth from trade and commerce helped make Muslim's Golden Age.

11. **2** The Commercial Revolution helped lead to the Industrial Revolution because during the Commercial Revolution new forms of business were developed. The Commercial Revolution marked the changes in the economy of Europe in the Middle Ages in which there was a growth of towns, banking systems, and trade among nations. As trade revived, merchants needed money to buy goods so they borrowed money from moneylenders. In time, the need for capital, or money, for investments led to the growth of the banking system. To raise large sums of money, joint stock companies were sometimes formed. These ventures were privately owned companies that sold stocks to investors hoping to make a profit. The joint stock companies, as a form of business organization, were the forerunners of the present-day corporations. Merchants also developed a system of insurance to help reduce costs. For a small fee, an underwriter would insure the merchants' shipments. Bankers also devised various new credit facilities. Bills of exchange for use in international trade enabled a merchant in one country to pay for goods purchased in another country. Bank notes, or paper money, issued by the banks were used as a convenient substitute for gold and silver. Limited by guild restrictions, Europe's textile producers proved unable to meet the demands for goods both in Europe and overseas. To increase output, manufacturers employed the domestic system of sending out raw materials to be worked on in the home. These new methods of doing business were part of the Commercial Revolution that transformed the medieval economy and laid the foundation for the Industrial Revolution of the 19th century.

WRONG CHOICES EXPLAINED:
(1) The Commercial Revolution did not help to institute the barter system. The barter system is one in which one set of goods is exchanged for another. The Commercial Revolution led to the rise of the banking system, which required the need for money to purchase goods for trading among different countries.

(3) Socialism was introduced in Europe in the 19th century to address the economic problems created by the Industrial Revolution. The Commercial Revolution began with the expansion of trade between cities and towns around the 1200s.

(4) The Commercial Revolution did not promote subsistence agriculture. Subsistence agriculture is when a farmer produces just enough harvest to supply his personal needs with little or no surplus. The Commercial

Revolution required farmers to provide food to supply the growing population in the towns and cities that were developing along the trade route.

12. **3** Information in the map indicates that Kublai Khan and Genghis Khan extended Mongol influence to other parts of Asia. In the 13th century, Genghis Khan, which means "Supreme Ruler" (1167–1227), united the Mongols with his organization and discipline. The Mongol Empire imposed law and order across most of Eurasia. Under his fierce leadership, Genghis Khan took most of Asia from Korea in the east and spread his influence to the Caspian Sea in the west. His armies advanced into Persia, India, and even northern China. During the time of Genghis Khan, the empire extended from the Pacific Ocean to the Danube River in Europe. After the death of Genghis Khan, the huge Mongol Empire was divided among his sons and grandsons. In 1279, Kublai Khan, the grandson of Genghis Khan, extended Mongol power over all of China. He ruled not only China but Tibet and parts of Vietnam. Under Mongol rule, an uneasy mix of Chinese and foreign ways developed. Kublai Khan adapted a Chinese name for his dynasty, the Yuan dynasty. The Mongol Empire (1200–1350) created the largest land empire in history. However, by the late 14th century, the empire disintegrated into a number of independent states.

WRONG CHOICES EXPLAINED:

(1) and (2) The map does not provide any information about whether the Yuan dynasty kept China isolated or any information about how many Chinese people lived in the river valleys. This map shows the extent of the Mongol Empire.

(4) The map shows that the city of Sumarkand was part of the empire established by Genghis Khan but not part of the Yuan dynasty. The Yuan dynasty extended Mongol influence primarily in China.

13. **1** Machiavelli's belief that "the end justifies the means" meant that leaders may use any methods to achieve what is best for the state. Niccolo Machiavelli was an Italian born in Florence, Italy, in 1469 and he lived until 1527. He served the Florentine Republic as secretary and diplomat. In his book *The Prince*, published in 1513, Machiavelli combined his personal experience of politics with his knowledge of the history of Ancient Rome and offered ways in which a strong ruler might seize and hold power. Citizens were given only those rights that the ruler wanted to grant. He advised the ruler to be as powerful as a lion, as cunning as a fox, and kind and generous when necessary. He urged the ruler to do whatever was necessary to achieve his goal of power. Machiavelli taught that "the end justifies the means" as long as the ruler gains control. On the issue of honesty in government, he advised that results were more important than promises. His work continues to spark ethical debates about the nature of government, and the word *Machiavellian* has come to mean shrewd and cunning. Machiavelli's belief was that a ruler can ignore right or wrong as long as the ruler maintains power.

WRONG CHOICES EXPLAINED:

(2) Machiavelli had little interest in whether the general public acts in its own best interest. For Machiavelli, what was good for the ruler would be good for the people or the public good.

(3) Machiavelli believed that a leader did not have to worry about pleasing all of the people at any given time. A ruler's concern was how to promote the needs of the state. A ruler acted only to help him maintain power, not to please the citizens.

(4) Machiavelli claimed that the leaders act not for the common good but for the good of the ruler. The needs of the ruler superceded the common good of the people.

14. **2** Venice in Europe, Mogadishu in Africa, and Canton in China emerged during the 13th century primarily as important centers of trade. During the 1200s, the cities of Venice, Mogadishu, and Canton achieved prominence because their locations were favorable for trade. Located at the northern end of the Adriatic Sea, Venice was ideally situated to maintain a trade monopoly with Asia. Renewed interest in products of the East, such as silk, perfume, and sugar, allowed Venice to serve as a link between western Europe and Asia. The bustling port city also attracted traders from all over the world. These advantages made Venice the wealthiest and most powerful city-state during the late Renaissance. At the height of its power, Venice stretched from the Adriatic Sea in the east to Milan in the west. Mogadishu was the capital city of Somalia along the coast of eastern Africa. Mogadishu was a thriving trading port on the Indian Ocean. By riding the monsoon winds, merchant vessels sailed to India between April and August and returned to East Africa between December and March. Mogadishu controlled the flow of gold from Southeast Asia and ivory from East Asia. In his visit to the city of Mogadishu in 1333, the North African scholar Ibn Battuta described the thriving commercial activities of the city. After Mogadishu lost much of its trading power, it was still a port of call for the Chinese Imperial Fleet in 1416 and 1419 when they were trading with other countries in the regions. The Chinese city of Canton, known today as Guangzhou, is located more than 90 miles inland from the South China Sea and is on the delta formed by the Hsi River. Like Venice and Mogadishu, Canton became an important center for world trade. The city became the first Chinese port regularly visited by Europeans. By the early 1500s, the Portuguese sent traders to Canton. Later, other European countries were allowed to trade with the Chinese in Canton but only under strict limits and supervision. The Europeans traded for silk and other spices of China. However, the Chinese demanded payment in gold and silver because they considered European products inferior.

WRONG CHOICES EXPLAINED:

(1), (3), and (4) None of these cities were ever considered important centers of agriculture, manufacturing, or mining. These cities were primarily commercial centers and did not develop any other forms of economic activities that attracted people.

15. **4** One influence of Mongol rule on the history of Russia was that Russian leaders adopted the idea of strong, centralized control of the empire. The Mongols ruled Russia for over 240 years from the 13th to the 15th centuries. The Mongols set an example of autocratic rule for Russia. The absolute power of the Mongols served as a model for later Russian rulers. Russian princes developed a strong desire to centralize their own power without interference from nobles, clergy, or wealthy merchants. The Romanov family, which ruled Russia for over 300 years until the Communist Revolution in 1917, continued the centralization of power that dominated the country throughout its history.

WRONG CHOICES EXPLAINED:

(1) Mongol rule did not increase contact with other kingdoms in western Europe. Mongol rule fostered cultural and social stagnation.

(2) The Russians never adopted the Chinese system of writing. The Russians used the Cyrillic alphabet from the Byzantine Empire.

(3) The Mongols tolerated Orthodox Christianity, and the Russians did not convert to Islam. During the period of Mongol rule, Orthodox Christianity grew more powerful. Eventually, the Orthodox Church would become an important part of the state's power when the Mongols were forced out of Russia.

16. **2** A generalization made from these statements is that some African societies achieved a high level of economic and cultural development. One of the major cities of the Mali Empire (1200–1450) was Timbuktu, which became a center of great learning and trade. Mansa Musa, who ruled from 1307 until his death in 1337, promoted peace and prosperity by opening up trade and protecting the caravan routes with a powerful standing army. On a voyage to Mecca, he invited As-Sahili to return to Mali. Mansa Musa built mosques and other fine buildings in the capital of Timbuktu. Timbuktu became the center of Muslim culture. The city had three universities and 50,000 residents at the height of its power. The walls of Great Zimbabwe reveal a powerful and rich society. The Great Zimbabwe originated from the Shona branch of the Bantu people. The Bantu translation for Zimbabwe is "house of stone." The Great Zimbabwe was situated on fertile land. The Shonas farmed many crops, benefiting their civilization. In addition to agriculture, the citizens herded livestock such as cattle. Great Zimbabwe became the capital civilization of Central Africa. Around A.D. 1100, the Shonas built the famous stone monument. The monument consists of three main parts. The first part is the Hill Complex, which provides a center for religion. The second part, known as the Great Enclosure, consists of two sets of large parallel walls. These walls were built without mortar. Each large block of granite was cut precisely to fit into the walls. The highest portion of this wall is 36

feet tall and 20 feet thick. The parallel walls form a passage leading to a large, tower-shaped cone. The community's king was believed to have lived under the protection of these walls. The third part is the Valley Ruins. Remains of these mud huts were found outside the Great Enclosure. These huts were believed to have housed the many citizens of this thriving community. In the beginning of the 1800s, the Zulu warriors destroyed this ancient civilization. The Benin kingdom rose in the rain forests on the Guinea coast. The forest people carved out farming villages and traded pepper, ivory, and later slaves to their neighbors in the savanna. The rulers of Benin organized their kingdom in the 1300s, building on the achievements of an earlier forest culture. An oba, or king, was both a political and religious leader. A three-mile-long wall surrounded the capital city, and the broad avenues had a great palace decorated with elaborate brass plaques and sculptures. According to tradition, earlier forest people had taught the people of Benin to cast bronze and brass. Benin sculptors developed their own style for representing human face and form. Most of their works depicted warriors armed for battle and Benin rulers.

WRONG CHOICES EXPLAINED:
(1), (3), and (4) None of these generalizations provide any information about the religious beliefs of these African societies. These statements do not give an insight into which societies were more advanced or whether African technology was behind that of Asian societies.

17. **3** The major reason that Portugal and Spain established water routes to Asia's spice markets was to avoid the overland routes that were controlled by Muslim traders. In the 1300s, Europe depended on spices from Asia and India. Spices such as pepper and cinnamon were in great demand. In the 1400s, Arab and Venetian merchants controlled the spice trade. Chinese and Indian merchants sold spices to the Arab merchants who then shipped the cargoes overland to Europe and reaped huge profits by selling the spices to Venetian merchants. Traders from Venice and other Italian cities then carried the precious cargoes to European markets. The Europeans were eager to amass a quick fortune and began to look for quicker routes to Asia to the spice markets. By the mid-1300s, the Mongols could no longer guarantee safe passage for traders on overland routes, so Europeans were forced to consider the sea as a possible route to Asia. Portugal and then Spain, the Atlantic powers, sought routes to Asia that bypassed the Mediterranean. In the early 1400s, Prince Henry of Portugal began exploratory voyages down Africa's west coast. These voyages were the foundation for what became in the 1500s the Portuguese Empire. In 1487, Bartholomew Dias rounded the Cape of Good Hope at the southern tip of Africa. In 1498, Vasco Da Gama followed the route Dias took around the Cape of Good Hope and traveled across the Indian Ocean to an Indian port. Da Gama returned home with Asian spices that he sold at a high profit. The Portuguese had established a successful all-water route to Asia. The success

of Portugal led Spain to try to gain a share of the rich spices in the East. In 1492 Christopher Columbus sailed west in search of the riches of the east. Although Columbus failed to reach the Indies, his voyage spurred the exploration of the New World, laying the foundation for the Spanish Empire. Through the efforts of Portugal and Spain, the Muslim domination of the spice trade was ended.

WRONG CHOICES EXPLAINED:

(1) The new technology such as the astrolabe and the sextant was not the major reason why Portugal and Spain established water routes to Asia. The astrolabe and the sextant enabled sailors to measure latitude and helped to make ocean voyages less dangerous, thus letting explorers travel beyond their borders.

(2) Neither Portugal nor Spain sought a direct route to Asia in order to provide jobs for navigators, cartographers, and shipbuilders. These people benefited from the exploration, but the main goal of Portugal and Spain was to reap the lucrative profits from the spice trade.

(4) The discovery of new continents, plants, and animals was not a major reason for establishing a direct water route to Asia. The Columbian Exchange, which brought new foods and products to Europe and the Americas, as well as the discovery of the Americas, were indirect results of the Age of Exploration.

18. **2** The Magna Carta can be described as a list of feudal rights that limited the power of the English monarchy. In 1215, King John signed the Magna Carta (Great Charter). The king could not raise taxes without the consent of the Great Council, which was composed of the nobles in the kingdom. The Magna Carta also stated that the king could not fine or imprison any free persons except by the judgment of his peers or according to the law of the land. Originally, the Magna Carta was designed to protect feudal nobility against royal tyranny. In time, the charter's protection was extended to all English people. The Magna Carta is considered to be the cornerstone of English democracy.

WRONG CHOICES EXPLAINED:

(1) The Magna Carta was not a journal about English feudal society. The Magna Carta addressed the issue of the power of the king.

(3) The Magna Carta was not a census of all tax-paying nobility in feudal England. The nobles wanted the king to sign the document to ensure that they could not be taxed without their consent.

(4) The Magna Carta was concerned with the grievances of the nobility, not the middle class. In feudal society, no middle class existed.

19. **4** The conclusion that can be drawn is that the Inca city of Macchu Picchu had a government with laws, leadership, and a military force. Macchu Picchu is an Incan city located in the Andes Mountains, 2000 miles above the

Urubamba Valley. Machu Picchu means "old peak" and is sometimes called the Lost City of the Incas. It is the most familiar symbol of the Inca Empire. The city was probably built by the Sap Inca Pachacuti starting in about 1440 and was inhabited until the Spanish conquest of Peru in 1532. Archeological evidence shows that Macchu Picchu was not a conventional city but a country retreat for Incan nobility. The site has large palaces and temples to Incan deities around a courtyard, with other buildings for support staff. These structures, carved from the gray granite of the mountaintop, are wonders of architecture. Many of the building blocks weigh 50 tons or more. However, they are so precisely sculpted and fitted together with such exactness that the mortarless joints will not permit the insertion of even a thin blade of grass. Invisible from below and completely self-sufficient, the city was surrounded by agriculture terraces sufficient to feed the population and was watered by natural springs. One of Macchu Picchu's primary functions was that of an astronomical observatory. All of these activities would indicate that there was a form of government to supervise them. The city was not rediscovered until 1911.

WRONG CHOICES EXPLAINED:

(1) The map indicates that religious activities were not prohibited in the city. There were sacred temples, which were sanctuaries for the different gods such as the Sun, as well as a sanctuary for the high priest of Incan society.

(2) The city may have been a ceremonial city but it was also a place of permanent settlements. The map shows that most of the people lived in the eastern part and that agriculture terraces existed to feed the population. An estimated 750 people resided in Macchu Picchu at any one time. Probably only a small fraction of the people lived in the town during the rainy season.

(3) The map shows that there was a community way of life in the city. Macchu Picchu had a temple, burial grounds, permanent settlements, and a prison. All of these facts show that there was an organized society in the city.

20. **1** Diagram (1) shows the correct social hierarchy of Spain's colonial empire in the Western Hemisphere. These colonies had a rigid social system with no social mobility. The highest class was the peninsulares, who were born in Spain and sent by the king to rule the colonies. Peninsulares included high government officials and church leaders. This small but powerful group controlled the economic life of the colonies. Below the peninsulares were the creoles, who were born in the colonies but whose ancestors came from Europe. This group included many wealthy landowners and lesser government officials. They were supposed to have the same rights as the peninsulares, but the king did not appoint them to top positions in the government. Together these two groups made up less than one-fifth of the population but controlled most of the wealth. Below them were the common people, which included mestizos, mulattoes, Native Americans, and African slaves. The mestizos were people of mixed European and Indian descent. Mulattoes were of European and African ancestry. These two groups formed the peasants and working class. Native Americans were employed as agricultural

workers on the large plantations. The last class was the African slaves, who did not gain their freedom until the 19th century.

WRONG CHOICES EXPLAINED:

(2) In the second diagram, the natives are at the top of the social scale. The peninsulares should be the highest class and the natives the lowest one.

(3) In the third diagram, the creoles are at the top of the social scale. The peninsulares were the highest class in colonial Latin America.

(4) In the fourth diagram, the natives, not the creoles, belong on the bottom of the social scale.

21. **3** Philosophers of the Enlightenment period believed that society could best be improved by applying reason and the laws of nature. The philosophers of the Enlightenment promoted the need for the use of reason for rational and logical thinking. The Enlightenment was an intellectual and cultural movement of the 18th century that tied together the ideas of the Scientific Revolution. The philosophers and writers of the Enlightenment argued that just as natural laws govern the physical universe, laws must exist to govern human society. They believed that through reason and logic one could explain the laws of society and also improve society. They also thought that this scientific approach would ensure the progress of civilizations and lead to better societies. Philosophers such as Montesquieu and Rousseau criticized the abuses of society and government and proposed ways to improve them.

WRONG CHOICES EXPLAINED:

(1) Philosophers rejected the notion of relying on faith and divine right to improve society. They criticized faith for not promoting intellectual development and the notion that the king was responsible only to God.

(2) The philosophers of the Enlightenment brought together the ideas of the Renaissance, which borrowed from the civilizations of the Greeks and Romans. However, the Enlightenment looked to the Scientific Revolution based on reason and logic, not to Greece and Rome, as their model to improve society.

(4) Philosophers did not believe that studying the practices of successful leaders could improve society. They believed that leaders could justify their position by claiming to govern in the people's interest.

22. **1** The Andes Mountains made unifying South America difficult. The Andes Mountains are the longest chain of mountains, stretching along the entire west coast of South America for a distance of 4,500 miles. The Andes are divided into three regional zones. The northern Andes include the mountains that run through Colombia, Venezuela, Ecuador, and part of Peru. The central Andes include parts of the range that run through Bolivia, the rest of Peru, northern Argentina, and Chile. The southern Andes include the mountains that run through southern Chile, Argentina, and Patagonia and then travel down to the southernmost tip of South America, Tierra del Fuego.

Mountains limit contact among areas and contribute to strong local traditions that divide the people within the region. For example, in the 19th century, Simon Bolivar failed to unify Colombia and Venezuela because the Andes Mountains divided the Colombians and Venezuelans. Geography creates barriers to unity.

WRONG CHOICES EXPLAINED:

(2) The Straits of Magellan did not make unifying South America difficult. The Straits of Magellan are a navigable route immediately south of the mainland of South America. The straits are arguably the most important natural passage between the Pacific and Atlantic Oceans.

(3) The Gulf of Mexico is a major body of water bordered and nearly landlocked by North America. The gulf does not have any impact on unity in South America.

(4) The Argentinian pampas, which stretch from Argentina to Uruguay, are not barriers to unity in South America. The farmers and ranchers of these areas may have different interests than the business class in Buenos Aires and Montevideo, but the pampas do not geographically divide the country.

23. **2** Laissez-faire economists of the 19th century argued that individuals should be allowed to pursue their self-interests in a free market. The economic theory of laissez-faire capitalism proposes that government should not interfere with business. Laissez-faire stemmed from the economic ideas of 18th-century Enlightenment philosophers who argued that government regulation only interfered with the production of wealth. They claimed the economy would prosper without government regulations. The economic ideas of laissez-faire were presented by Adam Smith in his book *Wealth of Nations.* Smith argued that the free market—the natural forces of supply and demand—should be allowed to operate and regulate business. The free market would produce more goods at lower prices and make them affordable to everyone. A growing economy would also encourage capitalists to reinvest new profits in new ventures. Smith and other capitalists argued that the marketplace was better off without any government regulation. However, Smith believed that the government had a duty to protect society and administer justice.

WRONG CHOICES EXPLAINED:

(1) Laissez-faire economists did not believe that the government should regulate the economy and foreign trade. They wanted the economy to be free from government interference.

(3) Laissez-faire economists did not argue that government should develop a state-run banking system to prevent instability. These economists believed that private individuals should establish and own banks. They believed the government should take a hands-off attitude toward the economy.

(4) Laissez-faire economists argued about how businesses should operate. They were not concerned about whether universal male suffrage would create anarchy.

24. **1** The conclusion best supported by the information on the map is that England's natural resources led to the growth of industrial cities. Although England is a small nation in area, it is rich in natural resources. It has a plentiful supply of coal, which was used to power steam engines, and iron ore, which was used to build the factories and run the machines. England was also rich in raw materials secured from the colonies and world-wide trade. This led to the growth of the Industrial Revolution and brought about the rapid urbanization or growth of cities in England. Overnight, small towns around coal or iron mines mushroomed into cities. Other cities grew up around the factories that entrepreneurs built in once-quiet market towns. The map shows that the city of Glasgow had a population of over 300,000, which meant that it had tripled in size from 100,000 because of its location near iron ore deposits. The new cities of Sheffield and Birmingham became important iron-smelting centers and along with Manchester formed the center of England's bustling cotton industry. During the 1800s, Manchester experienced rapid growth. In 1760, the population of this market town was around 45,000. By 1830, the city had swelled to over 300,000 people. The combined population of these cities threatened the industrial leadership of London, the capital of England. The rapid growth of the cities occurred because workers were migrating to the areas that contained the natural resources necessary for industrialization.

WRONG CHOICES EXPLAINED:

(2), (3), and (4) The map supports none of these conclusions. The map provides information only about natural resources and the growth of cities. No information is shown about balance of trade, whether prosperity unified the people, or if people migrated from Great Britain because of pollution.

25. **1** Karl Marx predicted a revolution of the proletariat would first occur in industrial Europe. In 1848, Karl Marx, in collaboration with Freidrich Engels, wrote *The Communist Manifesto* in which he called for a worldwide revolution to end the abuses of capitalism created by the Industrial Revolution in Europe. Marx proposed a scientific theory of history in which economic conditions determined history. He wrote that history is a struggle between the haves and have-nots. In ancient times, the struggle occurred between the patricians and the plebeians. During the Middle Ages, the struggle was between the lords and serfs. In industrial society, it was between the capitalists (factory owners), who are the haves, and the proletariat (workers), who are the have-nots. Capitalists exploited the workers by paying them just enough to keep them alive. Marx believed that industrialization created prosperity for few and poverty for many. Since class struggle was international, workers in each nation faced the same problems and the same capitalist oppressors. Marx predicted that a worldwide violent revolution by the workers would overthrow the capitalists in the industrial countries of the world.

WRONG CHOICES EXPLAINED:

(2), (3), and (4) Marx did not predict that a revolution would occur in independent Latin America, colonial Africa, or agricultural Russia. According to Marx, a country had to evolve into an industrial society before a communist revolution would occur. In Russia, where the first communist revolution occurred, Lenin modified Marxism. He claimed that there needed to be "a dictatorship of the proletariat" before Russia would become a communist state.

26. **4** The statement that best expressed the Western perspective regarding Rudyard Kipling's "white man's burden" is that Europeans had a duty to introduce the benefits of their civilization to non-European peoples. Rudyard Kipling (1865–1936) was an English writer whose poems and stories such as "The White Man's Burden" offered a justification for imperialism. Kipling was one of the most popular writers in the English-speaking world. He was born in British-ruled India. After being educated in England, he returned to India as a journalist for a number of years. Kipling expressed the belief that the white imperialists had a duty to spread to the undeveloped areas the blessings of Western culture, including medicine, law, and Christian religion. Written in 1899, "The White Man's Burden" glorified imperialism as a romantic adventure. His other poems such as "The Ballad of East and West" and "Gunga Din" reinforced the glorification of imperialism as a noble adventure.

WRONG CHOICES EXPLAINED:

(1) Rudyard Kipling's poem rejected the idea that Europeans should preserve traditional culture in Africa and Asia. His poem is based on the belief that the European race is the dominant race and had to transform the inferior cultures of Africa and Asia into that of Western civilization.

(2) Europeans were not interested in protecting existing African and Asian economies. The imperial nations such as England and France wanted the colonies to provide raw materials and markets for their manufactured goods and industrial economies.

(3) Kipling's "The White Man's Burden" was not about how Europeans suffered great hardships in exploring new trade routes to Asia. The poem was written to justify imperialism in Africa and Asia.

27. **3** The phrase that correctly completes this diagram is the failure of the Boxer Rebellion. The reasons for the decline of the Manchu dynasty can be traced to the opium trade. During the late 1700s, British merchants began to trade opium with the Chinese, who became addicted to the drug. In 1836, the Chinese government appealed to Queen Victoria to help them stop the opium trade. In 1839, when the Chinese outlawed the drug, the British went to war. The conflict, which became known as the Opium War, demonstrated the weakness of the Chinese. The British easily defeated the Chinese, who had refused to adapt to the new technology created by the Industrial

Revolution. The Opium War, which was fought primarily at sea, demonstrated the weakness of the Chinese. Chinese fleets armored with the type of cannons used in the 1300s were no match for the well-armed British gunboats that were equipped with the latest firepower. The Chinese defeat in the Opium War marked the beginning of a century of humiliation. China's weakness made it a victim of Japanese imperialism. In 1894, the Japanese fought China over Korea and easily won. Japan also annexed Taiwan. The Boxer Society was a secret Chinese nationalist society formed in 1899. The Manchu government supported them. Their goal was to drive out the foreign devils that were destroying the Chinese way of life and to return China to isolation. In 1900, the Boxers attacked foreign communities as well as Chinese Christians across China. They also attacked the foreign embassies in Beijing. In response, the Western powers and Japan formed a multinational force of 25,000 troops. Within two weeks, they crushed the Boxers and rescued the foreigners besieged in Beijing. The Boxer Rebellion failed, and it convinced the Chinese that reforms were necessary. In 1911, the Manchu emperor was overthrown.

WRONG CHOICES EXPLAINED:

(1), (2), and (4) None of these choices are the reasons for the decline of the Manchu dynasty. The export of tea to Europe dealt with the commercial trade with the West. The spread of Confucian principles reinforced the importance of respect for the emperor. The expanding power of Mao Zedong was one of the reasons that led to the rise of Communism in 1947, not the decline of the Manchu dynasty.

28. **4** The movement started by journalist Theodor Herzl to promote an independent Jewish state in Palestine is referred to as Zionism. Zionism was a Jewish movement that arose in the late 19th century in response to the growing anti-Semitism in Europe and sought to reestablish a Jewish homeland in Palestine. The name Zionism is derived from the hill Zion, on which the Temple in Jerusalem was situated. The founder of Zionism was Theodor Herzl, a Hungarian Jewish journalist who lived in France and was upset by the pogroms in Russia and the *Dreyfus* case in France. In 1894, Herzl was sent to cover the Dreyfus trial. Alfred Dreyfus was a French Jewish captain accused of treason for selling military secrets to Germany. Herzl soon realized that Dreyfus became the scapegoat for the frustrations of the French people, who had just suffered a defeat in the Franco-Prussian war. The Dreyfus trial unleashed a wave of anti-Semitism in France. Herzl believed that the growing hatred of Jews in Europe and the slow assimilation of Jewish culture into wider European culture could be stopped only by the establishment of a Jewish homeland. He launched modern Zionism and outlined his pogrom of political Zionism in his first major book, *Der Judenstaat (The Jewish State)*. In 1897, Herzl organized the First Zionist Congress in Basel, Switzerland. Almost 50 years after the First Zionist Congress, as he forecasted, the state of Israel was established.

WRONG CHOICES EXPLAINED:

(1) The Reconquista refers to the efforts by Christian leaders to drive the Muslims out of Spain. The Reconquista lasted from the 1100s to 1492, when the Muslims were expelled from Spain.

(2) The Diaspora was the dispersal of the Jews from their homeland in Palestine throughout the world. The defeat of the Jewish Revolt against the Romans and the Roman destruction of the Temple in Jerusalem contributed to the scattering of Jewish communities throughout Europe and North Africa.

(3) Utopianism was a 19th-century socialist movement that sought to establish an ideal society in which all members worked for and shared equally in the economic success for the common good.

29. **2** The success of the women's suffrage movement in 20th-century Europe resulted in part from women working in factories during World War I. World War I was a total war, which meant that the government turned for help from women as never before. As more and more men went to war, millions of women replaced them in the factories. Women worked in war industries, manufacturing weapons and supplies. Women also plowed fields, paved streets, dug ditches, and kept the soldiers supplied with food and clothing. When food shortages threatened Britain, volunteers in the Women's Land Army went to the field to grow their own food. Although most women left the workforce when the war ended, they had changed many people's views of what women were capable of doing. Women had challenged the idea that they were too delicate for demanding and dangerous jobs. Women's work in the war effort was one of the decisive factors that won them the right to vote. After World War I, women's suffrage became law in Britain, Sweden, Austria-Hungary, and Czechoslovakia.

WRONG CHOICES EXPLAINED:

(1) Holding high political offices did not contribute to the success of women's suffrage. Women needed to gain the right to vote before they could seek political office in Europe. Although many women gained suffrage after World War I, they did not begin to impact European politics until the end of the 20th century.

(3) Encouraging women to have large families did not contribute to the success of the suffrage movement. The focus on women having children would reinforce the traditional role of women in society rather than on the new spirit of independence that arose after World War I.

(4) Women did not serve in combat positions during World War I. Women worked near the front lines as nurses, but they did not participate in the fighting.

30. **1** This statement held appeal for nationalists in areas under colonial control because it suggested national self-determination. Self-determination means allowing people to decide for themselves which type of government they wish to have. In January 1918, President Woodrow Wilson of the United

States issued the Fourteen Points, a plan for resolving World War I and future wars. The plan included an end to secret treaties, freedom of the seas, and a reduction of the national army and navy. Seven of these points were specific suggestions for changing borders and creating new nations. The guiding idea behind these points was self-determination regarding the right of any national group to set up an independent state. The principle of self-determination resulted in a band of new nations emerging where German, Austrian, and Russian empires had once ruled. These nations included the Baltic states of Estonia, Lithuania, and Latvia. Poland regained independence after more than 10 years of foreign rule. Three new republics, Czechoslovakia, Austria, and Hungary, rose out of the old Hapsburg Empire. In the Balkans, the new state of Yugoslavia became an independent nation, dominated by the Serbs. European colonial leaders thought that the Paris Peace Conference would bring new respect and an end to imperial rule. European colonies in Africa, Asia, the Middle East, and the Pacific looked to the Paris Peace Conference with high hopes. They took up Wilson's call for self-determination. The Arabs expected a United Arab State to emerge from the Ottoman Empire under the leadership of Hussein-bin-Ali, a direct descendent of the Prophet Muhammad. Ho Chi Minh, the future leader of Vietnam, wanted to represent Vietnam at the Paris Peace Conference but failed to gain a meeting with President Wilson. The leaders of Europe applied self-determination to parts of Europe, but outside Europe the victorious Allies added territories to their empires. The treaties created a system of mandated territories, administered by Western powers. Britain and France gained mandates over German colonies in Africa and the Ottoman Empire. The mandates were to be held until the colonies were modernized and were able to stand alone. European colonialism disguised itself as the mandate system and continued in Asia, Africa, and the Middle East. From Africa to the Middle East and across Asia, colonized people felt that they had been betrayed by Wilson's policy of self-determination.

WRONG CHOICES EXPLAINED:

(2) This statement addresses the issue of national freedom and not economic development. Wilson is promoting political freedom for colonial people.

(3) This statement does not suggest anything about a system of alliances. One of the Fourteen Points was an end to secret alliances. Wilson's call for a League of Nations was based on the idea of collective security to replace the Alliance system, which he believed was a major reason for World War I.

(4) This statement contains no reference to protection from terrorists. Wilson believed that self-determination would help to deal with the ethnic tensions in the Balkans and Central Europe. Wilson's concern was promotion of democracy, not protection from terrorists.

31. **1** In the 1920s and 1930s, Mustafa Kemal Atatürk changed the Turkish government by introducing democratic reforms. In 1922, a group of Turkish nationals overthrew the last Ottoman emperor. The leader of the rev-

olution was an army commander, Mustafa Kemal, who set up the first republic in the Middle East. Mustafa Kemal later called himself Kemal Atatürk,
which means "Father of the Turks." He was the founder of Turkey and
became its first president in 1923. He introduced a program of reforms to
modernize Turkey along Western lines. Kemal broke the close connection
between church and state that had existed under the sultan. He separated the
laws of Islam from the laws of the nation. He also replaced Islamic laws with
laws from various European nations. He banned polygamy, a custom allowing
men to have more than one wife. Under Kemal, women gained more freedoms. He granted women the right to vote and to hold public office. Kemal
also launched government-funded programs to industrialize Turkey and to
spur economic growth. By the time of Kemal's death in 1938, Turkey had a
firm sense of national identity.

WRONG CHOICES EXPLAINED:

(2) Mustafa Kemal Atatürk did not increase the power of the sultan but,
instead, overthrew the last Ottoman emperor in 1922.

(3) Mustafa Kemal Atatürk did not support absolutism. He set up a new
republic of Turkey that was the first republic in southwest Asia.

(4) Mustafa Kemal Atatrürk did not incorporate religious teachings into
civil law. He separated the laws of Islam from the civil laws and supported a
secular government.

32.   **2** Fascist leaders in Italy and Germany came to power in the 1920s
because they exploited economic hardships to gain popular support. After
World War I, the Italian people saw their living standards decline. They suffered from ruinous inflation that drove up prices, heavy taxes, and widespread unemployment. By promising to improve conditions, Mussolini and
the Fascist Party won the support of low-paid workers, the unemployed, and
the landless peasants. Many Germans declared that the country's economic
problems stemmed from the loss of its European territories, overseas
colonies, and reparation payment of $35 billion. Germany's rampant inflation
in the early 1920s, when 4 trillion marks were equivalent to one dollar, added
to the unrest. It was reported that in 1923 a loaf of bread cost 200 billion
marks. Eventually the marks became worthless. Although the economy
revived in the mid-1920s, the Great Depression destroyed any hope of recovery. In the 1930s, Germany turned to Adolf Hitler and the Nazi Party. He
gained popular support by promising to restore order to the economic chaos
created by the reparation payment and to provide a strong economy.

WRONG CHOICES EXPLAINED:

(1) The Fascist leaders did not support the League of Nations. In 1935,
Mussolini ignored the League's sanctions when Italy invaded Ethiopia. Hitler
had no respect for the League of Nations. He rearmed Germany and invaded
the Rhineland in violation of the Versailles Treaty. The League of Nations
took no action to stop him.

(3) The Fascist leaders promoted extreme nationalism. Mussolini claimed that he was going to restore the greatness of Italy, and Hitler insisted that the Germans were the master race.

(4) Both of the Fascist leaders ignored political traditions. Mussolini gained power in 1922 by marching on Rome and forcing Victor Emmanuel II to appoint him premier. In 1933, Hitler suspended all civil liberties and banned all political parties. Eventually, the Reichstag, the German Parliament, gave him absolute power.

33. **2** Geography affected both Napoleon's invasion and Hitler's invasion of Russia, because the climate created obstacles to success. In June 1812, Napoleon decided to invade Russia when Czar Alexander I withdrew from the Continental System that forbade European countries from trading with England. Alexander I refused to stop selling grain to Britain. While leading a huge army of 600,000 men, Napoleon marched into Russia. Czar Alexander pulled back his troops and refused to be trapped in a battle, causing Napoleon to overextend his supply lines. As the Russians retreated, they adopted a scorched-earth policy of burning crops and villages. Desperate soldiers deserted the French army to search for scraps of food. When Napoleon captured Moscow in September, he found the city in ashes. Russian patriots probably destroyed most of the city. By October, when the Czar did not make a peace offer, Napoleon was too late to advance and perhaps too late even to retreat. He could not feed and supply his army through the long Russian winter. In October, he ordered his starving army to retreat. The retreat from Moscow turned into a desperate battle. Russian raiders attacked Napoleon's ragged army. Soldiers staggered through the snow and dropped in their tracks as the temperature fell to –35 degrees Fahrenheit. A French soldier noted that many of the soldiers were walking barefoot, using pieces of wood as canes, but their feet were frozen so hard that they sounded like wooden clogs. By the middle of December, when the last survivors crossed the border out of Russia, Napoleon had lost three-fourths of his army. The 1,000-mile retreat from Moscow was a disaster and Napoleon's first great military defeat. On June 22, 1941, Hitler launched a major attack against Russia. The goal of the Russian invasion was to gain control of the Ukraine's vast wheat fields and the oil fields of the Caucasus. Hitler ordered a massive blitzkrieg of 3 million men along a 2,000-mile border, catching Stalin by surprise. By October 1941, German troops surrounded Leningrad in the north, which was within 25 miles of Moscow, and had conquered most of the Ukraine. Hitler's propaganda machine proclaimed the war to be over, but it was mistaken. Russia did not collapse; instead, history repeated itself. Like Napoleon's forces, the German invaders were not prepared for the cold Russian winter. In summer uniforms, the Germans froze to death when the temperature plunged to –20 degrees Fahrenheit. Their fuel and oil froze as trucks and weapons became useless. At the Siege of Leningrad, which lasted 900 days, the Russians fought valiantly. More than 1.5 million citizens died during this siege, and

some inhabitants even resorted to cannibalism to survive. Hitler's failure to conquer Russia drained Germany's resources and contributed to Germany's defeat.

WRONG CHOICES EXPLAINED:

(1) Deserts were not a geographic factor influencing Napoleon's and Hitler's invasions. Russia has no deserts.

(3) The tundra climate is found across northeastern Siberia. By December 6 of each year, the temperatures drop as far as –40 degrees Fahrenheit. The tundra hinders, not enables, the movement of troops.

(4) Warm-water ports in Russia did not prevent the flow of supplies. These ports are in the north and provide Russia with an outlet to the sea. Napoleon's and Hitler's invasions were at the heartland of Russia, and supplies had to be transported by land, not by sea.

34. **4** The Armenian massacre, the Holocaust, and the Rape of Nanking are examples of human rights violations. Human rights are those rights such as freedom of speech and press held by all people by virtue of belonging to a civil society. The United Nations' Universal Declaration of Rights adopted in 1948 states that these are the basic liberties and freedoms to which all people are entitled. The Armenian massacre refers to the atrocities committed against the Armenian people of the Ottoman Empire during World War I. By the 1890s, roughly 2.5 million Christian Armenians had begun to demand their freedom. As a result, relations between the group and its Turkish ruler grew strained. Throughout the 1890s, the Turkish troops killed tens of thousands of Armenians. When World War I broke out, the Armenians pledged their support to the Turkish enemies. In response, the Turkish government deported nearly 2 million Armenians between the years 1915 and 1918. Along the way, more than 600,000 died of starvation or were killed by Turkish soldiers. Women and children were abused, and the entire wealth of the Armenian people was expropriated. The Holocaust was a systematic destruction of more than two-thirds of the prewar Jewish population of Europe. Hitler began this policy of genocide by limiting the rights of the Jewish people. In 1935, the Nuremberg laws in Germany placed severe restrictions on the Jewish people. They were prohibited from marrying non-Jews or holding a teaching or government job. Violence against Jews was encouraged. On November 9, 1938, Kristallnacht (Night of Broken Glass) spread across Germany. Nazi-led mobs attacked Jewish communities, smashed windows, looted shops, and burned synagogues. Hitler finally set up concentration camps where the Jewish people were starved, shot, or gassed to death. An estimated 6 million Jews died in the Holocaust. The Rape of Nanking refers to the six-week carnage that occurred when the Japanese invaded the city in December 1937. Between December 1937 and March 1938, the Japanese army proceeded to murder more than half of the 600,000 civilians and soldiers in the city. During this six-week carnage, an estimated 80,000 women and girls were raped; many of them were then mutilated or murdered.

Thousands of victims were beheaded, bayoneted, buried alive, or disembow-eled. Throughout the city of Nanking, acts of murder occurred as soldiers frequently fired their rifles into panicked crowds of civilians. Some consider the Rape of Nanking the single worst atrocity during World War II in the Pacific theater of war.

WRONG CHOICES EXPLAINED:

(1) Appeasement policies were used by England and France to satisfy Hitler's demand for land during the 1930s.

(2) Resistance movements usually refer to the efforts of people to gain their independence from their colonial rulers.

(3) Russification efforts are used to describe the policy adopted by the Russian czar to unite the empire's many provinces. Czar Alexander III started this policy in 1882.

35. **3** During the Indian independence movement, many Muslims in India demanded a separate state of Pakistan to address concerns about their status as a religious minority. Hinduism is the major religion of India. The Muslims, a distinctive minority, had invaded India in 700 and by 1200 had established a Muslim empire in northern India. However, unlike other invaders, the Muslims were never absorbed into Hindu society. The differ-ence between the two religions was too great. The Hindus believed in many gods. Islam was based on the belief in one God. Islam taught that all Muslims were equal before God. Hinduism supported a caste system. Muslims were always a small percentage of the population. For example, in the 1940s, there were approximately 350 million Hindus and about 100 million Muslims. Initially, the Muslims and Hindus cooperated in their campaign for indepen-dence from Great Britain. However, Muslims grew distrustful of the Indian National Congress, which had been formed in 1885 to promote indepen-dence, because the organization was mostly Hindu. In 1906, the Muslim League was set up in India to protect Muslim interests. The leader of the Muslim League, Muhammad Ali Jinnah, insisted that the Muslims resign from the National Congress party. The Muslim League stated that they would never accept Indian independence if it meant rule by the Hindu-dom-inated Congress party. At their Lahore Conference in 1940, the Muslim League first officially proposed the partition of India into separate Hindu and Muslim nations. Most Muslims lived in the northwest and northeast of the subcontinent. When World War II ended, the British realized that they could no longer keep India. As independence approached, widespread rioting broke out between Hindus and Muslims in Calcutta, East Bengal, Bihar, and Bombay. In August 1946, four days of rioting left more than 5,000 people dead and 15,000 hurt. In 1947, the British parliament passed the Indian Independence Act. This act ended British rule in India but also provided for the partition or subdivision of the Indian subcontinent into two separate, independent nations. One nation was the Hindu-dominated India and the other was Pakistan, with a Muslim majority. Muhammad Ali Jinnah became

governor general of Pakistan. This partition led to an explosion of violence between Muslims and Hindus. Although India and Pakistan had promised each other religious toleration, distrust and fears were deep rooted. Close to 1 million died in the fighting. To escape death, millions of Muslims fled India to Pakistan and millions of Hindus left Pakistan. An estimated 15 million people took part in this mass migration that led to the establishment of separate states for the Hindus and Muslims.

WRONG CHOICES EXPLAINED:

(1) Pakistan did not want to remain under British control. The Muslim League favored independence from Great Britain. The Muslims claimed that the only thing that they had in common with the Hindus was their slavery to the British.

(2) Pakistan was never invaded by either Afghanistan or China.

(4) Muslims were not interested in protecting the sacred rivers, the Indus and the Ganges. These rivers are connected to Hinduism. The Muslims wanted a separate state so they could practice their own religion.

36. **2** This commemorative stamp was issued 50 years after the Marshall Plan. George Marshall was honored because he had proposed economic aid from the United States to rebuild the economies of European nations. World War II left Europe physically devastated and in a weak economic condition. In 1947, the United States Secretary of State John Marshall offered economic aid to all European countries. The Marshall Plan, officially known as the European Recovery Plan, provided over $13 billion in aid for foodstuffs, machinery, and raw materials. The goal of the program was to achieve recovery—not relief—to lessen the dangers of communism, and to strengthen democratic governments. Stalin forbade Eastern European countries from accepting this aid and promised that the Soviet Union would help them instead. The Marshall Plan helped to improve the battered economies of Western Europe. The close cooperation among European nations required by the Marshall Plan also promoted economic growth.

WRONG CHOICES EXPLAINED:

(1) The Marshall Plan was not intended to have Germany and the other Axis Powers pay for starting World War II. The plan was designed to improve the economies of Europe.

(3) George Marshall did not propose the European Union. The European Union was proposed by the French statesman Jean Monet and French Foreign Minister Robert Schuman in 1950.

(4) The Marshall Plan encouraged Western European nations to accept aid from the United States. The Soviet Union never proposed giving aid to Western European countries.

37. **1** A major cause of the civil wars in many Central American nations in the 1970s and 1980s was the economic differences between social classes.

The social class structure in Central America created deep divisions. Old landowning families and rich industrialists who dominated these societies opposed change. In rural areas, a few families owned the best farmlands. Poor peasants and Indians either scratched a living from tiny plots or worked on the estates of large landowners. Nowhere was the hold of the wealthy elite stronger than in Nicaragua. From 1936 to 1979, the Somoza family had governed Nicaragua. The Somozas were repressive but had close ties to the United States because of their anticommunist stance. In 1979, the Sandinistas, a group that included both reform-minded nationalists and communists, overthrew the Somoza government. Under Sandinista President Daniel Ortega, they introduced land reform and other socialist policies. They seized lands that belonged to wealthy Somoza supporters and turned them over to peasant groups. They also taught people to read and write and improved rural healthcare. However, the Sandinistas faced growing opposition from the upper- and middle-class Nicaraguans who had lost property to them and opposed the creation of a socialist dictatorship. With the help of the United States, which feared that Nicaragua might become a communist state like Cuba, the Contras or forces that opposed the Sandinistas fought a civil war that lasted over a decade and seriously weakened the economy. As the economic situation worsened, President Ortega agreed to hold free elections. In 1990, the Sandinistas handed over power to a freely elected president, Violeta Chamorro. Nicaragua still had to struggle to rebuild its economy. In El Salvador, an estimated 25 families controlled about 90 percent of the wealth. This unequal distribution of wealth brought a growing demand for change. In the 1970s, church leaders abandoned traditional ties to the elite and instead pressed for reform. Inspired by the ideas of liberation theology, Salvadorian priests supported the poor and revolutionary changes. During a vicious 12-year civil war, right-wing death squads slaughtered church workers, students, and labor leaders. In 1980, Archbishop Oscar Romero, who considered insurrection morally justified when all peaceful means had been exhausted, was gunned down as he celebrated mass in a chapel. Meanwhile, the United States pressed the conservative government to make some reforms. However, it also provided weapons and other aid to help the military fight the rebels, who the United States believed were under communist influence. Finally in 1991, both sides agreed to a U.N.-brokered peace. Over 70,000 people had died in the 12-year civil war. Another 1.5 million became refugees.

WRONG CHOICES EXPLAINED:

(2) The end of slavery in the encomienda system was not a major cause of the civil wars in Central America in the 1970s and 1980s. As countries modernized, land reform was a major issue. The uneven distribution of land led to civil war. For example, in Guatemala, 2 percent of the landowners held two-thirds of the land.

(3) The failure to institute rapid economic reform in the 1970s and 1980s led to civil war in many Central American countries.

(4) Central American countries were never affected by oil production policies. Nicaragua and El Salvador did not have large deposits of oil. These countries depended upon the export of cash crops such as bananas, sugar, and coffee.

38.   **1** One way in which Lech Walesa, Mikhail Gorbachev, and Nelson Mandela are similar is that each led the people of his nation toward a more democratic government. In the 1980s, Poland's economic hardships caused labor unrest. Lech Walesa, an electrician working in the Gdansk shipyard of Poland, led a strike for better wages and living conditions against the Communist government. He organized an independent trade union called Solidarity. With millions of members, Solidarity called for political change. It demanded that all unions be free of communist control. At first, the Soviet Union pressured the Polish government to outlaw Solidarity and arrest Walesa. Military rule was established. However, international pressure forced Poland to release Walesa, and martial law was lifted in 1983. The Communist government legalized Solidarity and held the first free elections in 50 years on June 4, 1989. The Solidarity candidates, who outpolled the Communists, became the first freely elected opposition in a communist country. In 1990, Lech Walesa was elected first president of a democratic Poland. In 1985, Mikhail Gorbachev came to power in the Soviet Union. At 54, he was the youngest Soviet leader since Stalin. Gorbachev also introduced a policy of glasnost, or openness, in Soviet society. New election laws gave voters a choice among candidates even though the Communist Party remained the only legal party. Censorship ended, and free speech was promoted. Attacks on the crimes of the Stalin era appeared often in Soviet plays and newspapers, and the works of writers who had been banned for many years were made available. In 1988, a new constitution was adopted calling for elections of a new legislative body. In the past, voters had merely approved candidates who were handpicked by the Communist Party. Now voters could choose from a list of candidates for each office. In 1989, the Soviet Union held its first elections with modified choices since 1917. In some areas where the Communist Party leaders ran unopposed, the people were so angry that they crossed off the ballots the names of party leaders and wrote in local candidates. By 1990, Gorbachev was forced to admit noncommunist parties into the political process. In August 1991, Gorbachev resigned and Boris Yelstin would eventually become the first directly elected president in Russian history. Nelson Mandela led the fight for independence in South Africa. For more than 350 years, the European minority had ruled the South Africans. Nelson Mandela, who was the leader of the African National Congress, was jailed in 1964 for his opposition to apartheid. This policy had resulted in the segregation of the two races. During his 27 years in jail, Mandela became a symbol of the struggle for freedom. In 1990, Mandela was released from prison and continued to fight for freedom. In 1994, South Africans of all races voted and the people elected Mandela as their first president.

WRONG CHOICES EXPLAINED:

(2) Only Nelson Mandela fought for power for the black majority over the white minority. Lech Walesa fought for democracy in Poland, and Mikhail Gorbachev promoted political freedom in the Soviet Union.

(3) Walesa was the only political leader who worked to end communism. Mandela promoted democratic reform, and Gorbachev tried to reform, not end, communism.

(4) None of these leaders refused to participate in the United Nations.

39. **3** These events are most closely associated with the Cold War. The Cold War was a period of political and economic struggle between the nations of the West led by the United States and the communist countries of the Soviet Union. The Cold War began in 1945 and ended with the collapse of the Soviet government in 1991. In 1946, the United States and other Western European countries considered communism an evil force creeping across Europe and threatening countries around the world. The United States adopted a policy of containment that was designed to give economic and military assistance to countries fighting against communism. In 1949, the United States and 12 other Western European nations formed the North Atlantic Treaty Organization (NATO) as an alliance against communism. They pledged to support each other in case any member nation was attacked. The alliance was formed after the Berlin Airlift and the division of west Germany from Communist East Germany. In 1955, the Soviet Union formed the Warsaw Pact in response to the creation of NATO. The Warsaw Pact included the Soviet Union and seven of its satellites in Eastern Europe. It was a defensive alliance promising mutual military cooperation. The Warsaw Pact ended with the collapse of communism in 1991. Between 1949 and 1961, more than 3 million East Germans fled to West Germany. Most of these refugees escaped by going from East Berlin to West Berlin. Suddenly on August 13, 1961, Premier Khrushchev ordered the construction of the Berlin Wall. The wall was made of concrete blocks and barbed wire. It extended 28 miles along the border between East and West Germany, sealing off East Berlin in violation of existing agreements. The Berlin Wall became a symbol of the Cold War. By 1989, East German leaders could no longer count on support from the Soviet Union. A rising wave of protests forced the Communist government from power. On November 9, 1989, the new East German leaders allowed people to leave East Germany. Within days, more than 2 million Germans had crossed the border. The crowds were so huge that the government bulldozed new openings in the Berlin Wall. The Berlin Wall was torn down by joyous Germans. In 1959, Fidel Castro overthrew the dictatorship of Fulgencio Batista and seized power. He denounced the United States as imperialist, forbade elections, and nationalized American investments without compensation. The United States reacted by breaking off trade. In 1961, Castro proclaimed his intention to transform Cuba into a communist state and threatened to export communism to other Latin

American countries. He wanted closer ties with the Soviet Union. The Cuban Missile Crisis of October 1962 developed when President John F. Kennedy announced that Castro was allowing the Soviet Union to build nuclear missile bases in his country, which was just 90 miles off the coast of Florida. If the plan succeeded, Soviet nuclear missiles would be within easy striking distance of major cities in the United States. President Kennedy blockaded Cuba and threatened to invade if the missiles were not withdrawn. After 13 days of intense negotiations, Premier Nikita Khrushchev of the Soviet Union agreed to withdraw the missiles in exchange for a pledge by President Kennedy that the United States would not invade Cuba.

WRONG CHOICES EXPLAINED:

(1), (2), and (4) None of these choices are associated with the Cold War. Events such as World War I (1914–1918) and World War II (1939–1945) occurred before the Cold War. The Persian Gulf War took place in the post–Cold War era that began after 1990 when the Soviet Union was no longer a threat.

40. **4** The activities of Mother Teresa are most closely associated with the needs of the poor and health care. Mother Teresa was born Agnes Gonxha in 1910 in Macedonia, and dedicated her life to helping the poor, the elderly, the disabled, and the dying. Mother Teresa joined a convent in Ireland with a mission in India. At 18, she headed to Calcutta, India, to teach at a girls' school. In 1948, she received permission from her superiors to leave the school and devote herself to working among the poorest people in the slums of Calcutta. In 1950, the Pope gave her permission to start a new order, the Missionaries of Charity, whose primary task was to love and care for the sick, needy, and unfortunate. Often dressed in her trademark outfit of a plain white sari with a blue border and a cross pinned to her sleeve, Mother Teresa became the worldwide symbol for helping the downtrodden. In 1965, the Missionaries of Charity became an International Religious Family and many orders were established in Africa, Asia, and Latin America. In 1979, Mother Teresa received the Nobel Peace Prize for her efforts on behalf of the homeless on the streets of Calcutta, India. Although she died in 1997, her mission continues to reach more than 25 countries.

WRONG CHOICES EXPLAINED:

(1) Mother Teresa was not associated with democracy and political freedom. Her focus was on how to improve the conditions of the needy.

(2) Mother Teresa's activities were not connected with industrialization and open markets. She was concerned about industrialization only in the way it would affect the poor in society.

(3) Nationalism and independence movements were not part of the mission of Mother Teresa's religious order. Its goal was to provide assistance for the unfortunate.

41. **1** The conclusion that can best be drawn from these statements is that modern technology can have serious negative effects. On April 25–26, 1986, the world's greatest nuclear power accident occurred at Chernobyl in the former U.S.S.R. (now Ukraine). The Chernobyl nuclear power plant, located 80 miles north of Kiev, had four reactors. While testing reactor number 4, numerous safety procedures were disregarded. The chain reaction explosion blew off the reactor's heavy steel and concrete lid. The nuclear accident released more than 30 to 40 times the radioactivity of the atomic bombs dropped on Hiroshima and Nagasaki. The Chernobyl accident killed more than 30 people immediately. As a result of the high radiation levels in the surrounding areas, 135,000 people had to be evacuated and billions of dollars were spent to relocate communities and decontaminate the rich farmlands. Chloroflourocarbons (CFCs) are a carbon-based combination of chlorine and fluorine used in aerosol spray cans, inhalers, and coolants. The release of these chemicals is a major cause of the depletion of the ozone level. An international organization named Greenpeace was founded in 1981. Its goal is to prevent environmental degradation and promote environmental awareness through direct nonviolent confrontations with polluting corporations and governmental authorities. In 1992, Greenpeace introduced Greenfreeze, an ozone and climate-safe refrigeration technology. Greenfreeze uses a mixture of propane and isobutene to decrease the release of CO_2 into the atmosphere. By 1996, Germany, the United States, and Canada had agreed to phase out CFC use. Rivers and seas have become polluted by human wastes, fertilizers, pesticides, and toxic chemicals. These substances may lead to the development of cancers and even cause death. Oil spills pollute vital waterways and kill marine life. Many nations have set standards on water quality to protect the environment.

WRONG CHOICES EXPLAINED:

(2), (3), and (4) None of these choices can be supported by the statements given. These statements do not give any information about environmental renewal or the location and origin of environmental problems.

42. **4** The cartoon highlights the difference between reading about world famine and experiencing famine. The cartoon shows one child in the United States who is asking his mom what is for supper and one child who is in Africa asking his mother what a supper is. Famine is a global problem that affects millions of people throughout Africa. In 2002, the United Nations estimated that close to 14 million southern and western African people were malnourished or victims of famine. In addition, the majority of Africa south of the Sahara Desert is in the World Bank's lowest income category of less than $765 Gross National Income (GNI) per person per year. The GNI in countries such as Ethiopia is as low as $90 per person. The economic condition of Africa is of such concern that in the summer of 2005, world leaders from eight countries met to address the problems confronting Africa—

including famine, health concerns, and other economic issues—in the G8 summit. As a result of the G8 summit, overall aid to the continent will double. The leaders pledged $50 billion in aid to bolster Africa's weakened economy and to help fight disease and other health concerns.

WRONG CHOICES EXPLAINED:

(1) The cartoon does not indicate that famine affects only Africa and the United States. Famine in Africa is a global concern and affects every country in the world, not just the United States. Many of the world's most powerful leaders have pledged their financial support to address famine in Africa.

(2) The cartoon does not show anything about pollution as the cause of famine. Although pollution negatively affects a society's health, this cartoon does not indicate that pollution is the main cause of famine in Africa.

(3) This cartoon does not indicate that African governments are unconcerned about famine in Africa. The cartoon does not show anything that represents government.

43. **1** One way in which Iran's Ayatollah Khomeini and Afghanistan's Taliban were similar is that they each established an Islamic state. The goal of an Islamic state is to return to the basic values of Islam and to reject the cultural values of the West. In 1979, the Ayatollah Khomeini returned from exile in France and overthrew the shah of Iran. The ayatollah was a religious leader who established an Islamic theocratic state reflecting the principles contained in the Koran. The Western system of laws introduced by the shah was replaced by Islamic law and punishment. Women were expected to dress and behave according to the religious laws of the Koran. The Ayatollah Khomeini died in 1989. The Taliban is a movement of Afghanistan tribespeople from the south. They combined the ideas of Sunni Islam with those of Mao Zedong. The movement began in the 1980s in refugee camps where people fled the fighting during the Soviet occupation of Afghanistan. The Soviets withdrew in 1989, and various resistance groups began to fight among themselves. The Taliban, under the leadership of Mullah Mohammad Omar, seized control of the country in 1996 and established an Islamic republic. The Taliban imposed severe restrictions on women. They were not allowed to leave the home without a male relative escort and were forced to wear the burqa (a garment covering the whole body). Girls were sold when they were young and often resold by husbands when they were tired of their wives. Women were banned from nonemergency hospital care. The Taliban banned music except for unaccompanied religious songs and songs in praise of the Taliban. Photography was forbidden as anti-Islamic because the images can serve as objects of worship. The government also required men to grow a Muslim beard and wear traditional clothing. Special religious peacekeepers were organized to enforce these orders. The United States' invasion of Afghanistan in October 2001 led to the downfall of the Taliban government.

WRONG CHOICES EXPLAINED:

(2) Neither the ayatollah nor the Taliban sponsored a United Nations Conference on Women's Rights. Women in Iran and Afghanistan were denied basic rights in these Islamic states.

(3) Iran has been a member of OPEC since 1960. Afghanistan was never a member of OPEC since it is not an oil-rich country.

(4) The Ayatollah Khomeini rejected communism and sought to create a theocracy based on the principle of the Koran. However, the Taliban incorporated the ideas of Chinese communism into their government.

44. **3** The factor most responsible for the international importance of the Middle East is its vital natural resources in a strategic location. The Middle East stands at the crossroads of three continents: Africa, Asia, and Europe. Since ancient times, it has connected major trade routes both on land and on the seas. Middle Eastern nations, such as Saudi Arabia, Kuwait, Iraq, and Iran, also sit atop a vast reserve of oil. Oil supplies about 40 percent of the world's energy and 96 percent of its transportation energy. As a result, the Middle East is strategically important. Egypt operates the Suez Canal. The canal links the Mediterranean Sea with the Red Sea, creating a water route to the Indian Ocean. The Strait of Hormuz at the mouth of the Persian Gulf is a strategic waterway in which tankers travel to deliver oil for industries. Oil is a vital part of the global economy; 66 percent of global oil reserves are in the hands of Middle Eastern regions. Saudi Arabia has about 25 percent of these reserves. As oil consumption continues to grow in the West as well as in China and India, the Middle East will continue to be important.

WRONG CHOICES EXPLAINED:

(1) The governments of the Middle East have failed to implement political and social reforms. Most of these governments have denied basic political and social rights to a majority of their people. Women in Kuwait received the right to vote only in 2003.

(2) The Middle East is not important for superior weapons technology. Saudi Arabia, with assistance from the United States, is one of the few countries with some sophisticated military technology.

(4) The Middle East is not important because of its advanced scientific and industrial development. In the 1970s, an increasing number of Muslims opposed industrialization and technology. Their movement wanted to return to a society based on the values of the Koran. This approach has not helped the area to develop a technologically advanced society.

45. **3** The condition described in this passage occurred during the Industrial Revolution. The Industrial Revolution is a historical event that began in the textile industry in England in the 18th century. The Industrial Revolution resulted in the shift from the manufacturing of goods by hand tools to complex machines and from human and animal power to steam power. The Industrial Revolution brought about changes in where people

lived and in how they worked. In 1750, the population of Manchester was 17,000 people, and by 1800, there were over 80,000 people. The rapid growth of cities contributed to deplorable living conditions. The working class or poor lived in crowded and unhealthy conditions with no running water, sewage, or sanitation systems and with garbage rotting in the streets. The Industrial Revolution led to the invention of complex machines such as the steam engine. These bulky machines had to be installed in factory buildings. These factories were poorly supervised, had unsafe working conditions, and children were regularly beaten and abused by factory owners. In addition, the average workday was 12 to 14 hours.

WRONG CHOICES EXPLAINED:

(1) The Age of Discovery refers to the period from 1400 to 1600 during which European monarchs sent explorers to find new trade routes and lands in Asia, Africa, and the Americas.

(2) The Renaissance, which means "rebirth," was a period of reawakened interests in the classical works of art, literature, and architecture of Greece and Rome. The Renaissance began in Italy and spread throughout all of Europe from the 1300s until the 1600s.

(4) The Green Revolution refers to 20th century technological advances in agriculture. These advances have led to increased food production on a limited parcel of land.

46. **3** The heading that best completes the partial outline is Turning Points in History. Turning points in history are times when decisive changes alter the course of history for nations and people. The fall of Constantinople in 1453 marked the end of the Christian Byzantine Empire. The Byzantine Empire was a symbol of the power and glory of Rome long after the Roman Empire had faded. The Byzantine Empire had preserved the heritage of the Greek and Roman Empires for nearly 1,000 years. In 1453, the Ottomans captured Constantinople and for the next 200 years, backed by military advances, built a large and powerful empire in Europe and the Middle East. The voyages of Columbus that began in 1492 started the European race to colonize the Americas. The interaction of Europe with the Americas had a great impact on food, people, plants, animals, technology, and diseases that spread among Europe, the Americas, and Africa. The posting of Martin Luther's Ninety-five Theses in 1517 ended the religious unity of Europe. Until 1517, the Roman Catholic Church was the only Christian religion in Europe. A series of religious wars in the 1520s between Catholics and Lutherans led to the Peace of Augsburg. The agreement signed in 1555 allowed the ruler of a country to decide the religion of the people. Thus, most of northern Europe and northern Germany became Protestant and southern Europe became Catholic. The collapse of communism in the Soviet Union in 1991 brought an end to the Cold War and initiated years of change in eastern Europe. The Soviet Union lost its role as a world superpower. The collapse of communism led to the formation of the Commonwealth of

Independent States consisting of 11 of the 15 republics that formed the old Soviet Union. In the Balkans, ethnic conflicts ripped the multinational state of Yugoslavia. After the fall of communism, Croatia, Slovenia, Bosnia-Herzegovina, and Macedonia separated from Yugoslavia and became independent states. Ethnic conflicts within the former Yugoslavia lasted for a decade.

WRONG CHOICES EXPLAINED:

(1), (2), and (4) None of these choices can complete the partial outline.

47. **4** The routes shown on the map reflect Atlantic trade during the Age of Mercantilism. Mercantilism was an economic policy adopted by European monarchs from the 15th to 18th centuries in their quest for colonies and trade. Mercantilism was an economic system in which colonies existed for the benefit of the colonial powers. Colonies provided raw materials for the mother country, and in return colonies were expected to serve as a market for manufactured goods. The Atlantic slave trade formed one part of a three-legged trade network known as triangular trade. Over one trade route Europeans transported manufactured goods to the west coast of Africa. There traders exchanged these goods for captured Africans. Africans were then transported across the Atlantic Ocean and sold in the West Indies. Merchants then bought sugar, coffee, and tobacco in the West Indies and sailed back to Europe to sell products. On another triangular route, merchants carried rum and other goods from the New England colonies to Africa. There they exchanged their merchandise for Africans. The traders then transported the Africans to the West Indies and sold them for sugar and molasses. They then sold these goods for rum products in New England. The triangular trade encompassed a network of trade routes crisscrossing the northern and southern colonies, the West Indies, England, Europe, and Africa.

WRONG CHOICES EXPLAINED:

(1) The Hellenistic Period was a period from about 350 to 140 B.C. when Greece was conquered by Rome. It was a period in which the cultures of ancient Greece, Persia, Egypt, and India mixed together.

(2) The Roman Empire began in 27 B.C. and ended in A.D. 176. The Golden Age of the empire lasted for more than 200 years.

(3) The early Middle Ages lasted from A.D. 500 to 1000. It is often referred to as the Dark Ages. Culture and learning almost disappeared in Europe as a result of confusion and lack of an organized government. The period was not completely dark as is proven by a study of the Medieval Church, the Byzantine Empire, and the Muslim Empire.

48. **2** A common element in the movements for German unification, Italian unification, and Indian independence was the strength of nationalist leaders. Otto Von Bismarck was a nationalist leader who helped unite Germany. Until the 1860s, there was no German nation but, instead, a number of small states to which their residents felt loyal. The two most important

states were Prussia and Austria. Austria did not want a united Germany because it would lose influence over German affairs. France opposed a united Germany because it would challenge her leadership in Europe. In 1862, Otto Von Bismarck became the chancellor of Prussia. Through his policy of blood and iron, he ended Austria's influence in Germany and annexed many northern German states. He defeated France in the Franco-Prussian War of 1871 and was able to get the southern states to consent to unification. By 1871, Germany was a united nation. For many years, Italy was divided into a number of small states and was considered a geographic expression rather than a united country. Italian nationalists such as Giuseppe Mazzini called for a united country. In 1852, Count Camillo di Cavour became prime minister of Piedmont (also known as the kingdom of Sardinia). He strengthened the country by promoting industry, enlarging the army, and improving agriculture. He was also successful in getting diplomatic assistance to free Italy from Austrian domination. In 1859, he secured support from Napoleon III of France if Austria attacked Sardinia. Cavour maneuvered Austria into war and with the help of France was successful in driving Austria out of northern Italy. Further to the south, Giuseppe Garibaldi and his volunteer army of 1,000 Red Shirts gained control of Naples and the Two Sicilies. Cavour joined Naples to enlarge the kingdom of Piedmont. By 1860, Italy had become a united nation. Cavour died in 1861 and is considered the brains of Italian unification. Venice, and later Rome, joined Italy in 1866 and 1870, respectively. Gandhi, who came from a middle-class Hindu family and was educated in England, led the fight against British rule in India. During the 1920s and 1930s, he became the leader of the Indian Nationalist Movement and led a series of nonviolent actions against British rule. One effective form of protest was the boycott in which Indians refused to buy British cloth and other manufactured goods. Gandhi urged Indians to begin spinning their own cloth and used the spinning wheel as the symbol of his nationalist movement. He rejected Western civilization because it undermined native Indian culture. In 1947, India was the first major country to achieve independence in the post–World War II era.

WRONG CHOICES EXPLAINED:

(1) The Catholic Church opposed the unification of Italy and was not a factor in either German unification or Indian independence.

(3) German and Italian unification and Indian independence were not influenced by the mediation of the League of Nations. The League of Nations was formed in the 1920s and was replaced by the United Nations in 1945. Germany and Italy were unified in the 19th century, and India gained independence in 1947.

(4) A democratic tradition did not exist in Germany, Italy, or India. None of these countries had a long history of democracy.

49. **4** The leader most closely associated with the use of civil disobedience in a struggle to end colonial rule is Mohandas Gandhi. Mohandas

Gandhi became the leader of the Indian nationalist movement that wanted independence from Great Britain. Gandhi was a pacifist who believed in the principle of *satyagraha*, which in English is called passive resistance or civil disobedience. Gandhi believed that one perfect civil resister was enough to win the battle of right and wrong. Gandhi launched his campaign of nonviolent civil disobedience to weaken the British government and its economic power in India. One effective method of protest was the boycott in which Indians refused to buy British cloth and other manufactured goods. Gandhi urged Indians to begin spinning their own cloth and used the spinning wheel as a symbol of his rejection of Western civilization. He also called on the people to refuse to attend government schools, pay taxes, or vote in elections. Gandhi used these nonviolent methods to show the British the futility of denying India its freedom. India would not achieve its independence until 1947, one year before Gandhi's assassination on January 30, 1948.

WRONG CHOICES EXPLAINED:

(1) Momar Khadafi has been the dictator of Libya since 1968 and is associated with promoting terrorism. Since the 1990s, he has sought to promote a more moderate image in the West. In October 2003, he announced that he was dismantling Libya's weapons of mass destruction.

(2) Saddam Hussein was the military dictator of Iraq from 1973 to 2003. He was responsible for numerous human rights violations against the Kurdish minority in northern Iraq.

(3) Ho Chi Minh was the founder of the Vietnamese Nationalist Communists who fought against the French and the United States in Vietnam. He died in 1969.

50. **4** One similarity between the Reign of Terror during the French Revolution and the Cultural Revolution in China was that both used violent methods to eliminate their opponents. A Committee of Public Safety led by the radical leader Maximilien Robespierre launched a Reign of Terror from 1793 to 1794. The Radicals were those French who wanted to establish a republic in France and save the revolution from foreign and domestic enemies. Robespierre believed that France could achieve a republic of virtue through terror. The guillotine, which was considered more humane because it worked swiftly, became the symbol of the horrors of the Reign of Terror. An estimated 40,000 people lost their lives to the guillotine or gunfire or were drowned on barges set out to sea. By 1794, the public rejected violence and Robespierre was executed, thus ending the Reign of Terror. In 1949, Mao Zedong and the Communist Party took control of China. In 1966, Mao launched the Cultural Revolution to revive people's loyalty to communism and to establish a more equitable society. Mao feared that the revolutionary peasants and workers were being replaced by intellectuals in running the country. He urged China's young people to learn revolution by making revolution. Millions of high school and college students left their classrooms and formed militia units called the Red Guards. The new heroes were the peasants

who worked with their hands. The life of the mind—intellectual and artistic activity—was considered useless. The Red Guards shut down colleges and schools. They attacked professors, government officials, factory managers, and even their own parents. Exiled intellectuals had to "purify" themselves by doing hard work in remote villages. Thousands of people were executed or died in jail. By 1976, Mao had to admit that the Cultural Revolution had to stop. With Mao's approval, the Red Guards were dissolved and order was restored.

WRONG CHOICES EXPLAINED:

(1) The Reign of Terror and Cultural Revolution did not seek to limit the power of absolute leaders. In France, absolute rule had ended in 1789 when Louis XVI was overthrown. In China, Mao was a dictator with absolute power.

(2) Neither the Reign of Terror nor the Cultural Revolution illustrated the power of public opinion in forming national policy. These movements were designed to deal with the enemies of the government.

(3) The Reign of Terror and Cultural Revolution sought to promote social equality, not social stability or economic growth. In France, the Reign of Terror led to inflation. In China, the Cultural Revolution contributed to economic chaos.

THEMATIC ESSAY: GENERIC SCORING RUBRIC

Score of 5:
- Shows a thorough understanding of the theme or problem
- Addresses all aspects of the task
- Shows an ability to analyze, evaluate, compare and/or contrast issues and events
- Richly supports the theme or problem with relevant facts, examples, and details
- Is a well-developed essay, consistently demonstrating a logical and clear plan of organization
- Introduces the theme or problem by establishing a framework that is beyond a simple restatement of the task and concludes with a summation of the theme or problem

Score of 4:
- Shows a good understanding of the theme or problem
- Addresses all aspects of the task
- Shows an ability to analyze, evaluate, compare and/or contrast issues and events
- Includes relevant facts, examples, and details, but may not support all aspects of the theme or problem evenly
- Is a well-developed essay, demonstrating a logical and clear plan of organization
- Introduces the theme or problem by establishing a framework that is beyond a simple restatement of the task and concludes with a summation of the theme or problem

Score of 3:
- Shows a satisfactory understanding of the theme or problem
- Addresses most aspects of the task or addresses all aspects in a limited way
- Shows an ability to analyze or evaluate issues and events, but not in any depth
- Includes some facts, examples, and details
- Is a satisfactorily developed essay, demonstrating a general plan of organization
- Introduces the theme or problem by repeating the task and concludes by repeating the theme or problem

Score of 2:
- Shows limited understanding of the theme or problem
- Attempts to address the task
- Develops a faulty analysis or evaluation of issues and events
- Includes few facts, examples, and details, and may include information that contains inaccuracies
- Is a poorly organized essay, lacking focus
- Fails to introduce or summarize the theme or problem

Score of 1:
- Shows very limited understanding of the theme or problem
- Lacks an analysis of evaluation of the issues and events
- Includes little or no accurate or relevant facts, examples, or details

• Attempts to complete the task, but demonstrates a major weakness in organization
• Fails to introduce or summarize the theme or problem

Score of 0: Fails to address the task, is illegible, or is a blank paper

PART II: THEMATIC ESSAY QUESTION

Throughout history, global problems have posed a major challenge for nations and regions. Some examples of global problems are the spread of disease and deforestation. The bubonic plague in the 14th century had serious effects on the people who lived during those times, and deforestations in the 20th century greatly impacted the areas in which they occurred.

The bubonic plague was a disease spread by fleas on rats. Black rats carried fleas from one area to another. In medieval times, people did not bathe and most of them had fleas and lice. In addition, medieval people threw their garbage and sewage into the streets. These unsanitary conditions became breeding grounds for more rats.

The fleas carried by rats leaped from person to person, thus spreading the bubonic plague with incredible speed. The plague began in Asia. By traveling the trade lanes, it infected most of Asia and the Muslim world. Inevitably, it reached Europe. In 1347, four Genovese ships arrived in Sicily from the Black Sea. Besides trade goods from Asia, the ship brought a dreaded cargo.

Victims of this terrible disease had a raging fever. Black swellings grew at their necks and joints. The name Black Death came from these swellings. From Italy, the outbreak followed trade routes to France, Germany, England, and other parts of Europe.

The plague brought terror and ripped apart the very fabric of society. The Italian poet Boccaccio in *The Decameron* described the social decay that he witnessed in Florence as people tried to avoid contracting the plague from neighbors and relatives. Frightened people looked around for scapegoats. Christians blamed the Jews for the plague, charging that they had poisoned the wells.

The bubonic plague took about four years to reach every corner of Europe. The Black Death claimed more lives than any war until the 20th century. Historians estimate that the Black Death killed a quarter to one-half the population of Europe or about 25 million people and many more millions in Asia and North Africa. In Cairo, one of the world's largest cities, the plague at its peak killed 7,000 people a day.

The economic effects of the plague were enormous. Whole villages disappeared. Trade declined and prices rose. Fewer people meant that workers were scarce everywhere. Serfs, who had often been unpaid or poorly paid for their labor, now demanded wages for their work. They left the manor in search of better wages. Thus, the old manorial system based on a fixed labor supply began to crumble.

The ruling class fought these changes. Nobles fiercely resisted peasants' demands for higher wages, causing peasant revolts in England, France, Italy, and Belgium. In each case, nobles ruthlessly put down the revolts. Although the peasants did not win, the revolts contributed to the end of the feudal society of the Middle Ages. With millions dead from the plague, the remnants of feudalism and its relationship of lord and serfs were no longer feasible.

The Church also suffered a loss of prestige when its prayers and penances failed to stop the onslaught of the plague. In addition, many clergy deserted their flocks or charged high fees to perform services for the dying. The bubonic plague had spread both death and social unrest and hastened the changes already in the making that led to the collapse of medieval society.

A global problem of the 20th century that still affects the world today is deforestation. Forests are one of the most valuable ecosystems in the world, containing over 60 percent of the world's biodiversity. Deforestation is the destruction of forests, especially tropical rain forests. The most important direct causes of deforestation include logging, the conversion of forest land for agriculture and raising cattle, urbanization, mining, and oil development. There has also been a tendency to highlight small-scale migratory farmers as another major cause of forest loss. Farmers settle along roads throughout the forest to clear a patch of land and to use it for growing subsistence crops. In tropical rain forests, such practices tend to lead to rapid soil degradation as most soils are too poor to sustain agriculture. Consequently, the farmers are forced to clear another patch of forest after a few years. The remaining soil is often used for a few years for raising cattle. This is a death sentence for the soil as cattle remove the last scarce traces of fertility. The result is an entire piece of barren land that will be unable to recover its original biomass for many years.

Although deforestation is a problem for nations like India, Indonesia, and regions such as Central Africa and British Columbia, the most widely publicized issue is the rapid destruction of the Amazon rain forest, which occupies more than a million square miles in the heart of Brazil. The basin covers 40 percent of the South American continent and includes parts of eight South American countries. Since the 1930s, Brazil has opened more and more of this area to development. By the 1970s and 1980s, vast traces of forests were being bulldozed and burned for farms, cattle ranches, highways, and even planned cities. The destruction of the Amazon rain forest has come at an enormous cost. The Amazon rain forest has been described as the "lungs of our planet" because it provides the essential world service of continuously recycling carbon dioxide into oxygen. More than 20 percent of the world's oxygen is produced in the Amazon rain forest.

More than half of the world's estimated 10 million species of plants, animals, and insects live in the tropical rain forest. Currently, 121 prescription drugs are sold worldwide from plant-derived sources. The National Cancer Institute has identified 300 plants that are active against cancer. The loss of these species may affect the development of medicine and natural remedies for diseases.

Deforestation is also a problem for tribal cultures living in the area. Isolation has protected bands of Native-American forest dwellers just like the flora and the fauna in Brazil. Land-hungry farmers, speculators, and foreign mining companies are threatening these ancient ways of life. Many Native Americans die of diseases introduced by the newcomers.

The destruction of the rain forests in Brazil and around the world is very important to the environment. In every one of these areas, cutting down trees would drastically change the ecosystem of the area by causing erosion and endangering species. The deforestation of the Amazon rain forest in Brazil affects the world. Fewer rain forests mean less rain and oxygen to breathe as well as an increase in global warming. In 1992, the U.N. sponsored the Earth Summit in Brazil. The United States and 34 nations issued the Rio Pact, which called for nations and industries to plan economic growth to meet global needs, without sacrificing the environmental needs of future generations.

The bubonic plague of the 14th century and deforestation of the 20th century posed global problems and major challenges. The plague brought about political and social changes because it helped to destroy medieval society. Deforestation threatens our ecosystem and the possibility of losing Earth's greatest biological treasures. The bubonic plague was a global issue because it spread from Asia through Europe. Deforestation is a global concern because the greenhouse effect influences everyone in our world's ecosystem.

PART III: DOCUMENT-BASED QUESTION

Part A: Short Answers

Document 1

One reason European knights and soldiers joined the Crusades was for religious motives. They wanted to fight for the Cross.

Note: This response receives full credit because it correctly identifies one of the reasons why European knights and soldiers joined the Crusades.

Document 2

2a One positive, unexpected outcome of the Crusades on Western civilization was that Western civilization greatly expanded its knowledge of the geography of the "mysterious East."

Note: This response receives full credit because it identifies a positive, unexpected outcome of the Crusades on Western civilization.

2b One positive, unexpected outcome of the Crusades on Muslim civilization was that Arab builders learned much about military masonry and copied the features from the Crusaders' castles.

Note: This response receives full credit because it states a positive, unexpected outcome of the Crusades on Muslim civilization.

2c One reason the West was disappointed with the outcome of the Crusades was that they were a military failure because Jerusalem was returned to the Muslims for good.

Note: This response receives full credit because it specifically shows how the West was disappointed with the outcome of the Crusades.

Document 3

According to this diagram, two reasons for World War I were:
(1) Militarism or arms race
(2) Imperialism

Note: This response receives full credit because it specifically cites two reasons for World War I as presented by the diagram.

Document 4

4a According to this document, France was repaid for losses suffered during World War I by reparations payment from Germany and Germany's ceding to France the coal mines in the Saar Basin.

Note: This response receives full credit because it states how France was repaid for losses suffered during World War I.

4b According to the document, a consequence of World War I for Germany was that Germany surrendered all her rights and titles to overseas possessions and accepted responsibility for loss and damages.

Note: This response receives full credit because it identifies a consequence of World War I for Germany.

Document 5

According to this document, one reason Adolf Hitler felt war was necessary was to get territory because territory cannot be won as a favor from other people.

Note: This response receives full credit because it identifies a reason why Adolf Hitler thought war was necessary.

Document 6

According to the Yalta Conference, two ways Europe was expected to change as a result of World War II were:

(1) Get rid of Nazism and Fascism and establish order in Europe.

(2) Establish a more democratic provisional government in Poland and allow people to choose the form of government under which they will be ruled.

Note: This response receives full credit because it describes two ways in which Europe was to change as a result of World War II, citing information from the document to support the explanation.

Document 7

According to this document, two reasons President George H. W. Bush was concerned about the Persian Gulf region in 1990 were:

(1) Iraq had invaded Kuwait and its takeover was not acceptable.

(2) Iraq had damaged the security and stability of the Persian Gulf area and the security and safety of Americans had to be protected abroad.

Note: This response receives full credit because it identifies two concerns George H. W. Bush had about the Persian Gulf region in 1990.

Document 8

Based on this 1998 cartoon, one unexpected outcome of the Persian Gulf War was that Saddam Hussein was threatening to build chemical and biological weapons labs.

Note: This response receives full credit because it cites one unexpected outcome of the Persian Gulf War as shown in the 1998 cartoon.

DOCUMENT-BASED QUESTION: GENERIC SCORING RUBRIC

Score of 5:
- Thoroughly addresses all aspects of the *Task* by accurately analyzing and interpreting at least **four** documents
- Incorporates information from the documents in the body of the essay
- Incorporates relevant outside information
- Richly supports the theme or problem with relevant facts, examples, and details
- Is a well-developed essay, consistently demonstrating a logical and clear plan of organization
- Introduces the theme or problem by establishing a framework that is beyond a simple restatement of the *Task* or *Historical Context* and concludes with a summation of the theme or problem

Score of 4:
- Addresses all aspects of the *Task* by accurately analyzing and interpreting at least **four** documents
- Incorporates information from the documents in the body of the essay
- Incorporates relevant outside information
- Includes relevant facts, examples, and details, but discussion may be more descriptive than analytical
- Is a well-developed essay, demonstrating a logical and clear plan of organization
- Introduces the theme or problem by establishing a framework that is beyond a simple restatement of the *Task* or *Historical Context* and concludes with a summation of the theme or problem

Score of 3:
- Addresses most aspects of the *Task* or addresses all aspects of the *Task* in a limited way, using some of the documents
- Incorporates some information from the documents in the body of the essay
- Incorporates limited or no relevant outside information
- Includes some facts, examples, and details, but discussion is more descriptive than analytical
- Is a satisfactorily developed essay, demonstrating a general plan of organization
- Introduces the theme or problem by repeating the *Task* or *Historical Context* and concludes by simply repeating the theme or problem

Score of 2:
- Attempts to address some aspects of the *Task*, making limited use of the documents
- Presents no relevant outside information
- Includes few facts, examples, and details; discussion restates contents of the documents

- Is a poorly organized essay, lacking focus
- Fails to introduce or summarize the theme or problem

Score of 1:
- Shows limited understanding of the *Task* with vague, unclear references to the documents
- Presents no relevant outside information
- Includes little or no accurate or relevant facts, details, or examples
- Attempts to complete the *Task*, but demonstrates a major weakness in organization
- Fails to introduce or summarize the theme or problem

Score of 0: Fails to address the *Task*, is illegible, or is a blank paper

Part B: Essay

Throughout history, wars have occurred because of many different reasons. The Crusades, World War I, and the Persian Gulf War were caused by social, economic, or political reasons. Each of these conflicts led to anticipated results as well as to unpredicted outcomes. The expected and unexpected results greatly affected the course of history.

Religion was one of the social causes of the Crusades. The goal of the Crusades (1096–1246) was to capture from the Muslims the Holy Land, which was the birthplace of Christianity. In 1095, the Byzantine emperor appealed to Pope Urban II for help against the Muslim Turks. The pope agreed to help because the Muslims had taken control of the Holy Land. The pope's call for the Crusades led to a tremendous outpouring of support. Many saw the Crusades as a religious journey because they were doing God's work (Doc. 1). If they were killed, the soldiers would be guaranteed salvation in heaven. Some knights were attracted by the prospect of conquest, plunder, and adventure (Doc. 1). The common people, especially the peasants, saw the war in the far-off lands as an opportunity to improve their lot in life.

Economic and political factors influenced the Crusades. Nobles and the Church leaders saw the Crusades as an opportunity to get rid of quarrelsome knights who fought each other. These knights threatened the peace of the kingdom as well as church property. Others who participated were younger sons of nobles, who unlike their oldest brother, did not stand to inherit their father's property due to primogeniture (Doc. 1). They were looking for land and a position in society.

Politically, some Church leaders saw the Crusades as a way not only to reclaim the Holy Land but also to unite Christendom. The prestige of stopping Muslim expansion would ensure the continued dominance of the Church in medieval society.

Like the Crusades, World War I was caused by economic, political, and social factors. Economic rivalries created competition between Great Britain and Germany (Doc. 3). By 1900, German factories were outproducing the

British, and Germany was challenging Great Britain in the world markets. Imperialism, motivated by the struggle for territory, markets, and resources in Asia and Africa, contributed to the economic friction between Great Britain and Germany (Doc. 3). Great Britain resented Germany for blocking her plans for a Cape-Cairo Railway, which would have connected the British African possessions from South Africa to Cairo, Egypt.

The spirit of nationalism was both a political and social cause that created jealously and hatred among European nations. In France, national pride was hurt by the loss of Alsace-Lorraine in the Franco-Prussian War. The French considered Germany their natural enemy. Other countries wanted to extend their territories to include people of their own race or background. Subject nationalities of Czechs, Yugoslavs, and Poles sought independence.

The politics of entangling alliances also led to World War I (Doc. 3). The alliance system divided into two armed camps. The Triple Entente consisted of France, Russia, and Great Britain. The Triple Alliance was composed of Germany, Austria-Hungary, and Italy. In 1914, when Archduke Ferdinand of Austria-Hungary was assassinated by a Serbian nationalist, Germany supported her ally when Austria-Hungary declared war on Serbia. Russia backed Serbia. The Russians, as the largest Slavic country, defended the rights of the people of similar backgrounds to unite and support their Slavic brothers in Serbia. The other nations joined different sides based on their alliances.

Nationalism and economics were a major cause of the Persian Gulf War. In 1990, Iraqi troops invaded the oil-rich country of Kuwait. Kuwait wanted to maintain its independence. However, Saddam Hussein argued that, historically, Kuwait was part of Iraq until the British separated it at the end of World War I.

President George H. W. Bush saw the invasion as a threat to the security and stability of the Persian Gulf (Doc. 7). The United States feared that Iraq's invasion endangered the balance of power in the Middle East. Iraq could also invade Saudi Arabia and threaten the flow of oil from the Persian Gulf. President George H. W. Bush also claimed that the goal of the United States was to protect American citizens and restore the autonomy of the Kuwaiti government (Doc. 7). When Iraq refused to withdraw from Kuwait, the Persian Gulf War began. The United States organized a coalition of American, European, and Arabian countries to drive out Iraqi forces.

The outcomes of all wars vary. It is expected that wars will lead to death, destruction, and the resolution of those issues that caused the war. However, sometimes wars have unexpected outcomes that can influence the course of history for many years.

The failure of the Crusades led to the expected outcome of the Muslims retaining control of the Holy Land (Doc. 2). Although the first crusaders captured Jerusalem in 1099, they were driven out in 1187 by the Muslim leader Saladin. The Europeans organized other Crusades to recapture Jerusalem, but the Muslims retained the city. The victory of the Muslims led to their dominance in the Middle East for the next two centuries.

Although the West did not expect the Crusades to be a military failure, these expeditions had numerous unexpected positive outcomes. Returning Crusaders brought back new fabrics, spices, perfumes, and knowledge. The veil of the mysterious East was lifted (Doc. 2). Trade increased during the Crusades. Italian merchants who had built fleets to transport the Crusaders used these same transports to keep trade open. Contact with the East spurred a new demand for luxury goods and other items that Europe had once been unable to obtain.

The increased trade and contact between Europe and the East led to a renewed interest in learning as Europe became aware of ancient civilizations and the advances of Arab civilization in the arts, sciences, and literature. This renewed curiosity led the Europeans to realize that millions of people lived in regions that they had never known. Soon a few curious Europeans visited far-off places like India and China. By the 1400s, a desire to trade led Europeans to a new age of exploration.

Although the Crusades left a legacy of hatred between Christians and Muslims, the Muslims gained unexpected knowledge about military masonry. In constructing the famed Citadel of Cairo, Saladin took some of the features of the Crusaders' castles that he had seen in the area of the Eastern Mediterranean (Doc. 2).

The Crusades indirectly contributed to the end of feudalism and manoralism. Feudalism was weakened by the absence of nobles who were fighting in the Crusades or were killed. Manoralism declined when serfs joined the Crusades in return for their freedom.

As a result of the Allied victory in World War I, England, France, and Italy expected to gain territories and resources from Germany. France gained control of the Saar Valley as reparations (Doc. 4). France also gained Alsace-Lorraine. England maintained its naval supremacy by restricting the German army and navy to 100,000 men and forbade Germany from having an air force. As the loser in the war, Germany also accepted sole responsibility as stated in Article 231, also known as the War Guilt Clause (Doc. 4).

World War I, however, led to numerous unanticipated results that contributed directly to World War II. World War I created conditions in Russia that helped spark the Communist Revolution of 1917. Russia was one of the Allied Powers in World War I that fought Germany. However, Russia was not ready to fight a war and the Russian government of Czar Nicholas II was unable to feed the people and provide supplies for the soldiers. This led to the end of the Romanov dynasty and the rise of communism.

The harsh conditions included in the Versaille Treaty contributed to the rise of Nazism in Germany and Fascism in Italy. Adolf Hitler and the Nazi Party claimed that the country's economic problems stemmed from the loss of its European colonies and from its reparations payment of $35 billion. Hitler claimed that Germany had been "stabbed in the back at Versailles" and that Germany would regain power by taking back territories that they had lost unjustly (Doc. 5). In Italy, Mussolini and the Fascist Party promised to regain the territory that had been denied to them at the Versailles Treaty. They wanted more land in the Balkans and in the Middle East. The Versailles Treaty, which had been signed in the hope of establishing lasting peace in Europe, failed. The treaty created the conditions that led to World War II in 1939.

In 1991, the Persian Gulf War began. The United States and its allies quickly won the war, and the legitimate government of Kuwait was restored (Doc. 7). The victory assured the world that there would be a continued flow of oil from the Persian Gulf. Despite the quick defeat of the Iraqi forces, there were some unexpected results. The United States had viewed Saddam Hussein as a dangerous force and hoped that the war would topple his dictatorship. However, he remained in power. He brutally suppressed all critics and persecuted Kurds and Shiites. To protect these minorities, the U.N. enforced no-fly zones, areas over which Iraqi aircraft were not permitted to fly. At the end of the war, the United Nations required that Iraq destroy its nuclear, biological, and chemical weapons as well as its missiles. The U.N. began a series of inspections to ensure compliance. Over a decade, Hussein tested the resolve of the United Nations by developing chemical and biological weapons (Doc. 8). In the late 1990s, Iraq expelled U.N. inspections teams and refused to allow further inspections. Eventually in 2003, the United States and England invaded Iraq because they claimed that Hussein was developing weapons of mass destruction. Saddam Hussein was overthrown, and the United States and Great Britain are helping the Iraqis set up a democratic form of government.

The Crusades, World War I, and the Persian Gulf War of 1990, like most wars in history, were motivated by economic, political, and social causes. Although historians always debate the most important causes, the outcomes of war have also led to many different viewpoints. The Crusades are considered a military failure for the West. However, they also changed the history of Europe by arousing Europe's curiosity about the East. The Allies in World War I thought the Versailles Treaty was fair. However, the German people believed that they had been betrayed by this harsh treaty. The Persian Gulf War of 1990 was considered a success for the United States. However, many believe it failed because Saddam Hussein still remained in power. All wars have expected and unexpected outcomes that are subject to different interpretations as time passes and other events are set into motion.

Topic	Question Numbers	Total Number of Questions	Number Wrong	°Reason for Wrong Answer
U.S. AND N.Y. HISTORY				
WORLD HISTORY	4, 5, 6, 9, 10, 15, 16, 20, 21, 26, 27, 29, 30, 34, 38, 39, 40, 45, 46, 47, 48, 49, 50	23		
GEOGRAPHY	1, 2, 3, 7, 12, 14, 17, 19, 22, 24, 33, 35, 36, 41, 42, 44	16		
ECONOMICS	11, 23, 25, 32, 37	5		
CIVICS, CITIZENSHIP, AND GOVERNMENT	8, 13, 18, 28, 31, 43	6		

°Your reason for answering the question incorrectly might be (a) lack of knowledge, (b) misunderstanding the question, or (c) careless error.

Actual Items by Standard and Unit

	1 U.S. and N.Y. History	2 World History	3 Geography	4 Economics	5 Civics, Citizenship, and Gov't	Number
Methodology of Global History and Geography						
UNIT ONE Ancient World		4, 5, 6, 9	1, 7		8	7
UNIT TWO Expanding Zones of Exchange		10	3			2
UNIT THREE Global Interactions		15, 16	12, 14		13	5
UNIT FOUR First Global Age		20, 47	17, 19, 22		18	6
UNIT FIVE Age of Revolution		21, 26, 27, 45	24	23, 25	28	8
UNIT SIX Crisis and Achievement (1900–1945)		29, 30, 34		32	31	5
UNIT SEVEN 20th Century Since 1945		38, 39, 49	35, 36	37		6
UNIT EIGHT Global Connections and Interactions		40	41, 42, 44		43	5
Cross topical		46, 48, 50	2, 33	11		6
Total # of Questions		23	16	5	6	50
% of Items by Standard		46%	32%	10%	12%	100%

Examination
August 2005
Global History and Geography

PART I: MULTIPLE CHOICE

Directions (1–50): For each statement or question, write in the space provided, the *number* of the word or expression that, of those given, best completes the statement or answers the question.

1 • Oceans are an important source of food in Japan.
  • Terrace farming is used in many parts of China.
  • Irrigation systems are widely used in India.

Which conclusion can best be drawn from these statements?

1 Many civilizations use irrigation to improve crop production.
2 People adapt to meet the challenges of their geography.
3 Fish provide adequate protein for the Japanese.
4 Most nations are dependent on the same food source.   1____

2 Which social scientists are best known for studying the physical artifacts of a culture?

1 geographers   3 economists
2 archaeologists   4 sociologists   2____

3 Which statement most accurately describes how geography affected the growth of the ancient civilizations of Egypt and Mesopotamia?

  1 River valleys provided rich soil to grow plentiful crops.
  2 Large deserts provided many mineral deposits.
  3 Access to the Atlantic Ocean provided trade routes.
  4 Large savanna areas provided protection from invaders.

  3 _____

4 One way in which the Five Relationships, the Ten Commandments, and the Eightfold Path are similar is that they

  1 promote polytheism
  2 establish gender equality
  3 provide codes of behavior
  4 describe secularism

  4 _____

5 The Phoenicians are often referred to as the "carriers of civilization" because they

  1 introduced Islam and Christianity to Central Africa
  2 established colonies throughout northern Europe
  3 developed the first carts with wheels
  4 traded goods and spread ideas throughout the Mediterranean region

  5 _____

6 The exchange of silks and spices and the spread of Buddhism along the Silk Roads are examples of

  1 cultural diffusion   3 ethnocentrism
  2 self-sufficiency   4 desertification

  6 _____

Base your answer to question 7 on the passage below and on your knowledge of social studies.

1. *In the name of Allah, Most Gracious, Most Merciful.*
2. Praise be to Allah, The Cherisher and Sustainer of the Worlds;
3. Most Gracious, Most Merciful;
4. Master of the Day of Judgement.
5. Thee do we worship, And Thine aid we seek.
6. Show us the straight way,
7. The way of those on whom Thou hast bestowed Thy Grace, Those whose (portion) Is not wrath, And who go not astray.

—'Abdullah Yūsuf 'Alī, ed.,
The Meaning of The Holy Qur'ān,
Amana Publications, 1999

7 Which concept is best reflected in this passage?

1 baptism
2 karma
3 monotheism
4 animism

7 _____

8 Which accomplishments are associated with the Gupta Empire?

1 adoption of democracy and construction of the Pantheon
2 defeat of the Roman Empire and adoption of Christianity
3 establishment of Pax Mongolia and founding of a Chinese dynasty
4 use of Sanskrit language and development of the concept of zero

8 _____

9 Kievian Russia adopted the Eastern Orthodox religion, the Cyrillic alphabet, and different styles of art and architecture through contact with

  1 traders from South Asia
  2 conquering invaders from Mongolia
  3 crusaders from western Europe
  4 missionaries from the Byzantine Empire   9 ____

10 Which statement about the Golden Age of Islam is a fact rather than an opinion?

  1 Islamic art was more abstract than Greek art.
  2 Muslims were the best early mathematicians.
  3 Islamic society preserved Greek and Roman culture.
  4 Muslim artists had more talent than European artists.   10 ____

11 Which economic activity was the basis for most of the wealth and power of the West African empires of Ghana and Mali?

  1 hunting and gathering
  2 farming and cattle ranching
  3 trading in salt and gold
  4 working in bronze and brass   11 ____

12 What was one reason that some Italian cities developed into major commercial and cultural centers during the 13th and 14th centuries?

  1 unified central government
  2 isolationist economic policies
  3 geographic location
  4 system of social equality   12 ____

13 Which two cultures most influenced the development of early Japan?

  1 Greek and Roman
  2 Chinese and Korean
  3 Egyptian and Mesopotamian
  4 Indian and Persian   13 _____

Base your answers to questions 14 and 15 on the quotation below and on your knowledge of social studies.

> ". . . Finally, gather together all that we have said, so great and so august [important], about royal authority. You have seen a great nation united under one man: you have seen his sacred power, paternal and absolute: you have seen that secret reason which directs the body politic, enclosed in one head: you have seen the image of God in kings, and you will have the idea of majesty of kingship.
>
> God is holiness itself, goodness itself, power itself, reason itself. In these things consists the divine majesty. In their reflection consists the majesty of the prince. . . ."

> —Jacques-Benigne Bossuet

14 Which concept is associated with this quotation?

  1 direct democracy   3 socialism
  2 imperialism   4 divine right   14 _____

15 Which individual most likely opposed the form of government described in this quotation?

  1 Ivan the Terrible   3 John Locke
  2 Thomas Hobbes   4 Louis XIV   15 _____

16 The foreign policy of many Russian rulers supported the country's desire for

1 access to inland cities
2 more mineral resources
3 extensive canal systems
4 warm-water ports   16 _____

Base your answer to question 17 on the map below
and on your knowledge of social studies.

Spread of the Black Death

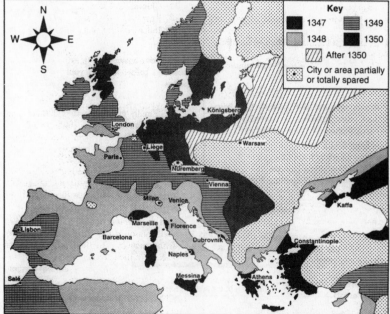

Source: Richard Bulliet et al., *The Earth and Its Peoples: A Global History*, Houghton Mifflin, 2001 (adapted)

17 Which area of Europe was *least* affected by the
Black Death?

1 southwestern Europe   3 eastern Europe
2 Mediterranean Coast   4 British Isles   17 _____

18 One way in which the Magna Carta, the Petition of Right, and the Glorious Revolution are similar is that each

1 strengthened the power of the pope
2 led to the exploration of Africa
3 limited the power of the English monarchy
4 settled religious conflicts

18 _____

19 The encomienda system in Latin America was a direct result of the

1 Crusades
2 Age of Exploration
3 Reformation
4 Age of Reason

19 _____

Base your answer to question 20 on the illustrations below and on your knowledge of social studies.

Aztec Civilization (A.D. 1200 to 1535)

Inca Civilization (A.D. 1200 to 1535)

Source: Sue A. Kime, *World Studies: Global Issues and Assessments*, N & N Publishing, 1995 (adapted)

20 These illustrations suggest that early Latin American civilizations

1 were based on European societies
2 used advanced technology to build complex structures
3 incorporated early Roman architectural design
4 were strongly influenced by Renaissance humanism   20 ____

21 Sir Isaac Newton, Galileo Galilei, and Johannes Kepler are all directly associated with the

1 Industrial Revolution
2 Scientific Revolution
3 English Revolution
4 Agricultural Revolution   21 ____

22 The Enlightenment and the American Revolution were both major influences on 19th-century uprisings in

1 Latin America   3 Vietnam
2 the Middle East   4 Japan   22 ____

23 Before the French Revolution, the people of France were divided into three estates based mainly on their

1 education level   3 social class
2 geographic region   4 religious beliefs   23 ____

24 One similarity in the leadership of Jomo Kenyatta, José de San Martín, and Sun Yixian (Sun Yat-sen) is that they

  1 supported nationalistic movements
  2 organized communist rebellions
  3 opposed trade with other nations
  4 established democratic rule in their countries   24 _____

25 The Opium Wars in China and the expedition of Commodore Matthew Perry to Japan resulted in

  1 the economic isolation of China and Japan
  2 an increase in Chinese influence in Asia
  3 the beginning of democratic governments in China and Japan
  4 an increase in Western trade and influence in Asia   25 _____

26 What was a direct result of the Meiji Restoration in Japan?

  1 Japan became a modern industrial nation.
  2 The Tokugawa Shogunate seized control of the government.
  3 Russia signed a mutual trade agreement.
  4 Japan stayed politically isolated.   26 _____

27 Which statement best describes a mixed economy?

  1 The government determines the production and distribution of goods and services.
  2 The products that consumers demand determine what goods are produced.
  3 Some industries are owned by the state, and others are privately owned.
  4 People produce the same goods, but in different amounts, every year.   27 _____

Base your answer to question 28 on the cartoon below and on your knowledge of social studies.

Source: Arcadio Esquivel, *La Nación*,
Cartoonists & Writers Syndicate (adapted)

28 This 2001 cartoon implies that nations in Central America are

  1 defeating enemies and overcoming all obstacles
  2 requesting assistance in the battle against drought
  3 facing several serious problems at the same time
  4 waiting patiently until the economic crisis is over   28 _____

29 Which leader based his rule on the ideas of Karl Marx and Friedrich Engels?

  1 Neville Chamberlain
  2 Vladimir Lenin
  3 Adolf Hitler
  4 Jiang Jieshi (Chiang Kai-shek)   29 _____

30 One reason for the outbreak of World War II was the

    1 ineffectiveness of the League of Nations

    2 growing tension between the United States and the Soviet Union

    3 conflict between the Hapsburg and the Romanov families

    4 refusal of the German government to sign the Treaty of Versailles

30 _____

31 Which United States foreign policy was used to maintain the independence of Greece and Turkey after World War II?

    1 containment   3 nonalignment

    2 neutrality   4 militarism

31 _____

32 Which important principle was established as a result of the Nuremberg trials?

    1 Defeated nations have no rights in international courts of law.

    2 Individuals can be held accountable for "crimes against humanity."

    3 Soldiers must follow the orders of their superiors.

    4 Aggressor nations must pay war reparations for damages caused during wars.

32 _____

33 Which statement about the European Union (EU) is most accurate?

1 The European Union dissolved because of disagreements among its members.

2 The goal of the European Union is to improve the economic prosperity of Europe.

3 Some nations are now being forced to become members of the European Union.

4 The European Union has recently expanded to include North African nations.

33 _____

Base your answer to question 34 on the cartoon below and on your knowledge of social studies.

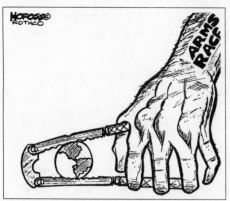

Source: Ellis and Esler, *World History: Connections to Today*, Prentice Hall, 2001 (adapted)

34 What is the main idea of this cartoon?

1 Proliferation of military weapons could destroy the world.

2 The world's population is growing faster than its food supply.

3 The land masses of the Northern and Southern Hemispheres are shifting.

4 Military technology is making the world a smaller place.

34 _____

35 ". . . I saw that the whole solution to this problem lay in political freedom for our people, for it is only when a people are politically free that other races can give them the respect that is due to them. It is impossible to talk of equality of races in any other terms. No people without a government of their own can expect to be treated on the same level as peoples of independent sovereign states. It is far better to be free to govern or misgovern yourself than to be governed by anybody else. . . ."

—Kwame Nkrumah, *Ghana: The Autobiography of Kwame Nkrumah*, Thomas Nelson & Sons, 1957

Which idea is expressed in this statement by Kwame Nkrumah?

1 free trade
2 collective security
3 self-determination
4 peaceful coexistence

35 _____

36 Most of the world's known oil reserves are located near which geographic area?

1 Persian Gulf
2 North Sea
3 Ural Mountains
4 Gulf of Mexico

36 _____

37 The policy of strict racial separation and discrimination that was implemented in the Republic of South Africa is called

1 collectivization
2 apartheid
3 intifada
4 communism

37 _____

38 Which statement best describes a problem facing India today?

1 Democracy has failed to gain popular support.
2 Religious and ethnic diversity has continued to cause conflict.
3 A decrease in population has led to labor shortages.
4 Lack of technology has limited military capabilities.

38 _____

Base your answer to question 39 on the cartoon below and on your knowledge of social studies.

Teamwork

Source: Jim Morin, *The Miami Herald*,
King Features Syndicate, 1989

39 Which concept is illustrated by the cartoon?

  1 scarcity   3 revolution
  2 capitalism   4 interdependence   39 ____

---

40 **"India Strives for Grain Self-Sufficiency by 1970"**

  "New Wheat Variety Grows in Arid Climate"

  "Chemical Fertilizer Use Rises 10% in 1960"

  "Sri Lanka's Rice Production Increases 25% in Three Years"

These newspaper headlines from the 1960s and 1970s describe some of the results of the

  1 Sepoy Mutiny   3 Green Revolution
  2 Kashmir crisis   4 Computer Revolution 40 ____

Base your answer to question 41 on the diagram below and on your knowledge of social studies.

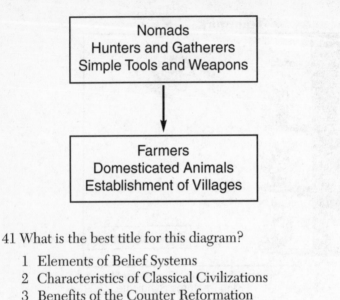

41 What is the best title for this diagram?

1 Elements of Belief Systems
2 Characteristics of Classical Civilizations
3 Benefits of the Counter Reformation
4 Changes during the Neolithic Revolution   41____

42 The treatment of the Armenians by Ottoman Turks in the late 19th and early 20th centuries and the treatment of Muslims by the Serbs of Yugoslavia in the 1990s are both examples of

1 coalition rule   3 universal suffrage
2 liberation theology   4 human rights violations   42____

43 The doctrines of the Roman Catholic, Eastern Orthodox, and Protestant churches are all based on the

1 concept of reincarnation
2 principles of Christianity
3 teachings of Muhammad
4 leadership of the pope   43____

44 Which factor contributed to the success of the
Hanseatic League, the Kingdom of Songhai, and
the British East India Company?

1 location in the Middle East
2 imperialism in Europe
3 development of trade with other regions
4 growth of the Ottoman Empire 44____

45 Heavy military losses in World War I, food and fuel
shortages, and opposition to the czar led to the

1 French Revolution
2 Russian Revolution
3 Chinese Revolution
4 Cuban Revolution 45____

46 Which geographic factor in Russia played a role in
Napoleon's defeat in 1812 and Hitler's defeat at
Stalingrad in 1944?

1 Siberian tundra   3 arid land
2 Caspian Sea   4 harsh climate 46____

47 • Scholars take civil service examinations for government positions.
• Students form Red Guard units to challenge
counterrevolutionaries.
• Students demonstrate for democratic reforms in
the capital and are killed by government troops.

These statements describe the changing role of students in which nation?

1 Japan   3 Russia
2 China   4 India 47____

Base your answer to question 48 on the map below
and on your knowledge of social studies.

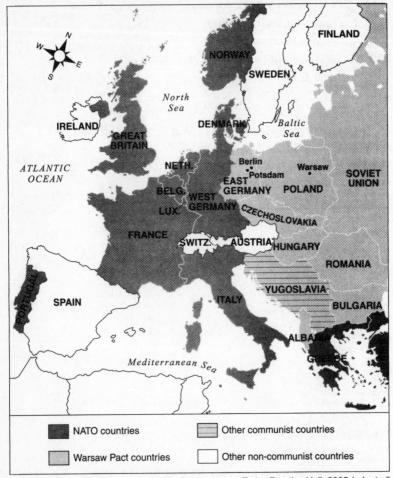

NATO countries

Warsaw Pact countries

Other communist countries

Other non-communist countries

Source: Ellis and Esler, *World History: Connections to Today,* Prentice Hall, 2005 (adapted)

48 Which time period is represented in this map of
Europe?

1 before the Congress of Vienna
2 during the Age of Imperialism
3 between World War I and World War II
4 during the Cold War

48 _____

Base your answers to questions 49 and 50 on the quotation below and on your knowledge of social studies.

". . . The daily tasks of the women are to milk the cattle in the morning and evening, and to fetch water as required. By using their donkeys it is possible for them to bring back enough water to last two or three days. When the settlement moves, on average about once every five weeks, each woman is responsible for moving her hut and rebuilding it. All the necessary movables, including hides, wooden containers and important struts in the framework of the hut, can normally be carried by two donkeys. Older women rely on their daughters, their younger co-wives, and their sons' wives for help in all these tasks. . . ."

Source: Paul Spencer, *The Samburu*,
University of California Press, 1965

49 Which type of economy would most likely be found in this society?

1 command   3 free market
2 traditional   4 manorial   49_____

50 Based on this passage, the Samburu people would be classified as

1 commercial farmers   3 nomads
2 urban dwellers   4 serfs   50_____

In developing your answer to Part II, be sure to keep these general definitions in mind:

- (a) <u>describe</u> means "to illustrate something in words or tell about it"
- (b) <u>discuss</u> means "to make observations about something using facts, reasoning, and argument; to present in some detail"

PART II: THEMATIC ESSAY QUESTION

Directions: Write a well-organized essay that includes an introduction, several paragraphs addressing the task below, and a conclusion.

Theme: Change

> Throughout history, the actions of leaders have changed the society in which they lived.

Task:

> Identify *two* leaders who changed the society in which they lived and for *each*
> - Describe *one* situation the leader attempted to change
> - Describe *one* action the leader took to change this situation
> - Discuss the impact of that action on the society in which the leader lived

You may use any leader from your study of global history and geography *except* **Johann Gutenberg** and **James Watt**. Some suggestions you might wish to consider include Martin Luther, Queen Elizabeth I, Toussaint L'Ouverture, Napoleon Bonaparte, Simón Bolívar, Otto von Bismarck, Mohandas Gandhi, Mao Zedong, Ho Chi Minh, Fidel Castro, and Nelson Mandela.

You are *not* limited to these suggestions.

Do *not* use a leader from the United States in your answer.

Guidelines:

In your essay, be sure to:

- Develop all aspects of the task
- Support the theme with relevant facts, examples, and details
- Use a logical and clear plan of organization, including an introduction and a conclusion that are beyond a restatement of the theme

---

In developing your answers to Part III, be sure to keep this general definition in mind:

(a) <u>explain</u> means "to make plain or understandable; to give reasons for or causes of; to show the logical development or relationships of"

(b) <u>discuss</u> means "to make observations about something using facts, reasoning, and argument; to present in some detail"

PART III: DOCUMENT-BASED QUESTION

This question is based on the accompanying documents. It is designed to test your ability to work with historical documents. Some of the documents have been edited for the purposes of the question. As you analyze the documents, take into account the source of each document and any point of view that may be presented in the document.

Historical Context:

Throughout history, changes in technology have had a great influence on society. Development of the **printing press**, **steam-powered machinery**, and the **atomic bomb** had a major impact on specific societies and the world.

Task:

Using the information from the documents and your knowledge of global history, answer the questions that follow each document in Part A. Your answers to the questions will help you write the Part B essay in which you will be asked to

---

Identify *two* of the technological changes mentioned in the historical context and for *each*

- Explain how the new technology changed the existing technology
- Discuss the impact of this new technology on a specific society *or* the world

---

Part A: Short-Answer Questions

Directions: Analyze the documents and answer the short-answer questions that follow each document in the space provided.

Document 1a

Medieval Scriptorium

Source: www.hrc.utexas.edu/exhibitions/permanent/
gutenberg/2a.html

Document 1b

The Book Before Gutenberg

> The earliest books were written on scrolls. From the Second Century A.D. to the present time, however, most books have been produced in the familiar codex format—in other words, bound at one edge. During the Middle Ages, manuscript books were produced by monks who worked with pen and ink in a copying room known as a scriptorium. Even a small book could take months to complete, and a book the size of the Bible could take several years. . . .

Source: www.hrc.utexas.edu/exhibitions/permanent/gutenberg/2a.html

1 According to these documents, how were books made before the development of the Gutenberg press? [1]

_____

_____

Document 2

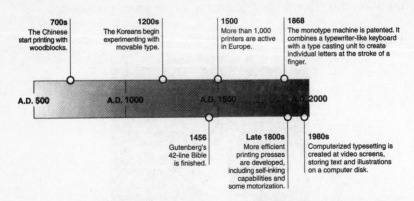

Source: Stephen Krensky, *Breaking Into Print, Before and After the Invention of the Printing Press*,
Little, Brown and Company, 1996 (adapted)

2 Based on this document, state *two* advances in printing technology that took place between 500 and 2000. [2]

(1) _____

_____

(2) _____

_____

Document 3

> . . . Gutenberg's methods spread with stunning rapidity. By 1500 an estimated half million printed books were in circulation: religious works, Greek and Roman classics, scientific texts, Columbus's report from the New World. An acceleration of the Renaissance was only the first by-product of the Gutenberg press. Without it, the Protestant movement might have been stillborn [failed], as well as the subsequent political and industrial revolutions. Gutenberg, however, got none of the glory. His brainchild [idea] bankrupted him; the year his Bible was published, a creditor took over his business. Little more is known of the inventor — in part because he never put his own name into print. . . .

Source: Robert Friedman, ed., *The Life Millennium: The 100 Most Important Events & People of The Past 1,000 Years,* Time, 1998

3 Based on this document, state *two* effects of Gutenberg's invention. [2]

(1) _____

_____

(2) _____

_____

Document 4

Woman Spinning

Source: *The Costume of Yorkshire*, Richard Jackson, Publisher

4 According to this document, what technology was used in cloth production in the early 1700s? [1]

_____

_____

Document 5a

Invention	Description
Improved steam engine (James Watt)	Improved version of steam engine that used coal rather than water power. First used to pump water from mines and to forge iron. By the late 1780s, powered machines in cotton mills.

Source: Ellis and Esler, *World History: Connections to Today*, Prentice Hall, 1999 (adapted)

Document 5b

Power Loom Weaving

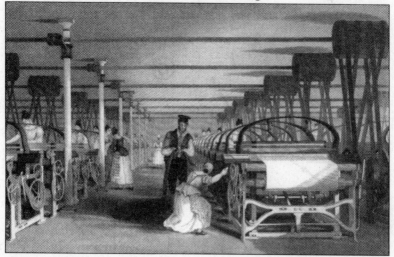

Drawn by T. Allom   Engraved by J. Tingle

Source: Edward Baines, *History of the Cotton Manufacture in Great Britain*, Fisher, Fisher, and Jackson, 1835 (adapted)

5 According to these documents, how did the steam engine promote the growth of the factory system? [1]

_____

_____

Document 6

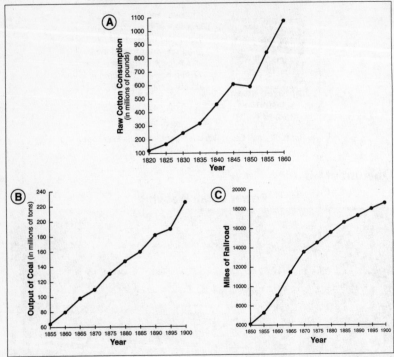

Selected Factors of Industrial Production in Great Britain

Source: Brian Mitchell, *Abstract of British Historical Statistics*, Cambridge University Press, 1962 (adapted)

6 What do these graphs imply about the effect of steam-powered machinery on industrial production in Great Britain? [1]

_____

_____

Document 7

This is an excerpt from a tape-recorded conversation of Kathleen Brockington in August 1994.

Kathleen's Story
Bombed out in the London Blitz, 1940

> . . . When the bomb dropped I wasn't even under the table! I heard the plane and recognised it was a Jerry (that's what we called them) [Germans] because I'd heard so many. There was a tremendous BANG! and I ducked. All the windows came in and the ceiling and a couple of walls came in and there was incredible smoke everywhere. I was shaking like a leaf but I wasn't hurt.
>
> I tried to get out but the door was stuck and I had to climb through where one of the windows had been. I could see there were lots of houses affected, glass everywhere in the street so I knew it was a big'un.
>
> I ran to the Air Raid Post but the Warden said "look missus, we're gonna be busy digging bodies out, if you've got a roof you're better off where you are. There's lots worse off than you". Funnily enough he was wrong; about 50 houses were badly damaged and a couple of them just turned into heaps of rubble, but nobody was actually killed. . . .

Source: http://timewitnesses.org/english/blitz.html (adapted)

7 Based on this document, state *one* effect of the bombing of London by German planes. [1]

_____

_____

Document 8

. . . In both cities the blast totally destroyed everything within a radius of 1 mile from the center of explosion, except for certain reinforced concrete frames as noted above. The atomic explosion almost completely destroyed Hiroshima's identity as a city. Over a fourth of the population was killed in one stroke and an additional fourth seriously injured, so that even if there had been no damage to structures and installations the normal city life would still have been completely shattered. Nearly everything was heavily damaged up to a radius of 3 miles from the blast, and beyond this distance damage, although comparatively light, extended for several more miles. Glass was broken up to 12 miles.

In Nagasaki, a smaller area of the city was actually destroyed than in Hiroshima, because the hills which enclosed the target area restricted the spread of the great blast; but careful examination of the effects of the explosion gave evidence of even greater blast effects than in Hiroshima. Total destruction spread over an area of about 3 square miles. Over a third of the 50,000 buildings in the target area of Nagasaki were destroyed or seriously damaged. The complete destruction of the huge steel works and the torpedo plant was especially impressive. The steel frames of all buildings within a mile of the explosion were pushed away, as by a giant hand, from the point of detonation. The badly burned area extended for 3 miles in length. The hillsides up to a radius of 8,000 feet were scorched, giving them an autumnal appearance. . . .

Source: "The Atomic Bombings of Hiroshima and Nagasaki,"
Manhattan Engineer District, United States Army, June 29, 1946

8 Based on this document, state *two* effects of the atomic bombings on Hiroshima and Nagasaki. [2]

(1) _____

_____

(2) _____

_____

Document 9a

Nuclear Countries – November 2002

Declared Nuclear States	Estimates of Nuclear Weapons Stockpiled
United States	10,640
Russia	8,600
China	400
France	350
United Kingdom	200
Israel	100–200
Pakistan	24–48
India	30–35
North Korea*	1–2

Source: Natural Resources Defense Council (NRDC), 2002
(adapted); *Bulletin of Atomic Scientist, 2003

Document 9b

Countries with Nuclear Power Reactors in Operation or Under Construction – December 2002

Argentina	Finland	Korea, Republic of	Slovenia
Armenia	France	Lithuania	South Africa
Belgium	Germany	Mexico	Spain
Brazil	Hungary	Netherlands	Sweden
Bulgaria	India	Pakistan	Switzerland
Canada	Iran	Romania	Ukraine
China	Japan	Russian Federation	United Kingdom
Czech Republic	Korea, Dem. Peoples Rep. of	Slovakia	United States

Source: "Nuclear Technology Review," International Atomic Energy Agency (IAEA), 2003 (adapted)

9 Based on these charts, state *two* ways countries have used nuclear technology. [2]

(1) _____

_____

(2) _____

_____

Part B: Essay

Directions: Write a well-organized essay that includes an introduction, several paragraphs, and a conclusion. Use evidence from *at least four* documents to support your response.

Historical Context:

Throughout history; changes in technology have had a great influence on society. Development of the **printing press**, **steam-powered machinery**, and the **atomic bomb** had a major impact on specific societies and the world.

Task:

Using the information from the documents and your knowledge of global history, write an essay in which you

---

Identify *two* of the technological changes mentioned in the historical context and for *each*
- Explain how the new technology changed the existing technology
- Discuss the impact of this new technology on a specific society *or* the world

---

Guidelines:

In your essay, be sure to:
- Develop all aspects of the task
- Incorporate information from *at least four* documents
- Incorporate relevant outside information
- Support the theme with relevant facts, examples, and details
- Use a logical and clear plan of organization, including an introduction and a conclusion that are beyond a restatement of the theme

Answers
August 2005
Global History and Geography

Answer Key

PART I (1–50)

1. 2	14. 4	27. 3	40. 3
2. 2	15. 3	28. 3	41. 4
3. 1	16. 4	29. 2	42. 4
4. 3	17. 3	30. 1	43. 2
5. 4	18. 3	31. 1	44. 3
6. 1	19. 2	32. 2	45. 2
7. 3	20. 2	33. 2	46. 4
8. 4	21. 2	34. 1	47. 2
9. 4	22. 1	35. 3	48. 4
10. 3	23. 3	36. 1	49. 2
11. 3	24. 1	37. 2	50. 3
12. 3	25. 4	38. 2	
13. 2	26. 1	39. 4	

PART II: Thematic Essay See answers explained section.

PART III: Document-Based Essay See answers explained section.

Answers Explained

PART I

1. **2** The conclusion that can best be drawn from these statements is that people adapt to meet the challenges of their geography. More than four-fifths of Japan is mountainous. The rugged terrain limits the amount of arable lands to coastal plains and narrow river valleys. The Japanese learned to use the sea as a source of food. Fish is the main source of protein in the Japanese diet. In the rich waters off the coasts, the Japanese catch sardines, herring, salmon, and cod. They also harvest shellfish and vitamin-rich seaweed in the inlets and bays. Only about 20 percent of China is level land, including the coastal plains and the river valleys. Yet only about half of the level land is good for farming. To create more farmland, the Chinese have constructed terraces, or small flat fields, built into the sides of mountains. The terraces hold the soil in place so that the farmers can plant crops to feed the Chinese population. Although rain is plentiful in India, most of it falls during the monsoon season from June to October. During the dry season, farmers use water from the rivers to irrigate crops. They dig wells to tap underground water. Finding water on the Deccan Plateau is made more difficult because the water lies in rocks below the ground. To reach water for irrigation, farmers must dig wells at least 200 feet deep. In addition, the government of India promotes building dams to increase the water supply. In the 1940s, the government supported the Narmada Valley Project (NVP), but it was delayed until the 1970s. The NVP was designed to supply water to irrigate farmlands for over 30 million people and called for the building of 30 major dams and more than 3,000 smaller dams. These efforts by the people in Japan, China, and India demonstrate how geography forces people to make adjustments to their way of life.

WRONG CHOICES EXPLAINED:

(1), (3), and (4) None of these conclusions can be applied to all of these statements. Civilizations that use irrigation to improve crop production refer to India. Fish is an important source of protein for the Japanese but does not explain the importance of terrace farming. None of these nations depend upon the same food source for their development.

2. **2** Social scientists that are best known for studying the physical artifacts of a culture are archaeologists. Archaeologists learn about early civilizations by excavating and studying the traces of early settlements. The objects or artifacts left by the early people include tools, weapons, pottery, clothing, and jewelry. By analyzing artifacts, archaeologists draw conclusions about the beliefs, values, and activities of earlier civilizations or our ancestors. For

example, temples and religious objects show that people had a well-developed belief system.

WRONG CHOICES EXPLAINED:

(1) Geographers study the link between people and the environment. They examine how the environment and the resources of an area affect the population. Geographers have developed five basic themes to help understand the link between people and the earth. These themes are location, place, interaction between people and their environment, movement, and region.

(3) Economists examine how people make a living. They study how goods and services are produced and how these goods and services satisfy people's needs.

(4) Sociologists study the origin and evolution of human societies and civilizations as well as the laws and institutions that control a society.

3. **1** The statement that most accurately describes how geography affected the growth of the ancient civilizations of Egypt and Mesopotamia is that river valleys provided rich soil to grow plentiful crops. In Egypt, the land would be a desert without the Nile River. Each year the overflowing of the Nile River deposited fertile soil that enabled farmers to grow large amounts of food and allowed permanent settlements. The first river valley civilization developed in Mesopotamia in the regions located along the Tigris and Euphrates Rivers. Although the area was hot and dry, people learned to irrigate the land by diverting water from these rivers, which allowed settlements to grow and increased food supplies. The overflowing of these rivers created a rich deposit of fertile soil that encouraged permanent settlements, ultimately fostering the development of civilizations.

WRONG CHOICES EXPLAINED:

(2) The large deserts did not contain mineral products to foster the growth of ancient civilizations. The desert areas on either side of the Nile River served as a natural barrier between Egypt and other lands. The deserts shut out invaders and spared the country the constant warfare that plagued the Fertile Crescent or the land along the Tigris and Euphrates Rivers.

(3) Neither of these civilizations has direct access to the Atlantic Ocean. The Atlantic Ocean influenced the growth of Europe.

(4) Large savanna areas did not provide protection from invaders. The savannas are largely grassland regions. These civilizations were primarily in desert areas, which provided protection from invasion.

4. **3** One way in which the Five Relationships, the Ten Commandments, and the Eightfold Path are similar is that they provide codes of behavior. The Five Relationships taught by Confucius encouraged people to maintain social and political order. Confucius, who lived between 551 and 479 B.C., was one of China's greatest philosophers and formulated an ethical code of behavior. The purpose of his code was to improve society and build and maintain good government. Confucius believed that harmony could be achieved by the

proper behavior of each member of a family or society. He taught that individuals should be guided by the following virtues: careful observance of ancient traditions; reverence for learning; respect for honesty; devotion to parents, family, and friends; obedience to the rulers; and respect for ancestors. He believed that these traditions could help maintain social peace and harmony. Each person's social role brings a number of obligations. If everyone fulfilled these roles by meeting their responsibilities, people and society would be in harmony. Confucius's followers collected his sayings and put them into a book entitled *The Analects*. The Ten Commandments are the religious and moral laws of the Hebrews. The Jews believed that God gave the commandments to Moses. The laws set out both religious duties toward God and rules for moral conduct toward other people. The Ten Commandments forbid immoral conduct, such as murder and stealing, but they do not provide for any punishment if any of the commandments are violated. The Eightfold Path is part of the basic teaching of Buddhism. Siddhartha Gautama, the 6th-century Indian prince who became known as Buddha, or the Enlightened One, taught that only by rejecting worldly goods, which are the cause of suffering and pain, could one find peace and harmony in life. He encouraged his followers to adopt the Eightfold Path by giving up material pleasures, controlling emotions, meditating selflessly, respecting all living creatures, acquiring knowledge, cultivating goodness, speaking truths, and acting generously. If Buddhists follow these rules, they will enter into nirvana, a state in which the soul merges with the universe.

WRONG CHOICES EXPLAINED:

(1) Neither the Five Relationships nor the Eightfold Path promotes polytheism, a belief in many gods. These belief systems stress the importance of righteous living. The Ten Commandments stress monotheism, which is the belief in one God.

(2) None of these systems establish gender equality.

(4) None of these beliefs describe secularism, which de-emphasizes the importance of religion in society. These belief systems promote the ideal that moral behavior and religion are important in society.

5. **4** The Phoenicians are often referred to as the carriers of civilization because they traded goods and spread ideas throughout the Mediterranean region. Phoenicia was mainly the area now known as Lebanon. Phoenicians never united into a country. Instead, they set up small city-states along the eastern Mediterranean coast and earned a living through commerce and trade. They never built an empire. Phoenician traders sailed the Mediterranean Sea, planting colonies from North Africa to Spain. Some historians believe that the Phoenicians traded for tin with the inhabitants of the southern coast of Britain. The Phoenicians spread the culture of the Middle East across a wide area. The Phoenicians developed an alphabet. As merchants, they needed a simple alphabet to ease the burden of keeping records. They replaced the existing cumbersome alphabet of 550 characters with a

phonetic alphabet, based on distinct sounds, consisting of 22 letters. After further alterations by the Greeks and Romans, this alphabet became the one that we use today.

WRONG CHOICES EXPLAINED:

(1) The Phoenicians never introduced Islam and Christianity to Central Africa. The Phoenicians prospered from 1200 B.C. to 800 B.C., many years before the birth of Christianity and Islam.

(2) The Phoenicians never established colonies throughout northern Europe. They traded primarily in the Mediterranean region.

(3) The Phoenicians did not develop the first carts with wheels. Earlier unknown people invented the wheel. The Sumerians made the first wheeled vehicles.

6. **1** The exchange of silks and spices and the spread of Buddhism along the Silk Road are examples of cultural diffusion. Cultural diffusion is the spread of ideas, customs, and technology from one area or region to another. The Han Dynasty (A.D. 206 to A.D. 220) in China opened a trade route that became known as the Silk Road because traders made a fortune carrying Chinese silk to the West. The Silk Road went through central Asia, connecting China to the Middle East and Rome. Over these routes, China exported silk, iron, and bronze in exchange for gold, linens, cloth, glass, horses, monkeys, and parrots. The religion of Buddhism began in India around 600 B.C. Contact with India led to the introduction of Buddhism in China. Buddhism became popular during the Han Dynasty. Missionaries also helped to spread Buddhism to Tibet, Korea, and Japan.

WRONG CHOICES EXPLAINED:

(2) Self-sufficiency is when a society is economically able to survive by itself. The medieval manor was self-sufficient in that its inhabitants raised crops and livestock for food, spun wool for clothing, tanned leather for shoes, and cut lumber for furniture and buildings.

(3) Ethnocentrism is the belief that a particular culture is superior to other cultures or ways of life.

(4) Desertification is the process by which fertile or semidesert land becomes a desert.

7. **3** The concept that is best reflected in this passage is monotheism. Like Judaism and Christianity, Islam is a monotheistic religion based on the belief in one God. In Arabic, Islam means "submission to the will of Allah." The followers of Islam are called Muslims. Muslim means "one who has submitted." Muhammad was the prophet who founded Islam. Muhammad became convinced that he was the last prophet and taught that Allah was the one and only God and that all other gods must be abandoned. Muslims also believe that Allah is compassionate and all-powerful.

WRONG CHOICES EXPLAINED:

(1) Baptism refers to the Christian symbol of initiation. Baptism symbolizes rebirth and purification.

(2) Karma is the Hindu belief that every mental or physical deed in this life affects a person's fate in the future life.

(4) Animism is a traditional African religion. It is the belief that the spirit dwells in all living and nonliving things.

8. **4** The accomplishments associated with the Gupta Empire are the use of the Sanskrit language and development of the concept of zero. The Gupta Dynasty, embracing northern India, came to power in India in A.D. 320 and ruled until A.D. 550. By restoring law and order, the Guptas revived the prosperity of their civilization. In literature, Gupta writers produced fine poems and dramas. These fables, folk tales in the Sanskrit language, were collected and recorded. These stories were carried west to Persia, Egypt, and Greece. The best-known poet and playwright was Kalidasa, who wrote *Shakuntala*. This romantic comedy about the love between a king and a forest maiden is still performed today. Gupta scholars contributed significantly to mathematics, making major advances in developing the principles of algebra. They also explained the concept of infinity and invented the concept of zero. The symbols they created for the numbers 1 to 9 were adopted by traders from the Middle East and were called "Arabic numerals" in the West. The Gupta period is considered the Golden Age of India.

WRONG CHOICES EXPLAINED:

(1) The Greeks developed democracy and constructed the Pantheon.

(2) The defeat of the Roman Empire is associated with the invasion by the Germanic tribes in western Europe in A.D. 476. The Roman Emperor Constantine helped to make Christianity the official religion of the Roman Empire in A.D. 313.

(3) The Mongols were a central Asian nomadic tribe who built the largest empire in the world. Mongol power reached its height in the 14th century and its rule stretched throughout central Asia and China, into Russia and Europe, and into southwest Asia and India. The period of stability under Mongol rule is known as Pax Mongolia, which allowed for an exchange of goods and ideas between East and West. One of the most famous Mongol rulers was Kublai Khan, who completed the conquest of China in A.D. 1279.

9. **4** Kievian Russia adopted the Eastern Orthodox religion, the Cyrillic alphabet, and different styles of art and architecture through contact with missionaries from the Byzantine Empire. The first Russian state was established in the A.D. 800s. This early Russian state was centered in the city of Kiev, in present-day Ukraine. Kiev's location on the Dnieper River made the city easily accessible to Byzantine traders and contributed to its prosperity and the growth of an educated class. In A.D. 863, the Byzantine Empire introduced Orthodox Christianity to Russia. The Byzantine emperor sent two

Greek monks, Cyril and Methodius, to convert the Slavic people. These missionaries adapted the Greek alphabet to translate the Bible into the Slavic language. The Cyrillic alphabet, named after Cyril, became the written language of Russia. It is still used today in Russia and the Ukraine. In A.D. 988, Prince Vladimir and all his subjects converted to Orthodox Christianity. Kiev, which was already linked to Byzantium by trade, now looked to Constantinople for religious guidance. Russian rule continued the autocratic tradition of the Byzantine emperors. Autocratic rulers in Russia took the title of czar, which is the Russian word for caesar. Russia also adapted Byzantine religious art, music, and architecture. Byzantine domes capped with colorful, carved "helmets" became the onion domes of Russian churches.

WRONG CHOICES EXPLAINED:

(1) Kievian Russia did not trade with South Asia. The city of Kiev traded primarily with Constantinople and other Slavic groups in eastern Europe.

(2) The conquering invaders from Mongolia did not influence the religion, alphabet, or architectural style of Russia. The Mongols, who ruled Russia for over 250 years until the 14th century, destroyed and burned the city of Kiev in the 1200s.

(3) The crusaders from western Europe appeared in the 11th century, and their goal was to capture the Holy Land. They never traveled to Russia.

10. **3** The statement about the Golden Age of Islam that is a fact rather than an opinion is that Islamic society preserved Greek and Roman culture. The Golden Age of Muslim culture occurred after the Abbasid Dynasty was established and lasted from A.D. 750 to about A.D. 1200. The Muslims founded great universities, especially in Cairo, Egypt and Baghdad, Mesopotamia. During the Golden Age, Baghdad became the center of the Muslim Empire and exceeded the size and wealth of Constantinople, the capital of the Byzantine Empire. These universities preserved and taught Greco-Roman culture. Muslim scholars translated the works of the Greeks and Romans. Muslim advances in mathematics, astronomy, and medicine were also partly based on their study of Greek and Indian knowledge. The Arab scholars borrowed the concept of zero from India and developed Arabic numbers that were eventually adapted worldwide. In philosophy, the scholar Iban Rushd, who was known in Europe as Averroes, strongly influenced medieval Christian scholars with his writings on Aristotle. The advances of Muslim civilization that contained elements of the Greco-Roman culture gradually reached Christian Europe in the Middle Ages through the Crusades.

WRONG CHOICES EXPLAINED:

(1), (2), and (4) None of these statements can be supported by facts. These statements are opinions based on what people think rather than on what is known to be true. It is an opinion that Islamic art was more abstract than Greek art or that the Muslims were the best early mathematicians since the Indians developed the concept of zero. It would be hard to get a consensus that Muslim artists had more talent than European artists.

11. **3** The economic activity that was the basis for most of the wealth and power of the West African empires of Ghana and Mali was trading in salt and gold. Each of these kingdoms controlled the trade routes of salt and gold. The first western African empire was Ghana. Its period of greatest power was from the 8th to the 11th centuries. Ghana's wealth came from gold, and its rulers controlled the supply of gold from nearby mines. Ghanayan traders exchanged gold, ivory, and slaves for salt and copper brought by Muslim traders. Muslim merchants also brought their religion and ideas to Ghana. The king had Muslim officials and was influenced by Muslim ideas. The income from trade also enabled the king to control and expand his kingdom. It was reported that the kings of Ghana were so rich that they armed their personal guards with gold swords. At the height of its power in the 10th century, the empire of Ghana was about the size of Texas. In Mali, King Mansa Musa, who ruled from 1312 to 1337, was able to make Timbuktu a wealthy center of commerce due to its control of the trade routes. Mansa Musa converted to Islam, basing his system of justice on the Koran. On his return from Mecca, Mansa Musa brought back many talented people who helped to make Timbuktu a center of Muslim learning. The city had three universities and 50,000 residents at the height of its power. Travelers to the city were also impressed by its many commercial activities and by the law and order that Mansa Musa had established.

WRONG CHOICES EXPLAINED:

(1) The kingdoms of Ghana and Mali were settled communities that had advanced beyond the stage of hunting and gathering. A royal palace and complex domed buildings dominated the capital of Ghana.

(2) The kingdoms of Ghana and Mali were near the trade routes of the Sahara Desert, which were not suitable for farming and cattle ranching.

(4) In the 1300s, the West African kingdom of Benin, not Ghana and Mali, was noted for its work in bronze and brass.

12. **3** The one reason that some Italian cities developed into major commercial and cultural centers during the 13th and 14th centuries was geographic location. Italy was made up of numerous city-states that were geographically situated to benefit from the revival of trade that had developed as a result of the Crusades. The northern Italian cities of Venice, Florence, and Genoa acted as middlemen in the lucrative trade with Asia. Located at the northern end of the Adriatic Sea, Venice was ideally situated to maintain a trade monopoly with Asia. Renewed interest in products of the East such as silk, perfume, and sugar allowed Venice to serve as a link between western Europe and Asia. This bustling port city also attracted traders from all over the world. These advantages made Venice the wealthiest and most powerful city-state during the late Renaissance. At the height of its power, Venice stretched from the Adriatic Sea in the east to Milan in the west. The Medici family, who had made a fortune in wool trading and expanded into banking, dominated Florence for more than 30 years. Cosimo de Medici and his

grandson, Lorenzo the Magnificent (1469–1492), became the outstanding patrons of Renaissance art.

WRONG CHOICES EXPLAINED:

(1) Italy did not have a unified government in the 13th and 14th centuries. Italy was divided into a number of city-states and would not become a united country until the 19th century.

(2) During the 13th and 14th centuries, Italy did not follow isolationist economic policies. The Italian city-states were involved in transporting Crusaders to the Holy Land as well as other trading activities.

(4) There was no system of social equality in Italian cities during the 13th and 14th centuries. Social structure was based primarily on birth.

13. **2** The two cultures that most influenced the development of early Japan are Chinese and Korean. Japanese culture features a unique blend of its own original traditions and ideas borrowed from the nearby civilizations of Korea and China. Korea often acted as a bridge between China and Japan. During the 6th century, many Koreans migrated to Japan, bringing Chinese influences with them. Korean missionaries introduced Buddhism to Japan, and by the mid-700s, the Japanese imperial court officially accepted Buddhism in Japan. The Koreans also brought the Chinese system of writing, which became Japan's first written language. These early exposures to China's advanced civilization through the Koreans impressed the Japanese. In 607, Prince Shotoku of the Japanese imperial family sent a group of Japanese nobles to China. After many years, they returned home eager to share their knowledge. Chinese influence reached all levels of Japanese life. The Japanese modeled their government on Chinese ideas. They increased the authority of the state and set up elaborate court ranks like those in China. Japanese scholars studied Confucian and Daoism philosophies. Many Confucian ideas took root in China. These included ideas about family loyalty, honoring parents, and a respect for learning and the educated class. Peasants learned to use Chinese tools and farming methods and to raise Chinese crops. Japanese potters and weavers modeled their wares on Chinese samples. The Japanese courts adapted such Chinese customs as tea drinking and the tea ceremony. In addition, the Japanese built their Buddhist monasteries to resemble Chinese monasteries. Despite the massive borrowing, the Japanese preserved their own identify. For example, they never accepted the Chinese idea of Mandate of Heaven or the Chinese civil service system.

WRONG CHOICES EXPLAINED:

(1), (3), and (4) None of these cultures had any extended contact with Japan.

14. **4** The concept associated with this quotation is divine right. Bishop Jacques Bossuet, who was tutor to the son of King Louis XIV of France, summed up the theory of divine right in his book *Universal History*. According to his way of thinking, the king was the agent of God and his authority to rule

came primarily from God. The king was entitled to unquestioning obedience and was responsible only to God. The divine right theory was used to justify absolute rulers in Europe during the 1500s and 1600s.

WRONG CHOICES EXPLAINED:

(1) Direct democracy is a system of government in which the people have supreme power.

(2) Imperialism is control by one country of the political, economic, or cultural life of another country or region.

(3) Socialism is a system in which the government owns and operates major businesses and controls other parts of the economy.

15. **3** The individual who most likely opposed the form of government described in this quotation is John Locke. John Locke was a 17th-century English philosopher who wrote *Two Treatises of Government* to justify the Glorious Revolution. He believed that all people in the state of nature were happy and that all people possess natural rights. These rights include the right to life, liberty, and property. Locke claimed that people entered a social contract with a government to protect these rights. If a government does not protect these rights, the people have the right to overthrow it. Locke's ideas influenced Thomas Jefferson's Declaration of Independence and Jean-Jacques Rousseau's book *The Social Contract*.

WRONG CHOICES EXPLAINED:

(1) Ivan the Terrible was the absolute ruler of Russia from 1462 to 1505. He was the first Russian ruler to assume the title of czar as a mandate from heaven.

(2) Thomas Hobbes was an English thinker who wrote *The Leviathan* in 1651 to support the need for absolute government. He wrote that people are selfish and greedy by nature and would fall into chaos unless there was a strong absolute government to control and maintain order.

(4) Louis XIV was the absolute ruler of France from 1643 to 1715. He was known as the Sun King, and he exercised unlimited power that he claimed had been bestowed upon him by God.

16. **4** The foreign policy of many Russian rulers supported the country's desire for warm-water ports. Climate and location have influenced Russia's relations with other nations. Since its northern ports froze during the winter, Russia sought warm-water ports in the south, especially seaports on the Black Sea to gain access to the Mediterranean Sea and, eventually, the Atlantic Ocean. Peter the Great, who ruled Russia from 1682 to 1725, created a strong army in Europe to expand Russia and gain ports on the Black Sea. In a long war with Sweden, he won territories adjoining the Baltic Sea. Here he built his new seaport and capital, St. Petersburg, his "window to the west." Peter failed in his goal to gain a port that would not be closed due to freezing in the winter. He fought the Ottoman Turks to gain a warm-water port on the Black Sea but did not succeed. However, in 1795, Catherine the Great, another absolute ruler, gained the right of Russian ships to sail from the

Black Sea into the Mediterranean Sea by traveling through the Turkish-controlled Dardanelles.

WRONG CHOICES EXPLAINED:
(1) Russian rulers sought to provide their landlocked country with access to water routes to western Europe, not inland cities.

(2) Russia has an abundance of mineral resources. Russian leaders have always been concerned about how to use their resources effectively to make them a powerful country.

(3) Russian rulers did not seek to develop extensive canal systems. The harsh winters in Russia and permafrost conditions in regions like Siberia make creating a canal system difficult.

17. **3** The map shows that eastern Europe was least affected by the Black Death. Eastern Europe was struck by the plague but not as seriously as elsewhere in Europe. The kingdom of Poland and its capital city, Warsaw, were partially spared. By 1351, when the plague was moving in that direction along the rivers and through the Baltics, the epidemic was 2 1/2 years old. By then, the bacteria may have been in a less virulent form. Geography also played a role in limiting the spread of the disease in eastern Europe. For example, regions like Poland and Bohemia were landlocked areas and were not major trading centers. Few rats lived there, and fewer could have been imported. Furthermore, the cold temperature of eastern Europe may have contributed to limiting the spread of the bacteria. Finally, there have been speculations that King Casimir III of Poland may have stopped the plague. His 40-day quarantine of foreigners and free distribution of food may have also prevented the Black Death from spreading in Poland.

WRONG CHOICES EXPLAINED:
(1), (2), and (4) The legend on the map shows that southwestern Europe, the Mediterranean Coast, and the British Isles were directly affected by the Black Death between 1347 and 1350.

18. **3** One way in which the Magna Carta, the Petition of Rights, and the Glorious Revolution are similar is that each limited the power of the English monarchy. In 1215, King John signed the Magna Carta (Great Charter). The king could not raise taxes without the consent of the Grand Council. The king could also not fine or imprison any free person except by the judgment of his peers or according to the law of the land. The Magna Carta showed that the king's power was limited by law and became the cornerstone of English democracy. In the 1600s, the Stuart kings tried to rule by divine right and without consulting Parliament. In the Petition of Rights (1628), Parliament protested the despotism of Charles I and reaffirmed that the king, according to English law, could not levy taxes without Parliament's consent. The king was also prohibited from imprisoning persons without specific charges and without providing a jury trial. By withholding new tax laws,

Parliament compelled Charles I to sign the Petition of Rights. The Glorious Revolution of 1689 refers to the nonviolent transfer of power from James II to William and Mary of Orange. Parliament invited these monarchs to rule provided that they agreed to submit all legislation to Parliament for approval. The monarchs could not suspend laws made by Parliament.

WRONG CHOICES EXPLAINED:

(1) None of these documents was designed to strengthen the power of the pope. The underlying issue behind these documents was primarily political, not religious.

(2) The Magna Carta, the Petition of Rights, and the Glorious Revolution contained no references that led to the exploration of Africa.

(4) These documents did not settle religious conflicts. The issue behind these events was whether Parliament or the king had absolute power. Although many supporters of the king were Catholic and many supporters of Parliament were Puritans, the main issue was political.

19. **2** The encomienda system in Latin America was a direct result of the Age of Exploration. The Age of Exploration refers to the period from 1400 to 1600 during which European monarchs sent explorers to find trade routes, resources, and land in Asia, Africa, and the Americas. During the 1500s, the Spanish established an empire in the Americas stretching from California to South America and brought great wealth to their nation. The Spanish created the encomienda system to make their colonies profitable and to obtain labor and taxes from the native peoples in the Spanish colonies. To make the Spanish colonies profitable, Spain closely controlled the economic activities of the colonies. The Spanish set up large plantations to grow cash crops, such as sugarcane and coffee, to be shipped to Spain. Finding the large number of workers needed to make the plantations profitable was a problem. During the early 1500s, the Spanish king created the encomienda system. The Spanish granted the conquistadors the right to demand taxes or labor from the people living on the land. In return, the Spanish were to pay the Native Americans for their work, look after their health, and teach them about Christianity. The Spanish used the system to enslave Native Americans. Bartolome de las Casas, a Dominican priest, spoke out against the horrors of the encomienda system, and in 1542, Spain passed a law forbidding the enslavement of Native Americans.

WRONG CHOICES EXPLAINED:

(1) The Crusades were religious wars between Christian Europe and the Muslims for control of the Holy Land. The Crusades lasted from 1096 to 1246.

(3) The Reformation, which began in 1517, was a religious revolt against the authority and certain doctrines of the Catholic Church.

(4) The Age of Reason, or the Enlightenment, began in the 18th century. The Enlightenment thinkers believed that reason could be used to solve and understand the world around them.

20. **2** These illustrations suggest that early Latin American civilizations used advanced technology to build complex structures. The Aztecs, who lived in the valley of Mexico, built the capital city of Tenochtitlan located in Lake Texcoco in 1325. Aztec engineers connected it to the mainland by causeways. In the heart of the city was the Grand Pyramid of the Sun, which was the center of activities for the people. By 1519, the year the Spaniards arrived, the city had a population of more than 150,000 and covered more than 4.6 square miles. The Inca Empire that developed along the Andes Mountains and extended over much of present-day Peru, Ecuador, and Bolivia was connected by a remarkable system of roads. The 14,000-mile-long network of roads and bridges went through rugged mountains and harsh deserts. These roads allowed the Inca emperor to control his vast empire. Cuczo was considered the center of the Inca Empire from the 14th century until the Spanish conquests in 1533. The Incan capital was known for its fine streets, plazas, and palaces. At the center of the city stood the Temple of the Sun, its interior filled with gold. Although they had no iron tools and did not use the wheel, Incan builders fitted the huge blocks of stone so perfectly that they needed no mortar. Many of these buildings have remained intact, undisturbed by the region's earthquakes.

WRONG CHOICES EXPLAINED:

(1), (3), and (4) None of these illustrations provide any information to show whether European societies, Roman architecture, or the Renaissance influenced the Latin American civilizations of the Aztecs and Incas.

21. **2** Sir Isaac Newton, Galileo Galilei, and Johannes Kepler are all directly associated with the Scientific Revolution. The Scientific Revolution of the 16th and 17th centuries changed the way educated people looked at the world. Influenced by the critical period of the Renaissance, these men used the scientific method—a method of reaching conclusions based on observation and experimentation, rather than on past authority—to solve problems. The English scholar Sir Isaac Newton used mathematics to show that all motion or force in the universe could be measured exactly. Newton called this force gravity. Newton eventually theorized that nature follows uniform laws. Galileo Galilei was an Italian astronomer and physicist. He built his own telescope, and his observation of the heavens proved that Copernicus's heliocentric theory of the universe was correct. Copernicus had challenged the Catholic Church's view that Earth was the center of the universe by asserting that the Sun was the center of the universe. Galileo published his findings, but the Catholic Church banned his ideas. Johannes Kepler was a German astronomer and mathematician who showed that the planets follow an elliptical, not a circular, orbit in revolving around the Sun. Kepler's findings help explain the path followed by human-made satellites today. All of these men challenged traditional authority and reached their conclusions through the scientific method.

WRONG CHOICES EXPLAINED:

(1) The Industrial Revolution refers to the historical event that began in the textile industry in England during the 18th century, resulting in the shift from the manufacturing of goods by hand to the use of machinery.

(3) The English Revolution occurred during the 17th century and describes the struggle between the king and Parliament for absolute power. The Glorious Revolution of 1689 ended the idea of absolute rule in England.

(4) The Agricultural Revolution refers to the changes in farming methods in England during the 1600s. These changes dramatically increased farm production.

22. **1** The Enlightenment and the American Revolution were both major influences on 19th-century uprisings in Latin America. In the 1700s, educated Creoles (American-born descendants of Spanish settlers) read the works of Voltaire, Rousseau, and Montesquieu. These Enlightenment writers supported the idea that the people had a right to rebel against unjust rulers. Some Creoles also traveled through Europe and were inspired by the ideas of the French Revolution. Simon Bolivar, who had studied in Europe, became an admirer of Enlightenment ideas and the French Revolution. He vowed to fight Spanish rule in Latin America. Bolivar earned the title "Liberator" for his role in the struggle for Latin American independence. In a series of battles from 1810 to 1824, Bolivar won the freedom for the present-day countries of Columbia, Panama, Bolivia, Ecuador, and Venezuela. He tried to combine the ideals of the Enlightenment and the French Revolution into the governments of these countries.

WRONG CHOICES EXPLAINED:

(2), (3), and (4) None of these areas was influenced by either the Enlightenment or the French Revolution. World War I influenced the struggle for independence in the Middle East and Vietnam. Japan was greatly influenced by the technological advances of the West in the 19th century rather than the ideas of the Enlightenment or the French Revolution.

23. **3** From the Middle Ages to just before the French Revolution, the people of France were divided into three estates based mainly on their social class. The clergy of the Catholic Church represented about 1 percent of the population but owned about 10 to 15 percent of the land. They paid no direct taxes to the government. The clergy of the First Estate included bishops and abbots but not the parish priests. The Second Estate included the titled nobility and landowners in France. They represented less than 2 percent of the population but owned about 20 percent of the land. They were also exempt from taxes. The Third Estate was composed of the middle class, urban city workers, and peasant farmers who comprised 97 percent of the population but owned only about 60 to 70 percent of the land. The majority of the Third Estate were the peasants who lived on the land. The bulk of the

taxes fell on the Third Estate. These inequalities among the three classes created the dissatisfaction that contributed to the French Revolution.

WRONG CHOICES EXPLAINED:

(1) The three estates were not divided by education. Many nobles in the Second Estate were not educated but were included in that estate because of their birthright.

(2) Geographic region did not determine how people were divided in France. Before the French Revolution, the bishops and nobles were divided into their specific estate by whether they were members of the clergy, nobility, or poor.

(4) The three estates in France were not divided according to religious beliefs. The First Estate consisted of members who had to be part of the Catholic clergy. The members of the Second Estate were determined by birth. Those in the Third Estate were determined by economic status.

24. **1** One similarity in the leadership of Jomo Kenyatta, José de San Martín, and Sun Yixian (Sun Yat-sen) is that they supported nationalistic movements. Jomo Kenyatta was the nationalist leader of Kenya. After World War II, Kenyatta, who had been educated and living in England, became a spokesperson for Kenya's independence. In 1947, Kenyatta was chosen as the leader of the Kenyan African Union, a political movement for independence. Other Africans formed a group that the Europeans called the Mau Mau. This secret group was made up of Kikuyu farmers who were forced out of the highlands by the British who had passed laws to ensure their domination. The goal of the Mau Mau was to force the British off the land. They began to carry out attacks against European settlers, such as burning farms and destroying livestock. Kenyatta, who was Kikuyu, had no connection to the Mau Mau but refused to condemn these actions. The British took military action against the movement and jailed Kenyatta, whom they accused of leading the movement. More than 10,000 black Kenyans and some white Kenyans were killed during the struggle for independence. In 1963, Britain granted Kenya its independence. Kenyatta was elected the first prime minister and he held office until his death in 1978. He worked hard to unite all the different ethnic and language groups in the country. José de San Martín was a nationalist leader in Latin America. San Martín was an Argentinian Creole (an American-born descendant of Spanish settlers) whose parents sent him to Spain to serve as an officer in the Spanish Army. In 1812, San Martín returned to Argentina to fight for freedom. By 1816, Argentina had won independence. San Martín then attempted to liberate Chile. With the help of Chilean patriot Bernardo O'Higgins, San Martín helped Chile to gain independence in 1818. Then San Martín headed north to help end Spanish rule in Ecuador and Peru. In the early 1900s, China was ripe for revolution. Foreign countries had humiliated China and controlled China's trade and economic resources. Many Chinese believed that modernization and nationalism held the country's key to survival. The Kuomintang, or Nationalist

Party, founded by Sun Yixian (Sun Yat-sen), a physician educated in British Hong Kong and American Hawaii, succeeded in overthrowing the last emperor of the Manchu (Qing) Dynasty in 1911. In 1912, Sun became president of the new Republic of China. He advocated a government based on Three Principles of the People: nationalism (an end to foreign control), democracy (people's rights), and people's livelihood (economic security for China by adopting Western industrial and agricultural ways). Unfortunately, Sun was never able to bring China completely under his control before his death in 1925. China would be torn by civil war or foreign invasion until 1949.

WRONG CHOICES EXPLAINED:

(2) None of these leaders organized communist rebellions. Jomo Kenyatta and Sun Yixian (Sun Yat-sen) did not support communism. José de San Martín believed in democracy.

(3) None of these leaders opposed trade with other nations.

(4) Sun Yixian (Sun Yat-sen) and José de San Martín believed in democracy but were not successful in establishing democracy in their countries. Jomo Kenyatta established a one-party system in Kenya from 1963 until 1978.

25. **4** The Opium Wars in China and the expedition of Commodore Matthew Perry to Japan resulted in an increase in Western trade and influence in Asia. In the late 1700s, British merchants began to trade opium in China. The Chinese became addicted to the drug, and in 1836, the Chinese government appealed to Queen Victoria to help them stop the opium trade. In 1839, when the Chinese tried to outlaw the drug, the British went to war. This conflict, which became known as the Opium Wars, demonstrated the weaknesses of the Chinese. In 1842, England and China signed the Treaty of Nanking. For China, the Treaty of Nanking marked the beginning of a century of humiliation. The British annexed Hong Kong and won the right to trade at four Chinese ports besides Canton. China was required to pay a $100 million indemnity for the opium it had destroyed. The trade in opium continued, and Britain received the privilege of extraterritoriality. Extraterritoriality meant that the British did not have to obey Chinese laws and were subject only to British laws and courts. In subsequent years, other European countries established spheres of influence, or control, in China. Japan was another Asian country to encounter Western influence in the late-19th century. Japan, like China, had almost completely cut itself off from European trade. The Tokugawa Shoguns, or rulers, allowed trade only with the Dutch at Nagasaki. In 1853, the United States sent Commodore Matthew Perry, with a naval squadron of four ships, to halt the mistreatment of shipwrecked American sailors. Perry also came to ask the Japanese to open their country to foreign trade. The United States also sought to develop new markets and to establish a port where Americans could obtain supplies on their way to China. The Japanese, who lived in what is now Tokyo Harbor, were astounded by ships made of iron and powered by steam. They were also shocked by the cannons and rifles that could easily destroy their samurai warriors. Fearing what had

happened to China, Japanese leaders signed a treaty that opened their ports to trade. By 1860, Japan, like China, had to negotiate similar trade agreements with the British, Russians, and Dutch.

WRONG CHOICES EXPLAINED:

(1) The Opium Wars in China and the expedition of Commodore Matthew Perry to Japan did not end the economic isolation of China and Japan. These events forced China and Japan to increase their trade with the Western countries.

(2) The Opium Wars led to a decline, not an increase, in Chinese influence in Asia. China's defeat in the Opium Wars revealed to the world her military weakness. In the late 19th and early 20th centuries, Japan, not China, increased its influence in Asia.

(3) Neither the Opium Wars nor the expedition of Commodore Matthew Perry to Japan resulted in the beginning of democratic government. The Manchu Dynasty in China ruled until 1911, and the Japanese replaced the weak feudal leaders and established a strong central government that gave the emperor autocratic power.

26. **1** A direct result of the Meiji Restoration in Japan was that Japan became a modern industrial nation. During the Meiji Restoration from 1862 to 1912, Japan reversed its policy of isolation, ended feudalism, and began to modernize by borrowing from the Western powers. The goal of the Meiji leader, or enlightened ruler, was to make Japan a strong military and industrial power. The Meiji emperor realized that the nation had to modernize to avoid becoming a victim of imperialism. Japanese leaders sent students abroad to Western countries to learn about their form of government, economics, technology, and customs. The government also brought foreign experts to Japan to improve industry. The Japanese adopted a constitution based on the model of Prussia with the emperor as the head. The new government was not intended to bring democracy but to unite Japan and make it equal to Western powers. The Meiji government established a banking system, modern shipyards, and factories for producing cement, glass, and textiles. The leaders also built up a modern army based on a draft and constructed a fleet of steam-powered iron ships. By imitating the West, Japan remained independent but also became an imperial power.

WRONG CHOICES EXPLAINED:

(2) The Tokugawa Shogunate did not seize control of the government as a result of the Meiji Restoration. In 1867, the samurai led a rebellion that removed the Tokugawa Shogunate from power and established the emperor as the leader of the country.

(3) Russia did not sign a mutual trade agreement with Japan as a result of the Meiji Restoration. From 1904 to 1905, Japan fought the Russo-Japanese war with Russia after the interests of the two nations conflicted in Korea.

(4) The Meiji Restoration did not politically isolate Japan. The Japanese borrowed Western ideas and adapted them to fit Japanese society. Japan was

also forced to follow a more aggressive foreign policy in Asia because it needed the raw materials of other nations to support its growing industrial economy.

27. **3** The statement that best describes a mixed economy is that some industries are owned by the state and others are privately owned. A mixed economy is an economic system that combines government regulation of industries with private enterprise or capitalistic characteristics. Most Western countries have some form of a mixed economy. For example, in Great Britain, the state owns some industries but allows others to be in private hands.

WRONG CHOICES EXPLAINED:

(1) A command economy is an economic system in which the government determines the production and distribution of goods and services.

(2) A market economy is one in which the products that consumers demand determines what it produces.

(4) A traditional economy describes an economy in which basic economic decisions are made according to customs or habits.

28. **3** This 2001 cartoon implies that nations in Central America are facing several serious problems at the same time. In October 1998, Hurricane Mitch, one of the most destructive storms of the century, swept across most of Central America. Widespread flooding and mudslides killed thousands. Some regions received up to two feet of rain a day during Hurricane Mitch. In Honduras, there were over 5,000 deaths and estimated property loss of $3,725 million. The countries of Nicaragua, Guatemala, and El Salvador also suffered great losses. Nicaragua lost 3,045 people with an estimated property loss of $969 million. Guatemala lost 268 people with a property loss of $698 million. El Salvador lost 240 people with a property loss of $334 million. Unfortunately, earlier deforestation contributed to devastating mudslides with a high death toll and economic losses. Roaring floodwaters and fast-flowing rivers carried away entire villages. These countries have also experienced a severe drought that crippled the region's subsistence farmers, producing hunger and malnourishment throughout the poorest areas in each country. It has been estimated that 1.4 million farmers lost between 80 percent and 100 percent of their corn, beans, and other crops that comprise their staple foods. The global glut of coffee has forced the prices of this important Central American commodity to plummet, making the situation even more difficult. The United Nations World Food Program (WFP) has called on governments and international organizations to send food aid to Central America. It has been estimated that the economy of Central America will take at least two decades to recover from all of these problems.

WRONG CHOICES EXPLAINED:

(1), (2), and (4) None of these choices can be supported by the cartoon. There is no information about obstacles, requesting assistance, or waiting patiently during the economic crisis.

29. **2** The leader who based his rule on the ideas of Karl Marx and Friedrich Engels was Vladimir Lenin. Karl Marx is considered to be the father of communism. Friedrich Engels was a 19th-century political philosopher who helped Marx write the *Communist Manifesto.* Vladimir Lenin is referred to as the father of Russian communism. Lenin adapted Marxist ideas to fit the Russian conditions. Marx had predicted that a communist revolution was inevitable only in an industrial society that had an urban working class, such as those in Western Europe or the United States. Russia did not have a large urban working class and was too poorly educated to stage a revolution. However, Lenin believed that an elite group of revolutionaries called the Bolsheviks could guide the revolution and establish communism. In 1917, Lenin gained the support of the people by making promises of "peace, land, and bread." The Bolsheviks promised an end to World War I, an end to food shortages, and land reforms. In November 1917, Lenin and the Bolsheviks seized control of Russia. In 1918, the Bolshevik Party became officially known as the Communist Party.

WRONG CHOICES EXPLAINED:

(1) Neville Chamberlain was prime minister of England from 1937 to 1940. He supported a policy of appeasement, which meant giving into the demands of Germany or Italy in order to avoid war.

(3) Adolf Hitler was the Nazi dictator of Germany from 1933 to 1945. Hitler's basic ideas were opposed to Marxism and democracy.

(4) Jiang Jieshi (Chiang Kai-shek) became the military leader of the Chinese Nationalist Party in 1925 after the death of Sun Yixian (Sun Yat-sen). He was involved in a civil war with the Communists from 1925 to 1949 and was exiled to Taiwan after his defeat by the Communists.

30. **1** One reason for the outbreak of World War II was the ineffectiveness of the League of Nations. In the 1930s, Japan, Italy, and Germany took aggressive actions to pursue their goal for an empire. The League of Nations was weak. Western countries were recovering from the Great Depression and did not want any more wars. In 1931, the Japanese invaded Manchuria. When the League of Nations condemned the aggression, Japan withdrew from the organization. In 1935, Italy invaded Ethiopia. The Ethiopian emperor Haile Selassie appealed to the League of Nations for help. The League condemned the attack and put an embargo on Italy. All goods were banned except for oil. Many members, however, did not honor the agreement. Britain continued to let Italian troops and supplies pass through the British-controlled Suez Canal. Britain and France hoped to keep the peace in Europe by giving into Mussolini in Africa. In 1935, Hitler began to remilitarize in violation of the Versailles Treaty, and in 1936, Hitler occupied the Rhineland in defiance of the Versailles Treaty. In both instances, the League of Nations did nothing to stop Hitler. The ineffectiveness of the League of Nations led to a lack of faith in the ability of the League to preserve peace in the world and also led to the outbreak of World War II in 1939.

WRONG CHOICES EXPLAINED:

(2) There was no growing tension between the United States and the Soviet Union in the years preceding the outbreak of World War II in 1939. In 1933, the United States officially recognized the Soviet Union in the hope of developing trade with them.

(3) Conflict between the Hapsburg Dynasty and the Romanov families did not lead to the outbreak of World War II. The Hapsburg Dynasty collapsed at the end of World War I, and the Russian Revolution destroyed the Romanov family in 1917.

(4) The German government already signed the Treaty of Versailles in 1919.

31. **1** The United States foreign policy used to maintain the independence of Greece and Turkey after World War II was containment. Containment was a policy of the United States toward the Soviet Union during the Cold War to prevent the spread of communism in the world. In 1947, the government of Greece was in serious danger of being overthrown by the force of Greek Communists. If Greece fell, Turkey could also be in danger of becoming a Soviet puppet state. Britain informed the United States that it was unable to help Greece, and the United States accepted the challenge. In March 1947, President Truman asked Congress for $400 million in United States military aid for Greece and Turkey. The Truman Doctrine was the opening shot in the Cold War, and it asserted that the United States would support any country that rejected or resisted communism. Truman proclaimed, "the policy of the United States would be to support free people who were resisting attempted subjugation by armed minorities." The United States declared that its goal was to contain communism or limit communism to the areas already under Soviet control. Aid from the United States helped to keep Greece and Turkey from falling under Communist control.

WRONG CHOICES EXPLAINED:

(2) Neutrality is a policy of not supporting any one side in a conflict.

(3) Nonalignment is a policy that some third-world nations followed during the Cold War of not supporting either the United States or the Soviet Union.

(4) Militarism is a policy of glorifying the armed forces and one that supports aggressive military preparedness.

32. **2** An important principle established as a result of the Nuremberg Trials is that individuals can be held accountable for "crimes against humanity." At a wartime meeting, the Allies had agreed that war criminals were to be brought to trial. In Germany, the Allies held war crime trials in Nuremberg where Hitler had staged mass rallies in the 1930s. In 1946, the International Military Tribunal, representing 23 nations, put a total of 177 Germans and Austrians on trial, and 142 were found guilty. Twelve top Nazis were sentenced to death, and others were imprisoned. These trials showed that political and military leaders could be held accountable for their actions in wartime. The trials also exposed the evils of Nazism.

WRONG CHOICES EXPLAINED:

(1) and (3) The Nuremberg Trials never discussed the rights of defeated nations or whether aggressor nations had to pay war reparations. These issues were addressed by the victorious nations in the treaties that ended World War II.

(4) The Nuremberg Trials rejected the idea that soldiers must follow the orders of their superiors. The trials pointed out that just following orders did not excuse a soldier from moral responsibility for war crimes.

33. **2** The statement about the European Union (EU) that is most accurate is that the goal of the European Union is to improve the economic prosperity of Europe. The European Union was established under that name in 1992 by the Maastricth Treaty. However, many aspects of the EU date back to the 1950s. The European Economic Community was formed in 1958 by six industrialized nations to expand trade and end trade restrictions among nations. By 1992, it combined with other European nations to become the EU and increased its membership to 15 nations. Its goal has been to end all tariff barriers and ensure the free movement of manufactured goods, farm products, and people among member nations. There are now 25 EU member states since 10 states joined in May 2004. Eight of these nations are former Russian satellites. In 2007, Bulgaria and Romania are expecting to join the European Union. The EU has a common banking system, and the euro has become the official currency of 12 member states. As of December 2004, the EU is the seventh largest country in the world by area and the third largest by population after China and India. The European Union has approximately 46 million citizens and represents the largest market for a variety of United States products that include toys, precious metals, software, fighter jets, and bananas. The EU is the second largest provider of goods and services (after Canada) to the United States. According to the International Monetary Fund, the European Union has the largest gross domestic product in the world.

WRONG CHOICES EXPLAINED:

(1) There is no possibility that the European Union will dissolve because of disagreements among members. Member states have disagreed about future enlargement of the European Union and about foreign policy, but no efforts have been made to dissolve the Union. Member nations are discussing whether to admit Turkey and Croatia in the future.

(3) No nation is being forced to become a member of the European Union. New countries such as Romania and Bulgaria will be admitted provided they meet the conditions for membership such as guaranteeing democracy and a respect for human rights.

(4) The European Union has not expanded to include North African nations. The European Union includes only states in Europe. Some European nations are split over whether Turkey should be considered a European nation.

34. **1** The main idea of this cartoon is that the proliferation of military weapons could destroy the world. The proliferation of military, especially nuclear, weapons has raised fear in the world community. Nuclear proliferation is defined as the spread of nuclear weapons to nations or states that had not previously maintained nuclear forces. In May 1998, India set off five nuclear tests, surprising the international community, which widely condemned India's pronuclear stance. Despite international urging for restraint, Pakistan responded by conducting several nuclear tests of its own. Both of these nations have refused to sign the Nuclear Non-Proliferation Treaty. The United States slapped sanctions on both countries. However, many people in India and Pakistan were jubilant because they believe that the possession of nuclear weapons makes them part of the elite nuclear club that is composed of the United States, England, France, Russia, and China. The international community is fearful that India and Pakistan will rely entirely on nuclear weapons to maintain their security. North Korea has tried to develop nuclear weapons and power plants. In September 1998, North Korea launched a test missile over Japan, claiming it was simply a scientific satellite. This created fear in Japan and the world about North Korea's intentions. Under intense pressure from the United States, in 1999, North Korea agreed to end its nuclear program and to allow the United States to conduct ongoing inspections. In exchange, the United States increased food and oil exports to the country. North Korea revoked its signature after a dispute with inspectors over monitoring nondeclared nuclear facilities. In February 2005, North Korea publicly declared that it does possess nuclear weapons and pulled out of the six-nation talks hosted by China to find a diplomatic solution to the issue. Although talks resumed in July 2005, there has been no progress. Iran is another country that is under suspicion for developing an active nuclear program. Iran says it merely wants to develop nuclear power, but Western nations fear that proliferation of nuclear weapons could lead to further bloodshed and conflicts in the Middle East.

WRONG CHOICES EXPLAINED:
(2), (3), and (4) None of these ideas are depicted in the cartoon.

35. **3** The idea expressed in this statement by Kwame Nkrumah is self-determination. *Self-determination* means allowing people to make their own decisions about their political and economic development. The British colony of the Gold Coast became the first African colony south of the Sahara to achieve independence. In 1957, Kwame Nkrumah led the Gold Coast to independence. Inspired by the writings of Mohandas Gandhi and by Pan-Africanism (cooperation among African states), Nkrumah organized a political party. He organized strikes and boycotts and was often imprisoned by the British government. In 1957, the British granted the Gold Coast independence, and Nkrumah became its first prime minister. Nkrumah renamed the country Ghana to honor famous West African kingdoms of the past. In 1963, Nkrumah created the Organization of African Unity to promote Pan-Africanism

and the end of colonialism in Africa. Nkrumah was deposed in 1966 because his dictatorial policies had created resentment among the people.

WRONG CHOICES EXPLAINED:

(1) Free trade is the removal of trade restrictions among nations.

(2) Collective security is a system in which groups of nations act as one to preserve the peace of all. The United Nations is an example of a collective security organization.

(4) Peaceful coexistence was a Soviet policy adopted by Nikita Khrushchev in the 1950s. Peaceful coexistence is the belief that communism and democracy could exist with each other peacefully.

36. **1** Most of the world's known oil reserves are located near the geographic area of the Persian Gulf. The Persian Gulf in the Middle East region is an extension of the Gulf of Oman located between Iran and the Arabian Peninsula. Countries with a coastline on the Persian Gulf are Iran, United Arab Emirates, Saudi Arabia, Qatar, Kuwait, Iraq, and Bahrain. The Persian Gulf and its coastal areas are the largest single source of oil in the world. Oil supplies about 40 percent of the world's energy and 96 percent of its transportation energy. The Persian Gulf contains 715 billion barrels of proven oil reserves, representing 57 percent of the world's oil reserves. The Persian Gulf countries also maintain almost all of the world's excess oil production capacity, which is located in Saudi Arabia. Saudi Arabia exports the most oil of any Persian Gulf country, followed by Iran, United Arab Emirates, Kuwait, Qatar, and Iraq. Finally, about 90 percent of the oil in the Middle East is exported from the Persian Gulf by tankers through the Strait of Hormuz for industries throughout the world.

WRONG CHOICES EXPLAINED:

(2) Oil was discovered in the North Sea in 1971. However, Norway's vast oil reserves in the North Sea are dwindling, and the government believes that the area has only about a 50-year supply of oil.

(3) The areas near the Ural Mountains contain only about 60 million barrels of oil, which is less than the 715 million barrels in the Persian Gulf region.

(4) The Gulf of Mexico, including the reserves of the state of Texas, contains about 25 percent of the United States' oil reserves. The United States holds only 2.2 percent of the world's proven oil reserves.

37. **2** The policy of strict racial separation and discrimination that was implemented in the Republic of South Africa is called apartheid. Apartheid, which is the Afrikaan word for apartness, was the official policy of strict segregation of the races practiced in South Africa. In 1948, Dutch-speaking white South Africans, known as Afrikaners or Boers, instituted the policy of apartheid. Blacks were forbidden to ride on white buses, swim at white beaches, or eat at white restaurants. Blacks were also required to live in certain

sections of the city and attend separate schools. They were also not allowed to vote. International pressure and the leadership of Nelson Mandela led to the repeal of apartheid in 1990. In 1994, a multiracial election was held, and Nelson Mandela was elected president of South Africa.

WRONG CHOICES EXPLAINED:

(1) Collectivization was a system under communism in which many small farms were combined into large farms and operated by the government. Peasants worked these farms. Joseph Stalin began collectivization in Russia during the late 1920s.

(3) Intifada was a series of violent demonstrations by young Palestinians in 1987 in the Israeli-controlled territories of the West Bank and Gaza Strip.

(4) Communism is an economic system in which all means of production are owned by the people. Private property does not exist, and all goods and services are shared.

38. **2** The statement that best describes a problem facing India today is that religious and ethnic diversity has continued to cause conflict. Sikhs, who live in the Punjab (the northeast region of India), demand a state of their own. The Sikhs are a religious group that blend elements of Islam and Hinduism. They make up 2 percent of the population. In 1984, Sikh extremists in Armistar occupied the Golden Armistar, their holiest shrine, and refused to leave. Indira Gandhi, Prime Minister of India, crushed their rebellion by sending tanks and troops. Many Sikhs were killed. Outraged by the violation of the holy shrine, two of Gandhi's personal guards (who were Sikhs) assassinated her. The conflict between Muslims and Hindus also continues to exist. Although many Muslims fled to Pakistan in 1947, about 100 million still live in India. In 1992, Hindu fundamentalists called for the destruction of a Muslim mosque in Ayodhya. This conflict touched off rioting, and the mosque was destroyed. Recently, the report of Indian archaeologists that they found evidence of a Hindu temple under the ruins of a 16th-century mosque added to the tensions between Hindus and minority Muslims. Some believe the two bombings in Bombay in August 2003 were due to militant Islamic groups who are critical of these findings. At least 45 people were killed in these blasts. The Tamil, an ethnic group living in southern India and in northern and eastern Sri Lanka, have also created problems. In the 1980s, ethnic conflict between Sri Lankan Sinhalese in the south and Sri Lankan Tamils in the north escalated, and Tamil separatists established bases in this part of India. In 1987, India signed an accord with Sri Lanka to settle the conflict. India agreed to send a peacekeeping force and to hold elections to accommodate Tamil demands for autonomy and to repatriate Tamil refugees in India and Sri Lanka. Eventually, in 1990, India withdrew its forces from the area. These religious and ethnic differences continue to challenge the democratic system in India.

WRONG CHOICES EXPLAINED:

(1) Democracy has popular support in India. India has been a democratic nation since its independence in 1947. It is the largest democracy in the world.

(3) There has not been a decrease in the population of India nor a labor shortage. According to the United States population bureau, India's population will virtually double in the next 40 years. It is estimated that the population will reach about 2 billion. This growth in population will lead to a surplus, not a shortage, of labor.

(4) In May 1998, India set off five nuclear tests and has also developed an impressive space program, which demonstrates that it does not lack the technology to become an important military country.

39. **4** The concept illustrated by the cartoon is interdependence. Interdependence is the mutual way in which the economies of countries are dependent on resources, goods, and knowledge from other parts of the world. In our global economy, all countries are part of a team connected together. The cartoon illustrates this concept by demonstrating that all are united together by the symbol of the rope and if one person jumps or falls, all the other people will be affected.

WRONG CHOICES EXPLAINED:

(1) Scarcity is a fundamental economic problem describing limited resources combined with unlimited wants and needs.

(2) Capitalism is a free-market economic system in which the means of production are owned and operated by individuals for profit.

(3) Revolution is a sudden and drastic change resulting in the overthrow of the existing government or political system by force, such as in the Russian Revolution. Revolution can also refer to change in cultural systems such as the Industrial or Computer Revolutions.

40. **3** These newspaper headlines from the 1960s and 1970s describe some of the results of the Green Revolution. The term *Green Revolution* refers to an increase in worldwide food and agricultural resources. The goal of the Green Revolution was to solve chronic food shortages through the use of technology. During the 1960s, scientists used genetically improved seeds, fertilizers, and pesticides to develop new kinds of rice and other grains that yielded more food per acre than older strains. The Green Revolution doubled the food supply in India and Indonesia, thus helping these countries to avoid famines. In India, the production of rice rose from 350,000 metric tons in the 1960s to 750,000 metric tons in the 1990s. Research efforts in Mexico developed a short-stemmed disease-resistant wheat that excelled at utilizing fertilizer and water for a high-yield crop. This pampered seed boosted Mexican wheat production. In Sri Lanka, the Green Revolution has enabled the country to improve rice production to an estimated output of 2.5 million tons by 2004.

WRONG CHOICES EXPLAINED:

(1) The Sepoys were Indian soldiers in the British Army. In 1857, a large number of Sepoys rebelled against the British because they refused to use cartridges greased from animal fats either from cows, which Hindus considered sacred, or from pork, which was forbidden to Muslims. The British crushed the mutiny.

(2) The Kashmir crisis refers to the struggle of the Muslims to gain independence from predominantly Hindu India.

(4) The Computer Revolution is a central feature of the 20th century. It has dramatically altered how businesses, schools, and society obtain information. The invention of silicon chips have made it possible to build computers that perform millions of calculations in a second and fit on one's lap.

41. **4** The best title for this diagram is "Changes during the Neolithic Revolution." Early hunters and gatherers were nomadic groups whose food supply depended on hunting animals and collecting plant food. Nomads wandered from place to place rather than making a permanent settlement. Historians call this earliest period of human history the Old Stone Age or Paleolithic Age, which began more than 2 million years ago. During the Paleolithic Age, people lived in small hunting and food-gathering bands numbering 20 or 30 people. In general, men hunted or fished. Women, with their small children, gathered berries, fruit, and even shellfish. They moved from place to place as they followed game animals and ripening fruit. They took shelter where they could, often in caves. Environmental changes brought new climate patterns that contributed to the end of the Old Stone Age. Warmer weather allowed plants to grow where previously sheets of ice had dominated the landscape. About 10,000 years ago, Neolithic humans began to grow food and domesticate animals. These developments led to the Neolithic or Agricultural Revolution, which meant that people no longer had to search for food. Food would now be abundant and permanent settlements were established. These changes marked the beginning of the Neolithic Revolution because farming and domesticated animals changed the way people lived.

WRONG CHOICES EXPLAINED:

(1), (2), and (3) None of these titles are supported by the diagram. Belief systems refer to religious ideas. There are no references to either classical civilizations or the benefits of the Counter-Reformation in the 16th century.

42. **4** The treatment of the Armenians by Ottoman Turks in the late-19th and early-20th centuries and the treatment of Muslims by the Serbs of Yugoslavia in the 1990s are both examples of human rights violations. Human rights are basic rights and freedoms, such as freedom of expression and religion, that belong to all individuals in any society. From the 16th century until World War I, a major portion of Armenia was controlled by the Ottoman Turks under whom the Armenians experienced discrimination, religious persecution, and heavy taxation. By the 1880s, the roughly 2 million Christian

Armenians in the Ottoman Empire began to demand their freedom. Throughout the 1890s, Turkish troops killed tens of thousands of Armenians in response to their nationalist stirrings. When World War I erupted in 1914, the Armenians pledged their support to the Turks' enemies. In April 1915, the Turks ordered the deportation of the nearly 2 million Armenians to the deserts of Syria and Mesopotamia. Along the way, more than 600,000 died of starvation or were killed by Turkish soldiers. Many women and children were seized by Turkish officials and sold into slavery. The breakup of Yugoslavia in 1991 and 1992 sparked ethnic violence. In Bosnia, fighting erupted among Serbs and Muslims. The Serbs, who dominated Yugoslavia, began a policy of ethnic cleansing that was designed to destroy and drive out all Muslims from the parts of the country that the Serbs claimed. In 1997, Slobodan Milosevic, the Yugoslav president who was Serbian, sent troops to fight ethnic Albanians who were self-ruled in Kosovo. As the conflict raged, Serbs also mounted a brutal campaign of ethnic cleansing against Muslim Kosovans. In 1999, President Milosevic was forced to retreat after a NATO military campaign of 72 days. In 2001, Milosevic was handed over to the Hague Tribunal and has been charged with war crimes.

WRONG CHOICES EXPLAINED:

(1) Coalition rule is when different political parties form together to organize a government.

(2) Liberation theology was a movement in the Catholic Church in Latin America in the late 1970s and 1980s. The goal of liberation theology was to urge the clergy to take an active role in changing the social conditions of the poor.

(3) Universal suffrage is the right of all adults to vote.

43. **2** The doctrines of the Roman Catholic, Eastern Orthodox, and Protestant churches are all based on the principles of Christianity. All three religions believe in one God and that Jesus was the Son of God whose mission was to bring salvation and eternal life to anyone who followed his teaching. They all believe that the sacred text is the Bible, which is divided into the Old and New Testaments. For the first thousand years of Christianity, both the Roman Catholic and Eastern Orthodox Churches were united. In 1054, the Great Schism developed between the Roman Catholic and Eastern Orthodox churches over papal authority. In 1517, Martin Luther led the Protestant Reformation that grew out of his rejection of papal authority as well as his belief that the Bible, not the clergy, was essential to gain eternal life. Despite the differences among these religions, they all accept the belief in one God and the role of Jesus in creating Christianity.

WRONG CHOICES EXPLAINED:

(1) Hinduism is associated with the concept of reincarnation, which is the belief that a soul is reborn in different forms and indicates whether a person had led a good or bad life.

(3) The teachings of Muhammad reject the belief of these three religions that Jesus is the Son of God. Muslims believe that Jesus was only a prophet. However, Muslims believe in a monotheistic god, Allah.

(4) Both the Eastern Orthodox and Protestant churches reject the leadership of the pope.

44. **3** The factor that contributed to the success of the Hanseatic League, the Kingdom of Songhai, and the British East India Company is the development of trade with other regions. In the late 1200s, a group of towns in northern Germany began to cooperate in defending their mutual trading interests. This group became known as the Hanseatic League. From the 1200s to the 1400s, the League monopolized trade in the Baltic and North Seas. It controlled trade of such basic goods as fish, fur, and salt. At the end of the 15th century, Songhai became the most powerful West African kingdom. It grew rich from trade across the Sahara Desert. Songhai became the largest of the West African kingdoms as trade expanded to Europe and Asia. The British East India Company was established in 1600 to challenge the Dutch-Portuguese monopoly of the spice trade. With the approval of the local Indian rulers, the British East India Company established trading posts in Madras, Bombay, and Calcutta. By 1720, the British East India Company controlled 15 percent of Britain's imports, which came from India. The British East India Company dominated trade with India until the 19th century.

WRONG CHOICES EXPLAINED:
(1), (2), and (4) None of these choices contributed to the success of the Hanseatic League, the Kingdom of Songhai, or the British East India Company. None of them was located in the Middle East, affected by imperialism in Europe, or contributed to the growth of the Ottoman Empire.

45. **2** Heavy military losses in World War I, food and fuel shortages, and opposition to the czar led to the Russian Revolution. World War I created many problems for Czar Nicholas II. The loss of millions of men on the battlefield combined with food shortages made the Russian people desperate. Food shortages had developed because a large number of men had been taken from the farms for service in the army. The transportation system collapsed, making the movement of troops, food, and other supplies difficult. Continued military reverses demoralized the troops. Nicholas II ignored the demands to withdraw and did nothing about the poverty and starvation caused by the war. In March 1917, the Russian Revolution began when the soldiers defied the government order to fire on a crowd, and Nicholas II was forced to abdicate. When the provisional government was unable to provide cities with food and failed to withdraw from the war, the Bolsheviks (Communists) gained control. On November 7, 1917, Lenin, under the banner of "peace, land, and bread," seized power. He ended the war with Germany and established a Communist government. The Bolsheviks killed Nicholas II and his family, ending the Romanov Dynasty that had ruled Russia for more than 300 years.

WRONG CHOICES EXPLAINED:

(1) The French Revolution occurred in the 19th century and addressed the injustices of French society under the old regime.

(3) The Chinese Communist Revolution took place in 1949 and was led by Mao Zedong. The Communists claimed to be fighting against the economic injustices of the nationalist regime of Jiang Jieshi (Chiang Kai-shek).

(4) Fidel Castro was the leader of the Cuban Revolution. The revolution was designed to end the economic and political injustices under the Batista government.

46. **4** The geographic factor in Russia that played a role in Napoleon's defeat in 1812 and Hitler's defeat at Stalingrad in 1944 is the harsh climate. In June 1812, Napoleon marched into Russia with an army of 600,000. Czar Alexander pulled back his troops and refused to be trapped in a battle, causing Napoleon to overextend his supply lines. As the Russians retreated, they adopted a scorched-earth policy of burning crops and villages. Desperate soldiers deserted the French army to search for scraps of food. When Napoleon captured Moscow in September, he found the city in ashes; Russian patriots had destroyed most of it. By October, when the czar did not make a peace offer, Napoleon was too late to advance and perhaps too late even to retreat. He could not feed and supply his army through the long Russian winter. In October, he ordered his starving army to retreat. The 1,000-mile retreat from Moscow turned into a desperate battle. Russian raiders attacked Napoleon's ragged army. Soldiers staggered through the snow and dropped in their tracks as the temperatures fell to 35 degrees below zero. A French soldier noted that many of the soldiers were walking barefoot, using pieces of wood as canes, but their feet were frozen so hard that they sounded like wooden clogs. By the middle of December when the last survivors crossed the border out of Russia, Napoleon had lost three-fourths of his army. The 1,000-mile retreat from Moscow was a disaster and Napoleon's first great military defeat. In June 1941, Hitler launched a major attack against Russia called Operation Barbarossa, which was named after the German king who had participated in the First Crusade during the 11th century. By October 1941, Hitler's army of over 3 million men had surrounded Leningrad in the north, which was within 25 miles of Moscow. Russia did not collapse. The German invaders were not prepared for the cold Russian winter. Germans, in summer uniform, froze to death as the temperature plummeted to 20 degrees below zero. Their fuel and oil froze as trucks and weapons became useless. At the siege of Leningrad, which lasted 90 days, the Russians fought valiantly. More than 1.5 million citizens died during this siege, and some inhabitants even resorted to cannibalism. Hitler then turned south to try to take Stalingrad. Russian troops and a freezing winter caused the German invaders to surrender. The Germans lost over 300,000 men. After the Battle of Stalingrad in 1943, the Russian army slowly began to drive the Germans out of the Soviet Union. The harsh Russian winter had contributed to the failure of both Napoleon and Hitler to conquer Russia.

WRONG CHOICES EXPLAINED:

(1), (2), and (3) None of these geographic factors affected Napoleon in 1812 or Hitler in 1944. The Siberian tundra is located in the northeastern part of Russia. These men did not invade that area. Neither the Caspian Sea nor the arid land contributed to Napoleon's and Hitler's defeats. Both of these men invaded with large land forces, and there were no battles near the Caspian Sea or on arid land.

47. **2** These statements describe the changing role of students in the nation of China. The Chinese philosopher Confucius placed a great emphasis on education. Chinese rulers relied on Confucian ideas and chose Chinese scholars as officials. As early as the first century B.C., Chinese emperors had begun granting government jobs to scholars who passed an examination on the Five Classics of Confucius. Candidates for high office had to pass three grueling exams. The candidates who passed became government officials. They collected taxes, kept peace, and advised the emperor. In theory, anyone (except women) could rise in government by doing well on the exams. In practice, however, these systems favored the wealthy men or gentry because they were the only ones who could afford an education. The Chinese emperors used the examination system for over 1,000 years. The Red Guard were the frontline revolutionaries of the Chinese Cultural Revolution of the 1960s. In 1966, Mao Zedong launched the Great Cultural Revolution to purge China of the evil forces that were destroying the Communist Party. Mao feared that the revolutionary peasants and workers were being replaced by intellectuals in running the country. The Red Guards were youngsters in their mid-teens who were urged by Mao to protect the Communist Party. Waving copies of the *Little Red Book* of Mao's sayings, Red Guards attacked professors, government officials, and factory managers. The accused were either exiled or executed. By 1969, the Red Guard was dismantled. Mao feared civil war and had the army restore order. Many Red Guards were sent to work on communes. After the death of Mao Zedong in 1976, Deng Xiaoping introduced reforms to modernize the economy. The government was willing to grant economic but not political reforms. In April 1989, 100,000 students gathered in Tiananmen Square to protest against official corruption and demand more civil liberties and better conditions at Chinese universities. In the following weeks, factory workers joined the students, and demonstrations spread to other cities. Some Communist officials expressed support for the students. After six tense weeks, Deng Xiaoping sent out tanks and troops to crush the demonstrations in Tiananmen Square. Many students were killed or wounded. The government hunted down all dissidents and stifled all political dissent.

WRONG CHOICES EXPLAINED:

(1), (3), and (4) None of these statements describes the role of students in Japan, Russia, or India. Japanese, Russian, and Indian students were never scholars who took civil service exams for government positions or members of a group known as the Red Guard. None of the students in these countries have been killed by their government in demonstrating for democratic reforms.

48. **4** The time period represented in this map of Europe is during the Cold War. The Cold War was a period of tension and hostility between the United States and the Soviet Union that began after World War II in 1945 and ended with the collapse of the Soviet government in 1991. The Cold War was an ideological and economic struggle of democracy and capitalism versus communism. During the Cold War, the United States and the Soviet Union competed for worldwide influence without an actual armed conflict. The term *Iron Curtain* referred to the Soviet-made barrier that split Europe into communist and noncommunist countries. In 1950, 12 western noncommunist countries—France, Great Britain, Italy, Belgium, Denmark, Iceland, Luxembourg, the Netherlands, Norway, Portugal, Canada, and the United States—formed the North Atlantic Treaty Organization (NATO) as a defensive alliance designed to protect Europe from communist aggression. In 1955, the Soviet Union formed the Warsaw Pact. In Eastern Europe, the communist-controlled countries or satellites, such as Hungary and Poland, became members of the Warsaw Pact. Like NATO, it was a defensive alliance by the communist countries to help each other in case of any attack by Western powers. Yugoslavia was the only nonaligned communist country that did not become a member of the Warsaw Pact. These Cold War divisions lasted until 1991.

WRONG CHOICES EXPLAINED:
(1), (2), and (3) None of these choices refers to the time period represented in this map, which represents the Europe during the era of the Cold War from 1945 to 1991. The Congress of Vienna was from 1814 to 1815. The Age of Imperialism was from 1870 to 1914. The years between World War I and World War II were from 1920 to 1939.

49. **2** The type of economy that would most likely be found in this society is traditional. In a traditional economy, people produce most of what they need to survive. Hunting and gathering, farming, and cattle herding are the bases of a traditional economy. People hunt for the food they eat or raise it themselves. Often they make their own clothing and tools. If they produce more food than they need, they trade the surplus or extra food for goods made by others.

WRONG CHOICES EXPLAINED:
(1) Command economy is an economic system in which the government or central authority makes all the production decisions on what to produce, how much to produce, and who will receive the goods.

(3) A free-market economy is a system in which individuals and private businesses have the freedom to operate for profit with little or no government interference.

(4) A manorial economy describes the economic and social system in medieval Europe. It was a self-sufficient community in which the serfs were bound to the land and required to work on the lord's manor.

50. **3** Based on this passage, the Samburu people would be classified as nomads. Nomads wandered from place to place rather than making a permanent settlement. Early people who moved frequently as they searched for the food they needed for survival were called hunters and gatherers. Hunters and gatherers were nomadic groups whose food supply depended on hunting animals and collecting plant food. Historians call this earliest period of human history the Old Stone Age, or Paleolithic Age. The Paleolithic or Old Stone Age began more than 2 million years ago. During the Paleolithic Age, people lived in small hunting and food-gathering bands numbering 20 or 30 people. In general, men hunted or fished. Women, with their small children, gathered berries, fruit, and even shellfish. They moved from place to place as they followed game animals and ripening fruit. As a result, people migrated across a wide area. They also learned to adapt to different climates and landforms.

WRONG CHOICES EXPLAINED:

(1) The Samburu people were not commercial farmers. They were subsistence farmers who grew just enough food to support themselves. Commercial farmers are those who have surplus food to sell for a profit.

(2) The Samburu people were not urban or city dwellers. They lived in rural areas and moved constantly.

(4) Serfs were peasants who were bound to the soil. They lived in the Middle Ages.

THEMATIC ESSAY: GENERIC SCORING RUBRIC

Score of 5:
- Shows a thorough understanding of the theme or problem
- Addresses all aspects of the task
- Shows an ability to analyze, evaluate, compare and/or contrast issues and events
- Richly supports the theme or problem with relevant facts, examples, and details
- Is a well-developed essay, consistently demonstrating a logical and clear plan of organization
- Introduces the theme or problem by establishing a framework that is beyond a simple restatement of the task and concludes with a summation of the theme or problem

Score of 4:
- Shows a good understanding of the theme or problem
- Addresses all aspects of the task
- Shows an ability to analyze, evaluate, compare and/or contrast issues and events
- Includes relevant facts, examples, and details, but may not support all aspects of the theme or problem evenly
- Is a well-developed essay, demonstrating a logical and clear plan of organization
- Introduces the theme or problem by establishing a framework that is beyond a simple restatement of the task and concludes with a summation of the theme or problem

Score of 3:
- Shows a satisfactory understanding of the theme or problem
- Addresses most aspects of the task or addresses all aspects in a limited way
- Shows an ability to analyze or evaluate issues and events, but not in any depth
- Includes some facts, examples, and details
- Is a satisfactorily developed essay, demonstrating a general plan of organization
- Introduces the theme or problem by repeating the task and concludes by repeating the theme or problem

Score of 2:
- Shows limited understanding of the theme or problem
- Attempts to address the task
- Develops a faulty analysis or evaluation of issues and events
- Includes few facts, examples, and details, and may include information that contains inaccuracies
- Is a poorly organized essay, lacking focus
- Fails to introduce or summarize the theme or problem

Score of 1:
- Shows very limited understanding of the theme or problem
- Lacks an analysis of evaluation of the issues and events
- Includes little or no accurate or relevant facts, examples, or details

- Attempts to complete the task, but demonstrates a major weakness in organization
- Fails to introduce or summarize the theme or problem

Score of 0: Fails to address the task, is illegible, or is a blank paper

PART II: THEMATIC ESSAY QUESTION

Throughout the ages, powerful individuals have brought about changes that have affected the development of history. These people have changed everything from politics to the economy and most certainly society itself. Otto von Bismarck of Germany and Mohandas Gandhi in India were strong leaders who found ways to influence the world and alter the society in which they lived.

Otto von Bismarck was a strong nationalist leader from Prussia. He molded society and politics to transform Prussia and the German states into a united German nation. Germany was the last of the great European powers to achieve political unity. In the early 1800s, German-speaking people lived in a number of medium-size states. Between 1807 and 1812, Napoleon's invasion unintentionally aided the growth of nationalism by abolishing the Holy Roman Empire and by reducing the more than 300 German states to about 100. In 1815, the Congress of Vienna reduced the number of German states to about 39 and organized them into the German Confederation, a weak body dominated by Austria.

The failure of the German Confederation to provide effective leadership stirred German nationalists to seek a unified Germany. Austria and Prussia competed for control of the German Confederation. In 1834, Prussia created an economic union called the Zollverein. With the exception of Austria, all the German states were joined into a single economic union. Still, Germany remained politically fragmented.

In 1862, Otto von Bismarck was appointed chancellor of Prussia. Bismarck was a Junker, a conservative landowning class. Bismarck despised democracy and claimed that Germany could be united only by "blood and iron," not by speeches. He believed that the only way to unite the German states was through war and industrialization.

From 1864 to 1871, Bismarck led Prussia into three wars, which would unite Germany and increase the prestige of Prussia as the dominant power in a united Germany. In the Danish War of 1864, Bismarck allied with Austria to seize land from Denmark. In the Austro-Prussia War of 1866, Prussia turned against Austria to gain more land. Prussia defeated Austria in seven weeks. It took control of northern Germany. In 1867, the remaining northern states joined a North German Confederation that Prussia dominated. Now only four southern German states remained outside of the Confederation.

In 1870, Bismarck used nationalism and the bitter memories of Napoleon's conquest to stir up support for war against France. Prussia and its German allies easily defeated France. During the war, the four southern states agreed to unite with Prussia. The Franco-Prussian War of 1870 was the

final stage of German unification. Bismarck had achieved Prussian dominance in Germany and had united the country.

Through Germany's unification, Bismarck helped to make Germany a
major power. Germany's rich natural resources strengthened its industries,
which would later contribute to the rise of imperialism. In 1870, Bismarck
called the Berlin Conference because he feared that Germany was losing the
race for colonies in Africa. European countries saw Africa as a source of raw
materials and markets for its industrial economy. The Berlin Conference led
to the Scramble for Africa and created tension between Germany and
England for economic and political dominance in Europe.

Bismarck managed to unite the German people into a strong nation that
he believed had a role to play in the world. The struggle for Germany to gain
its place in the Sun would create the friction that led to World War I in 1914
and upset the peace of Europe that had existed since the early 1800s.

Another nationalist leader whose actions changed society was Mohandas
Gandhi. Gandhi was a middle-class Hindu who was educated in England and
resented British colonial rule in India. In 1914, Gandhi returned to India.
Within a few years he emerged as a key figure in the Indian struggle for independence. Gandhi, called "The Saintly One" or "Mahatma," became the
leader of the Indian National Congress.

In 1919, Gandhi and other Indian nationalists were angry at the British for
the Amristar Massacre. British soldiers had fired without warning on a crowd
of 10,000 Hindus and Muslims who had come together to fast, pray, and listen
to speeches against government policies. When the British failed to punish the
officers, Gandhi urged the Indian National Congress to follow a policy of noncooperation. Ghandhi called this method *sat yagrapha*, or truth force.

Gandhi's ideas about nonviolence and respect for life were rooted in
Hindu beliefs and Christian traditions. The writings of the American philosopher Henry David Thoreau influenced Gandhi as well. Thoreau had practiced civil disobedience, the refusal to obey unjust laws. To Gandhi, the goal
of nonviolence was to make the world aware of British injustices by accepting
punishment without striking back. He hoped to awaken in the British a sense
of their own wrongdoings.

During the 1920s, Gandhi traveled around India urging nonviolent resistance to British rule. He urged Indians to boycott or stop buying British-
made goods, especially textiles. Gandhi urged Indians to begin spinning their
own cloth and used the spinning wheel as the symbol of his nationalist movement. He rejected Western-style clothing and dressed in the dhoti, the simple white garment traditionally worn by village Indians.

In 1930, Gandhi organized a demonstration to defy the hated Salt Acts.
According to these British laws, Indians could buy salt only from the government. They also had to pay a sales tax on salt. Gandhi led followers in a
protest of a 200-mile march from his home to the seacoast. Thousands joined
the march along the way. At the coast, they began to make their own salt by
collecting salt water and letting it evaporate. This peaceful protest, called the

Salt March, sparked discontent across India. Gandhi and an estimated 60,000 Indians were arrested. Although the government kept its salt tax, the campaign increased world support for Indian nationalists.

When World War II began, the Indians refused to support Great Britain unless Britain promised immediate independence. When the British refused, Gandhi and other Congress members joined a Quit India movement. They urged Indians to follow a policy of noncooperation with the British. The British responded by arresting more than 20,000 Congress members. At the end of the war, the British realized that they could no longer keep India. Gandhi's campaign of passive resistance had embarrassed Britain on the international level. In 1947, Gandhi's dream of an independent India became a reality. Unfortunately, he was killed by a Hindu fanatic in early 1948.

Gandhi's leadership influenced India. In his struggle for independence against England, he also fought for an end to the caste system. He demanded better treatment for the untouchables, whom he called *Haijan* or "children of God." However, Gandhi's dream of uniting Hindus and Muslims was unsuccessful. He had hoped that Hindus and Muslims would work together in an independent India. In 1947, the subcontinent was divided into the Muslim state of Pakistan and the Hindu state of India. Partition led to violence. Estimates indicate that more than 500,000 people died in the fighting between Hindus and Muslims. Sickened by the violence, Gandhi refused to celebrate India's independence on August 15, 1947.

Throughout history, many individuals have changed society by their actions. Otto von Bismarck and Mohandas Gandhi are two excellent examples of how individuals shaped the outcome of a nation or the society in which they lived. Otto von Bismarck was the driving force that helped to unite Germany and to make the country one of the dominant powers in Europe. Bismarck's actions also resulted in a struggle for power in Europe with Great Britain that had a lasting impact on the peace of the world. Gandhi's leadership and policy of civil disobedience were instrumental in getting Indian independence and in fostering equality. Both Bismarck and Gandhi were definitely leaders who took actions that had a lasting impact on the world.

PART III: DOCUMENT-BASED QUESTION

Part A: Short Answers

Documents 1a and 1b

According to these documents, before the development of the Gutenberg press, books were made by monks who copied them by hand or wrote them on scrolls.

Note: This response receives full credit because it correctly states how books were made before the development of the Gutenberg press.

Document 2

Based on this document, two advances in printing technology that took place between 500 and 2000 are:

(1) The Chinese started printing with woodblocks.

(2) More efficient printing presses were developed that included self-inking capabilities and some motorization.

Note: This response receives full credit because it identifies two specific advances that took place in printing between 500 and 2000.

Document 3

Based on this document, two effects of Gutenberg's invention are:

(1) An estimated half-million printed books were in circulation by 1500.

(2) The Protestant Movement might have been stillborn (failed) without the Gutenberg press.

Note: This response receives full credit because it specifically cites two effects of Gutenberg's invention.

Document 4

According to this document, the technology used in cloth production in the early 1700s was the spinning wheel.

Note: This response receives full credit because it identifies the technology used in cloth production in the 1700s.

Documents 5a and 5b

According to these documents, the steam engine promoted the growth of the factory system because by powering these machines with coal, they did not have to be located near streams and could be used in the cotton mills.

Note: This response receives full credit because it cites evidence in the documents to support the importance of the steam engine in promoting the growth of the cotton mills.

Document 6

These graphs imply that an effect of steam-powered machinery on industrial production in Great Britain was the increased consumption of raw cotton.

Note: This response receives full credit because it correctly states the effect of steam-powered machinery on industrial production in Great Britain.

Document 7

Based on this document, one effect of the bombing of London by German planes was that houses were destroyed and glass was everywhere, but nobody was actually killed.

Note: This response receives full credit because it specifically identifies the effect of the bombing of London by German planes.

Document 8

Based on this document, two effects of the atomic bombings on Hiroshima and Nagasaki are:

(1) Everything was destroyed within a radius of one mile in Hiroshima, and over a fourth of Hiroshima's population was killed.

(2) The burned area extended for three miles in Nagasaki, and the torpedo plant was also completely destroyed.

Note: This response receives full credit because it correctly cites the specific effects on the cities of Hiroshima and Nagasaki.

Documents 9a and 9b

Based on these charts, two ways countries have used nuclear technology are:

(1) Countries have stockpiled nuclear weapons.

(2) Countries are building nuclear power reactors.

Note: This response receives full credit because it correctly states two ways in which countries have used nuclear technology.

DOCUMENT-BASED QUESTION: GENERIC SCORING RUBRIC

Score of 5:
- Thoroughly addresses all aspects of the *Task* by accurately analyzing and interpreting at least **four** documents
- Incorporates information from the documents in the body of the essay
- Incorporates relevant outside information
- Richly supports the theme or problem with relevant facts, examples, and details
- Is a well-developed essay, consistently demonstrating a logical and clear plan of organization
- Introduces the theme or problem by establishing a framework that is beyond a simple restatement of the *Task* or *Historical Context* and concludes with a summation of the theme or problem

Score of 4:
- Addresses all aspects of the *Task* by accurately analyzing and interpreting at least **four** documents
- Incorporates information from the documents in the body of the essay
- Incorporates relevant outside information
- Includes relevant facts, examples, and details, but discussion may be more descriptive than analytical
- Is a well-developed essay, demonstrating a logical and clear plan of organization
- Introduces the theme or problem by establishing a framework that is beyond a simple restatement of the *Task* or *Historical Context* and concludes with a summation of the theme or problem

Score of 3:
- Addresses most aspects of the *Task* or addresses all aspects of the *Task* in a limited way, using some of the documents
- Incorporates some information from the documents in the body of the essay
- Incorporates limited or no relevant outside information
- Includes some facts, examples, and details, but discussion is more descriptive than analytical
- Is a satisfactorily developed essay, demonstrating a general plan of organization
- Introduces the theme or problem by repeating the *Task* or *Historical Context* and concludes by simply repeating the theme or problem

Score of 2:
- Attempts to address some aspects of the *Task*, making limited use of the documents
- Presents no relevant outside information
- Includes few facts, examples, and details; discussion restates contents of the documents

ANSWERS August 2005   503

- Is a poorly organized essay, lacking focus
- Fails to introduce or summarize the theme or problem

Score of 1:
- Shows limited understanding of the *Task* with vague, unclear references to the documents
- Presents no relevant outside information
- Includes little or no accurate or relevant facts, details, or examples
- Attempts to complete the *Task*, but demonstrates a major weakness in organization
- Fails to introduce or summarize the theme or problem

Score of 0: Fails to address the *Task*, is illegible, or is a blank paper

Part B: Essay

Throughout history, technological changes have greatly influenced societies and affected the world. The invention of the printing press in the 15th century and the development of steam-powered machinery in the 18th century led to political, economic, and social changes that helped shape the world.

The invention of the printing press greatly affected society. The earliest books were written on scrolls (Doc. 1). During the Middle Ages, books were written by monks in a scriptorium (Doc. 1a, 1b). These books took months and even years to complete (Doc. 1b). As a result, not many books were available, and they were very expensive. The nobles, who were wealthy and made up a small part of the population, were the few who could own them. Thus, the literacy rate was very low in society.

Methods of paper making and printing reached Europe from China about 1300. The Chinese had invented block printing in the 700s, and the Koreans had experimented with a movable type in the 1200s (Doc. 2). In the 1400s, German printers began to use movable type. Then in 1455, the German printer Johann Gutenberg invented the printing press. By using this invention, Gutenberg printed the Gutenberg Bible in 1456 (Doc. 2). It was the first full-size book printed with movable type. By 1500, the invention of the printing press led to an increase in the number of printers in Europe. Eventually by the 1800s, some motorization of the presses replaced handwork (Doc. 2).

The invention of the printing press had a revolutionary impact on European society. It enabled printers to produce hundreds of copies, all exactly alike, of a single work. By 1500, an estimated half-million printed books were in circulation (Doc. 3). For the first time, books were cheap enough that many people could buy them. The printing press quickly spread to other cities in Europe. Eventually, presses in over 250 cities had printed between 9 and 10 million books by the end of the 16th century. Since books were cheaper and more readily available, the literacy rate increased.

The increased circulation of books also helped to spread the ideas of the Renaissance (Doc. 3). As people began to read, they became more interested in the accomplishments of the classical civilizations of the Greeks and Romans, were hungry for new knowledge about science and medicine, and were curious about the reports by Christopher Columbus about the New World (Doc. 3).

Writing in the vernacular (the language of the country) also increased because even people who could not afford a classical education could now buy books. The vernacular replaced Latin as the language of the people. Printers now produced the Bible in the vernacular which allowed more people to read it. Previously, when books were scarce, most Christians had to depend completely on the priests to interpret the Bible. Now, people began to interpret the Bible for themselves and became more critical of the clergy and their behavior.

The printing press paved the way for the Protestant Reformation (Doc. 3). Martin Luther attacked the abuses of the Catholic Church and did not agree with the Church's interpretation of the Bible. When Luther posted his 95 Theses on the door of the Castle Church in Wittenberg in 1517, the printing press enabled his ideas to spread. Someone copied Luther's words and took them to a printer. Within six months, Luther's name was known all over Germany. Guttenberg's printing press enabled the ideas of the Reformation to spread and eventually ended the religious unity in Europe, which led to a decline in the power of the Catholic Church.

The printing press also enabled new scientific ideas, such as Newton's theory of gravity and Copernicus' heliocentric view of the universe, to spread quickly throughout Europe. These new ideas led to the rise of the Scientific Revolution and the Enlightenment in the 16th and 17th centuries. The ideas of the Enlightenment would influence political revolutions in Europe, North America, and Latin America (Doc. 3). Although the printing press bankrupted Gutenberg, his invention contributed to the spread of the Renaissance, the growth of the Protestant Reformation, and the subsequent birth of the political revolution of the 19th century.

Steam-powered machinery was another invention that greatly affected society. In the early 1700s, women produced cotton or wool thread with spinning wheels (Doc. 4). Working by hand at their wheels and looms, spinners and weavers made cloth that could be used for the family, and any surplus materials were sold. This domestic or cottage industry at home was dramatically changed when James Watt improved the steam engine (Doc. 5a). The use of coal rather than water power now meant that mills no longer had to be built near streams or bodies of water (Doc. 5a). Although the steam engine had first been used to pump water from mines and to forge iron, Watt adopted the steam engine to power machinery in cotton mills (Doc. 5a, 5b). By 1800, almost 500 steam engines were producing goods more efficiently than those by the hand-powered machinery of the spinning jenny.

The improved steam-powered engine could also run multiple machines at one time, which led to an increase in the production and consumption of cotton

(Doc. 6). The shift in production of goods from handmade to machine made resulted in the Industrial Revolution. The Industrial Revolution brought about many economic and social changes, with the most dramatic being the increased production and availability of goods. The increased purchase of goods brought riches to the factory owners and also led to the growth of more jobs. Families migrated to the cities as the demand for workers increased and businessmen built factories around small market towns. The population shifted from the rural areas to the urban regions. In 1750, the population of Manchester was 17,000 people, and by 1800, there were over 70,000 inhabitants.

Legislation, such as the Enclosure Acts that fenced off lands formerly shared by the peasants, also contributed to the growth of the cities. The unplanned growth of the cities contributed to deplorable living conditions. The working poor lived in crowded and unhealthy conditions with no running water, no sewage or sanitation systems, and garbage rotting in the city. Industrialization also affected the family structure. Before, entire families had worked together as a unit under the domestic system. Under the factory system, family members held different jobs and did not work together. Women and children frequently worked under horrible conditions and often labored for 12 to 14 hours per day. Factory owners were able to pay low wages because workers could easily be replaced. Furthermore, women and children provided a ready source of cheap labor.

The invention of steam-powered machinery did provide a ray of light for the workers. Goods that were mass produced were cheaper than those in preindustrial Europe, and therefore more people were able to purchase them. A new middle class emerged that would change the political and social structure of many countries. Workers began to form unions that led to an improvement in wages and working conditions. In 1821 in Great Britain, the Sadler Committee was appointed to investigate complaints that children were being beaten and abused by factory owners. This led to legislation to regulate the employment of children in factories.

The steam-powered machines also revolutionized railroad transportation. Thousands of passengers traveled between cities, and freight trains carried more goods than canals and road coaches combined. By 1890, railroad lines crisscrossed Britain (Doc. 6). By offering quick and reasonable cheap transportation, the railroads encouraged people to take distant city jobs. Industrialization swept across Great Britain in the 18th century to Holland, Belgium, France, and to the United States by 1830. By the 1850s, Germany, Italy, and Austria became industrialized. By the end of the 19th century, industrialization had spread to eastern Europe and Russia. In the 20th century, it spread to Asia, Africa, and Latin America.

Industrialization also led to the rise of imperialism as countries competed for markets for their manufactured goods, places to invest their excess capital, and raw materials for their economies. The early success of the Industrial Revolution in Great Britain contributed to the country's growth as the dominant power in the 19th century.

The invention of the printing press and steam-powered machines replaced existing technology and changed the historical development of society and the world. Many of these changes were positive. In some cases, though, they were negative, such as the growth of poor living and working conditions created by the abuses of industrialization. As technology continues to grow and change in the future, society will have to confront how the changes will affect people's way of life.

Topic	Question Numbers	Total Number of Questions	Number Wrong	*Reason for Wrong Answer
U.S. AND N.Y. HISTORY				
WORLD HISTORY	2, 4, 7, 8, 10, 13, 14, 15, 21, 23, 24, 30, 34, 35, 37, 38, 40, 41, 42, 43	20		
GEOGRAPHY	1, 3, 5, 6, 9, 12, 16, 17, 20, 25, 28, 32, 36, 46, 48, 50	16		
ECONOMICS	11, 19, 26, 27, 33, 39, 44, 45, 49	9		
CIVICS, CITIZENSHIP, AND GOVERNMENT	18, 22, 29, 31, 47	5		

*Your reason for answering the question incorrectly might be (a) lack of knowledge, (b) misunderstanding the question, or (c) careless error.

Actual Items by Standard and Unit

	1 U.S. and N.Y. History	2 World History	3 Geography	4 Economics	5 Civics, Citizenship, and Gov't	Number
Methodology of Global History and Geography		2	50	27, 49		4
UNIT ONE Ancient World		4, 7, 8, 41	1, 3, 5, 6, 9			9
UNIT TWO Expanding Zones of Exchange		10				1
UNIT THREE Global Interactions		13	12, 17	11		4
UNIT FOUR First Global Age		14	16, 20	19	18	5
UNIT FIVE Age of Revolution		15, 21, 23	25	26	22, 29	7
UNIT SIX Crisis and Achievement (1900–1945)		30	46	45		3
UNIT SEVEN 20th Century Since 1945		35, 37	28, 32, 36, 48	33	31, 47	9
UNIT EIGHT Global Connections and Interactions		34, 38, 40		39		4
Cross topical		24, 42, 43		44		4
Total # of Questions		20	16	9	5	50
% of Items by Standard		40%	32%	18%	10%	100%